Witnessing Lynching

Witnessing Lynching

American Writers Respond

Edited by Anne P. Rice

Foreword by Michele Wallace

RUTGERS UNIVERSITY PRESS
New Brunswick, New Jersey, and London

Library of Congress Cataloging-in-Publication Data

Witnessing lynching : American writers respond / edited by Anne P. Rice; foreword by
Michele Wallace.
    p. cm.
    Includes bibliographical references and index.
    ISBN 0-8135-3329-5 (cloth : alk. paper) — ISBN 0-8135-3330-9 (pbk. : alk. paper)
    1. Lynching—Literary collections. 2. Lynching—United States. 3. American
literature.   I. Rice, Anne P., 1961–
    PS509.L94W58 2003
    810.8'355—dc21
                          2003000228

British Cataloging-in-Publication information for this book is available from the British
Library

The publication program of Rutgers University Press is supported by the Board of Governors
of Rutgers, The State University of New Jersey.

Manufactured in the United States of America

To the memory of Kim A. Wilson

Contents

Illustrations

Foreword
Passing, Lynching, and Jim Crow

MICHELE WALLACE

In 1993, when I entered the Ph.D. program in Cinema Studies at New York University, I went in search of the historical roots of the stereotypical representations of blacks in contemporary cinema, television, and advertising. When I looked at the turn-of-the-century beginnings of film, and the political issues and social circumstances that seemed to me to help explain black images, I found three psycho-historical phenomena, each forming a world unto itself yet collaborative and interdependent with the others in myriad ways. These three phenomena I dubbed passing, lynching, and Jim Crow. And so I named my dissertation (and a book on silent film still in progress), in an attempt to encapsulate in simple terms the underlying emotional structure of the repertoire of images in visual art, material culture, photography, and film through the turn of the century. The most visually compelling of this three-pronged pitchfork, and the hardest to describe, incorporate, or morally justify, is lynching, also the subject of this important and groundbreaking collection of literature edited by my talented former student and present colleague Anne Rice.

Upon close consideration of the existing scholarship on lynching (see the excellent bibliography that accompanies this volume), I quickly came to the conclusion that lynching was, in fact, the cornerstone of conditions for Afro-Americans during the Jim Crow period. Jim Crow segregation and social policies would not have succeeded so well in keeping the black population in check without the de facto system that enforced lynching (which I define as the full range of racial violence and terrorism). During the period roughly following the demise of Reconstruction legislation in the late 1880s through the Depression, lynching was an everyday event in the South and a constant feature in newspapers all over the country.

Despite the fact that most of us know very little today about lynching—and even U.S. historians generally avoid the topic if at all possible—the masses of blacks were kept in a state of subjection under the constant and imminent threat of agonizing death and torture. The life they lived on the plantations in the fields and the kitchens of the South, working for scraps and peanuts, carefully shielded for the most part from the advantages of higher education, white-collar professionalism, and meaningful participation in politics, was circumscribed in the clearest terms from the tenderest age possible.

Lynching arose largely as an extralegal way of enforcing capital punishment, particularly in situations in which local official authorities were perceived as weak, ineffectual, inefficient, or wrongheaded. It seems likely that the hostility toward official national or federal authority—further strengthened by the loss of the South in the Civil War, the unsuccessful imposition of federal rule during Reconstruction, and the ongoing association of official law with intrusion and domination—helped to give lynching its irresistible flavor in the South in disputes between whites and blacks.

I think there is a tendency to regard the phenomenon of lynching as a monolithic event, inexplicable in terms of its origins in human motivations, agency, and intentions. On the one hand, we tend to think the victims were incapable of an adequate response. On the other hand, we consider that perhaps the perpetrators were provoked in a manner they found impossible to resist. Or was it just a matter of the dynamic of the collective, the things these people were able to do as part of a group? In any case, it is always about putting emotional and psychological distance between them and us. We could never do such things. If I am a sane person, I could never do such a thing. I could never experience such a thing being done to me. Since to me, as to most of us, black and white, the insane are inhuman, no one who ever participated in such an event—the victim, the spectators, the perpetrators—was ever fully human in the sense that I am and that others I know are.

Yet, I suspect it is very important to understand the mistake of this kind of thinking, because without so doing, not only we will never be able to grasp our particular historical legacy as Americans, as actors in the narrative of race, but also we will never be able to grasp our responsibilities as global citizens in the present. Such events—albeit not stemming from precisely the same circumstances—are going on right now. We are ourselves participating, suffering, or standing by watching. The continuum from helpless to conspiratorial watching must be endless as one sighs with relief and silently imagines oneself in the place of the victim.

I think it is important also never to forget the series of cultural practices that made it possible for blacks to live under such a regime. One of these is passing. No one knows how many black people who were sufficiently racially mixed in origin to look white passed on a periodic and strategic basis, for instance, when shopping or going to the movies—or perhaps when trying to move unnoticed through a lynch mob. No one knows either how many black people passed over permanently into the white community to escape the constant threat of harassment and violence.

Another thing that made life possible for blacks was the astonishing integrity and aesthetic fortitude of large portions of the subjected population. It is extremely important to remember this, and to remember it was precisely this beauty and fortitude that prompted such reactions of violence and force among hostile whites in the first place. Clearly, black people did not emerge from slavery and Reconstruction in a humble, complaisant, or docile frame of mind, as we are so often led to believe by American popular culture. They were angered by the withdrawal of Reconstruction's promises of protection and provision, and they continued to feel entitled to some recompense, even as they were clearly willing to work for everything they were given. The violent response of whites in the rural South where black populations were concentrated was a direct reaction to black people's dogged and persistent sense of entitlement to land, to dignity, to justice.

This integrity, beauty, and aesthetic fortitude are most familiar to many of us today via the extraordinary musical achievements of black Southerners of this period in the form of magnificent recordings of the blues, jazz, and gospel that survive. Also, much less well known but increasingly emerging into view are the extraordinary visual achievements of this era's so-called folk artists, or outsider artists, who worked on quilts, furniture, pottery, buildings, grave sites, gardens, and paintings and in myriad other forms still to be adequately researched.[1]

A third area of achievement, better known than the visual but not so well known as the music and performance, is literature. These days we are most familiar with the masterworks of African American literature, which focus in part on the Southern Jim Crow scenario: Zora Neale Hurston's *Their Eyes Were Watching God*, Richard Wright's *Black Boy*, Ralph Ellison's *Invisible Man*, Alice Walker's *The Color Purple*, and Maya Angelou's *I Know Why the Caged Bird Sings*, as well as many other works of fiction and poetry. Also in the sphere of the literary emerging from the black South, this volume anthologizes much less well known works by black writers that deal aggressively with the subject of lynching. Among these writers we find many names familiar to us from their other achievements: Frederick Douglass, perhaps the most famous living African American of the era; Charles Chesnutt, author of *The Marrow of Tradition*, which documents the catastrophic 1898 Wilmington, North Carolina, race riot; Ida B. Wells-Barnett, journalist and founder of the antilynching movement in the 1880s; Frances Harper and Pauline Hopkins, prominent novelists and journalists; poet, playwright, and lyricist Paul Lawrence Dunbar. After these came W.E.B. Du Bois in the beginning of the century; James Weldon Johnson, Claude McKay, and Angelina Grimke in the teens; poets Countee Cullen, Langston Hughes, and Jean Toomer in the twenties; and Sterling Brown and Richard Wright in the thirties. Add to these the less well known names of black writers Mary Powell Burrill, William Pickens, Anne Spencer, Sutton E. Griggs, and Walter White, as well as the few extraordinary white writers who raised their voices against lynching, among them Theodore Dreiser and Carl Sandburg, and you have some sense of the scope of creative resistance to the status quo mustered by blacks and their sympathizers. We should never forget this either, and Anne Rice's volume provides a useful beginning in this ongoing endeavor of recognizing the cultural contributions of the African American population who suffered the enormities of lynching and Jim Crow.

So that was the situation. When we start to mine the archive seriously, we unearth all kinds of supporting evidence. In 1999, James Allen collected lynching memorabilia for an exhibition and a book, *Without Sanctuary: Lynching Photography in America*, that included more than one hundred photographs of lynching victims. These were exhibited first at a small photography gallery on Manhattan's Eastside, where the lines of visitors stretched around the corner, then at the New York Historical Society, and then in Atlanta at its final home as part of the Emory University collection. Most of the lynching victims in these photographs are already dead, posed for the photographic lens, and sometimes surrounded by jubilant white onlookers who are not ashamed to appear complicit in the killing. Often as not, when we read the stories of these events as described by Allen and others, the victims have undergone harrowing deaths in which their bodies have been dragged, sometimes while still alive, from site to site in some bizarre ritual reenactment of mortification.

What these lynchings call to mind for me, more and more, is the mortification of Christ. As a visual historian, I have needed to call upon many years of appreciating the masterpieces of European religious painting, particularly of the Italian and northern Renaissances of the long-ago sacralized depictions of the hours preceding the crucifixion of Christ: the road to his death, along which he was forced to drag his own heavy wooden cross up to the mount, his body weeping blood from his crown of thorns and the cuts of the soldiers' whips; his torturously thin and nearly naked body nailed to the cross at feet and hands, his mother, Mary, kneeling at his feet; his words of forgiveness to the men hanging from the crosses on either side of him; and, finally, the moment of his death and implicit transcendence.

Thinking about the mortification of Christ and the mortification of these lynching victims has turned me into a confirmed opponent of the death penalty, because to inflict ritual death upon persons, regardless of their alleged crimes, is to use the force of the law in ways that are intrinsically pernicious to social mutuality and compassion. It is flagrantly to contradict all that makes us human in any meaningful way. Animals certainly do not engage in such torment of one another. To execute an alleged culprit turns that culprit into a victim and a martyr through the symbolism of the persecution of Christ, which pervades all Western representation. Moreover, I don't think this imagery represents a propagandistic or overly zealous misapprehension. To torture someone to death is to replace the victim's guilt with the torturers' own. Until there is a way to execute someone humanely without a trace of suffering, the executioner is complicit in a crime that far outweighs any other: the crime of pretending to be God.

We live in a time in which many people still take the necessity of the death penalty for granted. Some of them would shudder in horror at the thought of a lynching and can't bring themselves to look at the photographs or even to think about viewing documentaries on the subject. Some of them, I would wager, could find themselves lacking the guts to intervene or protest (even quietly to themselves) at a modern-day lynching. Hypocrisy. That's what lynching is all about. And it is still with us. We cannot afford to forget that just yet.

We obsess about the sordid details of genocide, torture, and assassination as if the bloodletting were beyond us, as if the devil were in the details. They are not; it is not.

If only we could finally as a group be rid of this fantasy of hygienic, rational acts of genocide and murder. We are too fond of killing in the hypothetical. Our death rows, our clamoring for prisons and executions, reveal the fact.

This book is filled with subtle, riveting examples of writers who have come to grips with the endless intricacies of lynching. I have many favorites here: Charles Chesnutt's "The Sheriff's Children," Ida B. Wells-Barnett's "Mob Rule in New Orleans," Paul Lawrence Dunbar's "The Lynching of Jube Benson," Countee Cullen's "Christ Recrucified," Jean Toomer's "Blood Burning Moon," Langston Hughes's "Christ in Alabama," and Erskine Caldwell's "Kneel to the Rising Sun." But every selection, as well as the meticulously written introductions to each author, will enhance your comprehension of the past and your compassion for the trials of the present.

Notes

1. J. William Harris, *Deep Souths: Delta, Piedmont, and Sea Island Society in the Age of Segregation* (Baltimore: Johns Hopkins UP, 2001); Karla F. C. Holloway, *Passed On: African American Morning Stories* (Durham: Duke UP 2002); Lucia Stanton, *Free Some Day: The African-American Families of Monticello* (Chapel Hill: U of North Carolina P/Thomas Jefferson Foundation, 2000); Mechal Sobel, *The World They Made Together: Black and White Values in Eighteenth-Century Virginia* (Princeton: Princeton UP, 1987); Laurie A. Wilkie, *Material Culture and African American Identity at Oakley Plantation, Louisiana, 1840–1950* (Baton Rouge: Louisiana State UP, 2000); Maude Southwell Wahlman, *Signs and Symbols: African Images in African American Quilts* (Atlanta: Tinwood Books, 2001); Cinda K. Baldwin, *Great and Noble Jar: Traditional Stoneware of South Carolina* (Athens: U of Georgia Press, 1993); Cuesta Benberry, *Always There: The African American Presence in American Quilts* (Louisville: Kentucky Quilt Project, 1992); Edward Campbell and Kym S. Rice, *Before Freedom Came: African American Life in the Antebellum South* (Charlottesville: Museum of the Confederacy/UP of Virginia, 1991); Helen Bradley Foster, *New Raiments of Self: African American Clothing in the Antebellum South* (Oxford: Oxford International, 1997); Gladys-Marie Fry, *Stitched from the Soul: Slave Quilts from the Ante-Bellum South* (New York: Museum of American Folk Art/Dutton Studio Books, 1990); John Michael Vlach, *The Afro-American Tradition in Decorative Arts* (Cleveland: Cleveland Museum of Art, 1978); Jacqueline Tobin, Raymond Dobard, and Cuesta Benberry, *Hidden in Plain View: A Secret Story of Quilts and the Underground Railroad* (New York: Doubleday, 1999).

Acknowledgments

My examination of the literary and historical records of lynching began as part of an assignment for David Greetham's textual scholarship seminar at the City University of New York Graduate Center in January 2001. I want to thank David for challenging me to dig deeper into the archive and to think harder about the significance of what I found there.

To Jane Marcus, I owe my gratitude and love for her generous encouragement and for educating me by example in the political value of scholarship. I would also like to thank Jane for recognizing the significance of my research and for introducing this project to Rutgers University Press.

I am extremely grateful to my editor at Rutgers, Leslie Mitchner, for her willingness to take on the project and for her patient guidance and understanding during manuscript preparation.

I want to thank Michele Wallace for sharing with me her important work on lynching and visual culture and for offering invaluable assistance in preparing this manuscript. I also want to thank Michele for being a wonderful mentor and friend.

Librarians at the Library of Congress, the New York Public Library, and the Schomburg Center for Research in Black Culture were generous with their knowledge and time.

Bill Seraile kindly offered his expertise on historical matters.

For my partner, Rory Donnelly, and our children, Rory, Liadan, and Brendan, I wish to express my love and to thank them for their help and for understanding time I spent away to bring this project to completion.

Witnessing Lynching

Introduction
The Contest over Memory

Lynching's Other Legacy

By the 1920s, the famous antilynching crusader Walter White charged that the lynching of African Americans had become "an almost integral part of our national folkways," with "mobbism" having "degenerated to a point where an uncomfortably large percentage of Americans can read in their newspapers of the slow roasting alive of a human being in Mississippi and turn, promptly and with little thought, to the comic strip or sporting page" ([1929] 2001, viii). In their fight against white supremacist hegemony, antilynching activists waged war on two fronts—in the legislature and at the bar of public opinion. On the one hand, activists relentlessly lobbied Congress and the White House to pass antilynching legislation, producing as evidence photographs of lynchings, witness statements from law enforcement and public officials and members of the mobs, and documents analyzing the causes and revealing the shocking death toll. Understanding, on the other hand, that lynching could not take place without the acquiescence of the majority of white Americans, antilynching crusaders battled fiercely to win over white American hearts and minds and to encourage and mobilize black America in their effort to do so. To read through successive issues of activist newspapers and periodicals from this era imparts a real sense of the state of emergency lynching produced in the African American community and of the extent to which poetry and description and analysis were deployed as weapons in the war to end it.

In the preface to her novel *Contending Forces*, Pauline Hopkins emphasized her special responsibility as an African American artist to dismantle destructive stereotypes: "No one will do this for us. We must ourselves develop the men and women who will faithfully portray the inmost thoughts and feelings of the Negro," as yet "unrecognized by writers of the Anglo-Saxon race" ([1900] 1988, 13–14). The deceitfulness of southern whites about black suffering under Jim Crow convinced Lizelia Augusta Jenkins Moorer that this "story must be told by a Negro—one who is a victim to the inconveniences of prejudice." Describing the origin of her protest poetry in her deep desire "for the world to know the unvarnished truth," Moorer added that "if by this effort, the slightest sentiment is generated, tending to call attention to the open sore of the body politic, my prayers will have been answered" ([1907] 1988, 5). In a famous essay published in

1926, "The Criteria of Negro Art," renowned intellectual and editor of the NAACP's *Crisis* magazine W.E.B Du Bois articulated the thoughts of many activists when he described his writing talent as a tool employed to advance "the right of black folk to love and enjoy. I do not care a damn for any art that is not used for propaganda. But I do care when propaganda is confined to one side while the other is stripped and silent" ([1926] 1999, 323–324).

Du Bois, Hopkins, and Moorer were well justified in their fears that the abscess of racial violence would be ignored, leaving African American suffering distorted, silenced, and erased in dominant history, politics, and culture. At the time they were writing, lynchings had evolved from clandestine operations carried out in the dead of night into widely publicized festivals held in the light of day and carefully choreographed, recorded, and marketed throughout the nation. After the Second World War, however, with the country's apotheosis as democratic standard-bearer and leader of the free world, a staggering historical amnesia set in concerning U.S. genocide, slavery, and racial violence. As Columbia law professor Patricia Williams puts it, lynching became "one of the more complicated public secrets of this nation's past," ignored until very recently by literary and cultural critics, relegated to a footnote in standard histories of the United States, and glossed over in the mainstream media, a silence David Levering Lewis compares to "the familiar plaint of a generation of Germans knowing nothing of the Holocaust" (Williams 2000, 9; Lewis 1997, 1263).

Certainly, African Americans never forgot lynching. Williams describes being shown lynching photographs by her aunt as a rite of passage, a common practice used "among many black families" to warn of the dangers of racism, or to memorialize "specific victims—often relatives," or to inspire activism in the next generation. In her 1984 book, *Exorcising Blackness*, literary historian and critic Trudier Harris discovered in every generation of black writers a compulsion to confront and to work through the historical trauma of lynching in order to address contemporary racial concerns. In his recent and important study of lynching, noted historian Philip Dray reminds us that "for many decades" the institution of lynching represented "an awesome and destructive power, murderous to some, menacing to a great many, a constant source of intimidation to all black Southerners young and old and a daily reminder of their defenselessness." He goes on to ask: "Is it possible for white America to really understand blacks' distrust of the legal system, their fears of racial profiling and the police without understanding how cheap a black life was for so long in our nation's history?" (2002, xi).

Another legacy of this era is the extraordinary heroism and courage of those who stood up against what *Crisis* magazine termed the "lynching industry." These men and women provide a powerful and inspiring example of Americans at their best, from the silent protest parade in Harlem that commemorated the 1917 East St. Louis massacre with a dignity and moral force that moved bigoted policemen to tears, to Walter White risking his life to pass as white in the South to gather evidence against lynchers, to Anne Spencer's writing of one of the finest protest poems of the twentieth century to commemorate the lynching of Mary Turner. Through this collection, I hope to reintroduce the voices of these antilynching crusaders into the literary and historical record. I hope we will listen to what they can tell us about how lynching was experienced by those who were its victims.

The collection brings together poetry, essays, and fiction that examined and recorded lynching's ongoing effects even as the brutal facts evaporated from official memory. Lynching remained one of the most pressing issues for African Americans well into the 1950s, and the 1998 murder of James Byrd in Jasper, Texas, by three white men who dragged him to death behind their pickup truck reveals that lynching has not disappeared as a white supremacist option. The collected texts, written between 1890 and 1935 (roughly within the time frame designated by many historians as the "lynching era"), illustrate major themes that surface in writings about lynching from this period and illuminate continuing racial divisions. While lynchings and race riots are often studied as separate but related phenomena, my selections reflect my agreement with Swedish sociologist Gunnar Myrdal's contemporary assessment of lynching-era race riots as "magnified or mass lynching" (1944, 566). (Myrdal refused to use the term "riot" to describe these episodes, preferring instead "terrorization" or "massacres.") The writers in this volume, moreover, did not split too many hairs emotionally over the difference between lynching and other lethal mob violence. This volume concentrates on lynching because it was at once the most evil manifestation and the most potent symbol of the system of violence established to control blacks in the South after the Civil War, which also included chain gangs, incarcerations, legal lynchings by the state, and peonage. Because so many of these selections respond to specific historical events, I have chosen a chronological arrangement for the texts. Readers may also usefully group these selections according to genre and to the themes explored later in this introduction.

While African Americans were in the frontlines of the fight to end lynching, both races put forth concerted efforts to raise political awareness, preserve the evidence of the slaughter, and commemorate those who died. Most selections in this anthology are written by African Americans, but I have included selections by white American authors who challenge or undermine the dominant narrative with their versions of lynching. These selections run the gamut from Theodore Dreiser's "Nigger Jeff," a tentative exploration of his own complicity as a reporter who witnesses but does not try to stop a lynching, to Erskine Caldwell's blistering condemnation of lynching as perpetuating the misery of blacks and poor whites alike in "Kneel to the Rising Sun." I have not included white supremacist depictions of lynchings because they represent the narrative that became dominant and that survives as both cause and backdrop for the counter-narratives assembled in this anthology. In bringing these texts together in this context for the first time, I hope to suggest further areas for investigation; to shed light on lynching's cultural impact, both immediately and on successive generations; and to deepen awareness of the many ways in which writers have used words to remember this U.S. atrocity.

The Battle with the Press

Historians trace lynching's origins in the United States to punishments of Loyalists and British sympathizers by tarring-and-feathering, whipping, or hanging during the Revolutionary War. Nineteenth-century mob violence included urban disorder in the North against African Americans, immigrants, Mormons, and Catholics; the southern lynching of abolitionists and rebellious slaves; and vigilante justice in western cities and mining camps. In the early to mid–nineteenth century, most victims of lynching were white. While lynching-era targets also included trade unionists, immigrants, German Americans, and Mexicans, by the end of the 1890s, the vast majority of those murdered were African American in a campaign of terror fueled by the nationwide dissemination of racist propaganda through the established press.

In the South, terrorism of African Americans by lynching had been well established before the Civil War. Slaveholders had often exhibited their power through physical brutality, particularly through severe public punishments designed to forestall rebellion. Because slaves were considered valuable property, these object lessons usually stopped short of murder, but mob violence was not unknown. In his book-length study of lynching, Walter White points out that beginning in the 1830s, lynching was a tool more frequently employed to forestall rebellion. Also, "in the decade beginning in 1850 the obviously incomplete records cite the lynching of twenty-six Negroes for killing their masters. Nine of the twenty-six, one of the nine a woman, were burned at the stake" ([1929] 2001, 92).

With the defeat of the Confederacy, southern racial violence became increasingly systematic, reflecting the shift from slavery to peonage and the desire of whites to maintain social, political, and economic control of the large black population. Following emancipation, explains Nell Painter, "the freed people insisted on being treated in a new way, no more as chattel but as people." They began to refuse the "whippings that had been their lot as slaves" and demanded that they be spoken to respectfully. For their part, white southerners could not "fathom the idea of black freedom." One investigator remarked on the persistence of the view that "the negro exists for the special object of raising cotton, rice, and sugar *for the whites*" (1976, 5–6, emphasis in the original). Many whites thus viewed as tantamount to insurrection any effort by blacks to assert their rights or improve their situation. From the earliest days of freedom, then, whites used organized violence to destroy African American autonomy. In the 1880s and 1890s, an explosion of rhetoric about black inhumanity, degeneracy, and mental deficiencies fueled a campaign of violence designed to end African American economic and political gains in the generation after Reconstruction.

By even the most conservative estimate, "on average a black man, woman or child was murdered nearly once a week, every week," in the South between 1882 and 1930 (Tolnay and Beck 1995, xi). Modern technology allowed news of a lynching to spread throughout the country within hours. During the lynching era, it would have been hard to find anyone in America who was not well aware of lynching. Lynchers did not try to hide their actions or cover their faces. They took out ads in newspapers and circulated flyers announcing upcoming murders. Special excursion trains were chartered to allow thousands of spectators, including reporters from national papers, to attend the events. At some lynchings, broadsheets were sold of ballads that had been composed in advance to celebrate the event. Photographers did a brisk business selling postcards and snapshots of the torture in progress and of carefully posed portraits of the lynch party with the charred and dismembered remains. They ignored with impunity the ban on sending violent material by mail, and their products crisscrossed the nation. Although concentrated in the South, racial violence took place throughout the country. Descriptions of lynchings were standard fare in nearly every newspaper in the United States. Lynchings sold papers.

In her examination of newspaper reports of lynchings, Grace Hale discovered that "no matter the specific characteristics," beginning in the 1880s, "representations of lynchings increasingly fell into a ritualistic pattern," with "the narratives constructed by witnesses, participants, and journalists" assuming "a standardized form." Although the number of lynchings declined after 1890, their cultural impact increased because "more people participated in, read about, saw pictures of, and collected souvenirs from lynchings even as fewer mob murders occurred" (1999, 207, 201). This lurid reportage or, to use Jacqueline Dowd Hall's phrase, "folk pornography," was matched by the novels of Thomas Dixon—*The Leopard's Spots* (1902) and *The Clansman* (1905)—which reversed reality to portray southern whites as innocent prey of a power-hungry and barbaric black populace. In white supremacist fiction, black men, no longer curbed by slavery's paternalism and encouraged by inadequate law enforcement, were obsessed with raping white women. The 1915 film version of *The Clansman,* D. W. Griffith's *Birth of a Nation*, popularized the widely accepted propaganda that lynching was an extreme but necessary response to the "one crime" of rape, muting criticism of the practice even among more liberal northerners.

At the same time, stunning gains in the black literacy rate (which had risen by the turn of the century from 18 to 46 percent) produced a flowering of African American newspapers that offered alternatives to the white-controlled press. Even papers like the *New York Times* with its relatively strong record of opposing racial violence routinely reproduced harmful racial stereotypes. During the 1880s and 1890s, Ida B. Wells-Barnett, a young reporter for the black-owned Memphis *Free Speech,* embarked on an extraordinary one-woman crusade to end lynching after the murder of her three friends Thomas Moss, Calvin McDowell, and Henry Stewart. The men had owned and operated a concern known as the People's Grocery Store that competed directly with a white man's store in a black neighborhood in Memphis. Jailed for defending their lives and property against a mob incited by their competitor, the men were removed from jail and shot to death. Wells-Barnett had previously accepted lynching as a regrettable response to the "one crime" of rape. But as she recalled in her autobiography, the deaths of Moss,

McDowell, and Stewart "opened my eyes to what lynching really was. An excuse to get rid of Negroes who were acquiring wealth and property and thus keep the race terrorized and 'keep the nigger down'" (Duster 1970, 64). As Wells-Barnett began to collect newspaper reports of lynching and to visit towns near Memphis where lynchings had occurred, she discovered that many reported cases of "rape" actually represented clandestine, consensual relationships between white women and black men that had inadvertently become public. In 1892, the Memphis *Free Speech* published an editorial in which Wells-Barnett dared to suggest that white women might be the sexual aggressors. Condemning "the old threadbare lie that Negro men rape white women," Wells-Barnett warned that "if Southern white men are not careful they will over-reach themselves and public sentiment will have a reaction; a conclusion will then be reached which will be very damaging to the moral reputation of their women" (quoted in *Southern Horrors,* 52). Luckily Wells-Barnett was out of town when the enraged citizens of Memphis discovered that she was the author of the unsigned piece. They had to content themselves with destroying the offices of her newspaper and issuing threats to lynch her if she dared ever to set foot in Memphis again.

Ignoring personal danger, Wells-Barnett embarked on a crusade of literary activism. To avoid charges of distortion or inaccuracy, she culled statistics from accounts of lynchings in white newspapers and published them in pamphlets that circulated around the world. Thereby, she publicized the names of the dead, carefully analyzing the reasons for their murders and marshaling international public opinion around her antilynching cause. She followed in the footsteps of Frederick Douglass's antislavery campaign with speaking tours throughout the British Isles, where audiences were shocked by the massive scale and barbarity of the lynchings Wells-Barnett reported. In her pamphlet *Southern Horrors,* Wells-Barnett debunked the notion that lynching was an unfortunate necessity to keep the libidos of black men in check. As she pointed out, most lynchings were punishments for murder; only 30 percent even purported to be punishments for the "one crime" of rape. Moreover, the definition of a sexual "assault" was elastic. On many occasions when intercourse took place, it had been consensual. Using the lynching statistics from the *Chicago Tribune,* Wells-Barnett was able to substantiate that blacks were in fact lynched for a variety of reasons besides rape and murder. These included trying to vote, being acquitted by a jury, being too prosperous, being related to the wrong person, appearing in the wrong place at the wrong time, and being "saucy" and refusing to remove their hats. In several cases, blacks were lynched as a warning to other blacks or for "no offense" at all.

In *The Hindered Hand* (1905), a frankly propagandistic novel by preacher activist Sutton Griggs excerpted in this volume, a local spectator at the lynching of a woman explains to a northern visitor that "the real 'one crime' that paves the way for a lynching whenever we have the notion, is the crime of being black." To recontextualize folk pornography and to humanize its victims, writers in this volume often created barely fictional accounts of famous lynchings. Griggs's description of the lynching of Bud and

Foresta Harper in *The Hindered Hand* parallels in nearly every detail newspaper accounts of the February 7, 1904, lynching of Luther Holbert and his wife in Doddsville, Mississippi. In the fictional version, after Bud Harper is wrongfully accused of killing a white woman, the couple escapes southward to Mississippi—the last place fugitives would be expected to flee—where they soon run into trouble when Foresta attempts to alleviate the wrenching poverty produced by peonage. The white farmers decide that the Fultons (as they are now known) are "rather undesirable neighbors" and calmly reach a decision "to put them out of the way." In an addendum to the novel entitled "Notes for the Serious," Griggs writes that "the details of the Maulville burning were given the author by an eyewitness to the tragedy, a man of national reputation among the Negroes." Explaining his decision to suppress only "the more revolting features" of the lynching for "decency's sake," Griggs argues that because the details of the lynching "have entered the thought life of the Negroes, . . . their influence must be taken into account" (1905, 136, 293). Social scientists Tolnay and Beck describe "vivid publicity" surrounding lynchings as, "in part, a weapon for the further psychological torment of the entire African American community" (1995, 23–24). The reframing of these events in Griggs's novel serves to explain to his African American audience the political and economic origins of this assault against them, to encourage them to develop strategies of resistance, and to provide a space where their psychological trauma might be acknowledged.

Antilynching activists understood that it was imperative for their message to reach not just the traumatized black community but also apathetic masses of white readers and voters who saw lynching as unpleasant, regrettable, but sometimes necessary. Formed in 1909 after a savage race massacre in Abraham Lincoln's hometown of Springfield, Illinois, the National Association for the Advancement of Colored People understood from the start that "the war against lynching would be to a great extent a contest of language" (Dray 2002, 177). Borrowing from and improving on the techniques of Wells-Barnett, the NAACP published detailed graphic accounts of lynchings that cited statistics and named names. In 1916, *Crisis* magazine sent a white suffragist named Elizabeth Freeman to Waco, Texas, to discover the facts behind the lynching and burning of Jesse Washington, a mentally handicapped teenager accused of murdering and raping his white employer. Found guilty in a sham trial attended and controlled by the mob, Washington was seized immediately after the verdict and dragged out to be burned. The lynch mob cut off his fingers, ears, toes, and penis before lowering him into the fire to roars of approval from the crowd. With a group of young boys dancing attendance, the lynchers then dragged Washington's charred corpse through the streets of Waco. Freeman found out that townspeople and the local press generally approved of the lynching but worried that the mutilation of Washington would hurt business by damaging Waco's reputation as a modern, progressive city.

Freeman's report on the results of her investigation became the basis for a lengthy article, included here, published as an eight-page supplement to the *Crisis* entitled "The Waco Horror." The article was illustrated with photographs taken for souvenir postcards by a local professional photographer who, by previous arrangement with the city fathers, had been perfectly positioned to view the event. Freeman's account used the residents' own testimony to provide a chilling chronicle of criminality, the photographs of the mob serving as a visual dossier of the active participation and widespread complicity of an entire community. In the largest antilynching publicity campaign thus far, the NAACP distributed copies of "The Waco Horror" to seven hundred newspapers, all forty-two thousand subscribers to the *Crisis*, both houses of Congress, and hundreds of influential individuals in the arts and political life. Elizabeth Freeman took her story on the road in a national lecture tour.

Along with journalism designed to interrupt the dominant lynching narrative were literary and poetic interventions. In "Morning Ride," published in 1927 and included in this volume, Irish American poet Lola Ridge depicts lynching's penetration into the everyday life of modern urban America. One of the most notorious southern lynchings involved Leo Frank, a Jewish factory manager in Atlanta, who in 1913 was accused of raping and murdering his thirteen-year-old employee Mary Phagan, even though evidence suggested an African American handyman as the culprit. Walter White recalls that "because of Frank's religion and place of birth the case developed into a clash of prejudice in which anti-Northern and anti-Semitic hatred had been whipped to such a frenzy that the usual anti-Negro prejudice was almost forgotten" (1995, 25). In 1915, Frank was abducted and lynched by the Ku Klux Klan while he was serving a life sentence for the crime, which he strenuously denied committing. Although Frank would not be officially pardoned by the State of Georgia until 1986, Ridge in her 1927 poem describes seeing headlines about evidence clearing Frank's name from a New York City elevated train. Juxtaposing the advertisement replaying Leo Frank's lynching (headlines used to sell the newspaper) with an ad slogan ("Say it with flowers") and brand names (Wrigley's Spearmint gum, Carter's Little Liver Pills), Ridge comments wryly on the commonplace commodification of lynching news. The poem, however, resists this commodification through its second-person invocation of an identification with Frank's last physical sensations as he waited for the lynchers to pull the rope.

Many of the authors in this volume, including Robert Bagnall, W.E.B. Du Bois, Carl Sandburg, Walter White, James Weldon Johnson, Nancy Cunard, and Erskine Caldwell, moved between factual exposés and subjective articulations of the horrors of lynching. Using literature to work through events he had reported on as a journalist, Theodore Dreiser explores in his short story "Nigger Jeff" the complicated and compromising position of the reporter as "hired witness" to mob violence; in the story he reproduces many of his own observations gathered when he covered a lynching for the *St. Louis Republic*. The story is told from the perspective of Davies, a naïve young reporter sent to a rural Missouri community to investigate reports of the impending lynching of an African American, Jeff Ingalls, who has allegedly attacked a neighboring farmer's daughter. Davies arrives to find the girl's father and brother heading a posse intent on lynching the youth. The sheriff captures Ingalls first and hides him in his own home in a nearby village, only to have the mob arrive, capture Ingalls, and bring him back to their community, where they hang him from a bridge. Dreiser's skillful retelling of the events forces the reader to see the lynching through the eyes of the reporter, whose position as "hired spectator" becomes increasingly untenable, his behavior at times merging with that of the rest of the crowd. While he recognizes the cowardice of the members of the lynching party—at first reluctant to act, then, "more horror stricken than gleeful at their own work," unable to end it—Davies remains silent, though deeply shocked by the brutality he witnesses.

Wishing to emphasize the unreliability of news flowing northward, Walter White ends his 1924 novel, *Fire in the Flint*, with an Associated Press dispatch to newspapers throughout the country. The item—supplied by the editor of the local paper, who acts as agent for the AP—reports the lynching of a local Negro named Doc for "attempted assault on a white woman." The truth of the story, as the reader knows, is that physician Kenneth Harper had been summoned to a severely ill white female's home by her husband (who feared the quackery of the local white doctor), and that his real transgression was trying to organize a sharecropper's union among his desperately poor patients. A similarly unreliable local source may have contributed an item that appeared in the December 21, 1919, *New York Times* reporting the lynching of a man in Georgia by a mob that "boarded so quietly" the crew of the train carrying the prisoner never even noticed. The item angered poet Leslie Pinckney Hill enough to inspire his poem "So Quietly," published two years later and included in this volume—an attack on the moral cowardice of that Georgia community, the national media, and, by extension, the entire nation.

In another selection, Esther Popel comments on the reception of lynching news in her 1934 poem "Flag Salute," inspired by an incident in a "Negro school" in which a pupil read a report of a horrific lynching for his "news topic during the opening exercises of the morning." The pupils briefly discussed the facts of the lynching, "after which the student in charge gave this direction: pupils, rise, and give the flag salute! They did so without hesitation!" As the words of the pledge alternate with flashbacks to the lynching story, Popel helps us imagine the children's thoughts while enacting this compulsory performance of obedience to a country that routinely sanctions the slaughter of African Americans.

Against the Wall and Fighting Back:
Militance and Masculinity

The texts in this volume reflect the pull of a range of possible responses to lynching, among them accommodation, migration (to the North or to Africa), nonviolent resistance, and militant rebellion. As lynchings became public entertainment, the killings escalated into depraved torture in which castration played an increasingly important part, even when rape had not been alleged. In "Lynch Law in the South," his 1892 article for the *North American Review* excerpted in this anthology, famous abolitionist and African American elder statesman Frederick Douglass denounces lynching as a backlash against the inevitable progress of the Negro race. Douglas predicts two possible solutions to the race hatred and persecution that gripped the South: Either the region will tire of violence and enter into the spirit of nineteenth-century progress, or the Negro will tire of patience and imitate the violence of his tormenters. Citing examples of African American bravery in combat, Douglass warns the South not to count too much on Negro cowardice in the face of brutalization.

In *Mob Rule in New Orleans,* published in 1900 and excerpted in this volume, Ida B. Wells-Barnett created the first case study of a lynching, detailing how an individual incident of black resistance escalated into a full-scale race riot. She deconstructs accounts from the white New Orleans press of the supposed rampage of Robert Charles, who was viciously assaulted by white police officers while having a quiet conversation with a friend and who then used his gun in self-defense. Aware that shooting an officer carried the penalty of lynching, Charles determined to exact a high price from the white mob for his death. When he was finally captured after three days at large, Charles had killed five of his would-be murderers, wounded nine others, and sent countless more fleeing for their lives. Wells-Barnett turns on its head the attempt of white reporters to condemn Robert Charles as a crazed marauder driven berserk by black propaganda as she analyzes in detail the content of each pamphlet found in his lodgings, describes the purpose of the emigration societies to which he belonged, and even solicits character testimonials from his friends. Disrupting derogatory stereotypes of black masculinity, a portrait emerges of a man of quiet integrity and passionate intensity, a striver and an activist, tireless in his pursuit to better himself and to improve the entire situation of his race. As Wells-Barnett concludes, Robert Charles provided a truly heroic figure for the African American people.

The resolve to die like a man rather than an animal, to meet escalating white violence with masculine force rather than passivity, forms a persistent refrain in these selections. French Wilson's "Jimmy," published in the *Crisis* in 1914, features a traumatized young boy's apocalyptic ascent into militant manhood. Before his rescue by an African American attorney and his wife, the twelve-year-old orphan had nearly died from horrendous torture inflicted by a white warden at a "reform farm." Although the boy gradually recovers a measure of physical and mental strength, he nurtures a dream of retribution in which, during a general uprising of his people, he kills his oppressor, whom he sees daily in their small town. The day of reckoning arrives when the ex-warden leads a mob past Jimmy's home, dragging an innocent man to be lynched.

Another selection, Mary Powell Burrill's 1919 play "Aftermath," dramatizes the masculine determination Du Bois celebrated in his famous challenge to African American troops returning from the First World War to "marshal every ounce of our brain and brawn to fight a sterner, longer, more unbending battle against the forces of hell in our own land." The play opens in a rural South Carolina cabin as an old woman, Mam Sue, and her granddaughter, Millie, discuss the end of the war and the return of Millie's brother John from battle. While John was fighting on the fields of France to make the world safe for democracy, an American lynch mob terrorized his family and burned his father alive in a dispute over wages. Against Mam Sue's advice, Millie has spared her brother this knowledge, fearing that his sorrow and despair would endanger his life in battle. John returns unexpectedly, clearly transformed by his battle experience and his exposure to life outside the Jim Crow South. Signaling the death of the old ways of dealing with racism, he moves aside his father's Bible to place his guns on the mantelpiece. (His grandmother's crooning of hymns to a militant Christ reinforces this message.) When a neighbor blurts out the news of his father's death, John picks up the guns, hands one to his younger brother, whom he castigates for surviving by running from trouble, and leads him out to seek revenge against their father's murderers.

This new spirit of determination and pride among African American veterans impressed Carl Sandburg during his investigation into conditions in Chicago's "black belt" shortly before the 1919 race terrorization there. He noted in *The Chicago Race Riots, July 1919* that in "one neighborhood are thousands of strong young men who have been talking to each other on topics more or less intimately related to the questions, 'What are we ready to die for? Why do we live? What is democracy? What is the meaning of freedom; of self-determination?'" Sandburg added that the "thought that seemed uppermost" is that having fought for America, the veterans want "to see our country live up to the constitution and the declaration of independence" ([1919] 1969, 8). When the shooting started in Chicago, African Americans defended themselves with guns and counterattacked with retaliatory fire against whites. As historian Herbert Shapiro explains, while "resistance by one means or another has always been the core of the black response to violence," in 1919 as racial violence erupted across the country, black "resistance was more often overt and directly defiant in its willingness to inflict as well as suffer casualties" (1988, 150).

As other texts show, the expectation of returning soldiers that heroic service to their country merited full recognition of their manhood was bitterly dashed, particularly in the South, where the courageous performance of African Americans on the battlefield caused great alarm. Some black men were lynched for daring to wear their uniforms, which were considered an encroachment upon and affront to a southern social order that required them to remain "boys." In the selection "The Black Draftee from Dixie," published in 1922—a poem dedicated to twelve southern blacks who had been lynched upon their return home from service overseas—Carrie Williams Clifford writes of a man lynched for seeking his democratic rights, a "hero-warrior" with black skin but a heart "white and loyal to the core" to Dixie. In another selection, "Lynching and Debt Slavery," an American Civil Liberties pamphlet issued in 1921, William Pickens describes massive retaliation from the white supremacist machine when Arkansas sharecroppers tried to organize a labor union to demand their share of dramatic wartime profits on the price of cotton.

Under this system, militance could mean simply asking for a fair accounting of wages. In poetry by Sterling Brown included in this volume—"He Was a Man" (1932) and "Let Us Suppose" (1935)—the stories of actual lynching victims provide compelling examples of dignity and heroism under Jim Crow. White writers who describe lynching scenarios, on the other hand, tell of a social order in which individual heroism is perceived less as threatening than as beyond the limits of possibility. Published in *Scribner's* in 1935, Erskine Caldwell's "Kneel to the Rising Sun" dramatizes how white masculinity categorically forbids solidarity with fellow laborers who are African American, even though the prohibition clearly violates the white worker's self-interest. The story begins as a white sharecropper, Lonnie, goes to the company store to beg for food for his family, who have been starving on short rations. Lonnie's employer, Arch Gunnard, intimidates all men except one of his black sharecroppers, Clem Henry, whom both black and white acknowledge as a natural leader. Everyone in the county suspects that a lynching is in the cards for Clem, yet it has clearly been held at bay while both sides observe a tension-laden ceasefire that allows the system of oppression to function smoothly.

Lynching and Womanhood

Overly laden with masculine coding, lynchings were also powerfully invested in policing female sexuality. Rationalizing their own interracial liaisons and rapes through the Jezebel myth that portrayed black females as passionate and sexually precocious, white men sought to compensate by creating a fiction of white women as sexless and incapable of miscegenation. Sex between black men and white women by definition, then, constituted black rape.

In his 1940 novel *Trouble in July,* Caldwell again demonstrates the powerful disciplinary effect of white supremacist ideology when a farmer finds no option as a white man beyond turning a frightened young boy over to a posse, even though he knows that the boy is innocent of the rape he is charged with and that the action will haunt him for the rest of his life. In a departure from the usual lynching narrative, the novel ends when the boy's accuser, a poor white girl from a disreputable family, recants her testimony and the mob turns from the boy they have just lynched and stones her to death.

Although lynching served primarily as a tool of economic and social terror, the myth of the black rapist allowed white men to violently police a status quo aimed at the social and economic subjugation of both black men and white women. Under the name of southern chivalry and for her own protection, the southern white woman found herself confined to housekeeping and childbearing, "a chattel of her husband and owner as precisely as a Negro slave was before the Civil War" (White [1929] 2001, 160). Just as slaveholders had the right to protect their property with violence if necessary, so did white southern men use the protection of women as a pretense for violence against black men and as a screen for their continuing sexual exploitation of black women and girls. It is no accident that eight of the twelve states that refused to ratify the Twentieth Amendment granting women the vote were from the South.

Yet, if it is true that white women were made to "pay a tremendous price for lynching," as Walter White wrote in 1929, it is equally true that they were offered a perverse power in the transaction ([1929] 2001, 162). As many of the selections here demonstrate, white women participated in lynchings by ritually identifying their attackers. Under duress, as Robert Bagnall's "The Unquenchable Fire" reflects, women often characterized even consensual relationships with black men as rape. Many times the identification of an unknown attacker was coerced or forced. Under segregation, race trumped class and even gender, allowing the poor white woman who cried rape to assume the mantle of a southern lady and to force groups of men to do her bidding. Not limiting themselves to testimony and accusation, white women participated in lynchings by firing at corpses, screaming and spitting at victims, and scrambling for souvenirs with their husbands and children. Many of the poetic memorializations of lynching in this volume document white women's presence as approving witnesses and as sadistic participants. In Claude McKay's "The Lynching" (1922), women push forward to observe the excruciating suffering of the victim, "but never a one" shows "sorrow in her eyes of steely blue." In Countee Cullen's "Christ Recrucified," published the same year, women join in "battling" for the victim's "black and brittle bones." In Bertha Johnston's "I Met a Little Blue-Eyed Girl" (1912) and Esther Popel's "Flag Salute" (1932), women and girls receive chivalric trophies of the teeth of lynching victims, which they hang on golden chains around their necks.

Many of the selections written by African American men reveal a deep anxiety about the mortal dangers of white women's sexuality. The lynching paraphernalia Richard Wright discovers at the site of a ritual burning includes, among other objects of oral pleasure, "butt-ends of cigars and cigarettes, peanut shells, a drained gin-flask, and a whore's lipstick." In his 1922 poem "The South," Langston Hughes represents the South as at once an atavistic, bestial idiot and a syphilitic and seductive whore. This allows him, on the one hand, to articulate the reality that commerce with a white woman is a sexually transmitted disease that ends in fatality, and on the other, to transfer accusations of bestiality and sexual depravity back onto a feminized southern society slowly rotting from its own corruption. In Jean Toomer's "Portrait in Georgia"(1923), the body of the southern belle dissolves into the body of a lynched black man, the union between the two collapsing at the instant it occurs into the violent ritual meant to prevent it:

> Hair—braided chestnut,
> coiled like a lyncher's rope,
> Eyes—fagots,
> Lips—old scars, or the first red blisters,
> Breath—the last sweet scent of cane,
> And her slim body, white as the ash
> of black flesh after flame.

In *Scottsboro Limited,* a 1932 pamphlet written to protest the legal lynching of the Scottsboro boys, Langston Hughes included a poem entitled "Justice" that depicts the blind goddess with "two festering sores" where her eyes might once have been. The wounds recall not only the castration of southern lynching victims, but also the twisted oedipal relations between black males and a white patriarchy responsible for the mass rape of their mothers. In "Christ in Alabama," also from *Scottsboro Limited,* Hughes describes a perverted family romance that reverses ordinary oedipal relations as the godlike southern patriarch violates the mother, then murders his own son. Written as a litany, "Christ in Alabama" summons the violated black woman through an invocation—"Mammy of the South, Silence your mouth"—that at the same time calls attention to her erasure from the conventional lynching narrative.

The selections in this volume show a pronounced refusal to "silence your mouth," documenting the forceful presence of African American women's voices from the beginning of the lynching era. Blaming lynching on the psychic fallout from slavery in her 1904 essay "Lynching from a Negro's Point of View" excerpted here, Mary Church Terrell expects little kindness from women raised on a tradition of white female cruelty to black women and children. She cannot help imagining, however, "what a tremendous influence for law and order, and what a mighty foe to mob violence Southern white women might be, if they would arise in the purity and power of their womanhood to implore their fathers, husbands and sons no longer stain their hands with the black man's blood."

In 1893 when civil rights activist and poet Frances Harper addressed the World's Congress of Representative Women at the Columbian Exposition in Chicago, she pictured her audience standing on "the threshold of a woman's era" and warned women of their moral responsibility to take away the power of "brutal and cowardly men" to "torture, burn, and lynch" people (Harper 1894, 433–437). In her poem published three years later and included in this volume, "An Appeal to My Countrywomen," Harper condemns her white sisters for their hypocritical neglect of the plight of the South; they weep easy tears over the "sad-eyed Armenian" and "the exile of Russia" while ignoring the "sobs of anguish" and "murmurs of pain" from African American sisters mourning their kin. White women will soon join in the weeping, Harper warns, not just for the African American, but for their own sons who must reap the bitter harvests their fathers have sown. In her autobiographical history of her time as an army nurse during the Civil War, Susie Baker King Taylor bristles at the hypocrisy of the ex-Confederate daughters' protesting the performance of *Uncle Tom's Cabin* because of the bad effect it will have on children, and recounts her own memories of seeing men, women, and children auctioned off without mercy. "Do these Confederate Daughters ever send petitions to prohibit the atrocious lynchings and wholesale murdering and torture of the negro?" Taylor demands to know. "Do you ever hear of them fearing this would have a bad effect on the children?"

In fact, Harper and Taylor anticipated one of the key issues that moved white women to take public action to prevent lynching. When Jessie Daniel Ames organized the Association of Southern Women for the Prevention of Lynching (ASWPL) in 1930, in what white feminist and civil rights activist Lillian Smith called a "magnificent uprising against the sleazy thing called 'chivalry,'" one of the founding concerns was the effect of lynchings on the young boys and girls who were allowed to witness them (1994, 146). They were also deeply concerned that many women watched and sometimes actively participated in the brutality. Above all, the ASWPL demanded an end to men's invoking female protection as a screen for their crimes. After six years, the number of women in the association grew from twelve to more than thirty-two thousand. Their intervention in local lynchings helped encourage its continued decline in the 1930s.

In addition to the low-key localized intervention of Jessie Daniel Ames and her southern ladies, the 1930s also witnessed a dramatic, internationally publicized attack by a southern white woman on the myth of chivalry and the vaunted purity of the white southern female in the Scottsboro Boys case. Nine black youths between the ages of twelve and nineteen were accused of raping two white women who had hopped the same freight train to look for work. The case turned into an international cause célèbre after the International Labor Defense (ILD), the legal arm of the Communist party, interceded on the youths' behalf. In the 1931 trial, the nation watched Victoria Price, a twice-married prostitute who had served time on charges of adultery and vagrancy, mount the witness stand and spin a lurid and highly improbable story of a gang rape by nine teenagers that left her without a bruise or even the slightest genital inflammation. (This testimony would receive a brilliant reenactment in Robert Mulligan's film version of Harper Lee's *To Kill a Mockingbird*.) Elevated through her testimony and that of her travelling companion, Ruby Bates, to the status of a white lady in need of protection, Price starred in a performance that inflamed mob passions to a fever pitch. The result was eight sentences of death and years of costly litigation for the state of Alabama before the last "boy" (now in middle age) would be freed.

The ILD represented the youths in appeals that reached all the way to the Supreme Court, and demonstrations were held in Britain, Moscow, and Berlin. In the second trial, Ruby Bates and Lester Carter, a white man who had also been on the train, testified that the charge of rape had been completely fabricated by Victoria Price to avoid a jail term. In "Scottsboro—and Other Scottsboros," her polemical account of the second trial published in 1934, poet and activist Nancy Cunard describes the reaction of the courtroom upon hearing Ruby Bates recant her testimony:

> "The Negroes never touched me, as they never touched Victoria Price."
> This is what Ruby Bates told the court. Though they had heard she was
> coming now to be a witness for the boys, and that she had publicly
> repudiated the rape lie, to hear this Southern white girl, one of
> themselves, utter this statement, made them aghast and convulsed with
> fury. It is the first great crack in the old Southern structure of white

supremacy. It will never be forgotten, it is a very high and splendid point
in the history of black and white. Realize too that it needed very great
courage, physical and moral, in these two young white Southerners,
Ruby Bates and Lester Carter. With their testimony they were piercing
the whole of the rotten Southern fabric of lies and race hatred, holding it
up to the entire world, tearing it inside out.

Ruby Bates joined the mothers of the Scottsboro Boys on many public platforms to
apologize for the great wrong she had done and to voice her concern that the boys' lives
not be lost because of her lie. The combination of the Scottsboro case with the famous
Scopes trial, in which the South fought against the teaching of evolution, led to increasingly critical coverage of southern backwardness, particularly in its racial relations. The
South dug into a defensive position against Yankees and Communists and especially
against Ruby Bates, who found herself shunned as a race traitor and whore who
deserved to be lynched.

Lynching and Whiteness

The racial and sexual mythology of southern apartheid demanded that even consensual
sex between a black man and a white woman be punished by death, and Ida B. Wells-
Barnett was herself almost lynched for suggesting that such a consensual relationship
was even possible. At the same time, as Wells-Barnett and many others pointed out, the
facts of miscegenation—often the result of white rape—were clearly marked in the various hues of the African American population. As Mrs. Smith says in Hopkins's *Contending Forces,* "There are strangely tangled threads in the lives of many colored
families." Some African Americans were undoubtedly lynched by mobs that included
their white relatives.

A number of the writers in this volume describe the problem of violence within
extended families that straddled the color line. In Charles Chesnutt's "The Sheriff's
Children" (1889), Sheriff Campbell, a well-educated man with a "high sense of responsibility pertaining to his office," prevents a lynch mob from taking a youth accused of
murdering a prominent community member. When a bullet from outside the jail dis-
tracts the lawman, the prisoner seizes his gun, threatens to shoot, and then reveals that
he is the sheriff's son by an enslaved woman whom he had sold down the river along
with the boy following a quarrel. Just as the prisoner takes aim to kill his father, the
sheriff's daughter arrives and wounds the young man in the arm. After dressing his
son's arm and promising to call the doctor in the morning, the sheriff goes home deeply
troubled.

In a society where "the baleful influence of human slavery poisoned the very fountains of life," the sheriff can consider himself a good man even after inflicting physical cruelty and deep psychological trauma on his lover and child. Faced with death,
the sheriff achieves enough moral clarity to admit his wrongdoing. Chesnutt makes

clear, however, that such an admission is not enough to resolve the deeper pain inflicted by a society where the youth's skin color means to wear "a badge of degradation" in his own country and where the mere accusation of crime condemns him to death at the hands of a mob or by the decree of the state. Chesnutt's story of near recognitions and misrecognitions proves a despairing parable about race relations in the South.

Although "The Sheriff's Children" was written nearly fifty years ahead of Langston Hughes's "Christ in Alabama," both show the bankruptcy of the white supremacist lawgiver as the despoiler of black women (who are silenced or sold down the river) and murderer of his own children (under the sign of religion or respectability). These intrafamily lynching tragedies underline the fact that segregation was from its inception an impossible rejection of southern reality that required increasingly pathological violence to maintain.

Perhaps the most pathological feature of the lynching epidemic was its strange mingling of barbarism with religiosity. Robert Penn Warren once wrote of an old southern "joke" that runs: "After the Saturday night lynching, the congregation generally turns up a little late" (1956, 57). The antecedents of this "joke" lie in white southern Protestantism's long complicity with the slave trade, vocal backing of segregation, and tacit as well as overt support for lynching. During slavery, preachers twisted the Bible to make God a white supremacist slave master, turning southern evangelical Protestantism from a religion of tolerance and brotherhood to a creed of bigotry against African Americans that was later revised to include Catholics and Jews. Walter White found it "exceedingly doubtful if lynching could possibly exist under any other religion than Christianity," singling out in particular the "violently emotional" evangelical revival services that whipped men and women into a frenzy of "emotions of cruelty," which sought "an outlet in lynching" ([1929] 2001, 40–43). Baptist and Methodist ministers were instrumental in the resurgence of the Klan, and ministers attended and sometimes even led lynchings.

Lynching's victims were also steeped in the Christian religion. Many prayed and sang hymns while dying, and others unsuccessfully implored their captors to show them Christian mercy. The lynching ritual naturally suggested the suffering and martyrdom of Christ on the cross to the African American community, and it would be nearly impossible to mention all the references to Christ in the antilynching literature. In the many representations of lynching as crucifixion, however, it is possible to identify two separate impulses. The first, as mentioned, comes from within the vocabulary of Christian belief, in which the innocent victim is equated with the martyred Christ, cut down but somehow transformed by contact with evil. The second impulse, not always separate from the first, ironically identifies the lynching victim with Christ to expose and critique white evangelical Protestantism's heart of darkness.

In *Rituals of Blood,* Orlando Patterson identifies "a substantial minority of lynchings" as partaking of a "cult of human sacrifice" in which victims became "burnt offerings to a Southern Christian God" whom worshippers sought "to assuage and propitiate after their humiliating defeat in the Civil War and their trauma of losing a cherished way of life." Patterson calls these blood rituals both religious and cannibalistic, with the sacrificed victim, "if not literally eaten," often "symbolically eaten, in that he was carved up and pieces of his body taken as sacred ritual mementos." Citing scientific findings that "taste and smell stimulants add up to the same sensation" and that "their effects are not perceived differently by the brain," he equates quite literally the experience "of being suffused with the odor of the lynch victim's roasting body" to the "cannibalistic devouring of his body" (1998, 185, 183, 199).

Although such rituals of human sacrifice represented a minority of lynchings, their psychological impact made them focal points for antilynching poetry and fiction. Many poems from this period capture the symbolic cannibalism of the lynching ritual. Edward S. Hardwick's "The Mob," which appeared in *Opportunity* in 1935, refers to the crowd that had been howling "in gibberish frenzy" leaving the lynching with "their pent up emotional bellies distended." James E. Andrews, in "Burnt Offering," published in *Opportunity* in 1939, describes the lynching victim as the "fatted calf" to be offered up. In this collection, Claude McKay's "The Lynching" begins with a direct reference to this ritual: "His spirit in smoke to heaven ascended." In this poem, the sadistic burning of the victim serves as both an initiation rite for "little lynchers to be" and a form of tribute to the cold, castrating white female spectator. Another selection, Countee Cullen's "Christ Recrucified," stages a crucifixion updated to an event in which "good" Christian men and women participate. As in so many lynching poems, "Christ Recrucified" re-enacts the ritual distribution of human remains, not as sacred relics but as the perverted spoils of an atrocity.

Unlike most antilynching poems, James Weldon Johnson's 1916 poem "Brothers," included here, features a lynching victim who is guilty of a "fiendish" crime. The question of guilt, however, quickly becomes complicated. The leader of the mob takes exquisite pleasure in the lynching, as he directs his subordinates not to pile the wood too high lest the flames obscure the "agony and terror" on the victim's face. Pleased at the shrieking, he orders water to prevent the man's burning too fast. No matter the crime the victim has committed, this savagery turns the judgment of beastliness back upon the lynch party. The dying man chastises his tormenters, calling them "brothers" in "spirit" and "deed," identifying his own depravity as a product of theirs. An earlier version of Richard Wright's "guilt of the nation" thesis in *Native Son*, Johnson's poem indicts white racism for warping this man into a demented criminal, showing how the construction of "blackness" itself constitutes a white crime.

A pivotal moment in much African American fiction concerns the sudden, violent realization of the societal imposition of "blackness." Many of the selections in this volume, however, chronicle an epiphany in which artists see "blackness" as a blessed haven from and opposition to white savagery, and they use their texts to express and explore the nature of blackness, while mourning the concentrated assault of evil directed against them in the name of whiteness. In "White Things," published in the *Crisis* in 1923, Anne Spencer expresses outrage over the lynching and burning of a pregnant woman named Mary Turner who tried to defend her husband from a Georgia mob. Spencer describes a race of mutants who steal onto the earth and in a nihilistic rampage bleach of beauty everything they find. Her reference to "white feathers of cowardice" recalls the women who during the First World War taunted conscientious objectors with white feathers, emphasizing that women too are implicated in a death-dealing culture of white supremacy that turns violently upon itself, as well as upon others. The poem recalls how this culture of violence destroyed the natural resources of the country to fuel its imperial industrial expansion, displacing the native populations. The white things consume people as well, burning "a race of black, black men" to "ashes white." The white skull of the black man, "a glistening awful thing" and a trophy for "a young one," becomes in Spencer's poem a prophetic symbol of the violent retribution that will inevitably rebound upon future generations.

"Litany at Atlanta," which W.E.B. Du Bois wrote in 1906 while traveling home to an Atlanta in the throes of a racial massacre, records a terrible struggle with the desire for vengeance in the face of massive evil. Du Bois's poem turns the image of human sacrifice back upon his white tormentors. At one point, he calls upon the Lord to "pile the pale frenzy of blood-crazed brutes who do such deeds high on Thine altar . . . and burn it in hell forever and forever." The poet cries out to God, then wonders if God is dead or, worse, if God is white, "a pale and bloodless thing." Although he turns from the suggestion of God's whiteness as blasphemy, he nevertheless experiences God's silence as "white terror to our heart." His last lines speak of a permanent loss of faith, at the same time that his entire composition remains a moving prayer that for the time being keeps at bay the "red and awful shape" of revenge.

In his memoir, Walter White describes how his childhood experience of the Atlanta riots left him "gripped by the knowledge" of his blackness when he and his father confronted a murderous mob. "I was sick with loathing for the hatred which had flared before me that night and come so close to making me a killer; but I was glad I was not one of those made sick and murderous by pride" (1995, 12). The fragile "blackness" of the light-skinned protagonist of James Weldon Johnson's *Autobiography of an Ex-Colored Man* (1912), however, dies an early death before the savage spectacle of a man being burned alive. Having had a troubled relation with the concept of race since realizing in childhood that he was "black," the talented musician has recently chosen to dedicate his life to collecting and preserving African American music, using its traditions to create great classical works. In the first part of the selection, he travels through the South to soak in the folk culture, attending a "Big Meeting," where he hears Negro spirituals associated with rebellion, escape, and perseverance.

Later that evening, however, the protagonist witnesses the burning alive of a dehumanized, dulled, and stupefied African American man. The violence elicits mixed reactions from the crowd. Some cheer triumphant rebel yells; others get sick; but the protagonist turns away, overwhelmed by "shame that I belonged to a race that could be so dealt with; and shame for my country, that it, the great example of democracy to the world, should be the only civilized, if not the only state on earth, where a human being would be burned alive. My heart turned bitter within me." He chooses no longer to be "identified with a people that could with impunity be treated worse than animals. For certainly the law would restrain and punish the malicious burning of animals." Johnson makes clear the tremendous courage it takes to live as a black man, and the temptations for those who have the ability and the desire to pass out of the race. And yet the protagonist is the poorer and less fortunate for his decision. He has turned his back on the one thing that would help him make sense of this persecution and of his life—the rich power of vernacular protest and affirmation embodied in the songs he had only just begun to learn.

The Haunting of the South

The white men and women responsible for southern lynchings were, as Mary Church Terrell pointed out, descendents of slaveholders and of poor whites themselves "brutalized" by the "slaveholding environment." A number of selections from this volume probe the damaging effects of generations of racial violence. A short story by NAACP field secretary and Episcopal priest Robert Bagnall, "The Unquenchable Fire," which appeared in the *Messenger* in 1924 and is included here, weaves a gothic tale of incest, murder, and haunting that reaches back to the sins of slavery. A traveler tells of the madness that ensues when a Kentucky farmer, John Tower, brings a mulatto housekeeper and her blue-eyed son to live with him and his daughter after the death of his wife. Tower treats the boy as if he were his own son, and the resemblance between the two suggests that this is indeed the case. The children grow up unaware of their relation to each other and fall in love. When he learns that his daughter is pregnant, Tower brutalizes her into declaring that she has been raped, and the boy is lynched. "Don't imagine that those lynched are the only ones who suffer from it," cautions the traveler. Remorse for her complicity in the lynching drives the girl into dementia, and she becomes a raving, disheveled affront to the ideal of southern womanhood. The boy's mother lives on in the house, openly seething with hatred for her employers. Haunted by his murdered son, Tower grimly endures each day in fear for his life and each night in sleepless terror, awaiting the boy's return.

In her short story "Beyond the Limit" (1903), the white writer Alice French describes the insidious aftermath of a lynching for an entire southern town. Supporting Mark Twain's thesis in "The United States of Lyncherdom" that many whites lynch because they fear their neighbors' disapproval, French's story represents a remarkable critique of the cult of white southern masculinity. The lynchers, who had believed themselves to be good men, are haunted by the memory of the victim's screams for mercy as he burned to death. Although French never calls into question the victim's guilt, she makes clear that the torture of a man who appears to have been mentally ill went way "beyond the limit." One by one, the lynchers' lives begin to unravel. Some young men who took part move quickly from harassing blacks for fun to burning the feet of a conductor on a train they have robbed. A prosperous farmer who had been part of the mob sells up and leaves town, and a temperance man turns into a vicious drunk. The story ends when a young man who has been forced to live alone since the lynching because his African American employees have fled, and who finds himself unable to quiet the screams inside his head, kills himself after he finds children trying to burn a cat to death as "punishment." Lynching's function as initiation for southern white children is a disturbing and recurrent theme in these texts, reflecting the preservation and renewal of a tradition of traumatic violence.

Many texts in this volume describe a southern landscape steeped in traumatic memory, focusing particularly on the haunted tree. Just as the lynching tree often assumed a symbolic importance in the white community—lynchers ritually returned with new victims to the spot—it became for African Americans a site of mourning and commemoration. In Paul Laurence Dunbar's poem "The Haunted Oak" (1903), based on a story he heard of an actual lynching, the branch upon which the victim hung dies in sympathy with him, never again to bear leaves. Dunbar records a lynching legend from African American oral culture using the English Border ballad form, which often involves the description of murders committed through evil influences. According to Bruce Baker, lynching ballads were an important part of the white community's "folk culture" of lynching. White supremacist ballads celebrated the power of the mob by advertising the name of the victim while preserving the anonymity of the murderers. Dunbar reverses this convention by identifying the sheriff and minister as members of the lynching party. In describing the haunting of the lynchers, moreover, Dunbar further undermines the notion of white violence as invincible and unanswerable. As Angelina Grimké would later do, Dunbar portrays the lynching tree as a living witness to the truth about events seen perhaps only by the murderers and the victim.

The special significance of trees in Angelina Weld Grimké's work informs her deceptively simple poem "Tenebris," which appears in this volume. Here the tree, whose shadow falls like a hand moving against the white man's house, functions as a complex figure for both traumatic violation and retribution. The title, Latin for "in darkness," refers to the moral state of the South as well as to the darkness of the night. Retribution and guilt, fingers on the hand, relentlessly work to destroy the house of pain built on the bodies of the tortured and enslaved. Grimké's use of the tree suggests that the consequences of lynching will be instrumental in pulling down this edifice.

Trees are also instrumental in Grimké's short story "Goldie," a largely neglected but important cultural representation of traumatic experience based on the same lynching that inspired Spencer's "White Things." For the crime of defending her husband, Mary Turner was hung by her feet, enabling her torturers to slice her open so that her child fell from her womb to the ground, where a member of the lynching party crushed its little skull under his heel. This event left the entire African American community profoundly outraged, horrified, and deeply, personally wounded. The slow pace and sheer length of "Goldie" enacts a post-traumatic deferral of knowledge as the protagonist, Vic Forrest, journeys toward the home where his pregnant sister has been murdered. The woods he must pass through seem a "boundless, deep, horrible, waiting sea," in which he wrestles to avoid a truth he already knows (that his sister has been lynched) and to deny the dread of a future he can already guess (his own death by lynching). Given the proximity between Turner's lynching and the publication of the story, it is likely that readers would also have been resisting the known fate of this "little mother." Certainly the number of times Grimké returned to the story in her work suggests her own use of fiction as a means of coming to terms with and working through knowledge of this terrible event.

In contrast to the traumatic deferral of "Goldie," the final selection in this anthology, Richard Wright's 1935 poem "Between the World and Me" features a sudden, traumatic flashback when the speaker stumbles upon the aftermath of a lynching in "a grassy clearing." Littered among the remnants of the night's festivities are the dead man's castoff clothes—"a vacant shoe, an empty tie, a ripped shirt, a lonely hat, and a pair of trousers stiff with black blood"; his bones are there too, and the sunlight pours through the eye sockets of his skull.

Dominic LaCapra believes that "certain forms of literature or art" may "provide a more expansive space" than historiography—"in psychoanalytical terms, a *relatively* safe haven"—for exploring responses to trauma, "including the role of affect and the tendency to repeat traumatic events." The "emergence of a traumatic realism" in particular allows "an often disconcerting exploration of disorientation, its symptomatic dimensions, and possible ways of responding to them" (2001, 185, 186). The disorientation of Wright's poem suggests a terrible haunting—a compulsion to endure these horrible events over and over again—that forms a part of lynching's powerful disciplinary effect upon the living. At the same time, however, by restoring the possibility of narrativity to the victim, by unmaking the lynch mob's absolute representative power, Wright's poem begins the work of healing the catastrophic psychological rupture within the larger community.

Witnessing Lynching

National identity depends as much on what we choose to forget as on what we remember. Nostalgia for an uncomplicated western frontier or the charms of the southern plantation screens traumatic memories of our genocidal and homicidal relations with Native Americans and African Americans. As Jacqueline Dowd Hall maintains, however, "atrocities banished from official memory are not in fact forgotten; rather . . . conflicting memories are buried near the surface of consciousness: real memories, secondhand memories, memories of silence, memories we are supposed to forget" (1997, 1268). Collectively, the bodies of lynching victims constitute an enormous if unacknowledged presence in the national psyche, a presence that seems to loom larger as these traumatic events recede in time. The crowds that flocked to a recent exhibit of lynching photography at New York's Roth Horowitz Gallery responded as if to the shock of the familiar. "These images make the past present," observed an editorial review in the *New York Times* on January 13, 2000. "They refute the notion that photographs of charged historical subjects lose their power, softening and becoming increasingly aesthetic with time. These images are not going softly into any artistic realm. Instead they send shock waves through the brain, implicating ever larger chunks of American society and in many ways reaching up to the present."

Literature plays a crucial role in the mourning of catastrophic events, particularly when there has been a radical forgetting in other areas of communication and in the preservation of history. As Dray points out, "Lynch mobs rather pointedly do not keep accounts; in a sense they seek to negate history itself" (2002, viii). There are no official records such as court transcripts or the depositions of witnesses. It is impossible to come up with an accurate estimate of the number of people killed in the lynching epidemic, although there is unanimous agreement that the actual number of the dead was much, much higher than the numbers routinely cited in the historical literature. In the face of such a gap of statistical evidence, the subjective and affective record created by these writers represents a vital source of knowledge in which the literary text carries the burden of remembering and working through the past.

The writers in this volume devoted their lives to preserving a different memory of lynching. Through their journalism, poetry, essays, and fiction, they worked to ensure that we would remember lynching not as a manly response to an epidemic of black rape, but as the preventable eruption of racist oppression and violence that had been building since the days of slavery and that continues to trouble our society today. They responded to lynching by recreating scenes of lynching as an act of protest designed to raise awareness for necessary social change, by enacting a public mourning ritual to commemorate the dead, and by effecting a cathartic release of the trauma of a lynching they had witnessed or narrowly avoided. Considered together, these representations reveal how thoroughly and deeply the nightmare of lynching penetrated the American psyche.

This anthology provides today's reader with an opportunity to witness lynching via the words of those who lived through it. Beginning more than a century ago, these writers interrogated the meanings of whiteness and blackness and calculated the terrible price the United States paid for maintaining caste privilege. It is striking how many of these writers accurately predicted racism's traumatic psychological impact on future American generations and its corrosive effect on negotiations of gender and class. It is also instructive to see how clearly African American commentators at the turn of the century could diagnose the influence of homegrown U.S. racism on our treatment of other nations. "The archive," as Derrida reminds us, "has always been a *pledge*, and like every pledge, a token of the future. . . . [W]hat is no longer archived the same way is no longer lived in the same way" (1996, 4n. 1). In reintroducing the individual and collective voice of these antilynching activists into the literary and historical record, I hope that readers will be inspired to seek a new way to live race in America.

1889–1900

Charles W. Chesnutt

1858–1932

The nation's most respected and influential African American writer at the turn of the century, Charles W. Chesnutt earned his fame through his innovative reworking of the "plantation tradition" of southern literature. Collected in *The Conjure Woman* in 1899, Chesnutt's plantation stories depict enslaved people responding to oppression with dignity and wit, often using "conjure," African American hoodoo, to outmaneuver their oppressors. Although he was born and died in Cleveland, Ohio, Chesnutt spent many of his formative years in Fayetteville, North Carolina, and much of his fiction reflects his experiences in the South. Trained as a lawyer, he built a prosperous stenography and court-reporting business, which he gave up in order to write full time but had to resume after disappointing sales of his more controversial works.

Chesnutt saw racism as a barrier to the moral progress of the American people, and he wanted his writing to effect a moral revolution by changing the minds of his white readers. In the years between 1899 and 1905, Chesnutt published two short-story collections, three novels, a biography of Frederick Douglass, and numerous essays and articles. His three novels chronicle the adversities and afflictions of African American existence in the New South. *The House behind the Cedars* (1900) examines the significant temptation for light-skinned blacks to try to pass as white. In *The Marrow of Tradition* (1901), Chesnutt follows the fraught relations between the black and white branches of a southern family in the midst of a brutal race riot closely based on the 1898 white supremacist revolution in Wilmington, North Carolina. Revealing the rotten "marrow" at the core of the New South's invented traditions, Chesnutt depicts lynching fever as provoked and manipulated by white elites hungry for power. Chesnutt's last novel, *The Colonel's Dream* (1905), tells the story of a white philanthropist who abandons the struggle to ameliorate racial conditions in his native North Carolina.

One of Chesnutt's earliest examinations of lynching, "The Sheriff's Children" was published in 1889 in the *Independent* and later collected in *The Wife of His Youth and Other Stories of the Color Line* (1899). A "voluntary" Negro—light enough to pass as white but choosing not to do so—Chesnutt explored in his fiction the moral, emotional, and psychological fallout from the enforced division of people into fixed racial categories. Eric Sundquist says of Chesnutt that "no writer between Stowe and Faulkner so completely made the family a means of delineating America's racial crisis, during slavery and afterwards" (1993, 394). In this story, as in Robert Bagnall's "The Unquenchable Fire," the sins of the patriarchy and the failure of the South's children to recognize each other as part of the same family produce a moral chaos in which lynching and self-destruction are the tragic but inevitable results.

—— The Sheriff's Children ——

[The story begins with a description of the physical and mental isolation of Branson County, North Carolina.]

A murder was a rare event in Branson County. Every well-informed citizen could tell the number of homicides committed in the county for fifty years back, and whether the slayer, in any given instance, had escaped either by flight or acquittal, or had suffered the penalty of the law. So, when it became known in Troy early one Friday morning in summer, about ten years after the war, that old Captain Walker, who had served in Mexico under Scott, and had left an arm on the field of Gettysburg, had been foully murdered during the night, there was intense excitement in the village. Business was practically suspended, and the citizens gathered in little groups to discuss the murder, and speculate upon the identity of the murderer. It transpired from testimony at the coroner's inquest, held during the morning, that a strange mulatto had been seen going in the direction of Captain Walker's house the night before, and had been met going away from Troy early Friday morning, by a farmer on his way to town. Other circumstances seemed to connect the stranger with the crime. The sheriff organized a posse to search for him, and early in the evening, when most of the citizens of Troy were at supper, the suspected man was brought in and lodged in the county jail.

By the following morning the news of the capture had spread to the farthest limits of the county. A much larger number of people than usual came to town that Saturday,—bearded men in straw hats and blue homespun shirts, and butternut trousers of great amplitude of material and vagueness of outline; women in homespun frocks and slat-bonnets, with faces as expressionless as the dreary sandhills which gave them a meagre sustenance.

The murder was almost the sole topic of conversation. A steady stream of curious observers visited the house of mourning, and gazed upon the rugged face of the old veteran, now stiff and cold in death; and more than one eye dropped a tear at the remembrance of the cheery smile, and the joke—sometimes superannuated, generally feeble, but always good-natured—with which the captain had been wont to greet his acquaintances. There was a growing sentiment of anger among these stern men, toward the murderer who had thus cut down their friend, and a strong feeling that ordinary justice was too slight a punishment for such a crime.

Toward noon there was an informal gathering of citizens in Dan Tyson's store.

"I hear it 'lowed that Square Kyahtah's too sick ter hol' co'te this evenin'," said one, "an' that the purlim'nary hearin' 'll haf ter go over 'tel nex' week."

A look of disappointment went round the crowd.

"Hit's the durndes', meanes' murder ever committed in this caounty," said another, with moody emphasis.

"I s'pose the nigger 'lowed the Cap'n had some greenbacks," observed a third speaker.

"The Cap'n," said another, with an air of superior information, "has left two bairls of Confedrit money, which he 'spected 'ud be good some day er nuther."

This statement gave rise to a discussion of the speculative value of Confederate money; but in a little while the conversation returned to the murder.

"Hangin' air too good fer the murderer," said one; "he oughter be burnt, stidier bein' hung."

There was an impressive pause at this point, during which a jug of moonlight whiskey went the round of the crowd.

"Well," said a round-shouldered farmer, who, in spite of his peaceable expression and faded gray eye, was known to have been one of the most daring followers of a rebel guerrilla chieftain, "what air yer gwine ter do about it? Ef you fellers air gwine ter set down an' let a wuthless nigger kill the bes' white man in Branson, an' not say nuthin' ner do nuthin', *I'll* move outen the caounty."

This speech gave tone and direction to the rest of the conversation. Whether the fear of losing the round-shouldered farmer operated to bring about the result or not is immaterial to this narrative; but, at all events, the crowd decided to lynch the negro. They agreed that this was the least that could be done to avenge the death of their murdered friend, and that it was a becoming way in which to honor his memory. They had some vague notions of the majesty of the law and the rights of the citizen, but in the passion of the moment these sunk into oblivion; a white man had been killed by a negro.

"The Cap'n was an ole sodger," said one of his friends solemnly. "He'll sleep better when he knows that a co'te-martial has be'n hilt an' jestice done."

By agreement the lynchers were to meet at Tyson's store at five o'clock in the afternoon, and proceed thence to the jail, which was situated down the Lumberton Dirt Road (as the old turnpike antedating the plank-road was called), about half a mile south of the court-house. When the preliminaries of the lynching had been arranged, and a committee appointed to manage the affair, the crowd dispersed, some to go to their dinners, and some to secure recruits for the lynching party.

It was twenty minutes to five o'clock, when an excited negro, panting and perspiring, rushed up to the back door of Sheriff Campbell's dwelling, which stood at a little distance from the jail and somewhat farther than the latter building from the courthouse. A turbaned colored woman came to the door in response to the negro's knock.

"Hoddy, Sis' Nance."

"Hoddy, Brer Sam."

"Is de shurff in," inquired the negro.

"Yas, Brer Sam, he's eatin' his dinner," was the answer.

"Will yer ax 'im ter step ter de do' a minute, Sis' Nance?"

The woman went into the dining-room, and a moment later the sheriff came to the door. He was a tall, muscular man, of a ruddier complexion than is usual among Southerners. A pair of keen, deep-set gray eyes looked out from under bushy eyebrows, and about his mouth was a masterful expression, which a full beard, once sandy in color, but now profusely sprinkled with gray, could not entirely conceal. The day was hot; the sheriff had discarded his coat and vest, and had his white shirt open at the throat.

"What do you want, Sam?" he inquired of the negro, who stood hat in hand, wiping the moisture from his face with a ragged shirt-sleeve.

"Shurff, dey gwine ter hang de pris'ner w'at's lock' up in de jail. Dey're comin' dis a-way now. I wuz layin' down on a sack er corn down at de sto', behine a pile er flour-bairls, w'en I hearn Doc' Cain en Kunnel Wright talkin' erbout it. I slip' outen de back do', en run here as fas' as I could. I hearn you say down ter de sto' once't dat you would n't let nobody take a pris'ner 'way fum you widout walkin' over yo' dead body, en I thought I'd let you know 'fo' dey come, so yer could pertec' de pris'ner."

The sheriff listened calmly, but his face grew firmer, and a determined gleam lit up his gray eyes. His frame grew more erect, and he unconsciously assumed the attitude of a soldier who momentarily expects to meet the enemy face to face.

"Much obliged, Sam," he answered. "I'll protect the prisoner. Who's coming?"

"I dunno who-all *is* comin'," replied the negro. "Dere's Mistah McSwayne, en Doc' Cain, en Maje' McDonal', en Kunnel Wright, en a heap er yuthers. I wuz so skeered I done furgot mo'd'n half un em. I spec' dey mus' be mos' here by dis time, so I'll git outen de way, fer I don' want nobody fer ter think I wuz mix' up in dis business." The negro glanced nervously down the road toward the town, and made a movement as if to go away.

"Won't you have some dinner first?" asked the sheriff.

The negro looked longingly in at the open door, and sniffed the appetizing odor of boiled pork and collards.

"I ain't got no time fer ter tarry, Shurff," he said, "but Sis' Nance mought gin me sump'n I could kyar in my han' en eat on de way."

A moment later Nancy brought him a huge sandwich of split corn-pone, with a thick slice of fat bacon inserted between the halves, and a couple of baked yams. The negro hastily replaced his ragged hat on his head, dropped the yams in the pocket of his capacious trousers, and, taking the sandwich in his hand, hurried across the road and disappeared in the woods beyond.

The sheriff reentered the house, and put on his coat and hat. He then took down a double-barreled shotgun and loaded it with buckshot. Filling the chambers of a revolver with fresh cartridges, he slipped it into the pocket of the sack-coat which he wore.

A comely young woman in a calico dress watched these proceedings with anxious surprise.

"Where are you going, father?" she asked. She had not heard the conversation with the negro.

"I am goin' over to the jail," responded the sheriff. "There's a mob comin' this way to lynch the nigger we've got locked up. But they won't do it," he added, with emphasis.

"Oh, father! don't go!" pleaded the girl, clinging to his arm; "they'll shoot you if you don't give him up."

"You never mind me, Polly," said her father reassuringly, as he gently unclasped her hands from his arm. "I'll take care of myself and the prisoner, too. There ain't a man in Branson County that would shoot me. Besides, I have faced fire too often to be scared away from my duty. You keep close in the house," he continued, "and if any one disturbs you just use the old horse-pistol in the top bureau drawer. It's a little old-fashioned, but it did good work a few years ago."

The young girl shuddered at this sanguinary allusion, but made no further objection to her father's departure.

The sheriff of Branson was a man far above the average of the community in wealth, education, and social position. His had been one of the few families in the county that before the war had owned large estates and numerous slaves. He had graduated at the State University at Chapel Hill, and had kept up some acquaintance with current literature and advanced thought. He had traveled some in his youth, and was looked up to in the county as an authority on all subjects connected with the outer world. At first an ardent supporter of the Union, he had opposed the secession movement in his native State as long as opposition availed to stem the tide of public opinion. Yielding at last to the force of circumstances, he had entered the Confederate service rather late in the war, and served with distinction through several campaigns, rising in time to the rank of colonel. After the war he had taken the oath of allegiance, and had been chosen by the people as the most available candidate for the office of sheriff, to which he had been elected without opposition. He had filled the office for several terms, and was universally popular with his constituents.

Colonel or Sheriff Campbell, as he was indifferently called, as the military or civil title happened to be most important in the opinion of the person addressing him, had a high sense of the responsibility attaching to his office. He had sworn to do his duty faithfully, and he knew what his duty was, as sheriff, perhaps more clearly than he had apprehended it in other passages of his life. It was, therefore, with no uncertainty in regard to his course that he prepared his weapons and went over to the jail. He had no fears for Polly's safety.

The sheriff had just locked the heavy front door of the jail behind him when a half dozen horsemen, followed by a crowd of men on foot, came round a bend in the road and drew near the jail. They halted in front of the picket fence that surrounded the building, while several of the committee of arrangements rode on a few rods farther to the sheriff's house. One of them dismounted and rapped on the door with his riding-whip.

"Is the sheriff at home?" he inquired.

"No, he has just gone out," replied Polly, who had come to the door.

"We want the jail keys," he continued.

"They are not here," said Polly. "The sheriff has them himself." Then she added, with assumed indifference, "He is at the jail now."

The man turned away, and Polly went into the front room, from which she peered anxiously between the slats of the green blinds of a window that looked toward the jail. Meanwhile the messenger returned to his companions and announced his discovery. It looked as though the sheriff had learned of their design and was preparing to resist it.

One of them stepped forward and rapped on the jail door.

"Well, what is it?" said the sheriff, from within.

"We want to talk to you, Sheriff," replied the spokesman.

There was a little wicket in the door; this the sheriff opened, and answered through it.

"All right, boys, talk away. You are all strangers to me, and I don't know what business you can have." The sheriff did not think it necessary to recognize anybody in particular on such an occasion; the question of identity sometimes comes up in the investigation of these extra-judicial executions.

"We're a committee of citizens and we want to get into the jail."

"What for? It ain't much trouble to get into jail. Most people want to keep out."

The mob was in no humor to appreciate a joke, and the sheriff's witticism fell dead upon an unresponsive audience.

"We want to have a talk with the nigger that killed Cap'n Walker."

"You can talk to that nigger in the courthouse, when he's brought out for trial. Court will be in session here next week. I know what you fellows want, but you can't get my prisoner to-day. Do you want to take the bread out of a poor man's mouth? I get seventy-five cents a day for keeping this prisoner, and he's the only one in jail. I can't have my family suffer just to please you fellows."

One or two young men in the crowd laughed at the idea of Sheriff Campbell's suffering for want of seventy-five cents a day; but they were frowned into silence by those who stood near them.

"Ef yer don't let us in," cried a voice, "we'll bu's' the do' open."

"Bust away," answered the sheriff, raising his voice so that all could hear. "But I give you fair warning. The first man that tries it will be filled with buckshot. I'm sheriff of this county; I know my duty, and I mean to do it."

"What's the use of kicking, Sheriff?" argued one of the leaders of the mob. "The nigger is sure to hang anyhow; he richly deserves it; and we've got to do something to teach the niggers their places, or white people won't be able to live in the county."

"There's no use talking, boys," responded the sheriff. "I'm a white man outside, but in this jail I'm sheriff; and if this nigger's to be hung in this county, I propose to do the hanging. So you fellows might as well right-about-face, and march back to Troy. You've had a pleasant trip, and the exercise will be good for you. You know *me*. I've got powder and ball, and I've faced fire before now, with nothing between me and the enemy, and I don't mean to surrender this jail while I'm able to shoot." Having thus announced his determination, the sheriff closed and fastened the wicket, and looked around for the best position from which to defend the building.

The crowd drew off a little, and the leaders conversed together in low tones.

The Branson County jail was a small, two-story brick building, strongly constructed, with no attempt at architectural ornamentation. Each story was divided into two large cells by a passage running from front to rear. A grated iron door gave entrance from the passage to each of the four cells. The jail seldom had many prisoners in it, and the lower windows had been boarded up. When the sheriff had closed the wicket, he ascended the steep wooden stairs to the upper floor. There was no window at the front of the upper passage, and the most available position from which to watch the movements of the crowd below was the front window of the cell occupied by the solitary prisoner.

The sheriff unlocked the door and entered the cell. The prisoner was crouched in a corner, his yellow face, blanched with terror, looking ghastly in the semi-darkness of the room. A cold perspiration had gathered on his forehead, and his teeth were chattering with affright.

"For God's sake, Sheriff," he murmured hoarsely, "don't let 'em lynch me; I didn't kill the old man."

The sheriff glanced at the cowering wretch with a look of mingled contempt and loathing.

"Get up," he said sharply. "You will probably be hung sooner or later, but it shall not be to-day, if I can help it. I'll unlock your fetters, and if I can't hold the jail, you'll have to make the best fight you can. If I'm shot, I'll consider my responsibility at an end."

There were iron fetters on the prisoner's ankles, and handcuffs on his wrists. These the sheriff unlocked, and they fell clanking to the floor.

"Keep back from the window," said the sheriff. "They might shoot if they saw you."

The sheriff drew toward the window a pine bench which formed a part of the scanty furniture of the cell, and laid his revolver upon it. Then he took his gun in hand, and took his stand at the side of the window where he could with least exposure of himself watch the movements of the crowd below.

The lynchers had not anticipated any determined resistance. Of course they had looked for a formal protest, and perhaps a sufficient show of opposition to excuse the sheriff in the eye of any stickler for legal formalities. They had not however come prepared to fight a battle, and no one of them seemed willing to lead an attack upon the jail. The leaders of the party conferred together with a good deal of animated gesticulation, which was visible to the sheriff from his outlook, though the distance was too great for him to hear what was said. At length one of them broke away from the group, and rode back to the main body of the lynchers, who were restlessly awaiting orders.

"Well, boys," said the messenger, "we'll have to let it go for the present. The sheriff says he'll shoot, and he's got the drop on us this time. There ain't any of us that want to follow Cap'n Walker jest yet. Besides, the sheriff is a good fellow, and we don't want to hurt 'im. But," he added, as if to reassure the crowd, which began to show signs of disappointment, "the nigger might as well say his prayers, for he ain't got long to live."

There was a murmur of dissent from the mob, and several voices insisted that an attack be made on the jail. But pacific counsels finally prevailed, and the mob sullenly withdrew.

The sheriff stood at the window until they had disappeared around the bend in the road. He did not relax his watchfulness when the last one was out of sight. Their withdrawal might be a mere feint, to be followed by a further attempt. So closely, indeed, was his attention drawn to the outside, that he neither saw nor heard the prisoner creep stealthily across the floor, reach out his hand and secure the revolver which lay on the bench behind the sheriff, and creep as noiselessly back to his place in the corner of the room.

A moment after the last of the lynching party had disappeared there was a shot fired from the woods across the road; a bullet whistled by the window and buried itself in the wooden casing a few inches from where the sheriff was standing. Quick as thought, with the instinct born of a semi-guerrilla army experience, he raised his gun and fired twice at the point from which a faint puff of smoke showed the hostile bullet to have been sent. He stood a moment watching, and then rested his gun against the window, and reached behind him mechanically for the other weapon. It was not on the bench. As the sheriff realized this fact, he turned his head and looked into the muzzle of the revolver.

"Stay where you are, Sheriff," said the prisoner, his eyes glistening, his face almost ruddy with excitement.

The sheriff mentally cursed his own carelessness for allowing him to be caught in such a predicament. He had not expected anything of the kind. He had relied on the negro's cowardice and subordination in the presence of an armed white man as a matter of course. The sheriff was a brave man, but realized that the prisoner had him at an immense disadvantage. The two men stood thus for a moment, fighting a harmless duel with their eyes.

"Well, what do you mean to do?" asked the sheriff with apparent calmness.

"To get away, of course," said the prisoner, in a tone which caused the sheriff to look at him more closely, and with an involuntary feeling of apprehension; if the man was not mad, he was in a state of mind akin to madness, and quite as dangerous. The sheriff felt that he must speak the prisoner fair, and watch for a chance to turn the tables on him. The keen-eyed, desperate man before him was a different being altogether from the groveling wretch who had begged so piteously for life a few minutes before.

At length the sheriff spoke:—

"Is this your gratitude to me for saving your life at the risk of my own? If I had not done so, you would now be swinging from the limb of some neighboring tree."

"True," said the prisoner, "you saved my life, but for how long? When you came in, you said Court would sit next week. When the crowd went away they said I had not long to live. It is merely a choice of two ropes."

"While there's life there's hope," replied the sheriff. He uttered this commonplace mechanically, while his brain was busy in trying to think out some way of escape. "If you are innocent you can prove it."

The mulatto kept his eye upon the sheriff. "I didn't kill the old man," he replied; "but I shall never be able to clear myself. I was at his house at nine o'clock. I stole from it the coat that was on my back when I was taken. I would be convicted, even with a fair trial, unless the real murderer were discovered beforehand."

The sheriff knew this only too well. While he was thinking what argument next to use, the prisoner continued:—

"Throw me the keys—no, unlock the door."

The sheriff stood a moment irresolute. The mulatto's eye glittered ominously. The sheriff crossed the room and unlocked the door leading into the passage.

"Now go down and unlock the outside door."

The heart of the sheriff leaped within him. Perhaps he might make a dash for liberty, and gain the outside. He descended the narrow stairs, the prisoner keeping close behind him.

The sheriff inserted the huge iron key into the lock. The rusty bolt yielded slowly. It still remained for him to pull the door open.

"Stop!" thundered the mulatto, who seemed to divine the sheriff's purpose. "Move a muscle, and I'll blow your brains out."

The sheriff obeyed; he realized that his chance had not yet come.

"Now keep on that side of the passage, and go back upstairs."

Keeping the sheriff under cover of the revolver, the mulatto followed him up the stairs. The sheriff expected the prisoner to lock him into the cell and make his own escape. He had about come to the conclusion that the best thing he could do under the circumstances was to submit quietly, and take his chances of recapturing the prisoner after the alarm had been given. The sheriff had faced death more than once upon the battlefield. A few minutes before, well armed, and with a brick wall between him and them he had dared a hundred men to fight; but he felt instinctively that the desperate man confronting him was not to be trifled with, and he was too prudent a man to risk his life against such heavy odds. He had Polly to look after, and there was a limit beyond which devotion to duty would be quixotic and even foolish.

"I want to get away," said the prisoner, "and I don't want to be captured; for if I am I know I will be hung on the spot. I am afraid," he added somewhat reflectively, "that in order to save myself I shall have to kill you."

"Good God!" exclaimed the sheriff in involuntary terror; "you would not kill the man to whom you owe your own life."

"You speak more truly than you know," replied the mulatto. "I indeed owe my life to you."

The sheriff started. He was capable of surprise, even in that moment of extreme peril. "Who are you?" he asked in amazement.

"Tom, Cicely's son," returned the other. He had closed the door and stood talking to the sheriff through the grated opening. "Don't you remember Cicely—Cicely whom you sold, with her child, to the speculator on his way to Alabama?"

The sheriff did remember. He had been sorry for it many a time since. It had been the old story of debts, mortgages, and bad crops. He had quarreled with the mother. The price offered for her and her child had been unusually large, and he had yielded to the combination of anger and pecuniary stress.

"Good God!" he gasped, "you would not murder your own father?"

"My father?" replied the mulatto. "It were well enough for me to claim the relationship, but it comes with poor grace from you to ask anything by reason of it. What father's duty have you ever performed for me? Did you give me your name, or even your protection? Other white men gave their colored sons freedom and money, and sent them to the free States. *You* sold *me* to the rice swamps."

"I at least gave you the life you cling to," murmured the sheriff.

"Life?" said the prisoner, with a sarcastic laugh. "What kind of a life? You gave me your own blood, your own features,—no man need look at us together twice to see that,—and you gave me a black mother. Poor wretch! She died under the lash, because she had enough womanhood to call her soul her own. You gave me a white man's spirit, and you made me a slave, and crushed it out."

"But you are free now," said the sheriff. He had not doubted, could not doubt, the mulatto's word. He knew whose passions coursed beneath that swarthy skin and burned in the black eyes opposite his own. He saw in this mulatto what he himself might have become had not the safeguards of parental restraint and public opinion been thrown around him.

"Free to do what?" replied the mulatto. "Free in name, but despised and scorned and set aside by the people to whose race I belong far more than to my mother's."

"There are schools," said the sheriff. "You have been to school." He had noticed that the mulatto spoke more eloquently and used better language than most Branson County people.

"I have been to school, and dreamed when I went that it would work some marvelous change in my condition. But what did I learn? I learned to feel that no degree of learning or wisdom will change the color of my skin and that I shall always wear what in my own country is a badge of degradation. When I think about it seriously I do not care particularly for such a life. It is the animal in me, not the man, that flees the gallows. I owe you nothing," he went on, "and expect nothing of you; and it would be no more than justice if I should avenge upon you my mother's wrongs and my own. But still I hate to shoot you; I have never yet taken human life—for I did *not* kill the old captain. Will you promise to give no alarm and make no attempt to capture me until morning, if I do not shoot?"

So absorbed were the two men in their colloquy and their own tumultuous thoughts that neither of them had heard the door below move upon its hinges. Neither of them had heard a light step come stealthily up the stairs, nor seen a slender form creep along the darkening passage toward the mulatto.

The sheriff hesitated. The struggle between his love of life and his sense of duty was a terrific one. It may seem strange that a man who could sell his own child into slavery should hesitate at such a moment, when his life was trembling in the balance. But the baleful influence of human slavery poisoned the very fountains of life, and created new standards of right. The sheriff was conscientious; his conscience had merely been warped by his environment. Let no one ask what his answer would have been; he was spared the necessity of a decision.

"Stop," said the mulatto, "you need not promise. I could not trust you if you did. It is your life for mine; there is but one safe way for me; you must die."

He raised his arm to fire, when there was a flash—a report from the passage behind him. His arm fell heavily at his side, and the pistol dropped at his feet.

The sheriff recovered first from his surprise, and throwing open the door secured the fallen weapon. Then seizing the prisoner he thrust him into the cell and locked the door upon him; after which he turned to Polly, who leaned half-fainting against the wall, her hands clasped over her heart.

"Oh, father, I was just in time!" she cried hysterically, and, wildly sobbing, threw herself into her father's arms.

"I watched until they all went away," she said. "I heard the shot from the woods and I saw you shoot. Then when you did not come out I feared something had happened, that perhaps you had been wounded. I got out the other pistol and ran over here. When I found the door open, I knew something was wrong, and when I heard voices I crept up stairs, and reached the top just in time to hear him say he would kill you. Oh, it was a narrow escape!"

When she had grown somewhat calmer, the sheriff left her standing there and went back into the cell. The prisoner's arm was bleeding from a flesh wound. His bravado had given place to a stony apathy. There was no sign in his face of fear or disappointment or feeling of any kind. The sheriff sent Polly to the house for cloth, and bound up the prisoner's wound with a rude skill acquired during his army life.

"I'll have a doctor come and dress the wound in the morning," he said to the prisoner. "It will do very well until then, if you will keep quiet. If the doctor asks you how the wound was caused, you can say that you were struck by the bullet fired from the woods. It would do you no good to have known that you were shot while attempting to escape."

The prisoner uttered no word of thanks or apology, but sat in sullen silence. When the wounded arm had been bandaged, Polly and her father returned to the house.

The sheriff was in an unusually thoughtful mood that evening. He put salt in his coffee at supper, and poured vinegar over his pancakes. To many of Polly's questions he returned random answers. When he had gone to bed he lay awake for several hours.

In the silent watches of the night, when he was alone with God, there came into his mind a flood of unaccustomed thoughts. An hour or two before, standing face to face with death, he had experienced a sensation similar to that which drowning men are said to feel—a kind of clarifying of the moral faculty, in which the veil of the flesh, with its obscuring passions and prejudices, is pushed aside for a moment, and all the acts of one's life stand out, in the clear light of truth, in their correct proportions and relations,—a state of mind in which one sees himself as God may be supposed to see him. In the reaction following his rescue, this feeling had given place for a time to far different emotions. But now, in the silence of midnight, something of this clearness of spirit returned to the sheriff. He saw that he had owed some duty to this son of his,—that neither law nor custom could destroy a responsibility inherent in the nature of mankind. He could not thus, in the eyes of God at least, shake off the consequences of his sin. Had he never sinned, this wayward spirit would never have come back from the vanished past to haunt him. As these thoughts came, his anger against the mulatto died away, and in its place there sprang up a great pity. The hand of parental authority might have restrained the passions he had seen burning in the prisoner's eyes when the desperate man spoke the words which had seemed to doom his father to death. The sheriff felt that he might have saved this fiery spirit from the slough of slavery; that he might have sent him to the free North, and given him there, or in some other land, an opportunity to turn to usefulness and honorable pursuits the talents that had run to crime, perhaps to madness; he might, still less, have given this son of his the poor simulacrum of liberty which men of his caste could possess in a slave-holding community; or least of all, but still something, he might have kept the boy on the plantation, where the burdens of slavery would have fallen lightly upon him.

The sheriff recalled his own youth. He had inherited an honored name to keep untarnished; he had had a future to make; the picture of a fair young bride had beckoned him on to happiness. The poor wretch now stretched upon a pallet of straw between the brick walls of the jail had had none of these things,—no name, no father, no mother—in the true meaning of motherhood,—and until the past few years no possible future, and then one vague and shadowy in its outline, and dependent for form and substance upon the slow solution of a problem in which there were many unknown quantities.

From what he might have done to what he might yet do was an easy transition for the awakened conscience of the sheriff. It occurred to him, purely as a hypothesis, that he might permit his prisoner to escape; but his oath of office, his duty as sheriff, stood in the way of such a course, and the sheriff dismissed the idea from his mind. He could, however, investigate the circumstances of the murder, and move Heaven and earth to discover the real criminal, for he no longer doubted the prisoner's innocence; he could employ counsel for the accused, and perhaps influence public opinion in his favor. An acquittal once secured, some plan could be devised by which the sheriff might in some degree atone for his crime against this son of his—against society—against God.

When the sheriff had reached this conclusion he fell into an unquiet slumber, from which he awoke late the next morning.

He went over to the jail before breakfast and found the prisoner lying on his pallet, his face turned to the wall; he did not move when the sheriff rattled the door.

"Good-morning," said the latter, in a tone intended to waken the prisoner.

There was no response. The sheriff looked more keenly at the recumbent figure; there was an unnatural rigidity about its attitude.

He hastily unlocked the door and, entering the cell, bent over the prostrate form. There was no sound of breathing; he turned the body over—it was cold and stiff. The prisoner had torn the bandage from his wound and bled to death during the night. He had evidently been dead several hours.

From *Independent*, November 7, 1889, 30–32.

Frederick Douglass

1817–1895

Rising from enslavement to international fame, Frederick Douglass was by the time of the Civil War black America's major leader and spokesperson and the confidant of many important white Americans, including Abraham Lincoln. Born in Tuckahoe, Maryland, the son of Harriet Bailey, a slave, and an unknown white man, Douglass largely taught himself to read and write. Christened Frederick Augustus Washington Bailey, he escaped slavery disguised as a sailor and renamed himself after a character from Sir Walter Scott's *Lady of the Lake*, an act emblematic of his lifelong reinvention of himself. Relocating to New Bedford Massachusetts, he discovered the *Liberator*, William Lloyd Garrison's abolitionist paper, which Douglass described as having a place in his heart "second only to the bible." From 1841 to 1845, Douglass worked as a fugitive-slave lecturer for the Massachusetts Anti-Slavery Society, using his life as an object lesson in the possibility of black advancement and a reminder to whites of their moral obligation to secure freedom and equality for all Americans. After publishing *Narrative of the Life of Frederick Douglass, An American Slave* in 1845, Douglass fled to England to avoid arrest under the Fugitive Slave Law. The book became an international best-seller, and Douglass spent the next two years lecturing throughout the British Isles before friends purchased his freedom from his former master. In 1847 he returned to America a free man. He began publishing a newspaper, first named the *North Star* and then *Frederick Douglass's Paper*. In 1859 he was forced to flee to Canada following accusations of complicity in John Brown's raid on Harper's Ferry.

During the Civil War, Douglass became a consultant to President Lincoln, urging him to allow former slaves to serve in the Union forces. Douglass went on to actively recruit black soldiers (among them his own sons), and he protested to Lincoln about these soldiers' unequal pay and treatment. After the war, Douglass fought for the passage of the Fifteenth Amendment and urged Lincoln's successors to adopt more equitable Reconstruction policies. He counseled against mass migration from the South, insisting that the answer to oppression lay in full civil rights for the freed people. When Reconstruction ended, Douglass went on to hold a number of government posts, serving as assistant secretary of the Santo Domingo Commission (1871), as marshal and recorder of deeds for the District of Columbia (1881–1886) and as U.S. minister and consul general to Haiti (1889–1891). A strong supporter of women's rights, Douglass much admired the work of Ida B. Wells-Barnett, becoming in the last years of his life a passionate antilynching activist.

In the selection excerpted here from "Lynch Law and the South," published in July 1892, Douglass asks his largely white audience to consider the consequences of American racial oppression. In his introduction to Ida B. Wells-Barnett's *Southern Horrors* written in October of that year, Douglass lamented the American indifference to the deaths of its black citizens: "It sometimes seems we are deserted by earth and Heaven—yet we must still think, speak, and work, and trust in the power of a merciful God for final deliverance."

—— Lynch Law in the South ——

The distressing circumstances in this revival of lynch law in different parts of the South is, that it shows that prejudice and hatred have increased in bitterness with the increasing interval between the time of slavery and now. I have been frequently asked to explain this phase of our national problem. I explain it on the same principle by which resistance to the course of a ship is created and increased in proportion to her speed. The resistance met by the negro is to me evidence that he is making progress. The Jew is hated in Russia, because he is thrifty. The Chinaman is hated in California because he is industrious and successful. The negro meets no resistance when on a downward course. It is only when he rises in wealth, intelligence, and manly character that he brings upon himself the heavy hand of persecution. The men lynched at Memphis were murdered because they were prosperous. They were doing a business which a white firm desired to do,—hence the mob and hence the murder. When the negro is degraded and ignorant he conforms to a popular standard of what a negro should be. When he shakes off his rags and wretchedness and presumes to be a man, and a man among men, he contradicts this popular standard and becomes an offence to his surroundings. He can, at the South, ride in a first-class car as a servant, as an appendage to a white man, but is not allowed to ride in his quality of manhood alone. So extreme is the bitterness of this prejudice that several States have passed laws making it a crime for a conductor to allow a colored man, however respectable, to ride in the same car with white men unless in the manner above stated.

To the question, What is to be the solution of this race hatred and persecution? I have two answers, one of hope and one of fear. There may come at the South satiety even in the appetite for blood. When a wall is raised to a height inconsistent with the law of gravitation, it will fall. The South is not all a wilderness. There are good men and good women there who will sooner or later make themselves heard and felt. No people can long endure the shame and disgrace of lynch law. The South, which has been compelled to keep step with the music of the Union, will also be compelled to keep step with the music of the nineteenth century, which is preeminently a century of progress. The grand moral forces of this century no barbarism can withstand. They met serfdom in Russia, and it fell before them. They will meet our barbarism against color, and *it* will fall before them. I am the more encouraged in this belief because, in various parts of the

North, and especially in the State of Massachusetts, where fifty years ago there existed the same proscription which at the present time prevails in the South, all men are now treated as equals before the law and are accorded the same civil rights.

I, however, freely confess that the present prospect has for me a gloomy side. When men sow the wind it is rational to expect that they will reap the whirlwind. It is evident to my mind that the negro will not always rest a passive subject to the violence and bloodshed by which he is now pursued. If neither law nor public sentiment shall come to his relief, he will devise methods of his own. It should be remembered that the negro is a man, and that in point of intelligence he is not what he was a hundred years ago. Whatever may be said of his failure to acquire wealth, it cannot be denied that he has made decided progress in the acquisition of knowledge; and he is a poor student of the natural history of civilization who does not see that the mental energies of this race, newly awakened and set in motion, must continue to advance. Character, with its moral influence; knowledge, with its power; and wealth, with its respectability, are possible to it as well as to other races of men. In arguing upon what will be the action of the negro in case he continues to be the victim of lynch law I accept the statement often made in his disparagement, that he is an imitative being; that he will do what he sees other men do. He has already shown this facility, and he illustrates it all the way from the prize ring to the pulpit; from the plow to the professor's chair. The voice of nature, not less than the Book of books, teaches us that oppression can make even a wise man mad, and in such case the responsibility for madness will not rest upon the man but upon the oppression to which he is subjected.

How can the South hope to teach the negro the sacredness of human life while it cheapens and profanes it by the atrocities of mob law? The stream cannot rise higher than its source. The morality of the negro will reach no higher point than the morality and religion that surround him. He reads of what is being done in the world in resentment of oppression and needs no teacher to make him understand what he reads. In warning the South that it may place too much reliance upon the cowardice of the negro, I am not advocating violence by the negro, but pointing out the dangerous tendency of his constant persecution. The negro was not a coward at Bunker Hill; he was not a coward in Haiti; he was not a coward in the late war for the Union; he was not a coward at Harper's Ferry, with John Brown; and care should be taken into goading him to acts of desperation by continuing to punish him for heinous crimes of which he is not legally convicted.

From *North American Review*, July 1892, 17–24.

Frances Ellen Watkins Harper

1825–1911

A contemporary of Frederick Douglass, William Wells Brown, and Harriet Jacobs, Frances Harper authored four novels and several volumes of poetry, becoming one of the most prolific and widely read African American writers in the nineteenth century. Born free in the slave state of Maryland, Harper was raised by her uncle, William Watkins, a civil rights activist who taught at the Academy for Negro Youth, which Harper attended until 1839.

Harper published her first poems in abolitionist periodicals, including Frederick Douglass's paper. Her first book of poems, *Forest Leaves*, was published in 1845, but no copies have survived. In 1850, Harper became the first woman to teach at Union Seminary (later Wilberforce University) in Columbus, Ohio. Unable to return to Maryland because of laws barring free blacks from entering the state, Harper moved to Philadelphia in 1853 to work on the Underground Railroad. Like Douglass, Harper was a professional speaker for the abolitionist cause, taking a position in 1854 with the Maine Anti-Slavery Society that entailed a grueling lecture schedule throughout the northern United States and southern Canada. A militant abolitionist, Harper helped raise money for the families of John Brown and his men after their raid on Harper's Ferry.

In 1854, Harper published *Poems on Miscellaneous Subjects*, which included poetry on abolition, temperance, women's rights, and Christianity. An immediate success, the volume was to be reprinted twenty times before 1900. Harper also served as editor of the *Anglo-African Magazine*, to which she contributed in 1859 a short story entitled "Two Offers," in which a feminist character tries to convince her cousin to reject both offers of marriages she has received because they represent business arrangements and thus a form of enslavement. In her own life, Harper did not allow marriage and children to end her literary and political activities.

After the Civil War, Harper went South to minister to the freed people, teaching them practical skills along with reading and writing. She lectured to integrated audiences across the South, insisting that racial unity was crucial for national survival. In 1870, Harper published *Sketches of Southern Life*, a collection of poems that introduced Aunt Chloe Fleet, a remarkable character who learns how to read, becomes involved in politics, and supervises the men's voting. Aunt Chloe helps build schools and churches and works to buy a cabin, which she enlarges to accommodate her children.

Scholarly, well read, courageous, and fiercely eloquent, Harper served as a mentor to Ida B. Wells-Barnett. The first name of the protagonist of Harper's 1892 novel, *Iola Leroy, or Shadows Uplifted*, is the name under which Wells-Barnett began her journalistic career. A tale of slavery, the Civil War, and Reconstruction, the novel refutes the idyllic picture of southern life created by writers like Thomas Nelson Page and includes critical debates about Ku Klux Klan lynchings during Reconstruction. The novel found a wide readership among members of the black women's organizations flourishing throughout the country.

Harper was a founding member of the National Association of Colored Women. One of four African American women to address the 1893 World's Congress of Representative Women at the Columbian Exposition in Chicago, it was Harper who announced: "Through weary, wasting years men have destroyed, dashed in pieces and overthrown, but to-day we stand on the threshold of a woman's era, and women's work is grandly constructive." Reminding women of all races of their moral obligation to do good, Harper made an impassioned plea for her sisters to inaugurate this woman's era by using the ballot to eradicate the evils of lynching. In "An Appeal to My Countrywomen," Harper attacks the hypocrisy of white female reformers who coldly ignore the plight of African Americans.

—— An Appeal to My Countrywomen ——

You can sigh o'er the sad-eyed Armenian
Who weeps in her desolate home.
You can mourn o'er the exile of Russia
From kindred and friends doomed to roam.

You can pity the men who have woven
From passion and appetite chains
To coil with a terrible tension
Around their heartstrings and brains.

You can sorrow o'er little children
Disinherited from their birth,
The wee waifs and toddlers neglected,
Robbed of sunshine, music and mirth.

For beasts you have gentle compassion;
Your mercy and pity they share.
For the wretched, outcast and fallen
You have tenderness, love and care.

But hark! from our Southland are floating
Sobs of anguish, murmurs of pain,
And women heart-stricken are weeping
Over their tortured and their slain.

On their brows the sun has left traces;
Shrink not from their sorrow in scorn.
When they entered the threshold of being
The children of a King were born.

Each comes as a guest to the table
The hand of our God has outspread,
To fountains that ever leap upward,
To share in the soil we all tread.

When ye plead for the wrecked and fallen,
The exile from far-distant shores,
Remember that men are still wasting
Life's crimson around your own doors.

Have ye not, oh, my favored sisters,
Just a plea, a prayer or a tear,
For mothers who dwell 'neath the shadows
Of agony, hatred and fear?

Men may tread down the poor and lowly,
May crush them in anger and hate,
But surely the mills of God's justice
Will grind out the grist of their fate.

Oh, people sin-laden and guilty,
So lusty and proud in your prime,
The sharp sickles of God's retribution
Will gather your harvest of crime.

Weep not, oh my well-sheltered sisters,
Weep not for the Negro alone,
But weep for your sons who must gather
The crops which their fathers have sown.

Go read on the tombstones of nations
Of chieftains who masterful trod,
The sentence which time has engraven,
That they had forgotten their God.

'Tis the judgment of God that men reap
The tares which in madness they sow,
Sorrow follows the footsteps of crime,
And Sin is the consort of Woe.

From *Poems* (Philadelphia: 1006 Bainbridge Street, 1896).

Ida B. Wells-Barnett

1862–1931

Investigative journalist, feminist, antilynching crusader, author, and civil rights activist, Ida B. Wells-Barnett did more than perhaps anyone else to change the way the world judged the U.S. habit of lynching its black citizens. Born in 1862 in the last few months of slavery, Wells-Barnett grew up in a family in which both her mother and grandmother bore terrible scars from whippings received when they were enslaved. The visible scars of her mother's whippings for insubordination deeply impressed upon the young Ida the cruelty of the white world—and the necessity of fighting back. She was educated at a local school for freed people and studied at Fisk University during summers. At the age of sixteen, Wells-Barnett lost both her parents and her youngest brother to yellow fever and assumed the burden of raising her four younger siblings.

When she accepted a teaching position outside Memphis, Wells-Barnett began to write for a local black paper, the *Living Way*, under the pen name Iola. Reflecting her lifelong blend of militant publicity and activism, her first article discussed her lawsuit against the Chesapeake, Ohio, and Southwestern Railroad. In 1883, Wells-Barnett refused a train conductor's direction to move from her seat in a ladies' car to a smoking car designated for black passengers. The conductor grabbed her arm. Wells-Barnett bit his hand and braced her feet against the seat in front of her. When the wounded conductor returned with reinforcements, it took three men to remove the five-foot-tall woman from her seat. In 1884, Wells-Barnett sued for five hundred dollars in damages and won, but the Tennessee Supreme Court struck down the decision, setting a precedent for segregation's "separate but equal" doctrine.

In 1889, Wells-Barnett purchased a one-third share in a black-owned Memphis weekly newspaper, the *Free Speech*. In March 1892, mobs in Memphis lynched her friends, Thomas Moss, Calvin McDowell, and Henry Stewart for wounding white men while trying to defend their property from attack by a mob bent on putting them out of business. Wells-Barnett responded with a series of articles that urged African Americans to flee from a city that refused to protect black lives, property, and civil liberties, and encouraged those who remained to boycott streetcars and white businesses. At least two thousand people followed her call. Wells-Barnett began to investigate the facts about lynching, traveling to towns where lynchings had taken place and poring over newspaper accounts. Later that year, she wrote an editorial that questioned the "threadbare lie" that most black men were lynched for raping white women, suggesting that "rape" was used to cover up consensual relations between black men and the white women who were attracted to them. Angry mobs destroyed her newspaper office and printing press, and her partner, J. L. Fleming, barely escaped with his life. They threatened Wells-Barnett, who was out of town at the time, with lynching should she ever return.

Wells-Barnett settled in New York and became part owner of T. Thomas Fortune's *New York Age*, which published the results of her investigations. She also published several pamphlet-length analyses of lynching: *Southern Horrors: Lynch Law in All Its Phases* (1892); *A Red Record: Tabulated Statistics and Alleged Causes of Lynching in the United States, 1892, 1893, and 1894* (1895); and *Mob Rule in New Orleans: Robert Charles and His Fight to Death: The Story of His Life, Burning Human Beings Alive (and) Other Lynching Statistics* (1900). Using accounts from the white press and lynching statistics from a respected white newspaper, the *Chicago Tribune*, Wells-Barnett analyzed lynching according to racial and regional patterns and compiled a list of reasons why African Americans had been lynched. Detailing the looting and destruction of black property and the mass arrests that often accompanied lynching, Wells-Barnett described lynching as a ritualistic act of terror designed to destroy black economic and political power. In 1893, Wells-Barnett co-wrote and published *The Reason Why the Colored American Is Not in the Columbian Exposition—the Afro-American's Contribution to the Columbiad*, a pamphlet that protested the racist underpinnings of U.S. consumerism, nationalism, and imperialism.

Wells-Barnett's power as a public speaker prompted the formation of antilynching leagues in both in Great Britain and the United States after her lectures. She made canny use of the press in her engagements abroad, turning her lectures into media events and using the high regard in which she was held by British elites to force U.S. legislators, clergy, and media to speak out on the issue of lynching. They did so, Wells-Barnett wrote, not out of "any latent spirit of justice voluntarily asserting itself, especially in those who do the lynching but because the entire American people now feel both North and South that they are objects in the gaze of the civilized world." Wells-Barnett worked hard to persuade northern and foreign investors that mob violence made the South a bad risk for business.

Marrying Ferdinand Barnett, a Chicago lawyer, in 1893, Wells-Barnett continued her life of activism while raising four children. One of the founders, in 1909, of the NAACP, Wells-Barnett routinely visited the scenes of race riots and lynchings. While involved in suffragism and women's club work, she established a kindergarten, a settlement house, and other organizations for black southern migrants in Chicago. She campaigned unsuccessfully for the Senate in 1930. Wells-Barnett continued throughout her life to write and to lecture against lynching.

Wells-Barnett saw lynching as a form of state-sponsored terrorism that allowed whites to kill with impunity, without the government intervening to protect black property or lives. After the Memphis lynchings, Wells-Barnett purchased a pistol, and she insisted that African Americans must be ready to act in their own defense. In *Southern Horrors*, she advised that "a Winchester rifle should have a place of honor in every Black home, and it should be used for that protection that the law refuses to give." It is little wonder, then, that she found the militant resistance of Robert

1. "The Reason." Reprinted from the *Crisis*, March 1920, 264.

Charles and the subsequent race terrorization in New Orleans to be worthy objects of study and worthy topics for distribution in pamphlet form. In *Mob Rule in New Orleans*, Wells-Barnett carefully reconstructs the facts behind this African American man's supposed rampage, showing that, far from the "monster" and "desperado" created in newspaper accounts, Charles exhibited all the hallmarks of American heroism: intelligence, pride, courage, and physical skill. (The first sentence in the excerpt refers to a massacre on March 14, 1891, when a New Orleans mob lynched eleven innocent Italian immigrants in revenge for the murder of Police Superintendent David C. Hennessey.)

—— Excerpt from *Mob Rule in New Orleans* ——

Shot an Officer

The bloodiest week which New Orleans has known since the massacre of the Italians in 1892 was ushered in Monday, July 24th, by the inexcusable and unprovoked assault upon two colored men by police officers in New Orleans. Fortified by the assurance born of long experience in the New Orleans service, three policemen, Sergeant Aucoin, Officer Mora and Officer Cantrelle, observing two colored men sitting on doorsteps on Dryades street, between Washington avenue and 6th streets, determined, without a shadow of authority, to arrest them. One of the colored men was named Robert Charles, the other was a lad of nineteen named Leonard Pierce. The colored men had left their homes, a few blocks distant, about an hour prior, and had been sitting upon the doorsteps for a short time talking together. They had not broken the peace in any way whatever, no warrant was in the policemen's hands justifying their arrest, and no crime had been committed of which they were the suspects. The policemen, however, secure in the firm belief that they could do anything to a Negro that they wished, approached the two men, and in less than three minutes from the time they accosted them attempted to put both colored men under arrest. The younger of the two men, Pierce, submitted to arrest, for the officer, Cantrelle, who accosted him, put his gun in the young man's face ready to blow his brains out if he moved. The other colored man, Charles, was made the victim of a savage attack by Officer Mora, who used a billet and then drew a gun and tried to kill Charles. Charles drew his gun nearly as quickly as the policeman, and began a duel in the street, in which both participants were shot. The policeman got the worst of the duel, and fell helpless to the sidewalk. Charles made his escape. Cantrelle took Pierce, his captive, to the police station, to which place Mora, the wounded officer, was also taken, and a man hunt at once instituted for Charles, the wounded fugitive.

In any law-abiding community Charles would have been justified in delivering himself up immediately to the properly constituted authorities and asking for a trial by a jury of his peers. He could have been certain that in resisting an unwarranted arrest he had a right to defend his life, even to the point of taking one in that defense, but Charles knew that his arrest in New Orleans, even for defending his life, meant nothing short of a long term in the penitentiary, and still more probable death by lynching at the hands of a cowardly mob. He very bravely determined to protect his life as long as he had breath in his body and strength to draw a hair trigger on his would-be murderers. How well he was justified in that belief is well shown by the newspaper accounts which were given of this transaction.

[Wells-Barnett here quotes wildly discrepant versions of the incident from the *Times-Democrat* and the New Orleans *Picayune*, the object of each being not to convey the truth, but to "justify the policemen in the absolutely unprovoked attack upon the two colored men."]

But the best proof of the fact that the officers accosted the two colored men and without any warrant or other justification attempted to arrest them, and did actually seize and begin to club one of them, is shown by Officer Mora's own statement. The officer was wounded and had every reason in the world to make his side of the story as good as possible. His statement was made to a Picayune reporter and the same was published on the 25th inst., and is as follows:

"I was in the neighborhood of Dryades and Washington streets, with Sergeant Aucoin and Officer Cantrell, when three Negro women came up and told us that there were two suspicious-looking Negroes sitting on a step on Dryades street, between Washington and Sixth. We went to the place indicated and found two Negroes. We interrogated them as to who they were, what they were doing and how long they had been here. They replied that they were working for some one and had been in town three days. At about this stage the larger of the two Negroes got up and I grabbed him. The Negro pulled, but I held fast, and he finally pulled me into the street. Here I began using my billet, and the Negro jerked from my grasp and ran. He then pulled a gun and fired. I pulled my gun and returned the fire, each of us firing about three shots. I saw the Negro stumble several times, and I thought I had shot him, but he ran away and I don't know whether any of my shots took effect. Sergeant Aucoin in the meantime held the other man fast. The man was about ten feet from me when he fired, and the three Negresses who told us about the men stood away about twenty-five feet from the shooting."

Thus far in the proceeding the Monday night episode results in Officer Mora lying in the station wounded in the hip; Leonard Pierce, one of the colored men, locked up in the station, and Robert Charles, the other colored man, a fugitive, wounded in the leg and sought for by the entire police force of New Orleans. Not sought for, however, to be placed under arrest and given a fair trial and punished if found guilty according to the law of the land, but sought for by a host of enraged, vindictive and fearless officers, who were coolly ordered to kill him on sight. This order is shown by the Picayune of the 26th inst., in which the following statement appears:

"In talking to the sergeant about the case, the captain asked about the Negro's fighting ability, and the sergeant answered that Charles, though he called him Robinson then, was a desperate man, and it would be best to shoot him before he was given a chance to draw his pistol upon any of the officers."

This instruction was given before anybody had been killed, and the only evidence that Charles was a desperate man lay in the fact that he had refused to be beaten over the head by Officer Mora for sitting on a step quietly conversing with a friend. Charles resisted an absolutely unlawful attack, and a gun fight followed. Both Mora and Charles were shot, but because Mora was white and Charles was black, Charles was at once declared to be a desperado, made an outlaw, and subsequently a price put upon his head and the mob authorized to shoot him like a dog, on sight.

The New Orleans Picayune of Wednesday morning said:

"But he has gone, perhaps to the swamps, and the disappointment of the bluecoats in not getting the murderer is expressed in their curses, each man swearing that the signal to halt that will be offered Charles will be a shot."

In that same column of the Picayune it was said:

"Hundreds of policemen were about; each corner was guarded by a squad, commanded either by a sergeant or a corporal, and every man had the word to shoot the Negro as soon as he was sighted. He was a desperate black and would be given no chance to take more life."

Legal sanction was given to the mob or any man of the mob to kill Charles at sight by the Mayor of New Orleans, who publicly proclaimed a reward of two hundred and fifty dollars, not for the arrest of Charles, not at all, but the reward was offered for Charles' body, "dead or alive." The advertisement was as follows:

"$250 REWARD.

"Under the authority vested in me by law, I hereby offer, in the name of the city of New Orleans, $250 reward for the capture and delivery, dead or alive, to the authorities of the city, the body of the Negro murderer,

"ROBERT CHARLES,

who, on Tuesday morning, July 24, shot and killed

"Police Captain John T. Day and Patrolman Peter J. Lamb, and wounded

"Patrolman August T. Mora.

"PAUL CAPDEVEILLE, Mayor."

This authority, given by the sergeant to kill Charles on sight, would have been no news to Charles, nor to any colored man in New Orleans, who, for any purpose whatever, even to save his life, raised his hand against a white man. It is now, even as it was in the days of slavery, an unpardonable sin for a Negro to resist a white man, no matter how unjust or unprovoked the white man's attack may be. Charles knew this, and knowing to be captured meant to be killed, he resolved to sell his life as dearly as possible.

The next step in the terrible tragedy occurred between 2:30 and 5 o'clock Tuesday morning, about four hours after the affair on Dryades street. The man hunt, which had been inaugurated soon after Officer Mora had been carried to the station, succeeded in running down Robert Charles, the wounded fugitive, and located him at 2023 4th street. It was nearly 2 o'clock in the morning when a large detail of police surrounded the block with the intent to kill Charles on sight. Capt. Day had charge of the squad of police. Charles, the wounded man, was in his house when the police arrived, fully prepared, as results afterward showed, to die in his own home. Capt. Day started for Charles' room. As soon as Charles got sight of him there was a flash, a report, and Day fell dead in his tracks. In another instant Charles was standing in the door, and seeing Patrolman Peter J. Lamb, he drew his gun, and Lamb fell dead. Two other officers, Sergeant Aucoin and Officer Trenchard, who were in the squad, seeing their comrades, Day and Lamb, fall dead, concluded to raise the siege, and both disappeared into an adjoining house, where they blew out their lights so that their cowardly carcasses could be safe from Charles' deadly aim. The calibre of their courage is well shown by the fact that they concluded to save themselves from any harm by remaining prisoners in that dark room until daybreak, out of reach of Charles' deadly rifle. Sergeant Aucoin, who had been so brave a few hours before when seeing the two colored men sitting on the steps talking together on Dryades street, and supposing that neither was armed, now showed his true calibre. Now he knew that Charles had a gun and was brave enough to use it, so he hid himself in a room two hours while Charles deliberately walked out of his room and into the street after killing both Lamb and Day. It is also shown, as further evidence of the bravery of some of New Orleans' "finest," that one of them, seeing Capt. Day fall, ran seven blocks before he stopped, afterwards giving the excuse that he was hunting for a patrol box.

At daybreak, the officers felt safe to renew the attack upon Charles, so they broke into his room, only to find that—what they probably very well knew—he had gone. It appears that he made his escape by crawling through a hole in the ceiling to a little attic in his house. Here he found that he could not escape except by a window which led into an alley which had no opening on 4th street. He scaled the fence and was soon out of reach.

It was now 5 o'clock Tuesday morning, and a general alarm was given. Sergeant Aucoin and Corporal Trenchard, having received a new supply of courage by returning daylight, renewed their effort to capture the man that they had allowed escape in the darkness. Citizens were called upon to participate in the man hunt and New Orleans was soon the scene of terrible excitement. Officers were present everywhere, and colored men were arrested on all sides upon the pretext that they were impertinent and "game niggers."

[Wells-Barnett goes on to describe the rising hysteria and mayhem as Charles remains at large. By Wednesday, with the city in the hands of the mob, black men, women, and children are indiscriminately beaten and slaughtered in the streets. It is only on Thursday, when the city fathers realize that the violence has lowered the price of state bonds on the New York market, that any serious attempt is made to restore order. Despite a posse of a thousand men deputized by the mayor to control the mob, rioting continues sporadically throughout Thursday night. The dead include Hannah Mabry, "an old Negress," shot while sleeping in the home she shared with her husband, children, and grandchildren.]

Death of Charles

Friday witnessed the final act in the bloody drama begun by the three police officers, Aucoin, Mora, and Cantrelle. Betrayed into the hands of the police, Charles, who had already sent two of his would-be murderers to their death, made a last stand in a small building, 1210 Saratoga street, and, still defying his pursuers, fought a mob of twenty thousand people, single-handed and alone, killing three more men, mortally wounding two more and seriously wounding nine others. Unable to get to him in his stronghold, the besiegers set fire to his house of refuge. While the building was burning Charles was shooting, and every crack of his death-dealing rifle added another victim to the price which he had placed upon his own life. Finally, when fire and smoke became too much for flesh and blood to stand, the long sought for fugitive appeared in the door, rifle in hand, to charge the countless guns that were drawn upon him. With a courage which was indescribable, he raised his gun to fire again, but this time it failed, for a hundred shots riddled his body, and he fell dead face fronting to the mob. This last scene in the terrible drama is thus described in the Times-Democrat of July 26th:

"Early yesterday afternoon at 3 o'clock or thereabouts, Police Sergeant Gabriel Porteus was instructed by Chief Gaster to go to a house at No. 1210 Saratoga street, and search it for the fugitive murderer, Robert Charles. A private 'tip' had been received at the headquarters that the fiend was hiding somewhere on the premises.

"Sergeant Porteus took with him Corporal John R. Lally and Officers Zeigel and Essey. The house to which they were directed is a small double frame cottage, standing flush with Saratoga street, near the corner of Clio. It has two street entrances and two rooms on each side, one in front and one in the rear. It belongs to the type of cheap little dwellings commonly tenanted by Negroes.

"Sergeant Porteus left Ziegel and Essey to guard the outside and went with Corporal Lally to the rear house, where he found Jackson and his wife in the large room on the left. What immediately ensued is only known by the Negroes. They say the sergeant began to question them about their lodgers and finally asked them whether they knew anything about Robert Charles. They strenuously denied all knowledge of his whereabouts.

"The Negroes lied. At that very moment the hunted and desperate murderer lay concealed not a dozen feet away. Near the rear, left-hand corner of the room is a closet or pantry, about three feet deep, and perhaps eight feet long. The door was open and Charles was crouching, Winchester in hand, in the dark further end.

"Near the closet door was a bucket of water, and Jackson says that Sergeant Porteus walked toward it to get a drink. At the next moment a shot rang out and the brave officer fell dead. Lally was shot directly afterward. Exactly how and where will never be known, but the probabilities are that the black fiend sent a bullet into him before he recovered from his surprise at the sudden onslaught. Then the murderer dashed out of the back door and disappeared.

"The neighborhood was already agog with the tragic events of the two preceding days, and the sound of the shots was a signal for wild and instant excitement. In a few moments a crowd had gathered and people were pouring in by the hundred from every point of the compass. Jackson and his wife had fled and at first nobody knew what had happened, but the surmise that Charles had recommenced his bloody work was on every tongue and soon some of the bolder found their way to the house in the rear. There the bleeding forms of the two policemen told the story.

"Lally was still breathing, and a priest was sent for to administer the last rites. Father Fitzgerald responded, and while he was bending over the dying man the outside throng was rushing wildly through the surrounding yards and passage-ways searching for the murderer. 'Where is he?' 'What has become of him?' were the questions on every lip.

"Suddenly the answer came in a shot from the room directly overhead. It was fired through a window facing Saratoga street, and the bullet struck down a young man named Alfred J. Bloomfield, who was standing in the narrow passage-way between the two houses. He fell on his knees and a second bullet stretched him dead.

"When he fled from the closet Charles took refuge in the upper story of the house. There are four windows on that floor, two facing toward Saratoga street and two toward Rampart. The murderer kicked several breaches in the frail center partition, so he could rush from side to side, and like a trapped beast, prepared to make his last stand.

"Nobody had dreamed that he was still in the house, and when Bloomfield was shot there was a headlong stampede. It was some minutes before the exact situation was understood. Then rifles and pistols began to speak, and a hail of bullets poured against the blind frontage of the old house. Every one hunted some coign of vantage, and many climbed to adjacent roofs. Soon the glass of the four upper windows was shattered by flying lead. The fusillade sounded like a battle, and the excitement upon the streets was indescribable.

"Throughout all this hideous uproar Charles seems to have retained a certain diabolical coolness. He kept himself mostly out of sight, but now and then he thrust the gleaming barrel of his rifle through one of the shattered window panes and fired at his besiegers. He worked the weapon with incredible rapidity, discharging from three to five cartridges each time before leaping back to a place of safety. These replies came from all four windows indiscriminately, and showed that he was keeping a close watch in every direction. His wonderful marksmanship never failed him for a moment, and when he missed it was always by the narrowest margin only.

"On the Rampart street side of the house there are several sheds, commanding an excellent range of the upper story. Detective Littleton, Andrew Van Kuren of the Work-house force and several others climbed upon one of these and opened fire on the upper windows, shooting whenever they could catch a glimpse of the assassin. Charles responded with his rifle, and presently Van Kuren climbed down to find a better position. He was crossing the end of the shed when he was killed.

"Another of Charles' bullets found its billet in the body of Frank Evans, an ex-member of the police force. He was on the Rampart street side firing whenever he had an opportunity. Officer J. W. Bofill and A. S. Leclerc were also wounded in the fusillade.

"While the events thus briefly outlined were transpiring time was a-wing, and the cooler headed in the crowd began to realize that some quick and desperate expedient must be adopted to insure the capture of the fiend and to avert what might be a still greater tragedy than any yet enacted. For nearly two hours the desperate monster had held his besiegers at bay, darkness would soon be at hand and no one could predict what might occur if he made a dash for liberty in the dark.

"At this critical juncture it was suggested that the house be fired. The plan came as an inspiration, and was adopted as the only solution of the situation. The wretched old rookery counted for nothing against the possible continued sacrifice of human life, and steps were immediately taken to apply the torch. The fire department had been summoned to the scene soon after the shooting began; its officers were warned to be ready to prevent a spread of the conflagration, and several men rushed into the lower right-hand room and started a blaze in one corner.

"They first fired an old mattress, and soon smoke was pouring out in dense volumes. It filled the interior of the ramshackle structure, and it was evident that the upper story would soon become untenable. An interval of tense excitement followed, and all eyes were strained for a glimpse of the murderer when he emerged.

"Then came the thrilling climax. Smoked out of his den, the desperate fiend descended the stairs and entered the lower room. Some say he dashed into the yard, glaring vainly for some avenue of escape; but, however that may be, he was soon a few moments later moving about behind the lower windows. A dozen shots were sent through the wall in the hope of reaching him, but he escaped unscathed. Then suddenly the door on the right was flung open and he dashed out. With head lowered and rifle raised ready to fire on the instant, Charles dashed straight for the rear door of the front cottage. To reach it he had to traverse a little walk shaded by a vine-clad arbor. In the back room, with a cocked revolver, was Dr. C. A. Noiret, a young medical student, who was aiding the citizens' posse. As he sprang through the door Charles fired a shot, and the bullet whizzed past the doctor's head. Before it could be repeated Noiret's pistol cracked and the murderer reeled, turned half around and fell on his back. The doctor sent another ball into his body as he struck the floor, and half a dozen men, swarming into the room from the front, riddled the corpse with bullets.

"Private Adolph Anderson of the Connell Rifles was the first man to announce the death of the wretch. He rushed to the street door, shouted the news to the crowd, and a moment later the bleeding body was dragged to the pavement and made the target of a score of pistols. It was shot, kicked and beaten almost out of semblance to humanity.

"The limp dead body was dropped at the edge of the sidewalk and from there dragged to the muddy roadway by half a hundred hands. There in the road more shots were fired into the body. Corporal Trenchard, a brother-in-law of Porteus, led the shooting into the inanimate clay. With each shot there was a cheer for the work that had been done and curses and imprecations on the inanimate mass of riddled flesh that was once Robert Charles.

"Cries of 'Burn him! Burn him!' were heard from Clio Street all the way to Erato street, and it was with difficulty that the crowd was restrained from totally destroying the wretched dead body. Some of those who agitated burning even secured a large vessel of kerosene, which had previously been brought to the scene for the purpose of firing Charles' refuge, and for a time it looked as though this vengeance might be wreaked on the body. The officers, however, restrained this move, although they were powerless to prevent the stamping and kicking of the body by the enraged crowd.

"After the infuriated citizens had vented their spleen on the body of the dead Negro, it was loaded into the patrol wagon. The police raised the body of the heavy black from the ground and literally chucked it into the space on the floor of the wagon between the seats. They threw it with a curse more hissed than uttered and born of the bitterness which was rankling in their breasts at the thought of Charles having taken so wantonly the lives of four of the best of their fellow-officers.

"When the murderer's body landed in the wagon it fell in such a position that the hideously mutilated head, kicked, stamped and crushed, hung over the end.

"As the wagon moved off, the followers, who were protesting against its being carried off, declaring that it should be burned, poked and struck it with sticks, beating it into such a condition that it was utterly impossible to tell what the man ever looked like.

"As the patrol wagon rushed through the rough street, jerking and swaying from one side of the thoroughfare to the other, the gory, mud-smeared head swayed and swung and jerked about in a sickening manner, the dark blood dripping on the steps and spattering the body of the wagon and trousers of the policeman standing on the step."

[Wells-Barnett goes on to document in detail the outbreak of mob brutality directed against every black man, woman, and child in the city: A gang of white longshoremen see an innocent black man walking along the levee and shoot him down. A group of Italians joins the mob and stabs him in the back and buttocks. All over the city, mobs pull black men off streetcars and lynch them; blacks spotted in public are brutally beaten and often killed; mobs break into the homes of defenseless black people and beat elderly men and women to death. No arrests are made in these murders, and those who have suffered police brutality during the rampage are "quickly called up before the courts and fined or sent to jail upon the statement of the police." A white man who has just arrived from New York and is heard sympathizing with the mob's victims is "fined $25 or thirty days" after telling the recorder that "he considered a Negro as good as a white in body and soul."

Wells-Barnett next moves to a consideration of whether Charles was a desperado, quoting newspaper accounts that try to twist his passions for improving himself intellectually and for escaping injustice through emigration to Liberia into evidence of a conspiracy against the white race. Her conclusions follow.]

Died in Self Defense

The life, character and death of Robert Charles challenges the thoughtful consideration of all fair-minded people. In the frenzy of the moment, when nearly a dozen men lay dead, the victims of his unerring and death-dealing aim, it was natural for a prejudiced press and for the civilians in private life to denounce him as a desperado and a murderer. But sea depths are not measured when the ocean rages, nor can absolute justice be determined while public opinion is lashed into fury. There must be calmness to insure correctness of judgment. The fury of the hour must abate before we can deal justly with any man or any cause.

That Charles was not a desperado is amply shown by the discussion in the preceding chapter. The darkest pictures which the reporters could paint of Charles were quoted freely, so that the public might find upon what grounds the press declared him to be a lawbreaker. Unquestionably the grounds are wholly insufficient. Not a line of evidence has been presented to prove that Charles was the fiend which the first reports of the New Orleans [press] charge him to be.

Nothing more should be required to establish his good reputation, for the rule is universal that a reputation must be assumed to be good until it is proved bad. But that rule does not apply to the Negro, for as soon as he is suspected the public judgment immediately determines that he is guilty of whatever crime he stands charged. For this reason, as a matter of duty to the race, and the simple justice to the memory of Charles, an investigation has been made of the life and character of Charles before the fatal affray which led to his death.

Robert Charles was not an educated man. He was a student who faithfully investigated all the phases of oppression from which his race has suffered. That he was a student is amply shown by the Times-Democrat [r]eport of the 25th, which says:

"Well-worn textbooks, bearing his name written in his own scrawling handwriting, and well-filled copy-books found in his trunk, showed that he had burned the midnight oil, and desired to improve himself intellectually in order that he might conquer the hated white race." From this quotation it will be seen that he spent the hours after days of hard toil in trying to improve himself, both in the study of textbooks and in writing.

He knew that he was a student of a problem which required all the intelligence that a man could command, and he was burning his midnight oil gathering knowledge that he might better be able to come to an intelligent solution. To his aid in the study of this problem he sought the aid of a Christian newspaper, The Voice of the Missions, the organ of the African Methodist Episcopal Church. He was in communication with its editor, who is a bishop, and is known all over this country as a man of learning, a lover of justice and the defender of law and order. Charles could receive from Bishop Turner not a word of encouragement to be other than an earnest, tireless and God-fearing student of the complex problems which affected the race.

For further help and assistance in his studies, Charles turned to an organization which has existed and flourished for many years, at all times managed by men of high Christian standing and absolute integrity. These men believe and preach a doctrine that the best interests of the Negro will be subserved by an emigration from America back to the Fatherland, and they do all they can to spread the doctrine of emigration and to give material assistance to those who desire to leave America and make their future homes in Africa. This organization is known as "The International Migration Society." It has its headquarters in Birmingham, Alabama. From this place it issues pamphlets, some of which were found in the home of Robert Charles, and which pamphlets the reporters of the New Orleans papers declare to be incendiary and dangerous in their doctrine and teaching.

Nothing could be further from the truth. Copies of any and all of them may be secured by writing to D. J. Flummer, who is President and in charge of the home office in Birmingham, Alabama. Three of the pamphlets found in Charles' room are named respectively:

First, "Prospectus of the Liberian Colonization Society;" which pamphlet in a few brief pages tells of the work of the society, plans, prices, and terms of transportation of colored people who choose to go to Africa. These pages are followed by a short, conservative discussion of the Negro question, and close with an argument that Africa furnishes the best asylum for the oppressed Negroes in this country.

The second pamphlet is entitled "Christian Civilization of Africa." This is a brief statement of the advantages of the Republic of Liberia, and an argument in support of the superior conditions which colored people may attain to by leaving the South and settling in Liberia.

The third pamphlet is entitled "The Negro and Liberia." This is a larger document than the other two, and treats more exhaustively the question of emigration, but from the first page to the last there is not an incendiary line or sentence. There is not even a suggestion of violence in all of its thirty-two pages, and not a word which could not be preached from every pulpit in the land.

If it is true that the workman is known by his tools, certainly no harm could ever come from the doctrines which were preached by Charles or the papers and pamphlets distributed by him. Nothing ever written in the "Voice of the Missions," and nothing ever published in the pamphlets above alluded to in the remotest way suggest that a peaceable man should turn lawbreaker, or that any man should dye his hands in his brother's blood.

In order to secure as far as possible positive information about the life and character of Robert Charles, it was plain that the best course to pursue was to communicate with those with whom he had sustained business relations. Accordingly a letter was forwarded to Mr. D. J. Flummer, who is president of the colonization society, in which letter he was asked to state in reply what information he had of the life and character of Robert Charles. The result was a very prompt letter in response, the text of which is as follows:

Birmingham, Ala., Aug. 21, 1900.

Mrs. Ida B. Wells Barnett, Chicago, Ill.:

Dear Madam—Replying to your favor of recent date requesting me to write you giving such information as I may have concerning the life, habits and character of Robert Charles, who recently shot and killed police officers in New Orleans, I wish to say that my knowledge of him is only such as I have gained from his business connection with the

International Migration Society during the past five or six years, during which time I was president of the society.

He having learned that the purpose of this society was to colonize the colored people in Liberia, West Africa, and thereby lessen or destroy the friction and prejudice existing in this country between the two races, set about earnestly and faithfully distributing the literature that we issued from time to time. He always appeared to be mild but earnest in his advocacy of emigration, and never to my knowledge used any method or means that would in the least appear unreasonable, and had always kept within the bounds of law and order in advocating emigration.

The work he performed for this society was all gratuitous, and apparently prompted from his love of humanity, and desires to be instrumental in building up a Negro Nationality in Africa.

If he ever violated a law before the killing of the policeman, I do not know of it. Yours very truly,

D. J. Flummer

Besides this statement, Mr. Flummer enclosed a letter received by the Society two days before the tragedy at New Orleans. This letter was written by Robert Charles, and it attests to his devotion to the cause of emigration which he had espoused. Memoranda on the margin of the letter show that the order was filled by mailing the pamphlets. It is very probable that these were the identical pamphlets which were found by the mob which broke into the room of Robert Charles and seized upon these harmless documents and declared they were sufficient evidence to prove Charles a desperado. In light of subsequent events the letter of Charles, which follows, sounds like a voice from the tomb:

New Orleans, July 30, 1900.

Mr. D. J. Flummer:

Dear Sir—I received your last pamphlets and they are all given out. I want you to send me some more, and I enclose you the stamps. I think I will go over in Greenville, Miss., and give my people some pamphlets over there. Yours truly,

Robert Charles

The last word of information comes from New Orleans from a man who knew Charles intimately for six years. For obvious reasons, his name is withheld. In answer to a letter sent him he answers as follows:

New Orleans, Aug. 23, 1900.

Mrs. Ida B. Wells Barnett:

Dear Madam—It affords me great pleasure to inform you as far as I know of Robert Charles. I have been acquainted with him about six years in this city. He never has, as I know, given any trouble to anyone. He was quiet and a peaceful man and was very frank in speaking. He was too much of a hero to die; few can be found to equal him. I am very sorry to say that I do not know anything of his birthplace, nor his parents, but enclosed find letter from his uncle, from which you may find more information. You will also find one of the circulars in which Charles was in possession of which was styled as a crazy document. Let me say, until our preachers preach this document we will always be slaves. If you can help circulate this "crazy" doctrine I would be glad to have you do so, for I shall never rest until I get to that heaven on earth; that is, the west coast of Africa, in Liberia.

With best wishes to you I still remain, as always, for the good of the race,

———

By only those whose anger and vindictiveness warp their judgment is Robert Charles a desperado. Their word is not supported by the statement of a single fact which justifies their judgment, and no criminal record shows that he was ever indicted for any offense, much less convicted of a crime. On the contrary, his work for many years had been with Christian people, circulating emigration pamphlets and active as an agent for a mission publication. Men who knew him say that he was a law-abiding, quiet, industrious, peaceable man. So he lived.

So he lived and so would he have died had he not raised his hand to resent un-provoked assault and unlawful arrest that fateful Monday night. That made him an out-law, and being a man of courage he decided to die with his face to the foe. The white people of this country may charge that he was a desperado, but to the people of his own race, Robert Charles will always be regarded as the hero of New Orleans.

From *Mob Rule in New Orleans: Robert Charles and His Fight to Death: The Story of His Life, Burning Human Beings Alive (and) Other Lynching Statistics* (Chicago: Author, 1900).

Pauline Elizabeth Hopkins

1859–1930

Born in Portland, Maine, Pauline Elizabeth Hopkins grew up in Boston and graduated from the renowned Boston Girls' High School. At fifteen, she won a contest associated with the famous author and abolitionist William Wells Brown for her essay supporting the temperance crusade. Her play *Slave's Escape, or The Underground Railroad*, performed in 1880 by the Hopkins Troubadours—a group that included her mother, stepfather, and Hopkins herself—reflects the deep admiration for the abolitionist movement that would inform her antilynching activism. For the next decade Hopkins toured with her family and continued writing plays. She supported herself by working as a stenographer.

Hopkins became a published author of narrative fiction at the age of forty with the inclusion of her short story "The Mystery within Us" in the inaugural issue of the *Colored American Magazine*. Between 1900 and 1905, she published four novels (three serialized in the *Colored American*), seven short stories, a historical pamphlet, twenty biographical sketches, and numerous essays and feature articles. One of the magazine's chief contributors, Hopkins served as literary editor of the *Colored American* from mid-1903 to 1904.

Contending Forces: A Romance Illustrative of Negro Life North and South was published in 1900 by the Colored Cooperative Publishing Company, which promoted it as "a race work" portraying actual incidents that could be "found in the archives of the Court House at Newboro, North Carolina." In *Contending Forces*, Hopkins links current oppressions to the past oppressions of slavery. A work of activist literature, the novel reaches out to white as well as black audiences to convince them that the lynching and raping of African Americans is a form of political terror that can best be cured through aggressive agitation in the abolitionist tradition.

Hopkins frames the novel's most overt political messages through various social meetings and public debates. In the chapter excerpted here, Will Smith discusses the causes and remedies for lynching at a meeting the Colored American League has called after the lynching of four men in an unnamed southern state. The meeting, which allows Hopkins to showcase and to respond to various positions in the lynching debate, begins with a speech by a white conservative politician, Herbert Clapp, who repeats standard myths about the unfitness of African Americans to vote, and the necessity of lynching to restrain black bestiality. He is followed by Dr. Arthur Lewis, whom Hopkins clearly meant to suggest Booker T. Washington in his advocacy of the avoidance of politics and the pursuit of industrial education as the best hope for the African American. Luke Sawyer speaks next. Describing a brutal rape and lynching inflicted on the family that had raised him after his own father was lynched for competing successfully with white traders, Sawyer passionately presses the case for violent retaliation. Will Smith, whose position echoes that of W.E.B. Du Bois and of Hopkins herself, has the last word. Smith's speech, which leaves "not a dry eye in that vast audience," provides an object lesson in the kind of agitation Hopkins sees as crucial to building the moral consensus necessary to put an end to lynching.

— Will Smith's Defense of His Race —

Thank God for the token!
Thank God that one man as a free
Man has spoken!
—Whittier [John Greenleaf Whittier (1807–1892), "Ritner"]

Someone at this moment began to sing that grand old hymn, ever new and consoling:

"Jesus, Lover of my soul,
Let me to thy bosom fly,
While the nearer waters roll,
While the tempest still is nigh."

When quiet once more reigned, amid intense silence the chairman arose and introduced Mr. William Smith as the last speaker of the evening. Tremendous applause greeted him, for he was known to be an able and eloquent debater.

"Friends," he said, "I shall not attempt a lengthy and discursive argument; I shall simply try to answer some of the arguments which have been advanced by other speakers. I have no doubt that they have spoken their honest convictions. Now let us look at the other side of the question.

"We know that the Negro question is the most important issue in the affairs of the American Republic today. We are told that there are but two ways of solving the vexed question of the equality of the two races: miscegenation by law, which can *never* take place, or complete domination by the white race—meaning by that *comparative servitude*.

"Miscegenation, either *lawful* or *unlawful,* we *do not want.* The Negro dwells less on such a social cataclysm than any other race among us. Social equality does not exist; no man is forced to receive another within the environments of intimate social life. 'Social position is not to be gained by pushing.' That much for miscegenation. The question now stands: Which race shall dominate within certain parallels of latitude south of Mason and Dixon's line? The Negro, if given his full political rights, would carry the balance of power every time. This power the South has sworn that he shall never exercise.

All sorts of arguments are brought forward to prove the inferiority of intellect, hopeless depravity, and God knows what not, to uphold the white man in his wanton cruelty toward the American Ishmael.

"We are told that we can receive education only along certain elementary lines, and in the next breath we are taunted with not producing a genius in science or art. A Southern white man will tell you that of all politicians the Negro is the vilest, ignoring the fact that for corrupt politics no race ever can or ever will excel the venality of a certain class of whites. Let us, for the sake of illustration, glance at the position of the Irish element in politics. They come to this country poor, unlettered, despised. Fifty years ago Pat was as little welcome at the North as the Negro at the South. What has changed the status of his citizenship? *Politics*. The Irishman dominates politics at the North, and there is no gift within the power of the government that does not feel his influence. I remember a story I heard once of an Irish man just landed at Castle Garden. A friend met him, and as they walked up the street said to him: 'Well, Pat, you are just in time to vote for the city government election.' 'Begorra,' replied Pat, 'an' is it a guviment they have here? Sure, thin, I'll vote agin it.'

"The Irish vote, then, is massed at certain strategic points in the North, and its power is feared and respected. The result has been a rapid and dazzling advance all along the avenues of education and wealth in this country for that incisive race. To the Negro alone politics shall bring no fruit.

"To the defense of slavery in the past, and the inhuman treatment in the present, the South has consecrated her best energies. Literature, politics, theology, history have been ransacked and perverted to prove the hopeless inferiority of the Negro and the design of God that he should serve by right of color and physique. She has convinced no one but herself. Bitterer than double-distilled gall was the Federal success which brought Negro emancipation, domination and supremacy.

"Disfranchisement is what is wanted by the South. Disfranchise the Negro and the South will be content. He, as the weaker race, can soon be crowded out.

"Many solutions of the question of Negro domination have been advanced; among them the deportation of the Negro to Africa has been most warmly advocated by public men all over the country. They argue that in this way the prophecy of the Bible will soonest be fulfilled; that 'Ethiopia shall stretch forth her hand and princes shall come out of Egypt.'

"The late Henry Grady* told us 'that in the wise and humane administration, in the lifting the slave to heights of which he had not dreamed in his savage home, and giving him a happiness he has not yet found in freedom—our fathers (Southern men) left their sons a saving and excellent heritage (slavery).' Another man, also a Southerner, has told us: 'In education and industrial progress this race has accomplished more than it could have achieved in centuries in different environment, without the aid of the

---

*Henry Grady (1850–1889) was a white political leader and editor of the *Atlanta Constitution*.

whites. The Negro has needed the example as well as the aid of the white man. In sections where the colored population is massed and removed from contact with the whites, the Negro has retrograded. Segregate the colored population and you take away the object-lesson.' Here, then is the testimony of two intellectual white men as to the dependence of the Negro upon his proximity to the whites for a continuance of what advancement he has made since the abolishment of slavery. Is such a race as this fit at the present time to carry enlightenment into a savage and barbarous country? Can the blind lead the blind? Would not the Negro gradually fall into the same habits of ignorance and savagery from which the white slave-trader so humanely rescued him when he transported him to the blissful lap of American slavery? The Negro cannot be deported.

"It is being argued that the Negro is receiving education beyond his needs or his capacity. In short that a Negro highly educated is a Negro spoiled. I agree with the gentleman on the other side that education alone will not produce a good citizen. But, of those who would curtail his endeavors to reach the highest that may be opened to him, I would ask: Of what use has education been to you in the upbuilding of the social and political structure which you designate the United States of America? What are the uses of education anyhow?

"To those who know the constitution of the brain as the organ of the moral and intellectual powers of man, education is of the highest importance in the formation of the character of the individual, the race, the government, the social life of any community under heaven. The objects presented to the mind by education stimulate in the same manner that the physical elements of nature do the nerves and muscles—they afford the faculties scope for action. Education is knowledge of nature in all its departments. The moment the mind discovers its own constitution and discerns the importance of the natural laws, the great advantage of moral and intellectual cultivation as a means of invigorating the brain and mental faculties, and of directing the conduct in obedience to the laws of God and man, is apparent. It is important that the Negro should not be hampered in his search after knowledge if we would eliminate from his nature any tendency toward vice that he may be thought to possess, and *which has largely increased by what he has imbibed from the example and the close,* IMMORAL ASSOCIATION *which often existed between the master and the slave.* From my own observation I should say that in this country today the science of man's whole nature—animal, moral and intellectual—was never more required to guide him than at present, when he seems to wield a giant's power, and in the application of it to display the selfish ignorance of an overgrown child.

"We come now to the crime of rape, with which the Negro is accused. For the sake of argument, we will allow that in one case out of a hundred the Negro is guilty of the crime with which he is charged; in the other ninety-nine cases the while man gratifies his lust, either of passion or vengeance. None of us will ever forget the tales told us tonight by Luke Sawyer; the wanton passions he revealed and which it has taken centuries of white civilization to develop, disclosing a dire hell to which the common crime of the untutored Negro is as white as alabaster. And it is from such men as these that the appeal comes for protection for woman's virtue! Do such examples as these render the Negro gentle and pacific? No; he sees himself traveling for years the barren Sahara of poverty, imprisonment, broken hopes and violated home ties; the ignorant, half-savage, irresponsible human animal who forms the rank and file of a race so recently emancipated from servitude, sees only revenge before his short-sighted vision.

"Rape is the outgrowth of a fiendish animus of the whites toward the blacks and of the blacks toward the whites. The Southern white is unable to view the feared domination of the blacks with the dispassionate reasoning of the unprejudiced mind. He exaggerates the nearness of that possibility, which is not desired by the blacks, and, like the physician sick of a mortal disease, is unable to prescribe for himself, and cannot realize that the simple remedy, gently applied, will lift him from his couch of pain. Lynch law prevails as the only such cure for the ills of the South.

" 'Lynchings are justifiable on two grounds,' says a thoughtful writer: 'First, if they are consonant with the moral dignity and well-being of the people; and secondly, if they stop, and are the only sure means of stopping, the crime they avenge.' Lynching does not stop crime; it is but a subterfuge for killing men. It is a good excuse, to use a rough expression, to 'go a-gunning for niggers.'

"Lynching was instituted to crush the manhood of the enfranchised black. Rape is the crime which appeals most strongly to the heart of the home life. Merciful God! Irony of ironies! *The men who created the mulatto race, who recruit its ranks year after year by the very means which they invoked lynch law to suppress,* bewailing the sorrows of violated womanhood!

"No; it is not rape. If the Negro votes, he is shot; if he marries a white woman, he is shot; if he accumulates property, he is shot or lynched—he is a pariah whom the National Government cannot defend. But if he defends himself and his home, then is heard the tread of marching feet as the Federal troops move southward to quell a 'race riot.'

"The South declares that she is no worse than the North, and that the North would do the same under like provocation. Perhaps so, if the offender were a Negro. Take the case of Christie Warden and Frank Almy, which occurred in New Hampshire only a few years ago. Where could a more atrocious crime be perpetrated? The refinement of intellectual pursuits, the elegancies of social intercourse, were the attributes which went to make up the personnel of the most brutal murderer that ever disgraced the history of crime. Centuries of culture and civilization were combined in his make-up. The community where the girl lived and was respected and beloved did not lynch the brute. The white heat of passion led men to lay aside all pursuits for days in order to hunt the criminal from his hiding-place. New Hampshire justice gave him counsel and every means to defend himself from the penalty of his horrid crime. *That was in the North!*

"Human nature is the same in everything. The characteristic traits of the master will be found in his dog. Black, devilish, brutal as they may picture the Negro to be, he but reflects the nature of his environments. *He is but the Hyde who torments the Dr. Jekyll of the white man's refined civilization!*

"My friends, it is going to take time to straighten out this problem; it will only be done by the formation of public opinion. Brute force will not accomplish anything. We must *agitate*. As the anti-slavery apostles went everywhere, preaching the word fifty years before emancipation, *so we must do to-day*. Appeal for the justice of our cause to every civilized nation under the heavens. Lift ourselves upward and forward in this great march of life until 'Ethiopia shall indeed stretch forth her hand, and princes shall come out of Egypt.'"

When he had finished there was not a dry eye in that vast audience. Every heart followed the words of the pastor as with broken utterance he invoked the divine blessing upon the meeting just ended. Slowly they dispersed to their homes, filled with thoughts that burn but cannot be spoken.

The papers said next day that a very interesting meeting occurred the night before at the church on X Street.

From *Contending Forces: A Romance Illustrative of Negro Life North and South*
(Boston: Colored Cooperative Publishing, 1900), 263–273.

1901–1910

Susie Baker King Taylor

1848–1912

Susie Baker King Taylor's 1902 autobiography, in spite of being entitled *Reminiscences of My Life in Camp with the 33rd United States Colored Troops Late 1st S.C. Volunteers*, chronicles her life from her birth (including her genealogy) to the turn of the century. Virtually everything known about Taylor comes from this remarkable text, which is at once a slave narrative, a history of a black regiment in the Civil War told from a woman's perspective, and an exposé of the condition of the African American in the post-Reconstruction South. The oldest of nine children, Taylor was born into slavery in Liberty County, Georgia, in 1848. At the age of seven, she was sent to Savannah to live with her maternal grandmother, Dolly Reed, who sent Taylor and her brother to a clandestine school for blacks, held in a freedwoman's kitchen. Taylor's later teachers included her white playmate and her landlord's high-school-aged son, who tutored her until he left to fight for the Confederacy in 1861.

During the war, Taylor and her family fled to the protection of the Union fleet and were eventually transported to St. Simon's Island, where she met and married Sergeant Edward King, an officer in the unit that would become the Thirty-third U.S. Colored Infantry. When orders were given to evacuate the island, Taylor enrolled in the army as a laundress, following her husband to Camp Saxon in Beaufort, South Carolina. Taking charge of the company mail, Taylor read and wrote letters for illiterate soldiers and taught them to read when she had time. She also worked as a nurse, met Clara Barton, and learned how to handle a musket and shoot it accurately. Taylor witnessed the reality of battle, including the slaughter of colored troops by "bushwhackers." "I can never and shall never forget that terrible war until my eyes close in death," she wrote.

After the war, Taylor returned with her husband to Savannah, where she opened a school. Edward King died in 1866 when Taylor was pregnant with their son. After finding work as a laundress with a family who went North, Taylor decided to settle in Boston. She married Russell L. Taylor in 1879. In 1886, her lifelong interest in the army led her to organize Corps Sixty-seven of the Women's Relief Corps, an auxiliary to the Grand Army of the Republic. In 1893 she became president of the organization.

Like many others, Taylor agonized over the meaning of the American part of her African American identity. Although she was fiercely patriotic and deeply proud of her contribution during the war, the racial violence that emerged afterward made her wonder whether the loss of so many lives had been worthwhile. Taylor offers her "thoughts on the present conditions," including lynching, Jim Crow segregation, the export of white supremacy with U.S. imperialism, and the New South's attempt to erase the historical memory of slavery.

—— Thoughts on the Present Conditions ——

Living here in Boston where the black man is given equal justice, I must say a word on the general treatment of my race, both in the North and South, in this twentieth century. I wonder if our white fellow men realize the true sense or meaning of brotherhood? For two hundred years we had toiled for them; the war of 1861 came and was ended, and we thought our race was forever freed from bondage, and that the two races could live in unity with each other, but when we read almost every day of what is being done to my race by some whites in the South, I sometimes ask, "Was the war in vain? Has it brought freedom, in the full sense of the word, or has it not made our condition more hopeless?"

In this "land of the free" we are burned, tortured, and denied a fair trial, murdered for any imaginary wrong conceived in the brain of the negro-hating white man. There is no redress for us from a government which promised to protect all under its flag. It seems a mystery to me. They say, "One flag, one nation, one country indivisible." Is this true? Can we say this truthfully, when one race is allowed to burn, hang, and inflict the most horrible torture weekly, monthly, on another? No, we cannot sing "My country, 'tis of thee, Sweet land of Liberty"! It is hollow mockery. The Southland laws are all on the side of the white, and they do just as they like to the negro, whether in the right or not.

I do not uphold my race when they do wrong. They ought to be punished, but the innocent are made to suffer as well as the guilty, and I hope the time will hasten when it will be stopped forever. Let us remember God says, "He that sheds blood, his blood shall be required again." I may not live to see it, but the time is approaching when the South will again have cause to repent for the blood it has shed of innocent black men, for their blood cries out for vengeance. For the South still cherishes a hatred toward the blacks, although there are some true Southern gentlemen left who abhor the stigma brought upon them, and feel it very keenly, and I hope the day is not far distant when the two races will reside in peace in the Southland, and we will sing with sincere and truthful hearts, "My country, 'tis of thee, Sweet land of Liberty, of thee I sing."

I have been in many States and cities, and in each I have looked for liberty and justice, equal for the black as for the white; but it was not until I was within the borders of New England, and reached old Massachusetts, that I found it. Here is found liberty in the full sense of the word, liberty for the stranger within her gates, irrespective of race or creed, liberty and justice for all.

We have before us still another problem to solve. With the close of the Spanish war, and on the entrance of the Americans into Cuba, the same conditions confront us as the war of 1861 left. The Cubans are free, but it is a limited freedom, for prejudice, deep-rooted, has been brought to them and a separation made between the white and black Cubans, a thing that had never existed between them before; but to-day there is the same intense hatred toward the negro in Cuba that there is in some parts of this country.

I helped to furnish and pack boxes to be sent to the soldiers and hospitals during the first part of the Spanish war; there were black soldiers there too. At the battle of San Juan Hill, they were in the front, just as brave, loyal, and true as those other black men who fought for freedom and the right; and yet their bravery and faithfulness were reluctantly acknowledged, and praise grudgingly given. All we ask for is "equal justice," the same that is accorded to all other races who come to this country, of their free will (not forced to, as we were), and are allowed to enjoy every privilege, unrestricted, while we are denied what is rightfully our own in a country which the labor of our forefathers helped to make what it is.

One thing I have noticed among my people in the South: they have accumulated a large amount of real estate, far surpassing the colored owners in the North, who seem to let their opportunity slip by them. Nearly all of Brownsville (a suburb of Savannah) is owned by colored people, and so it is in a great many other places throughout the State, and all that is needed is the protection of the law as citizens.

In 1867, soon after the death of my father, who had served on a gunboat during the war, my mother opened a grocery store, where she kept general merchandise always on hand. These she traded for cash or would exchange for crops of cotton, corn, or rice, which she would ship once a month, to F. Lloyd & Co., or Johnson & Jackson, in Savannah. These were colored merchants, doing business on Bay Street in that city. Mother bought her first property, which contained ten acres. She next purchased fifty acres of land. Then she had a chance to get a place with seven hundred acres of land, and she bought this.

In 1870, Colonel Hamilton and Major Devendorft, of Oswego, N.Y., came to the town and bought up a tract of land at a place called Doctortown, and started a mill. Mrs. Devendorft heard of my mother and went to see her, and persuaded her to come to live with her, assuring her she would be as one of the family. Mother went with her, but after a few months she went to Doctortown, where she has been since, and now owns the largest settlement there. All trains going to Florida pass her place, just across the Altamaha River. She is well known by both white and black; the people are fond of her, and will not allow any one to harm her.

Mr. Devendorft sold out his place in 1880 and went back to New York, where later he died.

I read an article, which said the ex-Confederate Daughters had sent a petition to the managers of the local theatres in Tennessee to prohibit the performance of "Uncle Tom's Cabin," claiming it was exaggerated (that is, the treatment of the slaves), and would have a very bad effect on the children who might see the drama. I paused and thought back a few years of the heart-rending scenes I have witnessed; I have seen many times, when I was a mere girl, thirty or forty men, handcuffed, and as many women and children, come every first Tuesday of each month from Mr. Wiley's trade office to the auction blocks, one of them being situated on Drayton Street and Court Lane, the other on Bryant Street, near the Pulaski House. The route was down our principal street, Bull Street, to the courthouse, which was only a block from where I resided.

All people in those days got all their water from the city pumps, which stood about a block apart throughout the city. The one we used to get water from was opposite the courthouse, on Bull Street. I remember, as if it were yesterday, seeing droves of negroes going to be sold, and I often went to look at them, and I could hear the auctioneer very plainly from my house, auctioning these poor people off.

Do these Confederate Daughters ever send petitions to prohibit the atrocious lynchings and wholesale murdering and torture of the negro? Do you ever hear of them fearing this would have a bad effect on the children? Which of these two, the drama or the present state of affairs, makes a degrading impression upon the minds of our young generation? In my opinion it is not "Uncle Tom's Cabin," but it should be the one that has caused the world to cry "Shame!" It does not seem as if our land is yet civilized. It is like times long past, when rulers and high officers had to flee for their lives, and the negro has been dealt with in the same way since the war by those he lived with and toiled for two hundred years or more. I do not condemn all the Caucasian race because the negro is badly treated by a few of the race. No! for had it not been for the true whites, assisted by God and the prayers of our forefathers, I should not be here to-day.

There are still good friends to the negro. Why, there are still thousands that have not bowed to Baal. So it is with us. Man thinks two hundred years is a long time, and it is, too; but it is only as a week to God, and in his own time—I know I shall not live to see the day, but it will come—the South will be like the North, and when it comes it will be prized higher than we prize the North to-day. God is just; when he created man he made him in his image, and never intended one should misuse the other. All men are born free and equal in his sight.

I am pleased to know at this writing that the officers and comrades of my regiment stand ready to render me assistance whenever required. It seems like "bread cast upon the water," and it has returned after many days, when it is most needed. I have received letters from some of the comrades, since we parted in 1866, with expressions of gratitude and thanks to me for teaching them their first letters. One of them, Peter Waggall, is a minister in Jacksonville, Fla. Another is in the government service at Washington, D.C. Others are in Darien and Savannah, Ga., and all are doing well.

There are many people who do not know what some of the colored women did during the war. There were hundreds of them who assisted the Union soldiers by hiding them and helping them to escape. Many were punished for taking food to the prison stockades for the prisoners. When I went into Savannah, in 1805, I was told of one of these stockades which was in the suburbs of the city, and they said it was an awful place. The Union soldiers were in it, worse than pigs, without any shelter from sun or storm, and the colored women would take food there at night and pass it to them, through the holes in the fence. The soldiers were starving, and these women did all they could towards relieving those men, although they knew the penalty, should they be caught giving them aid. Others assisted in various ways the Union army. These things should be kept in history before the people. There has never been a greater war in the United States than the one of 1861, where so many lives were lost,—not men alone but noble women as well.

Let us not forget that terrible war, or our brave soldiers who were thrown into Andersonville and Libby prisons, the awful agony they went through, and the most brutal treatment they received in those loathsome dens, the worst ever given human beings; and if the white soldiers were subjected to such treatment, what must have been the horrors inflicted on the negro soldiers in their prison pens? Can we forget those cruelties? No, though we try to forgive and say, "No North, no South," and hope to see it in reality before the last comrade passes away.

A Visit to Louisiana

The inevitable always happens. On February 3, 1898, I was called to Shreveport, La., to the bedside of my son, who was very ill. He was traveling with Nickens and Company, with "The Lion's Bride," when he fell ill, and had been ill two weeks when they sent to me. I tried to have him brought home to Boston, but they could not send him, as he was not able to sit and ride this long distance; so on the sixth of February I left Boston to go to him. I reached Cincinnati on the eighth, where I took the train for the south. I asked a white man standing near (before I got my train) what car I should take. "Take that one," he said, pointing to one. "But that is a smoking car!" "Well," he replied, "that is the car for colored people." I went to this car, and on entering it all my courage failed me. I have ridden in many coaches, but I was never in such as these. I wanted to return home again, but when I thought of my sick boy I said, "Well, others ride in these cars and I must do likewise," and tried to be resigned, for I wanted to reach my boy, as I did not know whether I should find him alive. I arrived in Chattanooga at eight o'clock in the evening, where the porter took my baggage to the train which was to leave for Marion, Miss. Soon after I was seated, just before the train pulled out, two tall men with slouch hats on walked through the car, and on through the train. Finally they came back to our car and stopping at my seat said, "Where are those men who were with you?" I did not know to whom they were speaking, as there was another woman in the car, so I made no reply. Again they asked me, standing directly in front of my seat, "Where are those men who came in with you?" "Are you speaking to me?" I said. "Yes!" they said. "I have not seen any men," I replied. They looked at me a moment, and one of them asked where I was from. I told him Boston; he hesitated a minute and walked out of our car to the other car.

When the conductor came around I told him what these men had said, and asked him if they allowed persons to enter the car and insult passengers. He only smiled. Later, when the porter came in, I mentioned it to him. He said, "Lady, I see you do not belong here; where are you from?" I told him. He said, "I have often heard of Massachusetts. I want to see that place." "Yes!" I said, "you can ride there on the cars, and no person would be allowed to speak to you as those men did to me." He explained that those men were constables, who were in search of a man who had eloped with another man's wife. "That is the way they do here. Each morning you can hear of some negro being lynched;" and on seeing my surprise, he said, "Oh, that is nothing; it is done all the time. We have no rights here. I have been on this road for fifteen years and have seen some terrible things." He wanted to know what I was doing down there, and I told him it was only the illness of my son that brought me there.

I was a little surprised at the way the poor whites were made to ride on this road. They put them all together by themselves in a car, between the colored people's coach and the first-class coach, and it looked like the "laborers' car" used in Boston to carry the different day laborers to and from their work.

I got to Marion, Miss., at two o'clock in the morning, arrived at Vicksburg at noon, and at Shreveport about eight o'clock in the evening, and found my son just recovering from a severe hemorrhage. He was very anxious to come home, and I tried to secure a berth for him on a sleeper, but they would not sell me one, and he was not strong enough to travel otherwise. If I could only have gotten him to Cincinnati, I might have brought him home, but as I could not I was forced to let him remain where he was. It seemed very hard, when his father fought to protect the Union and our flag, and yet his boy was denied, under this same flag, a berth to carry him home to die, because he was a negro.

Shreveport is a little town, made up largely of Jews and Germans and a few Southerners, the negroes being in the majority. Its sidewalks are sand except on the main street. Almost all the stores are kept either by the Jews or Germans. They know a stranger in a minute, as the town is small and the citizens know each other; if not personally, their faces are familiar.

I went into a jewelry store one day to have a crystal put in my watch, and the attendant remarked, "You are a stranger." I asked him how he knew that. He said he had watched me for a week or so. I told him yes, I was a stranger and from Boston. "Oh! I have heard of Boston," he said. "You will not find this place like it is there. How do you like this town?" "Not very well," I replied.

I found that the people who had lived in Massachusetts and were settled in Shreveport were very cordial to me and glad to see me. There was a man murdered in cold blood for nothing. He was a colored man and a "porter" in a store in this town. A clerk had left his umbrella at home. It had begun to rain when he started for home, and on looking for the umbrella he could not, of course, find it. He asked the porter if he had seen it. He said no, he had not. "You answer very saucy," said the clerk, and drawing his revolver, he shot the colored man dead. He was taken up the street to an office where he was placed under one thousand dollars bond for his appearance and released, and that was the end of the case. I was surprised at this, but I was told by several white and colored persons that this was a common occurrence, and the persons were never punished if they were white, but no mercy was shown to negroes.

I met several comrades, white and colored, there, and noticed that the colored comrades did not wear their buttons. I asked one of them why this was, and was told, should they wear it, they could not get work. Still some would wear their buttons in spite of the feeling against it. I met a newsman from New York on the train. He was a veteran, and said that Sherman ought to come back and go into that part of the country.

Shreveport is a horrid place when it rains. The earth is red and sticks to your shoes, and it is impossible to keep rubbers on, for the mud pulls them off. Going across the Mississippi River, I was amazed to see how the houses were built, so close to the shore, or else on low land; and when the river rises, it flows into these houses and must make it very disagreeable and unhealthy for the inmates.

After the death of my son, while on my way back to Boston, I came to Clarksdale, one of the stations on the road from Vicksburg. In this town a Mr. Hancock, of New York, had a large cotton plantation, and the Chinese intermarry with the blacks.

At Clarksdale, I saw a man hanged. It was a terrible sight, and I felt alarmed for my own safety down there. When I reached Memphis I found conditions of travel much better. The people were mostly Western and Northern here; the cars were nice, but separate for colored persons until we reached the Ohio River, when the door was opened and the porter passed through, saying, "The Ohio River! change to the other car." I thought, "What does he mean? We have been riding all this distance in separate cars, and now we are all to sit together." It certainly seemed a peculiar arrangement. Why not let the negroes, if their appearance and respectability warrant it, be allowed to ride as they do in the North, East, or West?

There are others beside the blacks, in the South and North, that should be put in separate cars while traveling, just as they put my race. Many black people in the South do not wish to be thrown into a car because all are colored, as there are many of their race very objectionable to them, being of an entirely different class; but they have to adapt themselves to the circumstances and ride with them, because they are all negroes. There is no such division with the whites. Except in one place I saw, the workingman and the millionaire ride in the same coaches together. Why not allow the respectable, law-abiding classes of the blacks the same privilege? We hope for better conditions in the future, and feel sure they will come in time, surely if slowly.

While in Shreveport, I visited ex-Senator Harper's house. He is a colored man and owns a large business block, besides a fine residence on Cado Street and several good building lots. Another family, the Pages, living on the same street, were quite wealthy, and a large number of colored families owned their homes, and were industrious, refined people; and if they were only allowed justice, the South would be the only place for our people to live.

We are similar to the children of Israel, who, after many weary years in bondage, were led into that land of promise, there to thrive and be forever free from persecution; and I don't despair, for the Book which is our guide through life declares, "Ethiopia shall stretch forth her hand."

What a wonderful revolution! In 1861 the Southern papers were full of advertisements for "slaves," but now, despite all the hindrances and "race problems," my people are striving to attain the full standard of all other races born free in the sight of God, and in a number of instances have succeeded. Justice we ask,—to be citizens of these United States, where so many of our people have shed their blood with their white comrades, that the stars and stripes should never be polluted.

From *Reminiscences of My Life in Camp with the 33rd United States Colored Troops Late 1st S.C. Volunteers* (Boston: Author, 1902).

Alice French (Octave Thanet)

1850–1934

Writing under the pseudonym Octave Thanet, Alice French was one of the most highly paid and widely read authors of fiction at the turn of the twentieth century. Between 1887 and 1911, she published nine short-story collections containing work previously published in magazines such as *Harper's Monthly*, *Scribner's Magazine*, *Century Magazine*, and *Atlantic Monthly*. Most famous for her short stories, French also wrote three novels, two volumes of sketches about Arkansas plantation life, and numerous essays commenting on social issues.

French was born in New England to a socially prominent and wealthy Anglo-American family that traced its ancestry back to the Pilgrims. When she was a girl, the family moved to Davenport, Iowa, for her father's health, but French returned east to attend Andover Academy and Vassar College. After Vassar, French went to live with her life companion, Jane Crawford, at Clover Bend, Crawford's plantation on the Black River in Arkansas. Most of French's fiction is set in either Iowa or Arkansas. The most conservative and elitist of any author in this volume, French was a complex figure who shared her life with another woman for fifty years, wrote extensively about the negative impact of marriage on women's independence and friendships with other women, supported herself through her writing, and was by all accounts a shrewd businesswoman—yet she actively supported the antisuffrage movement in Iowa.

French's local-color pieces about Arkansas use the patronizing and stereotypical language common to the Plantation School to describe her black sharecropping tenants, but in "Beyond the Limit" she breaks with that tradition to compose a powerfully persuasive argument against lynching for its negative impact on the white community (including the flight of black labor from the area). The story's title and the stance taken by the Yankee schoolmarm who provides its moral center seem to suggest that while hanging an accused rapist without a trial might be appropriate, the sadistic burning alive of a mentally retarded man goes way beyond all civilized limits and sets in motion the moral and psychological degeneration of an entire society. French's analysis goes even further, however, to indict southern codes of masculinity for nurturing and encouraging mob behavior and violence—anticipating the arguments made in the 1930s and 1940s by white southern female antilynching activists such as Jessie Daniel Ames and Lillian Smith.

—— Beyond the Limit ——

An atrocious crime had been as atrociously revenged. Long as the volunteer execution-ers might live they would remember the look of the blazing white disk, sinking through a smoldering sunset, behind the cypress-trees; the dark open space in the forest, with its winter-stung grass trampled by horses' hoofs into stiff mud; the horses incuriously gazing; the grim ring of men; the long shadows of water oaks and maples and gum-trees walling the "slash;" the inky blackness of the water in the "slash," save where it caught one horrible, wavering glow, not from the sun but from dying flames, which every puff of breeze drew out of a great mass of coals about a charred walnut-trunk.

Only a dying fire and graying coals, now! It was all over. It seemed hours since those agonized screams had ceased—hours through which they had stood in silence, steeling their hearts; yet, in reality, it was barely a single hour.

The silence grew more terrible than the sound to one man, a farmer, Sam Waller by name, living near. This strong, quiet young man was liked by his neighbors, although they saw but little of him.

He had joined the lynchers under the first impetus of horror at the crime. Bolles, his next neighbor, had brought him the news. He had known the little victim of the dead wretch, and was as crazed with fury as any man of them there. He had been tireless on the march, and foremost in the assault—though that says little; for the sheriff had daughters, and *he* barely fulfilled the forms of resistance. Bolles had been in an excess of excitement since noon, but now he was spent. So were they all.

Stealthily, he glanced from one to another familiar face wearing its mask of ruthless determination. Every man's brows met over the same stern eyes, every man's lips made a straight line above clenched teeth; and the same bluish pallor was on every man's skin.

All at once, Bolles shivered and coughed; and, as if he had twitched an electric wire, a shrug and cough ran through the half-circle. Waller had a fancy that it was a relief. A man apart from them, nearest the walnut trunk, unfolded his arms, and turned his head. His face was haggard, and his eyes had a peculiar, glassy stare. He took off his hat, as if at a funeral.

"I reckon that's all, gentlemen," he said. Bolles went up to him. Unconsciously, he walked on tip-toe, and his voice sank so the words were not audible.

The man's answer was louder, and in the same hushed tones: "No, it caynt ketch nothing; there'll be frost, and everything's sopping wet. Good evening, gentlemen." Bolles said something more, to which the man shook his head. Then Bolles shook hands before he slipped away, on tip-toe as before.

One obscure impulse sent every man present up to the lonely man, and forced each to wring his hand. It felt cold and hard like iron when Waller touched it; the chill clung to his fingers as he slunk back to his horse. But he did not ride away; he lingered, watching the others departing in twos and threes, no man riding alone, and no man speaking above his breath.

Directly Bolles nodded at his elbow; and they, too, set forth, together. At the first touch of the forest-road, they heard the thud of Reeve Miller's horse's hoofs. He was one of the village storekeepers—a man they did not like, but they welcomed him now. They saw that he was shivering, and his teeth rattled over his words like a wheel over stones.

"H—! Ain't it c—cold!" he chattered.

Miller was a zealous church-member, of rigid walk and conversation; there was something ghastly in the oath in his mouth.

"Say,"—in a minute he was talking again, although no word had been said—"We were just naturally *obliged* to do it, weren't we? I don't reckon he suffered—at least not so terrible much—those screeches were more being frightened, don't you reckon? They—they didn't last long—"

"Lookahere!"—Bolles twisted his head on him—"I don't wanter talk. He was a devil incarnate, and he's got his deservings. But, I tell you, I don't wanter talk! Now nor never!"

"Me neither," echoed Waller.

"Oh, of course, that's right; that's prudent!" Miller agreed, hastily; "only I keep hearing him—him—"

"*Will* you quit!" bawled Bolles, in sudden access of rage; and, inarticulately appeasing him, Miller rode on through the stiffening mud. There was no sound beyond the slump and plash of the horses' hoofs.

It grew colder—a damp, clinging, subtle cold that crept into Waller's bones. He began to strain his eyes to catch the red glow of his own lamps, the sight of the fences on the corner, and the willow thicket near the house, in whose kitchen Aunt Tilly and Uncle Noe had worked for the Wallers when his mother, the widow, was alive. They were a faithful pair, and they were good workers in the unhurried fashion of their race.

"B-r-r! I'm cold," said Miller, shudderingly. "Say, Sam, have you got any whiskey?"

This was an unusual question, and it made Bolles' under jaw drop with amazement, for Miller's father died of drinking; and Miller, ever since he had lived in the village (which was five years), had been the man who engineered the annual fight against the petition for license. It was Miller, too, who was suspected of helping the revenue officer capture Ned Annable, and destroy the still—that was why he was not liked. So Bolles stared. But Waller hardly caught the words; he was peering uneasily at the dark bulk of his own house. No light brightened the windows, no smoke drifted from the chimneys.

"Shorely, Aunt Tilly must have gone to town," he muttered. "Say! 'Light boys, won't you? We'll git a drink and a warm, for she'll be back directly."

They did alight. Bolles volunteered to look up Aunt Tilly in her cabin, while Waller and Miller went into the house. Waller went first. The air of the room was chill and damp. The fire was laid in the kitchen stove, ready for lighting. The coffee was ground, and ready to hand, beside the skilletful of pork and the sweet potatoes in the pan. Even the lamp stood on the table, its chimney removed as if to light the wick. Waller shivered as Miller had shivered before. But when Bolles returned to report that Uncle Noe and Aunt Tilly were gone, taking their clothes with them, he forced a laugh, and said: "Scared off, I reckon. They'll come back, all right. Jest chased off. Dror up boys. I've got a jug for Christmas egg-nog, and there's some left."

He put the jug on the table, and they all drank. Miller drank twice, but he did not cough or choke over his gulps, and his trembling hands began to grow steady. At Waller's pressing, they stayed with him for supper. They lighted all the lamps, and set the fires roaring up the chimneys. They had more whisky with their meal. They ate and drank in a kind of excited greed, tasting the savor of nothing, but eating in answer to some kind of craving faintness, such as drunkards will feel in the first stages of a debauch—they were sick with weakness, and they thought that they were hungry. They talked in gusts, with heavy falls of dumbness. Not a word was said of the afternoon's work.

Miller, who had been drinking far more than the others, grew loquacious and boastful in his cups, and told sly stories of his wild youth before he was converted, until Bolles and Waller exchanged frowning glances.

"Reckon I best git him home, and that mighty briefly," Bolles said to Waller.

The two had risen. Miller was still at the table, where he was puffing on an unlighted pipe, and plying a glass between the jug and his mouth.

"He kin ride all right—now," said Bolles; "but he's beginning to tell 'bout his mother, and his hearing her sing hymns, and pretty soon he'll be a-crying, and then he'll go to sleep; and there'll be no doing nothin' with him—"

"I don't mind keeping him!" interrupted Waller, quickly; "not a mite!"

"Well, I got to git home. There's my wife; and there's *his* wife, too—no, I got to git him home!"

So, presently, they helped Miller to his horse, a steady beast sure to go home safely, even with a rider who used the mane for a bridle; and the two rode away. Waller had declined Bolles' offer to send his eldest boy over for the night, declined it peevishly— what did he want a boy 'round for? Couldn't he wash his dishes and cook his breakfast himself?—and Bolles had not persisted. But after they had passed by the gate, Bolles turned in his saddle to see Waller fleeing toward the house like a hunted man; and all night long the lights burned. Bolles saw them. He had a bad night, himself; and, more than once, he looked out of his windows over the ragged cotton-fields at Waller's house, and the red glimmer fixed his eyes. He did not make any comment to Waller when they met.

A month later, as the wind drifted the dust and the dead oak-leaves down the untidy village sidewalk, and the wooden rectangles of the shop-fronts looked grim and weather-stained, two men met outside Miller's store. One of the men was Waller. He looked sallow and ill, but he was dressed with unusual care in a new suit, with a bright red cravat about a shining white collar. The other man looked even thinner and paler and sicklier than Waller, because of his shabby clothing. It was their first meeting since the lynching.

They looked at each other furtively. Their eyes dodged. In the glance of each was the same quality of shrinking and woeful curiosity. Each disguised it with the same affectation of indifference.

"Howdy, Dan? How's you-all?"

"Oh, we're all stirrin'!" You look like you b'en chillin'."

"Yes, sir; I have been chillin'—a right smart. I ain't been well."

"Say, is it all true 'bout the Dane boys holding up the train, and roasting the express messenger's feet to make him tell how to open the safe?"

"Yes, sir. They-all got the boys. Say, they'll git the 'pen,' shore! I wouldn't of thought it of Gather Dane; and doing the man that mean way—"

"Wasn't they out chasing niggers? I heard some pretty bad—"

"Oh, niggers! They scared more'n they hurt, I reckon; and, someway, I—I got a sick feelin' on me ever' black skin I see. I can't keer what happens to them!"

"God knows, that ain't strange!" interposed Waller; "but they ain't *all* mean!"

"I dunno," said Dan wearily; "I can't make myself keer no matter what happens to 'em! But—I wisht—I can't help feelin' it's be'n bad for our own folks. Miller, he's be'n drinkin' ever sence; says he hears screeches the plumb while if he ain't stiffed up with liquor! And more'n him is drinkin'; and here's Gather gittin' so bad. Sometimes wife says we hadn't oughter done it—says if we'd jest hanged him—I don't know myself, ef we hadn't orter jest burnt him up by our lones—anyhow not let boys like Gather help. School-teacher said it be'n right enough to kill him up, but we made ourselves low's him, torturin' him like savages. The women was awful mad at her, 'cept wife—she said she didn't understand. Kinder preyed on wife, though, for she thought a heap of School-teacher."

"She *is* a mighty nice young lady," Waller said, his color turning; but Dan was too sunken in his own dark musings to notice.

"I dunno how come sech a hellish thing could happen to me!" he burst out, suddenly. "I never done mean things, and I aimed to do right! I was honest, and I tried to raise my children honest, and, yit, if I'd be'n the wust devil on this earth I cudn't have suffered and be'n tortured more! It ain't fair—it ain't fair—" He choked with the flood of anguish that his words had unloosened, and his whole face quivered.

"Oh, you'll feel better by 'n' by," said Waller, who had grown pale, nevertheless.

"If I don't, I'll kill myself," Dan muttered savagely, as he wrung Waller's hand, and turned away. Waller watched him mount his horse, and trot down the street, his own face set in somber attention.

"If it's bad for him's it is for me, I don't blame him!" he thought.

Sighing deeply, he cast his eye over his own person. He brushed a smouch of dust from his coat. He straightened his shoulders.

"I reckon I best walk down to the post-office," he was thinking; "likely she'll be there for the mail." Again he sighed heavily. " 'Tleast she'll let me talk it over, and tell how it happened. Maybe it won't be so bad then."

As he walked, he observed the people on the streets. Some of them were men who had been with him that afternoon. Did he only fancy a change in their aspect, he wondered, wretchedly. Did *they* see a wriggling black shape in the sunset, and hear screams mingled with the wind in the trees? But they did not have to live alone.

He would have been lonely and miserable enough in any case, for his mother, his only relative, with whom he had lived and worked and been happy, had died only six months before; but now his haunted solitude was intolerable.

There was not even work to occupy his mind, as it was winter—the last bale of cotton had been picked. At first he made work for himself—very little repair, planned during the year, was finished; he chopped a woodpile, at which the passers-by stared—he was busy every hour of the day, but there grew upon him a most dreadful sensation of pursuit. Something awful was happening behind his back, and a formless Thing was stealthily dogging him, nearer, nearer! What it was, he could not tell; but he knew, once let it clutch his throat, there would be no to-morrow for him. He could not even tell how it had grown—this foolish and monstrous notion. He only knew it began in the sudden panic that fell on him when his companions rode away and left him in the night. All he knew was that he was afraid.

Nothing is so awful as to be afraid! To be afraid of *anything*, no matter how terrible, is little when compared to the nightmare horror of pure fear which is without reason or definition—or limit.

Waller was afraid. He began to sit down always against the wall. He never turned except slowly. It was as if he would give the Thing time to turn, also, and save his eyes from it. The only way that he could escape the sense of its presence was to have it out with the cause of his suffering, and try to justify himself. He was not a man likely to explain his own emotions—men of his sort seldom can explain what they feel. The nearest approach he made was a sentence which he often called aloud: "If we-all done right, you ain't got the *right* to ha'nt me!"

Therefore, he would sit, and let the drama of that awful twilight act itself over and over in a ghastly iteration.

Over and over, he would hear the negro pleading in the piteous, childish language of his half-developed race: "Oh, please! Oh *please*! Please lemme git cool a minnit!"

Again he would feel the impulse upon him to send one of his own bullets into the tormented wretch's heart. It was not fear of his comrade's rage which held his hand. It was, rather a shrinking from his squeamishness as unmanly and false to their trust.

The same emotion (which can be trusted as implicitly, to do the devil's work neatly, as any of the passions) gripped his throat, when he had sickened at the sight of the paraphernalia of torture, and it choked down a prayer in his mouth that they hang the man instead of burning him. Hanging would take the fiend off the earth; and that was the main thing. Waller did not, for an instant, doubt the righteousness of killing him. He *ought* to be killed, crazy or not! But killed like *that*! Why hadn't he interfered? He answered his memories fiercely. He gave back inch by inch—but he did give back. At first, he called the doom, itself, just. Then he admitted that they went too far, but what good would his talking have done? Who'd have harked to *him*? But every day was revealing to him the remorse of some one of the lynchers. Dan, himself, seemed troubled. Obscurely, Waller began to perceive that a mob is swayed as much by what men *think* their companions feel as by real feelings, and the savagery of a mob is fickle, because it has in it as much fear and contagion as rage. Dan's words this afternoon, had added a new argument against him.

The negro was not the only victim. The executioners did not go free. Waller, in his simple way, was a good citizen. He was a man who would haul a fallen tree out of the road. To be convinced he had helped men to do wrong, and had brought evil on his neighbors, was bitter to him. There *was* more drinking and fighting, cursing and wickedness. He thought of Dan's story, and remembered Gather's look at the lynching, and the way the boy had craned his head forward, and he shuddered. For he was wondering whether that afternoon's dreadful excitement had awakened sleeping devils in some of the spectators' souls. But he would not yield to the miserable confusion that darkened his mind; he still had a refuge of hope.

That morning he had jumped to his feet suddenly, with a loud cry.

"Why ain't I thought of her before!" he shouted. This accursed and ever-present trouble had even driven his sweetheart out of his mind. Yet until it happened, Waller had thought often of the new schoolteacher from Illinois. He had gone to church in the village only to see her pretty brown head, which never turned away from the minister, and, afterward, to catch the chance of walking home with her.

It was only a chance, for Waller was bashful, and did not know that he was handsome, and he did not realize that a girl would admire his strength; and he did not push himself before the assured young sparks of the village, who "lived on the railroad," and wore a necktie every-day, and felt that they knew the world.

Once or twice, he had caught her eye, had spoken to her, and had taken her away from them all. He would never forget the time he was driving the black colt, and met her on the road, and gave her a lift, and how she only laughed at the colt's antics—they would have frightened other girls. She told him that she had heard he was able to "gentle" anything, and of how kind he was to beasts. He told her about the old dog dying only a week after his mother, and he was even bold enough to tell her a little how he felt. Why hadn't he talked to *her*? He couldn't tell anybody else. She was a good girl—a girl his mother would have liked.

She was sorry, for she didn't understand. If he could explain that they lynched the negro not through cruelty but because they must protect their homes by a frightful warning! She didn't know niggers. It wasn't the subject to discuss with a young lady; but it seemed as if his heart would split with the weight of his trouble.

Who can tell what bright hopes and cravings of youth stirred in the young farmer's heart as he made the most careful toilet of his life? He scrubbed himself with a painstaking thoroughness, and he darned a minute hole in his best pair of stockings. Always, before he had gone into her presence, he paid her the tribute of his best attempt at dainty cleanliness.

At the door he paused, and cast a quick glance about the room, neat with a man's tasteless and cast-iron neatness. His face quivered with a remembrance of his mother, and he stepped back to softly stroke the cushion of the big rocking-chair in which she always used to sit. Although he brushed his hand over his eyes, he rode down the road more cheerfully than he had ridden in weeks. In this mood, he had met Dan; and, still strengthened by his acknowledged hope, he would not let Dan's disclosures dismay him utterly. He walked on toward the post-office. She would be there after school to get the mail. She never missed Thursdays, for she had a mother at home in Illinois struggling, with two half-grown brothers, on a little farm, and the letter from home came on Thursday.

Outside the office, he saw Bolles. He had not met Bolles often of late. He had fancied Bolles was not so cheerful as he had been. Bolles was a good-humored, jovial fellow, and gave prizes to his cotton-pickers, and picked more, himself, than the prize-winner. He was a carpenter of the "saw-and-hatchet" type, and he worked at his trade between crops, and he was considered a prosperous man. He stopped to shake hands with Waller, and tell him that he looked "pearter."

"Am I? You ain't joking?"

"I'm quit joking. Lookahere, Waller, you wanted to buy my farm last spring. I'll give it to you for a hundred down and long time for the rest, and same price you offered—"

"I—I ain't aiming to buy more land now," hesitated Waller.

"Fifty less."

Waller's jaw dropped. The contrast between Bolles' customary bargaining manner and this offer gave him a sick feeling.

"You ain't going away?"

"I want to," said Bolles. He squared his shoulders, and threw up his head, but his eyes went past Waller toward the sky where the golden glow was dulling into red. "I ain't right well, and my folks ain't; and I want to work at my trade. I can git a steady job down Morningstar way. Land's cheap there, too; and it's high ground. Say, I'll let you have the place for fifty down and long time's you want and—and—and a hundred off."

Waller shook his head. "I'd like to go, myself. Lookahere—do you ever see him, nights, like now?"

Bolles did not answer for a second. Waller had not the courage to look at him.

"Yes," Bolles said.

There was a pause. Both men heard the rattle of the twigs on the trees. "I reckon it's hoot-owls I hear, nights," said Waller, "but it sounds terrible like *him*!"

"Don't it?" said Bolles.

"Did you hear he was crazy?"

"Yes,—got hit on the head. I don't care; he deserved it."

"He shore did. But I—I wish we'd hung 'im or shot 'im."

"*I* felt like asking the boys to let him off with shooting; but it wouldn't done no good."

"Not a mite; you couldn't stop 'em," said Waller, eagerly.

Bolles kicked the clods of frosted earth about his feet. "Thar's a terrible sight of feeling, still, 'mong the women 'specially. You know the school-teacher?" he said.

"Yes," said Waller; he bit his dry lips.

"She said a right smart against it—said thar was a limit; this was beyond it; we might have the right to take life, but we hadn't the right to torture—"

"Do you reckon she was right? She—she's a nice young lady."

"She's the best school-teacher we ever did have, but the women run her off for jest that. Got at the school board, and sent her off. She's gone."

"*Gone!*" repeated Waller; his face was white.

"Plumb gone. Went yestiddy. I saw her, and toted her bag for her. I told her she'd got good friends here, who'd fight for her if she'd say the word; but she said she be'n glad to go, that even the little tricks at school talked of it. She said she was sorry for us, for she knew most of us only meant to do something that would be so awful that it would prevent sech things happenin' forevermore; but it wouldn't more than hanging; and the doing and seeing of it would work a whole heap of misery and wickedness."

"Where'd she go?" asked Waller.

"Dunno. Somewhere's in Indianny; they moved. I was kinder sorry for her; her folks lost their farm in Illinois, and I expect she hated to give up her job; for they-all need the money—where you going'?"

"I got to git home," said Waller. "Good evening."

"I 'lowed he was going for the mail," mused Bolles. "He changed his mind, maybe. He ain't looking so peart's I thought—must of be'n the way the sun struck him. Well I wisht he'd buy the farm!"

Waller went to the store where he had left his horse. He rode slowly homeward. Against the blood-red skies the forest spread a ragged fringe of black. *And he was afraid.*

It was a week or two later before Bolles saw Waller again. During the interval, Waller had been out of the place. It was a subject of discussion at the store why he went, some holding that it was on business, and others offering wagers as high as a pig that he went in search of the schoolmistress. These same gossips, also, were sure that he did not find her. Bolles, therefore, studied his neighbor's face with a certain curiosity. He was shocked at the change in it. It was the face of a hunted creature—thin to ghastliness, with great, bluish hollows in the cheeks and under the eyes. It was haggard and sunken and wan, and the eyes were like bits of smoked glass. The spectacle of a man who had been so erect and strong, riding with stooping shoulders and his head bowed on his chest, unnerved the kind-hearted Bolles.

"Lookahere, Waller," he cried, "what's the matter with you?"

"Nothing," returned Waller. His voice was the weak, hesitating voice of a sick man. "I ain't be'n sleeping right, that's all."

"But—but you slept when you was gone?"

"No," said Waller.

"It ain't—"

"Yes, sir. I run away to git rid of it. But you can't run away from the sunset; and *It* come, too."

"Take something to make you sleep," growled Bolles. "Go to a doctor. You're a plumb ijit!"

"That's what the doctor said. He don't know. It's no use talkin', Bolles. I be'n studying and studying. Has he got the right to ha'nt us? *Has* he? Not jes' for killing him that dreadful, cruel way, but for making the whole of us crueler and wickeder—"

"Oh quit your nonsense!" cried Bolles, laying a rough, kindly hand on his arm. "You're studying yourself crazy. We ain't nothing of the kind. I'm coming over to see you, and—"

"What's that?" gasped Waller, with a start.

It was the din of childish voices, penetrated by the screams of a cat.

"What the—what are them boys a-doing?" cried Bolles, angrily. "Look over thar! Over in Coles' field."

But Waller was riding furiously toward the field and a little group of small, black figures about a column of smoke. Bolles set his teeth, and followed. Coles' field had been Coles' farm. Years ago, the house had burned to the ground, and had never been rebuilt; the shell of a barn had been hacked away in bits for the lumber, the cotton-pen had sprawled its rotting logs about its crooked rectangle; and the fences had been stolen rail by rail until only a few rails, here and there amid the elbow-high brush, marked the line. The children were about a fire near the cotton-pen. Bolles could see that. They were jumping in frantic excitement, and their shrill yells almost drowned the outcry of the cat.

Suddenly, like a stone flung into a pool, Waller rode into the group, spattering it in every direction.

Wild screams of fright and pain in human notes succeeded the cat's wails. Bolles jumped off his horse, and caught one of the slowest-footed fugitives. The other children were flying in every direction. Bolles dragged his shrieking captive up to Waller, who was stamping out the fire. At that instant, he saw a cat that was leaping down the field, dragging a charred stick after her. The stick was chained to her by a little toy chain. Bolles' hand tightened on the trembling little shoulder.

"Is that stick afire?" he hissed. "You little—what you be'n doing?"

A burst of sobs answered him. "We—we—she eat up Tommy's mocking-bird! We-all was jest a-exercutin' of her like they done the nigger who tilled little Pearl. Tommy said his papa said 'twas all right—Lemme go!"

Bolles eyes dilated as for the first time he really looked at the child.

2. "A Little Klansman." (Photographs and Prints Division, Schomburg Center for Research in Black Culture, The New York Public Library, Astor, Lenox and Tilden Foundations.)

"My God! He's nothing but a—*baby*?" he groaned. "Git out! I hope the cat will han't you like the nigger ha'nts us!"

He was so unstrung by the horror of the thing that his voice stuck in his throat like a rusty saw. He did not know what he was saying—something about licking the little demons.

"They wasn't more than babies," said Waller. "And they laffed—*laffed*! Bolles, the wrath of God is on this country. We-all have sinned against our own folks worse'n against that nigger. He's got *leave* to ha'nt us."

Bolles felt the contagion of his gloom. The pith was gone out of his own courage, and his knees shook as he scrambled back in the saddle. Yet he tried feebly to hearten Waller, who did not say another word. Nearing the town, they perceived two men—acquaintances of both. Waller lifted his head. "I don't want to talk," said he. "I'm going home. Good-by, Bolles."

He turned his horse slowly (Bolles noticed what a wide circle he made), and then galloped away toward the forest and the blood-red west. Bolles uneasily watched him. Once he called his name, but Waller did not turn his head, and his horse's speed grew more and more rapid until a fall in the road snatched him from view.

There remained with Bolles an extraordinary impression of shock and disquietude. So unbearable did this become that after a little time he gave his anxiety to his friends; and he told them that he should go at once to Waller's to persuade him to go home with him for the night.

"Some of we-all has got to stay longer him till he gits better," he said. "Somebuddy—if we kin find him—wasn't in that d—d lynching! I tell you, boys, flesh and blood can't stand some things!"

The other men fell in with his mood, having, perhaps, their own reasons for sympathy. They agreed to ride, without delay, to Waller's farm. As they rode, an unacknowledged dread spurred them; they rode faster and faster, as Waller had ridden. When they came to the open highway, to the little hill beyond the forest, where Waller's house stood, the west was a sea of red, with a blazing white disk sinking through the glow. The cypress-fringe on the horizon was black, black as the buzzards, flying high in the steel blue sky, with languid wings. There was no light in the house, and the door stood open. Simultaneously they reined in their horses, for the air was ringing with the prolonged, bell-like howling of a hound.

"That's Waller's new dog," said one of the men. To save him he could not lift his voice above a whisper.

Bolles alighted. His face was gray, and, walking along the path to the house, he clenched his hands tightly.

When he came to the door, he hesitated; but immediately he went in, the others following.

Waller lay on the bed, his revolver at his side, the dog crouched near him, wistfully licking a nerveless hand. They had come too late! Waller was no longer afraid.

From *Cosmopolitan*, February 1903, 451–459.

Paul Laurence Dunbar

1872–1906

The first native-born African American poet to win international and national acclaim, by the time of his death at the age of thirty-three Paul Laurence Dunbar had published four novels, four short story collections, and six volumes of poetry. Born in Dayton, Ohio, to parents who had been enslaved, Dunbar was best known in his own time for lively verse written in black dialect. Named the "Poet Laureate of the Negro Race" by Booker T. Washington, Dunbar was popular with both black and white readers. Dunbar's poetry reflects a "double-voicedness" announced in poems such as "We Wear the Mask" and illustrated in his re-creation of the dialect sermon, in which simple speech carries a subversive message. Many of Dunbar's stories and essays confronted the effects of racism. Affected himself by the 1900 New York race riot, Dunbar considers the difficulties of migration from the rural South to the urban North in *The Sport of the Gods* (1903), a bleak portrait of black life in the U.S. city that some consider a forerunner to black militant novels of the sixties. In the same year, the *New York Times* published Dunbar's essay "The Fourth of July and Race Outrages," which attacks white America's hypocritical celebration of liberty while African Americans endured wage slavery, disfranchisement, race riots, and even burning at the stake.

"The Haunted Oak" was inspired by a story Dunbar heard from an elderly formerly enslaved man who lived on the grounds of Howard University. The man's nephew in Alabama had been falsely accused of rape, then dragged out of jail and hung from an oak tree. Shortly after the lynching, the branch that held the rope withered, while those around it continued to flourish. The poem was first printed in *Century Magazine* in 1900 only after a reluctant editor excised the last two stanzas, which depict the victim's merciless haunting of his white murderers. The complete version of the poem, printed in Dunbar's 1903 collection *Lyrics of Love and Laughter*, appears below.

"The Lynching of Jube Benson," the story that here follows the poem, appeared in Dunbar's 1904 short-story collection *The Heart of Happy Hollow*. In it, Dunbar describes how racism fuels a lynching when a young doctor fails to recognize the "black beast" stereotype as a stand-in for white depravity—including his own.

—— The Haunted Oak ——

Pray why are you so bare, so bare,
 Oh, bough of the old oak-tree;
And why, when I go through the shade you throw,
 Runs a shudder over me?

My leaves were green as the best, I trow,
 And sap ran free in my veins,
But I saw in the moonlight dim and weird
 A guiltless victim's pains.

I bent me down to hear his sigh;
 I shook with his gurgling moan,
And I trembled sore when they rode away,
 And left him here alone.

They'd charged him with the old, old crime,
 And set him fast in jail:
Oh, why does the dog howl all night long,
 And why does the night wind wail?

He prayed his prayer and he swore his oath,
 And he raised his hand to the sky;
But the beat of hoofs smote on his ear,
 And the steady tread drew nigh.

Who is it rides by night, by night,
 Over the moonlit road?
And what is the spur that keeps the pace,
 What is the galling goad?

And now they beat at the prison door,
 "Ho, keeper, do not stay!
We are friends of him whom you hold within,
 And we fain would take him away.

"From those who ride fast on our heels
 With mind to do him wrong;
They have no care for his innocence,
 And the rope they bear is long."

They have fooled the jailer with lying words,
 They have fooled the man with lies;
The bolts unbar, the locks are drawn,
 And the great door open flies.

Now they have taken him from the jail,
    And hard and fast they ride,
And the leader laughs low down in his throat,
    As they halt my trunk beside.

Oh, the judge, he wore a mask of black,
    And the doctor one of white,
And the minister with his oldest son,
    Was curiously bedight.

Oh, foolish man, why weep you now?
    'T is but a little space,
And the time will come when these shall dread
    The mem'ry of your face.

I feel the rope against my bark,
    And the weight of him in my grain,
I feel in the throe of his final woe
    The touch of my own last pain.

And never more shall these leaves come forth
    On a bough that bears the ban.
I am burned with dread, I am dried and dead,
    From the curse of a guiltless man.

And ever the judge rides by, rides by,
    And goes to hunt the deer,
And ever another rides his soul
    In the guise of a mortal fear.

And ever the man he rides me hard,
    And never a night stays he;
For I feel his curse as a haunted bough,
    On the trunk of a haunted tree.

From *Lyrics of Love and Laughter* (New York: Dodd, Mead, 1903).

—— The Lynching of Jube Benson ——

Gordon Fairfax's library held but three men, but the air was dense with clouds of smoke. The talk had drifted from one topic to another much as the smoke wreaths had puffed, floated, and thinned away. Then Handon Gay, who was an ambitious young reporter, spoke of a lynching story in a recent magazine, and the matter of punishment without trial put new life into the conversation.

"I should like to see a real lynching," said Gay rather callously.

"Well, I should hardly express it that way," said Fairfax, " but if a real, live lynching were to come my way, I should not avoid it."

"I should," spoke the other from the depths of his chair, where he had been puffing in moody silence. Judged by his hair, which was freely sprinkled with gray, the speaker might have been a man of forty-five or fifty, but his face, though lined and serious, was youthful, the face of a man hardly past thirty.

"What, you, Dr. Melville? Why, I thought that you physicians wouldn't weaken at anything."

"I have seen one such affair," said the doctor gravely, "in fact, I took a prominent part in it."

"Tell us about it," said the reporter, feeling for his pencil and note-book, which he was, nevertheless, careful to hide from the speaker. The men drew their chairs eagerly up to the doctor's, but for a minute he did not seem to see them, but sat gazing abstractedly into the fire, then he took a long draw upon his cigar and began:

"I can see it all very vividly now. It was in the summer time and about seven years ago. I was practising at the time down in the little town of Bradford. It was a small and primitive place, just the location for an impecunious medical man, recently out of college.

"In lieu of a regular office, I attended to business in the first of two rooms which I rented from Hiram Daly, one of the more prosperous of the townsmen. Here I boarded and here also came my patients—white and black—whites from every section, and blacks from 'nigger town,' as the west portion of the place was called.

"The people about me were most of them coarse and rough, but they were simple and generous, and as time passed on I had about abandoned my intention of seeking distinction in wider fields and determined to settle into the place of a modest country doctor. This was rather a strange conclusion for a young man to arrive at, and I will not deny that the presence in the house of my host's beautiful young daughter, Annie, had something to do with my decision. She was a beautiful young girl of seventeen or eighteen, and very far superior to her surroundings. She had a native grace and a pleasing way about her that made everybody that came under her spell her abject slave. White and black who knew her loved her, and none, I thought, more deeply and respectfully than Jube Benson, the black man of all work about the place.

"He was a fellow whom everybody trusted; an apparently steady-going, grinning sort, as we used to call him. Well, he was completely under Miss Annie's thumb, and would fetch and carry for her like a faithful dog. As soon as he saw that I began to care for Annie, and anybody could see that, he transferred some of his allegiance to me and became my faithful servitor also. Never did a man have a more devoted adherent in his wooing than did I, and many a one of Annie's tasks which he volunteered to do gave her an extra hour with me. You can imagine that I liked the boy and you need not wonder any more that as both wooing and my practice waxed apace, I was content to give up my great ambitions and stay just where I was.

"It wasn't a very pleasant thing, then, to have an epidemic of typhoid break out in the town that kept me going so that I hardly had time for the courting that a fellow wants to carry on with his sweetheart while he is still young enough to call her his girl. I fumed, but duty was duty, and I kept to my work night and day. It was now that Jube proved how invaluable he was as a coadjutor. He not only took messages to Annie, but brought sometimes little ones from her to me, and he would tell me little secret things that he had overheard her say that made me throb with joy and swear at him for repeating his mistress' conversation. But best of all, Jube was a perfect Cerberus, and no one on earth could have been more effective in keeping away or deluding the other young fellows who visited the Dalys. He would tell me of it afterwards, chuckling softly to himself. 'An', Doctah, I say to Mistah Hemp Stevens, "'Scuse us, Mistah Stevens, but Miss Annie, she des gone out," an' den he go outer de gate lookin' moughty lonesome. When Sam Elkins come, I say, "Sh, Mistah Elkins, Miss Annie, she done tuk down," an' he say, "What, Jube, you don' reckon hit de—." Den he stop an' look skeert, an' I say, "I feared hit is, Mistah Elkins," an' sheks my haid ez solemn. He goes outer de gate lookin' lak his bes' frien' done daid, an' all de time Miss Annie behine de cu'tain ovah' de po'ch des' a laffin' fit to kill.'

"Jube was a most admirable liar, but what could I do? He knew that I was a young fool of a hypocrite, and when I would rebuke him for these deceptions, he would give way and roll on the floor in an excess of delighted laughter until from very contagion I had to join him—and, well, there was no need of my preaching when there had been no beginning to his repentance and when there must ensue a continuance of his wrong-doing.

"This thing went on for over three months, and then, pouf! I was down like a shot. My patients were nearly all up, but the reaction from overwork made me an easy victim of the lurking germs. Then Jube loomed up as a nurse. He put everyone else aside, and with the doctor, a friend of mine from a neighbouring town, took entire charge of me. Even Annie herself was put aside, and I was cared for as tenderly as a baby. Tom, that was my physician and friend, told me all about it afterward with tears in his eyes. Only he was a big, blunt man and his expressions did not convey all that he meant. He told me how my nigger had nursed me as if I were a sick kitten and he my mother. Of how fiercely he guarded his right to be the sole one to 'do' for me, as he called it, and how, when the crisis came, he hovered, weeping, but hopeful, at my bedside, until it was safely passed, when they drove him, weak and exhausted, from the room. As for me, I knew little about it at the time, and cared less. I was too busy in my fight with death. To my chimerical vision there was only a black but gentle demon that came and went, alternating with a white fairy, who would insist on coming in on her head, growing larger and larger and then dissolving. But the pathos and devotion in the story lost nothing in my blunt friend's telling.

"It was during the period of a long convalescence, however, that I came to know my humble ally as he really was, devoted to the point of abjectness. There were times when for very shame at his goodness to me, I would beg him to go away, to do something else. He would go, but before I had time to realise that I was not being ministered to, he would be back at my side, grinning and pottering just the same. He manufactured duties for the joy of performing them. He pretended to see desires in me that I never had, because he liked to pander to them, and when I became entirely exasperated, and ripped out a good round oath, he chuckled with the remark, 'Dah, now, you sholy is gittin' well. Nevah did hyeah a man anywhaih nigh Jo'dan's sho' cuss lak dat.'

"Why I grew to love him, love him, oh, yes, I loved him as well—oh, what am I saying? All human love and gratitude are damned poor things; excuse me, gentlemen, this isn't a pleasant story. The truth is usually a nasty thing to stand.

"It was not six months after that that my friendship to Jube, which he had been at such great pains to win, was put to too severe a test.

"It was in the summer time again, and as business was slack, I had ridden over to see my friend, Dr. Tom. I had spent a good part of the day there, and it was past four o'clock when I rode leisurely into Bradford. I was in a particularly joyous mood and no premonition of the impending catastrophe oppressed me. No sense of sorrow, present or to come, forced itself upon me, even when I saw men hurrying through the almost deserted streets. When I got within sight of my home and saw a crowd surrounding it, I was only interested sufficiently to spur my horse into a jog trot, which brought me up to the throng, when something in the sullen, settled horror in the men's faces gave me a sudden, sick thrill. They whispered a word to me, and without a thought, save for Annie, the girl who had been so surely growing into my heart, I leaped from the saddle and tore my way through the people to the house.

"It was Annie, poor girl, bruised and bleeding, her face and dress torn from struggling. They were gathered round her with white faces, and, oh, with what terrible patience they were trying to gain from her fluttering lips the name of her murderer. They made way for me and I knelt at her side. She was beyond my skill, and my will merged with theirs. One thought was in our minds.

" 'Who?' I asked.

"Her eyes half opened, 'That black—'

She fell back into my arms dead.

"We turned and looked at each other. The mother had broken down and was weeping, but the face of the father was like iron.

" 'It is enough,' he said; 'Jube has disappeared.' He went to the door and said to the expectant crowd, 'She is dead.'

"I heard the angry roar without swelling up like the noise of a flood, and then I heard the sudden movement of many feet as the men separated into searching parties, and laying the dead girl back upon her couch, I took my rifle and went out to join them.

"As if by intuition the knowledge had passed among the men that Jube Benson had disappeared, and he, by common consent, was to be the object of our search. Fully a dozen of the citizens had seen him hastening toward the woods and noted his skulking air, but as he had grinned in his old good-natured way they had, at the time, thought nothing of it. Now, however, the diabolical reason of his slyness was apparent. He had been shrewd enough to disarm suspicion, and by now was far away. Even Mrs. Daly, who was visiting with a neighbour, had seen him stepping out by a back way, and had said with a laugh, 'I reckon that black rascal's a-running off somewhere.' Oh, if she had only known.

"'To the woods! To the woods!' that was the cry, and away we went, each with the determination not to shoot, but to bring the culprit alive into town, and then to deal with him as his crime deserved.

"I cannot describe the feelings I experienced as I went out that night to beat the woods for this human tiger. My heart smouldered within me like a coal, and I went forward under the impulse of a will that was half my own, half some more malignant power's. My throat throbbed drily, but water nor whiskey would not have quenched my thirst. The thought has come to me since that now I could interpret the panther's desire for blood and sympathise with it, but then I thought nothing. I simply went forward, and watched, watched with burning eyes for a familiar form that I had looked for as often before with such different emotions.

"Luck or ill-luck, which you will, was with our party, and just as dawn was graying the sky, we came upon our quarry crouched in the corner of a fence. It was only half light, and we might have passed, but my eyes had caught sight of him, and I raised the cry. We levelled our guns and he rose and came toward us.

"'I t'ought you wa'n't gwine see me," he said sullenly, 'I didn't mean no harm.'

"'Harm!'

"Some of the men took the word up with oaths, others were ominously silent.

"We gathered around him like hungry beasts, and I began to see terror dawning in his eyes. He turned to me, 'I's moughty glad you's hyeah, doc,' he said, 'you ain't gwine let 'em whup me.'

"Whip you, you hound,' I said, 'I'm going to see you hanged,' and in the excess of my passion I struck him full on the mouth. He made a motion as if to resent the blow against even such great odds, but controlled himself.

"'W'y, doctah,' he exclaimed in the saddest voice I have ever heard, 'w'y, doctah! I ain't stole nuffin' o' yo'n, an' I was comin' back. I only run off to see my gal, Lucy, ovah to de Centah.'

"'You lie!' I said, and my hands were busy helping the others bind him upon a horse. Why did I do it? I don't know. A false education, I reckon, one false from the beginning. I saw his black face glooming there in the half light, and I could only think of him as a monster. It's tradition. At first I was told that the black man would catch me, and when I got over that, they taught me that the devil was black, and when I had recovered from the sickness of that belief, here were Jube and his fellows with faces of menacing blackness. There was only one conclusion: This black man stood for all the powers of evil, the result of whose machinations had been gathering in my mind from childhood up. But this has nothing to do with what happened.

"After firing a few shots to announce our capture, we rode back into town with Jube. The ingathering parties from all directions met us as we made our way up to the house. All was very quiet and orderly. There was no doubt that it was as the papers would have said, a gathering of the best citizens. It was a gathering of stern, determined men, bent on a terrible vengeance.

"We took Jube into the house, into the room where the corpse lay. At sight of it, he gave a scream like an animal's and his face went the colour of storm-blown water. This was enough to condemn him. We divined, rather than heard, his cry of 'Miss Ann, Miss Ann, oh, my God, doc, you don't t'ink I done it?'

"Hungry hands were ready. We hurried him out into the yard. A rope was ready. A tree was at hand. Well, that part was the least of it, save that Hiram Daly stepped aside to let me be the first to pull upon the rope. It was lax at first. Then it tightened, and I felt the quivering soft weight resist my muscles. Other hands joined, and Jube swung off his feet.

"No one was masked. We knew each other. Not even the culprit's face was covered, and the last I remember of him as he went into the air was a look of sad reproach that will remain with me until I meet him face to face again.

"We were tying the end of the rope to a tree, where the dead man might hang as a warning to his fellows, when a terrible cry chilled us to the marrow.

"'Cut 'im down, cut 'im down, he ain't guilty. We got de one. Cut him down, fu' Gawd's sake. Here's de man, we foun' him hidin' in de barn!'

"Jube's brother, Ben, and another Negro, came rushing toward us, half dragging, half carrying a miserable-looking wretch between them. Someone cut the rope and Jube dropped lifeless to the ground.

"'Oh, my Gawd, he's daid, he's daid!' wailed the brother, but with blazing eyes he brought his captive in to the centre of the group, and we saw in the full light the scratched face of Tom Skinner—the worst white ruffian in the town—but the face we saw was not as we were accustomed to see it, merely smeared with dirt. It was blackened to imitate a Negro's.

"God forgive me; I could not wait to try to resuscitate Jube. I knew he was already past help, so I rushed into the house and to the dead girl's side. In the excitement they had not washed or laid her out. Carefully, carefully, I searched underneath her broken finger nails. There was skin there. I took it out, the little curled pieces, and went with it to my office.

"There, determinedly, I examined it under a powerful glass, and read my own doom. It was the skin of a white man, and in it were embedded strands of short, brown hair or beard.

"How I went out to tell the waiting crowd I do not know, for something kept crying in my ears, 'Blood guilty! Blood guilty!'

"The men went away stricken into silence and awe. The new prisoner attempted neither denial nor plea. When they were gone I would have helped Ben carry his brother in, but he waved me away fiercely, 'You he'ped murder my brothah, you dat was *his* frien', go 'way, go 'way! I'll tek him home myse'f.' I could only respect his wish, and he and his comrade took up the dead man and between them bore him up the street on which the sun was now shining full.

"I saw the few men who had not skulked indoors uncover as they passed, and I—I—stood there between the two murdered ones, while all the while something in my ears kept crying, 'Blood guilty! Blood guilty!' "

The doctor's head dropped into his hands and he sat for some time in silence, which was broken by neither of the men, then he rose, saying, "Gentlemen, that was my last lynching."

From *The Heart of Happy Hollow* (New York: Dodd, Mead, 1904), 223–240.

Mary Church Terrell

1863–1954

Prominent women's rights activist, peace activist, and civil rights leader, Mary Church Terrell was born into an affluent family in Memphis. Her father, Robert Reed Church, was a self-educated, formerly enslaved person whose shrewd real estate investments made him the South's first black millionaire. Terrell was sent north for her education, graduating from Oberlin College with a baccalaureate degree in 1884 and a master's degree in 1888. She became a teacher at Wilberforce University in Ohio and later moved to Washington, D.C., to teach Latin and German at Colored High School. After marrying Robert H. Terrell, a Harvard Law graduate who went on to distinguish himself as a municipal judge in Washington, Terrell had to quit her job because the District of Columbia barred married women from teaching in its schools. Robert Terrell was also an outspoken advocate of women's suffrage.

After leaving teaching, Terrell began an active public career as a writer, lecturer, and organizer devoted to winning struggles against injustice. Her life story reads as a succession of firsts: she was the first black woman to be offered the position of registrar at a white college; she served as the first woman president of the Bethel Literary and Historical Association and the first president of the National Association of Colored Women (which she helped found in 1896); her appointment to the board of education in Washington, D.C., in 1885 is thought to be the first such appointment of an African American woman in the United States. Terrell served as vice president of the International Council of Women of the Darker Races, led by Mrs. Booker T. Washington. From the 1890s until the ratification of the Nineteenth Amendment giving women the right to vote, Terrell was an active member of the National American Women's Suffrage Association. She forged important ties with white feminists, and she was a significant figure in the international women's movement. In 1904, she represented black women in the U.S. delegation to the International Congress of Women in Berlin, delivering her address in three languages. The Women's International League for Peace and Freedom selected her to be on the program of the 1919 Quinquennial International Peace Conference in Zurich. Terrell also addressed the International Assembly of World Fellowship of Faith in London.

A contemporary of Booker T. Washington, Terrell did not share his reticence on matters of discrimination. In 1906, she interceded with Secretary of War William Howard Taft on behalf of the black soldiers who were involved in the Brownsville,

Texas riot, and she protested their court-martial after they went to trial.* Although an ally in Booker T. Washington's fight to deny W.E.B. Du Bois the post of assistant superintendent of schools in Washington, D.C., Terrell allied herself with Du Bois in her later years. She became deeply involved in the 1949 case of Rosa Lee Ingram and her two sons, sharecroppers convicted of murder in a clear case of self-defense. As chair of the national committee to free the Ingrams, Terrell took her appeal to the United Nations. Instead of the death sentence, the three received life imprisonment and were finally freed in 1959. For many years vice-president of the Washington chapter of the NAACP, Terrell believed in challenging segregation at every opportunity. In 1949, she won her three-year battle to desegregate the Washington chapter of the American Association of University Women. When she was in her nineties, supporting herself by a cane, Terrell marched at the head of picket lines protesting Jim Crow segregation in the nation's capital.

In addition to delivering lectures throughout the nation and the world, Terrell wrote for many prominent journals and newspapers. "Lynching from a Negro's Point of View" appeared in the *North American Review* in 1904 to rebut an apologia for lynching written by white southern author Thomas Nelson Page. Presenting a gendered perspective on lynching, in the excerpt that follows Terrell reminds her audience of the particular vulnerability of black women to rape, of the black women who have been victims of lynching themselves, and of the culpability of white women in the violent system of segregation underpinning the Jim Crow South.

—— Excerpt from ——
"Lynching from a Negro's Point of View"

What, then, is the cause of lynching? At the last analysis, it will be discovered that there are just two causes of lynching. In the first place, it is due to race hatred, the hatred of a stronger people toward a weaker who were once held as slaves. In the second place, it is due to the lawlessness so prevalent in the section where nine-tenths of the lynchings occur. View the question of lynching from any point of view one may, and it is evident that it is just as impossible for the negroes of this country to prevent mob violence by any attitude of mind which they may assume, or any course of conduct which they may pursue, as it is for a straw dam to stop Niagara's flow. Upon the same spirit of intolerance and of hatred the crime of lynching must be fastened as that which called into being the Ku-Klux Klan, and which has prompted more recent exhibitions of hostility toward the negro, such as the disfranchisement acts, the Jim Crow Car laws, and the

---

*In the court-martial, 167 African American soldiers from the Twenty-fifth U.S. Army Infantry Regiment were dishonorably discharged as a form of collective punishment after a white man was killed in Brownsville, Texas. The incident took place after the all-black regiment had been severely harassed by local residents, and evidence was never produced to link individual soldiers to shooting. Despite appeals from the African American community, Theodore Roosevelt permitted the vigilante justice to proceed.

new slavery called "peonage," together with other acts of oppression which make the negro's lot so hard.

Lynching is the aftermath of slavery. The white men who shoot negroes to death and flay them alive, and the white women who apply flaming torches to their oil-soaked bodies to-day, are the sons and daughters of women who had but little, if any, compassion on the race when it was enslaved. The men who lynch negroes to-day are, as a rule, the children of women who sat by their firesides happy and proud in the possession and affection of their own children, while they looked with unpitying eye and adamantine heart upon the anguish of slave mothers whose children had been sold away, when not overtaken by a sadder fate. If it be contended, as it often is, that negroes are rarely lynched by the descendants of former slaveholders, it will be difficult to prove the point. According to the reports of lynchings sent out by the Southern press itself, mobs are generally composed of the "best citizens" of a place, who quietly disperse to their homes as soon as they are certain that the negro is good and dead. The newspaper who predicted that Sam Hose would be lynched, which offered a reward for his capture and which suggested burning at the stake, was neither owned nor edited by the poor whites. But if it be conceded that the descendants of slaveholders do not shoot and burn negroes, lynching must still be regarded as the legitimate offspring of slavery. If the children of the poor whites of the South are the chief aggressors in the lynching-bees of that section, it is because their ancestors were brutalized by their slaveholding environment. In discussing the lynching of negroes at the present time, the heredity and the environment, past and present, of the white mobs are not taken sufficiently into account. It is as impossible to comprehend the cause of the ferocity and barbarity which attend the average lynching-bee without taking into account the brutalizing effect of slavery upon the people of the section where most of the lynchings occur, as it is to investigate the essence and nature of fire without considering the gases which cause the flame to ignite. It is too much to expect, perhaps, that the children of women who for generations looked upon the hardships and degradation of their sisters of a darker hue with few if any protests, should have mercy and compassion upon the children of that oppressed race now. But what a tremendous influence for law and order, and what a mighty foe to mob violence Southern white women might be, if they would arise in the purity and power of their womanhood to implore their fathers, husbands and sons no longer to stain their hands with the black man's blood!

While the men of the South were off fighting to keep the negro in bondage, their mothers, wives and daughters were entrusted to the black man's care. How faithfully and loyally he kept his sacred trust the records of history attest! Not a white woman was violated throughout the entire war. Can a white woman of the South forget how black men bore themselves throughout that trying time? Surely it is not too much to ask that the daughters of mothers who were shielded from harm by the black man's constancy and care should requite their former protectors, by at least asking that, when the children of the latter are accused of crime, they should be treated like human beings and not like wild animals to be butchered and shot.

If there were one particularly heinous crime for which infuriated people took vengeance upon the negro, or if there were a genuine fear that a guilty negro might escape the penalty of the law in the South, then it might be possible to explain the cause of lynching on some other hypothesis than that of race hatred. It has already been shown that the first supposition has no foundation in fact. It is easy to prove that the second is false. Even those who condone lynching do not pretend to fear the delay or the uncertainty of the law, when a guilty negro is concerned. With the courts of law entirely in the hands of the white man, with judge and jury belonging to the superior race, a guilty negro could no more extricate himself from the meshes of the law in the South than he could slide from the devil-fish's embrace or slip from the anaconda's coils. Miscarriage of justice in the South is possible only when white men transgress the law.

In addition to lynching, the South is continually furnishing proof of its determination to wreak terrible vengeance upon the negro. The recent shocking revelations of the extent to which the actual enslavement of negroes has been carried under the peonage system of Alabama and Mississippi, and the unspeakable cruelties to which men, women and children are alike subjected, all bear witness to this fact. In January of the present year, a government detective found six negro children ranging in age from six to sixteen years working on a Georgia plantation in bare feet, scantily clad in rags, although the ground was covered with snow. The owner of the plantation is one of the wealthiest men in northeast Georgia, and is said to have made his fortune by holding negroes in slavery. When he was tried it was shown that the white planter had killed the father of the six children a few years before, but was acquitted of the murder, as almost invariably happens, when a white man takes a negro's life. After the death of their father, the children were treated with incredible cruelty. They were often chained in a room without fire and were beaten until the blood streamed from their backs, when they were unable to do their stint of work. The planter was placed under $5,000 bail, but it is doubtful whether he will ever pay the penalty of his crime. Like the children just mentioned hundreds of negroes are to-day groaning under a bondage more crushing and more cruel than that abolished forty years ago.

This same spirit manifests itself in a variety of ways. Efforts are constantly [in the] making to curtail the educational opportunities of colored children. Already one State has enacted a law by which colored children in the public schools are prohibited from receiving instruction higher than the sixth grade, and other States will, doubtless, soon follow this lead. It is a well-known fact that a Governor recently elected in one of the Southern States owes his popularity and his votes to his open and avowed opposition to the education of negroes. Instance after instance might be cited to prove that the hostility toward the negro in the South is bitter and pronounced, and that lynching is but a manifestation of this spirit of vengeance and intolerance in its ugliest and most brutal form.

To the widespread lawlessness among the white people of the South lynching is also due. In commenting upon the blood-guiltiness of South Carolina, the Nashville "American" declared some time ago that, if the killings in the other States had been in the same ratio to population as in South Carolina, a larger number of people would have been murdered in the United States during 1902 than fell on the American side in the Spanish and Philippine wars.

Whenever Southern white people discuss lynching, they are prone to slander the whole negro race. Not long ago, a Southern writer of great repute declared without qualification or reservation that "the crime of rape is well-nigh wholly confined to the negro race," and insisted that "negroes furnish most of the ravishers." These assertions are as unjust to the negro as they are unfounded in fact. According to statistics recently published, only one colored male in 100,000 over five years of age was accused of assault upon a white woman in the South in 1902, whereas one male out of every 20,000 over five years of age was charged with rape in Chicago during the same year. If these figures prove anything at all, they show that the men and boys in Chicago are many more times addicted to rape than are the negroes in the South. Already in the present year two white men have been arrested in the national capital for attempted assault upon little children. One was convicted and sentenced to six years in the penitentiary. The crime of which the other was accused was of the most infamous character. A short account of the trial of the convicted man appeared in the Washington dailies, as any other criminal suit would have been reported; but if a colored man had committed the same crime, the newspapers from one end of the United States to the other would have published it broadcast. Editorials upon the total depravity and the hopeless immorality of the negro would have been written, based upon this particular case as a text. With such facts to prove the falsity of the charge that "the crime of rape is well-nigh wholly confined to the negro race," it is amazing that any writer of repute should affix his signature to such a slander.

But even if the negro's morals were as loose and as lax as some claim them to be, and if his belief in the virtue of women were as slight as we are told, the South has nobody to blame but itself. The only object lesson in virtue and morality which the negro received for 250 years came through the medium of slavery, and that peculiar institution was not calculated to set his standards of correct living very high. Men do not gather grapes of thorns nor figs of thistles. Throughout their entire period of bondage colored women were debauched by their masters. From the day they were liberated to the present time, prepossessing young colored girls have been considered the rightful prey of white gentlemen in the South, and they have been protected neither by public sentiment nor by law. In the South, the negro's home is not considered sacred by the superior race. White men are neither punished for invading it, nor lynched for violating colored women and girls. In discussing this phase of the race problem last year, one of the most godly and eloquent ministers in the Methodist Episcopal Church (white) expressed himself as follows: "The negro's teachings have been white. It is from the white man the negro has learned to lie and steal. If you wish to know who taught the negro licentiousness, you have only to look into the faces of thousands of mulatto people and get your answer." When one thinks how the negro was degraded in slavery, which discouraged, when it did not positively forbid, marriage between slaves, and considers the bad example set them by white masters, upon whom the negroes looked as scarcely lower than the angels, the freedman's self-control seems almost like a miracle of modern times. In demanding so much of the negro, the South places itself in the anomalous position of insisting that the conduct of the inferior race shall be better, and its standards higher, than those of the people who claim to be superior.

The recent lynching in Springfield, Ohio, and in other cities of the North, show how rapidly this lawlessness is spreading throughout the United States. If the number of Americans who participate in this wild and diabolical carnival of blood does not diminish, nothing can prevent this country from becoming a byword and a reproach throughout the civilized world. When Secretary Hay appealed to Roumania in behalf of the Jews, there were many sarcastic comments made by the press of that country and of other foreign lands about the inhuman treatment of the negro in the United States. In November, 1903, a manifesto signed by delegates from all over the world was issued at Brussels, Belgium, by the International Socialist Bureau, protesting against the lynching of the negroes in the United States.

It is a source of deep regret and sorrow to many good Christians in this country that the church puts forth so few and such feeble protests against lynching. As the attitude of many ministers on the question of slavery greatly discouraged the abolitionists before the war, so silence in the pulpit concerning the lynching of negroes to-day plunges many of the persecuted race into deep gloom and dark despair. Thousands of dollars are raised by our churches every year to send missionaries to Christianize the heathen in foreign lands, and this is proper and right. But in addition to this foreign missionary work, would it not be well for our churches to inaugurate a crusade against the barbarism at home, which converts hundreds of white women and children into savages every year, while it crushes the spirit, blights the hearth and breaks the hearts of hundreds of defenceless blacks? Not only do ministers fail, as a rule, to protest strongly against the hanging and burning of negroes, but some actually condone the crime without incurring the displeasure of their congregations or invoking the censure of the church. Although the church court which tried the preacher in Wilmington, Delaware, accused of inciting his community to riot and lynching by means of incendiary sermon, found him guilty of "unministerial and unchristian conduct," of advocating mob murder and of thereby breaking down the public respect for the law, yet it simply admonished him to be "more careful in the future" and inflicted no punishment at all. Such indifference to lynching on the part of the church recalls the experience of Abraham Lincoln, who refused to join a church in Springfield, Illinois, because only three out of twenty-two ministers in the whole city stood with him in his effort to free the slave. But, however unfortunate may have been the attitude of some churches on the question of slavery before the war, from the moment the shackles fell from the black man's limbs to the present day, the American Church has been most kind and generous in its treatment of the backward and struggling race. Nothing but ignorance or malice could prompt one to disparage the efforts put forth by the churches in the negro's behalf. But, in the face of so much lawlessness to-day, surely there is a role for the Church Militant to play. When one reflects upon the large number of negroes who are yearly hurled into eternity, unshriven by priest and untried by law, one cannot help realizing that as a nation we have fallen upon grave times, indeed. Surely, it is time for the ministers in their pulpits and the Christians in their pews to fall upon their knees and pray for deliverance from this rising tide of barbarism which threatens to deluge the whole land.

How can lynching be extirpated in the United States? There are just a few ways in which this can be accomplished. In the first place, lynching can never be suppressed in the South, until the masses of ignorant white people in that section are educated and lifted to a higher moral plane. It is difficult for one who has not seen these people to comprehend the density of their ignorance and the depth of their degradation. A well-known white author who lives in the South describes them as follows:

"Wholly ignorant, absolutely without culture, apparently without even the capacity to appreciate the nicer feelings or higher sense, yet conceited on account of their white skin which they constantly dishonor, they make, when aroused, as wild and brutal a mob as ever disgraced the face of the earth."

In lamenting the mental backwardness of the white people of the South, the Atlanta "Constitution" expressed itself as follows two years ago: "We have as many illiterate white men over the age of twenty-one years in the South to-day as there were fifty-two years ago, when the 1850 census was taken." Over against these statistics stands the record of the negro, who has reduced his illiteracy 44.5 per cent. in forty years. The hostility which has always existed between the poor whites and the negroes of the South has been greatly intensified in these latter days, by the material and intellectual advancement of the negro. The wrath of a Spanish bull, before whose maddened eyes a red flag is flaunted, is but a feeble attempt at temper compared with the seething, boiling rage of the average white man in the South who beholds a well-educated negro dressed in fine or becoming clothes. In the second place, lynching cannot be suppressed in the South until all classes of white people who dwell there, those of high as well as middle and low degree, respect the rights of other human beings, no matter what may be the color of their skin, become merciful and just enough to cease their persecution of a weaker race and learn a holy reverence for the law.

It is not because the American people are cruel, as a whole, or indifferent on general principles to the suffering of the wronged or oppressed, that outrages against the negro are permitted to occur and go unpunished, but because many are ignorant of the extent to which they are carried, while others despair of eradicating them. The South has so industriously, persistently, and eloquently preached the inferiority of the negro, that the

North has apparently been converted to this view—the thousands of negroes of sterling qualities, moral worth and lofty patriotism to the contrary notwithstanding. The South has insisted so continuously and belligerently that it is the negro's best friend, that it understands him better than other people on the face of the earth and that it will brook interference from nobody in its method of dealing with him, that the North has been persuaded or intimidated into bowing to this decree.

Then, too, there seems to be a decline of the great convictions in which this government was conceived and into which it was born. Until there is a renaissance of popular belief in the principles of liberty and equality upon which this government was founded, lynching, the Convict Lease System, the Disfranchisement Acts, the Jim Crow Car Laws, unjust discriminations in the professions and trades and similar atrocities will continue to dishearten and degrade the negro, and stain the fair name of the United States. For there can be no doubt that the greatest obstacle in the way of extirpating lynching is the general attitude of the public mind toward this unspeakable crime. The whole country seems tired of hearing about the black man's woes. The wrongs of the Irish, of the Armenians, of the Roumanian and Russian Jews, of the exiles of Russia and of every other oppressed people upon the face of the globe, can arouse the sympathy and fire the indignation of the American public, while they seem to be all but indifferent to the murderous assaults upon the negroes in the South.

From *North American Review*, June 1904, 853–868.

Sutton E. Griggs

1872–1933

Born in Chatfield, Texas, to a prominent Baptist minister and his wife, Sutton E. Griggs also became a Baptist minister, serving in Virginia, Texas, and Tennessee. One of the most prolific African American writers of the early twentieth century, Griggs worked primarily outside mainstream white publishing companies, selling his novels, like Oscar Micheaux, from door to door to the working-class blacks who formed his primary audience. Along with racial and political tracts, Griggs published five novels: *Imperium in Imperio* (1899), *Overshadowed* (1901), *Unfettered* (1902), *The Hindered Hand; or, The Reign of the Repressionist* (1905), and *Pointing the Way* (1908). Like Pauline Hopkins and Frances Harper, Griggs viewed his fiction as a weapon in the battle to end racial oppression and to uplift his race. Critics have suggested that the simple language, melodramatic plots, and thin characterization of his fiction reflected a desire to convey his message to an audience that typically had little formal education. His primary themes include the unprotected state of black womanhood, the consequences of miscegenation, the crisis of lynching and mob violence, and the effects of peonage and political repression.

Griggs wrote between the Spanish American War and the First World War, when the novels of Thomas Dixon and Thomas Nelson Page and D. W. Griffith's film *Birth of a Nation* were inflaming racial violence by portraying blacks as sexual predators. Griggs claimed that he wrote *The Hindered Hand* because the National Baptist Convention requested that he respond to this racist onslaught. The novel indicts the "reign of the repressionist," revealing the persecution and propaganda through which white supremacy maintains its power.

In chronicling the troubles of the light-skinned Seabright family, *The Hindered Hand* weighs the options open to African Americans. The Seabrights send their dark-skinned daughter, Tiara, to live in the black community and then re-invent themselves as white—a decision that leads to tragedy and ultimately insanity. Tiara and her dark-skinned fiancé decide to emigrate to Liberia at the end of the novel—but the outcome of this decision remains uncertain. The novel's pessimism reflects the extremity of the days in which it was written—it records episodes of violence based on actual incidents. In this excerpt, "The Blaze," Foresta Crump, Tiara's friend, tries with her husband to make use of their education and industry to uplift the race—a decision that leads to their lynching. In these scenes, Griggs recreates in nearly exact detail the February 7, 1904, lynching of Luther Holbert and his wife in Doddsville, Mississippi.

—— The Blaze ——

Little Melville Brant stamped his foot on the floor, looked defiantly at his mother and said, in the whining tone of a nine-year old child,

"Mother, I want to go."

"Melville, I have told you this dozen times that you cannot go," responded the mother with a positiveness that caused the boy to feel that his chances were slim.

"You are always telling me to keep ahead of the other boys, and I can't even get up to some of them," whined Melville plaintively.

"What do you mean?" asked the mother.

"Ben Stringer is always a crowing over me. Every time I tell anything big he jumps in and tells what he's seen, and that knocks me out. He has seen a whole lots of lynchings. His papa takes him. I bet if my papa was living he would take me," said Melville.

"My boy, listen to your mother." said Mrs. Brant. "Nothing but bad people take part in or go to see those things. I want mother's boy to scorn such things, to be way above them."

"Well, I ain't. I want to see it. Ben Stringer ain't got no business being ahead of me," Melville said with vigor. The shrieking of the train whistle caused the fever of interest to rise in the little boy.

"There's the train now, mother. Do let me go. I ain't never seen a darky burned."

"Burned!" exclaimed Mrs. Brant in horror.

Melville looked up at his mother as if pitying her ignorance.

"They are going to burn them. Sed Lonly heard his papa and Mr. Corkle talking about it, and it's all fixed up."

"My Heavenly Father!" murmured Mrs. Brant, horror struck.

The cheering of the multitude borne upon the air was now heard.

"Mother, I must go. You can beat me as hard as you want to after I do it. I can't let Ben Stringer be crowing over me. He'll be there."

Looking intently at his mother, Melville backed toward the door. Mrs. Brant rushed forward and seized him.

"I shall put you in the attic. You shall not see that inhuman affair."

To her surprise Melville did not resist, but meekly submitted to being taken up stairs and locked in the attic.

Knowing how utterly opposed his mother was to lynchings he had calculated upon her refusal and had provided for such a contingency. He fastened the attic door on the inside and took from a corner a stout stick and a rope which he had secreted there. Fastening the rope to the stick and placing the stick across the small attic window he succeeded in lowering himself to the ground. He ran with all the speed at his command

and arrived at the railway station just in time to see the mob begin its march with Bud and Foresta toward the scene of the killing of Sidney Fletcher.

Arriving at the spot where Fletcher's body had been found, the mob halted and the leaders instituted the trial of the accused.

"Did you kill Mr. Sidney Fletcher?" asked the mob's spokesman of Bud.

"Can I explain the matter to you, gentlemen," asked Bud.

"We want you to tell us just one thing; did you kill Mr. Sidney Fletcher?"

"He tried to kill me," replied Bud.

"And you therefore killed him, did you?"

"Yes, sir. That's how it happened."

"You killed him, then?" asked the spokesman.

"I shot him, and if he died I suppose I must have caused it. But it was in self-defense."

"You hear that, do you. He has confessed," said the spokesman to his son who was the reporter of the world-wide news agency that was to give to the reading public an account of the affair.

"Well, we are ready to act," shouted the spokesman to the crowd.

Two men now stepped forward and reached the spokesman at about the same time.

"I got a fine place, with everything ready. I knew what you would need and I arranged for you," said one of the men.

"My place is nearer than his, and everything is as ready as it can be. I think I am en-titled to it," said the other.

"You want the earth, don't you?" indignantly asked the first applicant of the second.

Ignoring this thrust the second applicant said to the spokesman,

"You know I have done all the dirty work here. If you all wanted anybody to stuff the ballot box or swear to false returns, I have been your man. I've put out of the way every biggety nigger that you sent me after. You know all this."

"You've been paid for it, too. Ain't you been to the legislature? Ain't you been con-stable? Haven't you captured prisoners and held 'um in secret till the governor offered rewards and then you have brung 'em forward? You have been well paid. But me, I've had none of the good things. I've done dirty work, too, don't you forget it. And now I want these niggers hung in my watermelon patch, so as to keep darkies out of nights, being as they are feart of hants, and you are here to keep me out of that little favor."

The dispute waxed so hot that it was finally decided that it was best to accept neither place.

"We want this affair to serve as a warning to darkies to never lift their hands against a white man, and it won't hurt to perform this noble deed where they will never for-get it. I am commander to-day and I order the administration of justice to take place near the Negro church."

"Good! Good!" was the universal comment.

The crowd dashed wildly in the direction of the church, all being eager to get places where they could see best. The smaller boys climbed the trees so that they might see well the whole transaction. Two of the trees were decided upon for stakes and the boys who had chosen them had to come down. Bud was tied to one tree and Foresta to the other in such a manner that they faced each other. Wood was brought and piled around them and oil was poured on very profusely.

The mob decided to torture their victims before killing them and began on Foresta first. A man with a pair of scissors stepped up and cut off her hair and threw it into the crowd. There was a great scramble for bits of hair for souvenirs of the occasion. One by one her fingers were cut off and tossed into the crowd to be scrambled for. A man with a corkscrew came forward, ripped Foresta's clothing to her waist, bored into her breast with the corkscrew and pulled forth the live quivering flesh. Poor Bud her helpless husband closed his eyes and turned away his head to avoid the terrible sight. Men gathered about him and forced his eyelids open so that he could see all.

When it was thought that Foresta had been tortured sufficiently, attention was turned to Bud. His fingers were cut off one by one and the corkscrew was bored into his legs and arms. A man with a club struck him over the head, crushing his skull and forcing an eyeball to hang down from the socket by a thread. A rush was made toward Bud and a man who was a little ahead of his competitors snatched the eyeball as a souvenir.

After three full hours had been spent in torturing the two, the spokesman announced that they were now ready for the final act. The brother of Sidney Fletcher was called for and was given a match. He stood near his mutilated victims until the photographer present could take a picture of the scene. This being over the match was applied and the flames leaped up eagerly and encircled the writhing forms of Bud and Foresta.

When the flames had done their work and had subsided, a mad rush was made for the trees which were soon denuded of bark, each member of the mob being desirous, it seemed, of carrying away something that might testify to his proximity to so great a happening.

Little Melville Brant found a piece of the charred flesh in the ashes and bore it home.

"Ben Stringer aint got anything on me now," said he as he trudged along in triumph.

Entering by the rear he caught hold of the rope which he had left hanging, ascended to the attic window and crawled in.

The future ruler of the land!

On the afternoon of the lynching Ramon Mansford alighted from the train at Maulville in search of Bud and Foresta. He noted the holiday appearance of the crowd as it swarmed around the depot awaiting the going of the special trains that had brought the people to Maulville to see the lynching, and, not knowing the occasion that had brought them together, said within himself:

"This crowd looks happy enough. The South is indeed sunny and sunny are the hearts of its people."

At length he approached a man, who like himself seemed to be an onlooker. Using the names under which Mrs. Harper told him that Bud and Foresta were passing, he made inquiry of them.

The man looked at him in amazement.

"You have just got in, have you?" asked the man of Ramon.

"Yes," he replied.

"Haven't you been reading the papers?" further inquired the man.

"Not lately, I must confess; I have been so absorbed in unraveling a murder mystery (the victim being one very dear to me) that I have not read the papers for the last few days."

"We burned the people to-day that you are looking for."

"Burned them?" asked Ramon incredulously.

"Yes, burned them."

"The one crime!" gasped Ramon.

"I understand you," said the man. "You want to know how we square the burning of a woman with the statement that we lynch for one crime in the South, heh?"

The shocked Ramon nodded affirmatively.

"That's all rot about one crime. We lynch niggers down here for anything. We lynch them for being sassy and sometimes lynch them on general principles. The truth of the matter is the real 'one crime' that paves the way for a lynching whenever we have the notion, is the crime of being black."

"Burn them! The one crime!" murmured Ramon, scarcely knowing what he said. With bowed head and hands clasped behind him he walked away to meditate.

From *The Hindered Hand; or, The Reign of the Repressionist*
(Nashville: Orion Publishing, 1905), 129–136.

W.E.B. Du Bois

1868–1963

One of the twentieth century's great civil rights activists, William Edward Burghardt Du Bois was also an internationally acclaimed scholar, journalist, critic, novelist, essayist, and poet. Du Bois was born and raised in Great Barrington, Massachusetts, where he attended predominantly white elementary and secondary schools. In 1885, he left the Northeast to begin his studies at Fisk University in Tennessee, where he was shocked by the barbarism of southern racism. After graduating from Fisk in 1888, Du Bois entered Harvard, earning a second baccalaureate in philosophy, a master's degree in history, and the first Harvard Ph.D. awarded to an African American. From 1892 to 1894, Du Bois studied at the University of Berlin, where he first experienced life beyond the color line of U.S. racism.

He began teaching at Wilberforce University in Ohio and undertook research for the University of Pennsylvania that would be published in 1899 as *The Philadelphia Negro*, the first sociological study of the black population of a major U.S. city. In 1897, Du Bois joined the faculty of Atlanta University, where he began the Atlanta Conferences, a series of academic meetings that issued annual reports on such topics as African American mortality, landholding, religious worship, family structure, and migration. These reports, which provided a wealth of sociological data for public and private institutions, are seen by many as the foundation of twentieth-century black studies.

In 1899, the lynching of Sam Hose acted, in Du Bois's words, like a "red ray" cutting through his studies of the "Negro Problem." Sam Hose, an illiterate sharecropper in Palmetto, just southwest of Atlanta, killed his landlord in self-defense during a dispute over wages. An unfounded rumor that Hose had also raped his landlord's wife whipped the countryside into a lynching frenzy (which was kept in check long enough after Hose's capture to allow special excursion trains to arrive carrying four thousand spectators from Atlanta). Du Bois drafted a letter protesting the impending lynching and started for the office of the editor of the *Atlanta Constitution*, Joel Chandler Harris. As he related in his autobiography, Du Bois learned on the way there that Hose had been lynched and that "his knuckles were on exhibition" at a nearby grocery store. His realization that "one could not be a calm, cool, and detached scientist, while Negroes were lynched, murdered, and starved" changed the direction of his career and his life.

3. "Christmas in Georgia, A.D., 1916." Reprinted from the *Crisis*, December 1916, 78–79.

In 1903, Du Bois published *The Souls of Black Folk*, a collection of poetry and prose, history and sociology, that established him as one of the leading black intellectuals in the country. Dissatisfied with Booker T. Washington's accommodationism, in 1905 Du Bois organized the all-black Niagara Movement, which demanded voting rights, access to higher education, and freedom of the press and of speech for African Americans. The Niagara Movement was later absorbed into the National Association for the Advancement of Colored People, which was founded in 1909 after Abraham Lincoln's hometown, Springfield, Illinois, erupted in rioting in which two blacks were lynched, four whites killed, and more than seventy people injured. From its beginning, the NAACP mounted an aggressive campaign against racial violence, with a particular focus on ending lynching. Du Bois was appointed director of publicity and research and moved to New York in 1910 to found and edit the NAACP's *Crisis* magazine, which became the preeminent literary and political African American periodical, selling 100,000 subscriptions at its 1919 circulation peak. During his years at the *Crisis*, Du Bois published editorials on lynching, disfranchisement, and all other forms of racial oppression.

Du Bois served with the NAACP from 1910 to 1934, then returned to Atlanta University to chair the Department of Sociology. In 1935, he published *Black Reconstruction*, a history reclaiming Reconstruction as an important era of African American struggle. In *Dusk of Dawn: An Autobiography of a Concept of a Race* published in 1940, Du Bois advocated strategic separation, among other ideas, as the most effective avenue to political and economic freedom for blacks. During the 1940s, his politics became increasingly Marxist, anti-colonialist, and militant. Forced to retire from Atlanta University in 1944, Du Bois returned to the NAACP, but political and personal differences with executive secretary Walter White led him to resign in 1948. After serving for a time as vice chair of the anti-colonialist Council of African Affairs, Du Bois became in 1950 chair of the Peace Information Center, an organization opposed to nuclear weapons that Secretary of State Dean Acheson vilified as a front for the Soviet Union. In 1951, Du Bois was indicted as an un-registered "agent of a foreign principal." Although he was acquitted, the government refused to release his passport until 1958. In 1961, at the age of ninety-three, Du Bois joined the American Communist Party and accepted President Kwame Nkrumah's invitation to live in Ghana. He renounced his U.S. citizenship shortly before his death in 1963.

W.E.B. Du Bois viewed militant protest and agitation as absolutely imperative in the crisis facing African Americans and saw writing as an indispensable weapon in this struggle. Much of his finest writing mixes an explicitly political agenda with deeply personal emotion, including the poem "A Litany at Atlanta," written in 1906 as he sat in a Jim Crow car heading toward an Atlanta gripped by a terrible race massacre, in which his family's fate remained unknown.

The immediate cause of the "riot" was the hysteria that had been mounting throughout August and September as newspapers printed accounts, many of them false, of black men raping white women. The true cause, however, lies in the context of the white supremacist revolution between 1898 and 1908, which incited forty violent race riots in cities throughout the South to destroy black political and economic power. In the 1905–1906 Georgia gubernatorial campaign, Hoke Smith, a former populist and racial moderate, rode to victory on a white supremacist platform fueled by incendiary speeches in which he referred to the 1898 Wilmington riot In North Carolina, implicitly calling for another racial massacre. His message resonated in Atlanta with whites threatened by increased black political leverage, property ownership, and development of social and edu-cational institutions.

The chronic problem of southern police brutality was particularly severe in Atlanta. There had been incidents of collective self-defense during the 1880s and 1890s, when African American civilians liberated prisoners from the police or chased police officers from their neighborhood. As tension increased in the sum-mer and fall of 1906, law enforcement began antivagrancy and antivice campaigns targeted at shutting down black businesses and restricting African American move-ment in public spaces. During the night and early morning of September 22 and 23, an angry white mob began to attack every African American in sight. The mob grew to thousands of men, who indiscriminately assaulted black men, women, and chil-dren, beating, torturing, and killing their victims in a rampage that lasted four days. The *Atlanta Constitution* reported that "in some portions of the street, the sidewalks ran red with the blood of dead and dying Negroes." Published on October 11 in the *Independent* just days after the riot, "A Litany at Atlanta" comes closer than perhaps any other poem to expressing the inexpressible trauma of witnessing a massive catastrophic event.

—— A Litany at Atlanta ——

Done at Atlanta, in the Day of Death, 1906.

O Silent God, Thou whose voice afar in mist and mystery hath left our ears an-hungered in these fearful days—

Hear us, good Lord!

Listen to us, Thy children: our faces dark with doubt, are made a mockery in Thy sanctuary. With uplifted hands we front Thy heaven, O God, crying:

We beseech Thee to hear us, good Lord!

We are not better than our fellows, Lord, we are but weak and human men. When our devils do deviltry, curse Thou the doer and the deed: curse them as we curse them, do to them all and more than ever they have done to innocence and weakness, to womanhood and home.

Have mercy upon us, miserable sinners!

And yet whose is the deeper guilt? Who made these devils? Who nursed them in crime and fed them on injustice? Who ravished and debauched their mothers and their grandmothers? Who bought and sold their crime, and waxed fat and rich on public iniquity?

Thou knowest, good God!

Is this Thy justice, O Father, that guile be easier than innocence, and the innocent crucified for the guilt of the untouched guilty?

Justice, O Judge of men!

Wherefore do we pray? Is not the God of the fathers dead? Have not seers seen in Heaven's halls Thine hearsed and lifeless form stark amidst the black and rolling smoke of sin, where all along bow bitter forms of endless dead?

Awake, Thou that sleepest!

Thou art not dead, but flown afar, up hills of endless light through blazing corridors of suns, where worlds do swing of good and gentle men, of women strong and free—far from the cozenage, black hypocrisy, and chaste prostitution of this shameful speck of dust!

Turn again, O Lord, leave us not to perish in our sin!

From lust of body and lust of blood,

Great God, deliver us!

From lust of power and lust of gold,

Great God, deliver us!

From the leagued lying of despot and of brute,

Great God, deliver us!

A city lay in travail, God our Lord, and from her loins sprang twin Murder and Black Hate. Red was the midnight; clang, crack and cry of death and fury filled the air and trembled underneath the stars when church spires pointed silently to Thee. And all this was to sate the greed of greedy men who hide behind the veil of vengeance!

Bend us Thine ear, O Lord!

In the pale, still morning we looked upon the deed. We stopped our ears and held our leaping hands, but they—did they not wag their heads and leer and cry with bloody jaws: *Cease from Crime!* The word was mockery, for thus they train a hundred crimes while we do cure one.

Turn again our captivity, O Lord!

Behold this maimed and broken thing; dear God, it was an humble black man who toiled and sweat to save a bit from the pittance paid him. They told him: *Work and Rise.* He worked. Did this man sin? Nay, but some one told how some one said another did—one whom he had never seen nor known. Yet for that man's crime, this man lieth maimed and murdered, his wife naked to shame, his children, to poverty and evil.

Hear us, O heavenly Father!

Doth not this justice of hell stink in Thy nostrils, O God? How long shall the mounting flood of innocent blood roar in Thine ears and pound in our hearts for vengeance? Pile the pale frenzy of blood-crazed brutes who do such deeds high on Thine altar, Jehovah Jireh, and burn it in hell forever and forever!

Forgive us, good Lord; we know not what we say!

Bewildered we are, and passion-tost, made with the madness of a mobbed and mocked and murdered people; straining at the armposts of Thy Throne, we raise our shackled hands and charge Thee, God, by the bones of our stolen fathers, by the tears of our dead mothers, by the very blood of Thy crucified Christ: *What meaneth this?* Tell us the Plan; give us the Sign!

Keep not Thou silence, O God!

Sit no longer blind, Lord God, deaf to our prayer and dumb to our dumb suffering. Surely Thou too art not white, O Lord, a pale bloodless, heartless thing?

Ah! Christ of all the Pities!

Forgive the thought! Forgive these wild, blasphemous words. Thou art still the God of our black fathers, and in Thy soul's soul sit some soft darkenings of the evening, some shadowings of the velvet night.

But whisper—speak—call, great God, for Thy silence is white terror to our hearts! The way, O God, show us the way and point us the path.

Whither? North is greed and South is blood; within, the coward, and without, the liar. Whither? To Death?

Amen! Welcome dark sleep!

Whither? To life? But not this life, dear God, not this. Let the cup pass from us, tempt us not beyond our strength, for there is that clamoring and clawing within, to whose voice we would not listen, yet shudder lest we must,—and it is red, Ah! God! It is a red and awful shape.

Selah!

In yonder East trembles a star.

Vengeance is mine; I will repay, saith the Lord!

Thy will, O Lord, be done!

Kyrie Eleison!

Lord, we have done these pleading, wavering words.

We beseech Thee to hear us, good Lord!

We bow our heads and hearken soft to the sobbing of women and little children.

We beseech Thee to hear us, good Lord!

Our voices sink in silence and in night.

Hear us, good Lord!

In night, O God of a godless land!

Amen!

In silence, O silent God.

Selah!

From *Independent*, October 11, 1906, 856–858.

Lizelia Augusta Jenkins Moorer

Fl. 1907

Lizelia Augusta Jenkins Moorer taught at the Normal and Grammar Schools, Chaflin College, Orangeburg, South Carolina, from 1895 to 1899. Little else is known about her life beyond what may be inferred from her poetry. In her introduction to the facsimile edition of Moorer's *Prejudice Unveiled and Other Poems* (1907) published in 1988, Joan R. Sherman calls the first twenty-six poems the "best poems on racial issues written by any black woman until the middle of [the twentieth] century" because the "anger, bitterness, irony, and pain are passionately felt and genuinely integral to the verse" (Moorer [1907] 1988, xxxii–xxxiii). In *Prejudice Unveiled*, Moorer presents a comprehensive analysis of the sweeping nature of racial oppression. Her poetry targets lynching, debt peonage, white rape, Jim Crow segregation, and the hypocrisy of the church and the white press. While the scandal of lynching pervades her poetry, the collection includes three poems that take lynching as their primary subject: "Lynching" contrasts the graphic details of lynching with the nation's imperialistic "concern" about brutality in the Philippines and Cuba; "The Eutawville Lynching" describes the tragedy of an actual lynching; and in "Russia's Resentment," Russia answers outrage over a pogrom by insisting that the United States remove the "beam" of lynching from its own eye before criticizing other cultures.

In "Jim Crow Cars," Moorer targets an important symbol of the fight over the right of African Americans to freely inhabit public spaces. The doctrine of "separate but equal" was established in 1886 by the Supreme Court decision in *Plessy v. Ferguson*, which upheld the segregation of blacks on public transportation. The treatment of African American women in the segregated Jim Crow cars was a common plaint among female antilynching activists. In A *Voice from the South*, Anna Julia Cooper references "instances of personal violence to colored women travelling in less civilized areas of our country, where women have been forcibly ejected from cars, thrown out of seats, their garments rudely torn, their persons wantonly and cruelly injured" (1892, 91). The predicament of black women who used public transportation provided an example of and metaphor for their experience of life under the Jim Crow regime. In her poem, Moorer describes the humiliation and fear of travel in segregated railway cars, where at any moment lynching could be used to enforce white power over southern space.

—— Jim Crow Cars ——

If within the cruel Southland you have chanced to take a ride,
You the Jim Crow cars have noticed, how they crush a Negro's pride,
How he pays a first class passage and a second class receives,
Gets the worst accommodations ev'ry friend of truth believes.

'Tis the rule that all conductors in the service of the train,
Practice gross discriminations on the Negro—such is plain—
If a drunkard is a white man, at his mercy Negroes are,
Legalized humiliation is the Negro Jim Crow car.

'Tis a license given white men, they may go just where they please,
In the white man's car or Negro's will they move with perfect ease,
If complaint is made by Negroes the conductor will go out
Till the whites are through carousing, then he shows himself about.

They will often raise a riot, butcher up the Negroes there,
Unmolested will they quarrel, use their pistols, rant and swear,
They will smoke among the ladies though offensive the cigar;
'Tis the place to drink their whisky, in the Negro Jim Crow car.

If a Negro shows resistance to his treatment by a tough,
At some station he's arrested for the same, though not enough,
He is thrashed or lynched or tortured as will please the demon's rage,
Mobbed, of course, by "unknown parties," thus is closed the darkened page.

If a lunatic is carried, white or black, it is the same,
Or a criminal is taken to the prison-house in shame,
In the Negro car he's ushered with the sheriff at his side,
Out of deference for white men in their car he scorns to ride.

We despise a Negro's manhood, says the Southland, and expect,
All supremacy for white men—black men's rights we'll not protect,
This the Negro bears with patience for the nation bows to might,
Wrong has borne aloft its colors disregarding what is right.

This is called a Christian nation, but we fail to understand,
How the teachings of the Bible can with such a system band;
Purest love that knows no evil can alone the story tell,
How to banish such abuses, how to treat a neighbor well.

From *Prejudice Unveiled and Other Poems* (Boston: Roxburgh, 1907), 14–16

1911–1920

Bertha Johnston

1865–1953

A longtime advocate for women's and children's rights, Bertha Johnston was a member of the Women's Political Union, the New York City Suffrage League, and the Brooklyn Ethical Culture Society. After graduating from Framingham Normal School in 1885, Johnston became editor and publisher of the *Kindergarten Magazine* in Chicago, where she also worked at the Helen Heath Settlement House. In 1904, Johnston began publishing her magazine in Brooklyn and in 1909 renamed it the *Kindergarten-Primary Magazine*. She also wrote a column for the monthly *Everywhere*, as well as two books, *Home Occupations for Boys and Girls* and *Lyrical Lines for Lasses and Lads*.

In the headnote to her poem "I Met a Little Blue-Eyed Girl," published in the *Crisis* in 1912, Johnston recounts the disgust of a visitor from the North at the aftermath of a southern lynching carnival. In the poem, Johnston contrasts the angelic appearance of a female child with the gruesome relic she keeps close to her heart and traces the perversion of childhood innocence to the doctrines of white supremacist demagogues like James K. Vardaman and Cole Blease. Known as the "White Chief," Vardaman served as governor of Mississippi from 1904 to 1908, during which time he called for an end to Negro education and an intensification of Jim Crow segregation, proclaiming: "If it is necessary every Negro in the state will be lynched; it will be done to maintain white supremacy." While in the U.S. Senate from 1913 to 1919, Vardaman lobbied to rescind the Fourteenth and Fifteenth Amendments, which guarantee civil rights to African Americans. Senator Cole Blease of South Carolina shared Vardaman's view of such legal protections, announcing that "whenever the Constitution comes between me and the virtue of the white women of the South, I say to hell with the Constitution."

—— I Met a Little Blue-Eyed Girl ——

A certain element in the South takes pains to rear the children of the family faithfully in the doctrines of Blease and Vardaman. "A Negro had been lynched in the neighborhood," said a recently returned traveler, "and crowds went out to see what was left of his body. The people I was staying with went with the rest and took their children—all but one, who had been naughty and was kept home as a punishment."

I met a little blue-eyed girl—
   She said she was five years old;
"Your locket is very pretty, dear;
   And pray what may it hold?"

And then—my heart grew chill and sick—
   The gay child did not flinch—
"I found it—the tooth of a colored man—
   My father helped to lynch."

"And what had he done, my fair-haired child?"
   (Life and Death play a fearful game!)
"Oh, he did nothing—they made a mistake—
   But they had their fun just the same!"

From *Crisis*, July 1912, 147.

James Weldon Johnson

1871–1938

Educator, Broadway lyricist, poet, diplomat, novelist, and civil rights leader, James Weldon Johnson was born in Jacksonville, Florida. He attended Atlanta University Preparatory School and received his bachelor's degree from Atlanta University in 1894. Returning to Jacksonville, he served as principal of Staunton School, founded a weekly newspaper, the *Daily American*, and passed the Florida bar exam. In 1900, Johnson and his brother J. Rosamond collaborated on "Lift Every Voice and Sing," a song written to commemorate Lincoln's birthday that became known as the "Negro National Anthem." The Johnson brothers moved to New York City in 1902, where they formed with musician Bob Cole the successful songwriting team Cole Johnson, producing popular light operas, musical comedies, and more than two hundred songs, including "Under the Bamboo Tree" (1902) and "Congo Love Song" (1903).

In 1906, Johnson was appointed U.S. consul to Puerto Cabello, Venezuela, by Theodore Roosevelt. He assumed the post of consul in Corinto, Nicaragua, in 1909 and received praise for his aid to U.S. Marines in defeating a revolution there in 1912. Johnson left the consular service after Woodrow Wilson's election in 1913, because the new administration was hardly committed to the political advancement of African Americans. He moved back to New York in 1914, where he began to write a weekly column in the *New York Age*, which he used to rail against lynching and other racial violence.

In 1917, Johnson joined the staff of the NAACP. As field secretary, he established local branches throughout the South and raised membership numbers from ten thousand to forty-four thousand by the end of 1918. In 1920, he became the organization's first African American leader. For Johnson, the NAACP's most urgent priority was to expose and eradicate lynching, a goal he called saving black America's bodies and white America's souls. He spent considerable time in Washington lobbying for the passage of antilynching legislation, in particular the 1922 Dyer bill that would have made lynching a federal crime. Although the NAACP never secured an antilynching bill, the group's massive publicity campaign and intense lobbying efforts shoved the brutal facts of lynching in the face of the American people in a manner that made this crime difficult to dismiss. This campaign played an important role in the steep decline in lynchings by the time Johnson resigned from the NAACP in 1930.

During the 1920s, Johnson continued his literary efforts as one of the authors and supporters of the movement that we know as the Harlem Renaissance. Mentor to Claude McKay and Langston Hughes, he also compiled the important anthology *The Book of American Negro Poetry*, which helped set the standard for the "New Negro" movement. Musical publications included *The Book of American Negro Spirituals* (1925) and *The Second Book of American Negro Spirituals* (1926). *God's Trombones: Seven Negro Sermons in Verse* came out in 1927, as did the reissue of *The Autobiography of an Ex-Colored Man*, first published in 1912. *Black Manhattan* followed in 1930, the year Johnson left the NAACP to become professor of creative writing and African American literature at Fisk University. He published his autobiography, *Along This Way*, in 1933. Johnson died in an automobile accident in 1938.

Throughout his life, James Weldon Johnson fought to end the brutality and injustice inflicted upon African Americans throughout the United States. His passionate commitment to preventing lynching in the Jim Crow South began with his own deeply wounding experience. In *Along This Way*, Johnson describes how in 1900 he was nearly lynched by a mob of Jacksonville militiamen who had mistaken his light-skinned companion for a white woman. Were it not for his ability to remain calm, he knew that he surely would have been lynched. "For weeks and months the episode with all of its implications preyed on my mind and disturbed me in my sleep. I would wake often in the night-time, after living through again those few frightful seconds, exhausted by the nightmare of a struggle with a band of murderous, bloodthirsty men in khaki, with loaded rifles and fixed bayonets. It was not until twenty years after, through work I was then engaged in, that I was able to liberate myself completely from this horror complex" ([1933] 2000, 170).

A classic of African American literature that has remained in print since its 1927 reissue, *The Autobiography of an Ex-Colored Man* provides a richly complex portrait of a man searching to come to terms with the meaning of race during the country's lynching era. While the novel's unnamed protagonist should not be seen as an autobiographical figure—for one thing, the darker-skinned author never had the luxury of choosing his race—he does share Johnson's preoccupation with the vernacular tradition in word and song. Johnson's sympathetic (and at times ironic) portrayal reveals the dilemma facing "the voluntary negro," in which even a fascination with and reverence for black culture collides with the awful extremity of lynch law. In this excerpt from chapter 10, the unnamed light-skinned protagonist, raised in the North with little exposure to rural African American life, has just returned from a tour of Europe as the companion of a depressive and eccentric white millionaire. Determined to cast his lot with his black mother's race, he plans to devote his life to studying and collecting Negro folklore and music. The text follows the progress of his first research trip into the Deep South.

"Brothers," Johnson's widely anthologized antilynching poem that follows this excerpt, first appeared in print in 1916.

— Excerpt from —
The Autobiography of an Ex-Colored Man

In thus traveling about through the country I was sometimes amused on arriving at some little railroad-station town to be taken for and treated as a white man, and six hours later, when it was learned that I was stopping at the house of the colored preacher or school teacher, to note the attitude of the whole town change. At times this led even to embarrassment. Yet it cannot be so embarrassing for a colored man to be taken for white as for a white man to be taken for colored; and I have heard of several cases of the latter kind.

All this while I was gathering material for work, jotting down in my notebook themes and melodies, and trying to catch the spirit of the Negro in his relatively primitive state. I began to feel the necessity of hurrying so that I might get back to some city like Nashville to begin my compositions and at the same time earn at least a living by teaching and performing before my funds gave out. At the last settlement in which I stopped I found a mine of material. This was due to the fact that "big meeting" was in progress. "Big meeting" is an institution something like camp-meeting, the difference being that it is held in a permanent church, and not in a temporary structure. All the churches of some one denomination—of course, either Methodist or Baptist—in a county, or, perhaps, in several adjoining counties, are closed, and the congregations unite at some centrally located church for a series of meetings lasting a week. It is really a social as well as a religious function. The people come in great numbers, making the trip, according to their financial status, in buggies drawn by sleek, fleet-footed mules, in ox-carts, or on foot. It was amusing to see some of the latter class trudging down the hot and dusty road, with their shoes, which were brand-new, strung across their shoulders. When they got near the church, they sat on the side of the road and, with many grimaces, tenderly packed their feet into those instruments of torture. This furnished, indeed, a trying test of their religion. The famous preachers come from near and far and take turns in warning sinners of the day of wrath. Food, in the form of those two Southern luxuries, fried chicken and roast pork, is plentiful, and no one need go hungry. On the opening Sunday the women are immaculate in starched stiff white dresses adorned with ribbons, either red or blue. Even a great many of the men wear streamers of vari-colored ribbons in the buttonholes of their coats. A few of them carefully cultivate a forelock of hair by wrapping it in twine, and on such festive occasions decorate it with a narrow ribbon streamer. Big meetings afford a fine opportunity to the younger people to meet each other dressed in their Sunday clothes, and much rustic courting, which is as enjoyable as any other kind, is indulged in.

This big meeting which I was lucky enough to catch was particularly well attended; the extra large attendance was due principally to two attractions, a man by the name of

John Brown, who was renowned as the most powerful preacher for miles around; and a wonderful leader of singing, who was known as "Singing Johnson." These two men were a study and a revelation to me. They caused me to reflect upon how great an influence their types have been in the development of the Negro in America. Both these types are now looked upon generally with condescension or contempt by the progressive element among the colored people; but it should never be forgotten that it was they who led the race from paganism and kept it steadfast to Christianity through all the long, dark years of slavery.

John Brown was a jet-black man of medium size, with a strikingly intelligent head and face, and a voice like an organ peal. He preached each night after several lesser lights had successively held the pulpit during an hour or so. As far as subject-matter is concerned, all of the sermons were alike: each began with the fall of man, ran through various trials and tribulations of the Hebrew children, on to the redemption by Christ, and ended with a fervid picture of the judgment day and the fate of the damned. But John Brown possessed magnetism and an imagination so free and daring that he was able to carry through what the other preachers would not attempt. He knew all the arts and tricks of oratory, the modulation of the voice to almost a whisper, the pause for effect, the rise through light, rapid-fire sentences to the terrific, thundering outburst of an electrifying climax. In addition, he had the intuition of a born theatrical manager. Night after night this man held me fascinated. He convinced me that, after all, eloquence consists more in the manner of saying than in what is said. It is largely a matter of tone pictures.

The most striking example of John Brown's magnetism and imagination was his "heavenly march"; I shall never forget how it impressed me when I heard it. He opened his sermon in the usual way; then, proclaiming to his listeners that he was going to take them on the heavenly march, he seized the Bible under his arm and began to pace up and down the pulpit platform. The congregation immediately began with their feet a tramp, tramp, tramp, in time with the preacher's march in the pulpit, all the while singing in an undertone a hymn about marching to Zion. Suddenly he cried: "Halt!" Every foot stopped with the precision of a company of well-drilled soldiers, and the singing ceased. The morning star had been reached. Here the preacher described the beauties of that celestial body. Then the march, the tramp, tramp, tramp, and the singing were again taken up. Another "Halt!" They had reached the evening star. And so on, past the sun and moon—the intensity of religious emotion all the time increasing—along the milky way, on up to the gates of heaven. Here the halt was longer, and the preacher described at length the gates and walls of the New Jerusalem. Then he took his hearers through the pearly gates, along the golden streets, pointing out the glories of the city, pausing occasionally to greet some patriarchal members of the church, well-known to most of his listeners in life, who had had "the tears wiped from their eyes, were clad in robes of spotless white, with crowns of gold upon their heads and harps within their hands," and ended his march before the great white throne. To the reader this may sound ridiculous, but listened to under the circumstances, it was highly and effectively dramatic. I was a more or less sophisticated and non-religious man of the world, but the torrent of the preacher's words, moving with the rhythm and glowing with the eloquence of primitive poetry, swept me along, and I, too, felt like joining in the shouts of "Amen! Hallelujah!"

John Brown's powers in describing the delights of heaven were no greater than those in depicting the horrors of hell. I saw great, strapping fellows trembling and weeping like children at the "mourners' bench." His warnings to sinners were truly terrible. I shall never forget one expression that he used, which for originality and aptness could not be excelled. In my opinion, it is more graphic and, for us, far more expressive than St. Paul's "It is hard to kick against the pricks." He struck the attitude of a pugilist and thundered out: "Young man, your arm's too short to box with God!"

Interesting as was John Brown to me, the other man, "Singing Johnson," was more so. He was a small, dark-brown, one-eyed man, with a clear, strong, high-pitched voice, a leader of singing, a maker of songs, a man who could improvise at the moment lines to fit the occasion. Not so striking a figure as John Brown, but, at "big meetings," equally important. It is indispensable to the success of the singing, when the congregation is a large one made up of people from different communities, to have someone with a strong voice who knows just what hymn to sing and when to sing it, who can pitch it in the right key, and who has all the leading lines committed to memory. Sometimes it devolves upon the leader to "sing down" a long-winded or uninteresting speaker. Committing to memory the leading lines of all the Negro spiritual songs is no easy task, for they run up into the hundreds. But the accomplished leader must know them all, because the congregation sings only the refrains and repeats; every ear in the church is fixed upon him, and if he becomes mixed in his lines or forgets them, the responsibility falls directly on his shoulders.

For example, most of these hymns are constructed to be sung in the following manner:

Leader.	*Swing low, sweet chariot.*
Congregation.	*Coming for to carry me home.*
Leader.	*Swing low, sweet chariot.*
Congregation.	*Coming for to carry me home.*
Leader.	*I look over yonder, what do I see?*
Congregation.	*Coming for to carry me home.*
Leader.	*Two little angels coming after me.*
Congregation.	*Coming for to carry me home. . . .*

The solitary and plaintive voice of the leader is answered by a sound like the roll of the sea, producing a most curious effect.

In only a few of these songs do the leader and the congregation start off together. Such a song is the well-known "Steal away to Jesus."

The leader and the congregation begin with part-singing:

Steal away, steal away,
Steal away to Jesus;
Steal away, steal away home,
I ain't got long to stay here.

Then the leader alone or the congregation in unison:

My Lord he calls me,
He calls me by the thunder,
The trumpet sounds within-a my soul.

Then all together:

I ain't got long to stay here.

The leader and the congregation again take up the opening refrain; then the leader sings three more leading lines alone, and so on almost *ad infinitum*. It will be seen that even here most of the work falls upon the leader, for the congregation sings the same lines over and over, while his memory and ingenuity are taxed to keep the songs going.

Generally the parts taken up by the congregation are sung in a three-part harmony, the women singing the soprano and a transposed tenor, the men with high voices singing the melody, and those with low voices a thundering bass. In a few of these songs, however, the leading part is sung in unison by the whole congregation, down to the last line, which is harmonized. The effect of this is intensely thrilling. Such a hymn is "Go down, Moses." It stirs the heart like a trumpet call.

"Singing Johnson" was an ideal leader, and his services were in great demand. He spent his time going about the country from one church to another. He received his support in much the same way as the preachers—part of a collection, food and lodging. All of his leisure time he devoted to originating new words and melodies and new lines for old songs. He always sang with his eyes—or, to be more exact, his eye—closed, indicating the tempo by swinging his head to and fro. He was a great judge of the proper hymn to sing at a particular moment; and I noticed several times, when the preacher reached a certain climax, or expressed a certain sentiment, that Johnson broke in with a line or two of some appropriate hymn. The speaker understood and would pause until the singing ceased.

As I listened to the singing of these songs, the wonder of their production grew upon me more and more. How did the men who originated them manage to do it? The sentiments are easily accounted for; they are mostly taken from the Bible; but the melodies, where did they come from? Some of them so weirdly sweet, and others so wonderfully strong. Take for instance "Go down, Moses." I doubt that there is a stronger theme in the whole musical literature of the world. And so many of these songs contain more than mere melody; there is sounded in them that elusive undertone, the note in music which is not heard with the ears. I sat often with the tears rolling down my cheeks and my heart melted within me. Any musical person who has never heard a Negro congregation under the spell of religious fervor sing these old songs has missed one of the most thrilling emotions which the human heart may experience. Anyone who without shedding tears can listen to Negroes sing "Nobody knows de trouble I see, Nobody knows but Jesus" must indeed have a heart of stone.

As yet the Negroes themselves do not fully appreciate these old slave songs. The educated classes are rather ashamed of them and prefer to sing hymns from books. This feeling is natural; they are still too close to the conditions under which the songs were produced; but the day will come when this slave music will be the most treasured heritage of the American Negro.

At the close of the "big meeting" I left the settlement where it was being held full of enthusiasm. I was in that frame of mind which, in the artistic temperament, amounts to inspiration. I was now ready and anxious to get to some place where I might settle down to work, and give expression to the ideas which were teeming in my head; but I strayed into another deviation from my path of life as I had it marked out, which led me upon an entirely different road. Instead of going to the nearest and most convenient railroad station I accepted the invitation of a young man who had been present the closing Sunday at the meeting to drive with him some miles farther to the town in which he taught school, and there take the train. My conversation with this young man as we drove along through the country was extremely interesting. He had been a student in one of the Negro colleges—strange coincidence, in the very college, as I learned through him, in which "Shiny" was now a professor. I was, of course, curious to hear about my boyhood friend; and had it not been vacation time, and that I was not sure that I should find him, I should have gone out of my way to pay him a visit; but I determined to write to him as soon as the school opened. My companion talked to me about his work among the people, of his hopes and his discouragements. He was tremendously in earnest; I might say, too much so. In fact it may be said that the majority of intelligent colored people are, in some degree, too much in earnest over the race question. They assume and carry so much that their progress is at times impeded and they are unable to see things in their proper proportions. In many instances a slight exercise of the sense of humor would save much anxiety of soul. Anyone who marks the general tone of editorials in colored newspapers is apt to be impressed with this idea. If the mass of Negroes took their present and future as seriously as do the most of their leaders, the race would be in no mental condition to sustain the terrible pressure which it undergoes; it would sink of its own weight. Yet is must be acknowledged that in the making of a race overseriousness is a far lesser failing than its reverse, and even the faults resulting from it lean to the right.

We drove into the town just before dark. As we passed a large unpainted church, my companion pointed it out as the place where he held his school. I promised that I would go there with him the next morning and visit awhile. The town was of that kind which hardly requires or deserves description; a straggling line of brick and wooden stores on one side of the railroad track and some cottages of various sizes on the other side constituted about the whole of it. The young school teacher boarded at the best house in the place owned by a colored man. It was painted, had glass windows, contained "store bought" furniture, an organ, and lamps with chimneys. The owner held a job of some kind on the railroad. After supper it was not long before everybody was sleepy. I occupied the room with the school teacher. In a few minutes after we got into the room he was in bed and asleep; but I took advantage of the unusual luxury of a lamp which gave light, and sat looking over my notes and jotting down some ideas which were still fresh in my mind. Suddenly I became conscious of that sense of alarm which is always aroused by the sound of hurrying footsteps on the silence of the night. I stopped work and looked at my watch. It was after eleven. I listened, straining every nerve to hear above the tumult of my quickening pulse. I caught the murmur of voices, then the gallop of a horse, then of another and another. Now thoroughly alarmed, I woke my companion, and together we both listened. After a moment he put out the light and softly opened the window-blind, and we cautiously peeped out. We saw men moving in one direction, and from the mutterings we vaguely caught the rumor that some terrible crime had been committed. I put on my coat and hat. My friend did all in his power to dissuade me from venturing out, but it was impossible for me to remain in the house under such tense excitement. My nerves would not have stood it. Perhaps what bravery I exercised in going out was due to the fact that I felt sure my identity as a colored man had not yet become known in the town.

I went out and, following the drift, reached the railroad station. There was gathered there a crowd of men, all white, and others were steadily arriving, seemingly from all the surrounding country. How did the news spread so quickly? I watched these men moving under the yellow glare of the kerosene lamps about the station, stern, comparatively silent, all of them armed, some of them in boots and spurs; fierce, determined men. I had come to know the type well, blond, tall, and lean, with ragged mustaches and glittering gray eyes. At the first suggestion of daylight they began to disperse in groups, going in several directions. There was no extra noise or excitement, no loud talking, only swift, sharp words of command given by those who seemed to be accepted as leaders by mutual understanding. In fact, the impression made upon me was that everything was being done in quite an orderly manner. In spite of so many leaving, the crowd around the station continued to grow; at sunrise there were a great many women and children. By this time I also noticed some colored people; a few seemed to be going about customary tasks; several were standing on the outskirts of the crowd; but the gathering of Negroes usually seen in such towns was missing.

Before noon they brought him in. Two horsemen rode abreast; between them, half-dragged, the poor wretch made his way through the dust. His hands were tied behind him, and ropes around his body were fastened to the saddle horns of his double guard. The men who at midnight had been stern and silent were now emitting that terror-instilling sound known as the "rebel yell." A space was quickly cleared in the crowd, and a rope placed about his neck, when from somewhere came the suggestion, "Burn him!" It ran like an electric current. Have you ever witnessed the transformation of human beings into savage beasts? Nothing can be more terrible. A railroad tie was sunk into the ground, the rope was removed, and a chain brought and securely coiled around the victim and the stake. There he stood, a man only in form and stature, every sign of degeneracy stamped upon his countenance. His eyes were dull and vacant, indicating not a single ray of thought. Evidently the realization of his fearful fate had robbed him of whatever reasoning power he had ever possessed. He was too stunned and stupefied even to tremble. Fuel was brought from everywhere, oil, the torch; the flames crouched for an instant as though to gather strength, then leaped up as high as their victim's head. He squirmed, he writhed, strained at his chains, then gave out cries and groans that I shall always hear. The cries and groans were choked off by the fire and smoke; but his eyes, bulging from their sockets, rolled from side to side, appealing in vain for help. Some of the crowd yelled and cheered, others seemed appalled at what they had done, and there were those who turned away sickened at the sight. I was fixed to the spot where I stood, powerless to take my eyes from what I did not want to see.

It was over before I realized that time had elapsed. Before I could make myself believe that what I saw was really happening, I was looking at a scorched post, a smoldering fire, blackened bones, charred fragments sifting down through coils of chain; and the smell of burnt flesh—human flesh was in my nostrils.

I walked a short distance away and sat down in order to clear my dazed mind. A great wave of humiliation and shame swept over me. Shame that I belonged to a race that could be so dealt with; and shame for my country, that it, the great example of democracy to the world, should be the only civilized, if not the only state on earth, where a human being would be burned alive. My heart turned bitter within me. I could understand why Negroes are led to sympathize with even their worst criminals and to protect them when possible. By all the impulses of normal human nature they can and should do nothing less.

Whenever I hear protests from the South that it should be left alone to deal with the Negro question, my thoughts go back to that scene of brutality and savagery. I do not see how a people that can find in its conscience any excuse whatever for slowly burning to death a human being, or for tolerating such an act, can be entrusted with the salvation of a race. Of course, there are in the South men of liberal thought who do not approve of lynching, but I wonder how long they will endure the limits which are placed upon free speech. They still cower and tremble before "Southern opinion." Even so late as the recent Atlanta riot those men who were brave enough to speak a word in behalf of justice and humanity felt called upon, by way of apology, to preface what they said with a glowing rhetorical tribute to the Anglo-Saxon's superiority and to refer to the "great and impassable gulf" between the races "fixed by the Creator at the foundation of the world." The question of the relative qualities of the two races is still an open one. The reference to the "great gulf" loses force in the face of the fact that there are in this country perhaps three or four million people with the blood of both races in their veins; but I fail to see the pertinency of either statement subsequent to the beating and murdering of scores of innocent people in the streets of a civilized and Christian city.

The Southern whites are in many respects a great people. Looked at from a certain point of view, they are picturesque. If one will put oneself in a romantic frame of mind, one can admire their notions of chivalry and bravery and justice. In this same frame of mind an intelligent man can go to the theatre and applaud the impossible hero, who with his single sword slays everybody in the play except the equally impossible heroine. So can an ordinary peace-loving citizen sit by a comfortable fire and read with enjoyment of the bloody deeds of pirates and the fierce brutality of Vikings. This is the way in which we gratify the old, underlying animal instincts and passions; but we should shudder with horror at the mere idea of such practices being realities in this day of enlightened and humanitarianized thought. The Southern whites are not yet living quite in the present age; many of their general ideas hark back to a former century, some of them to the Dark Ages. In the light of other days, they are sometimes magnificent. Today they are cruel and often ludicrous.

How long I sat with bitter thoughts running through my mind I do not know; perhaps an hour or more. When I decided to get up and go back to the house, I found that I could hardly stand on my feet. I was as weak as a man who had lost blood. However, I dragged myself along, with the central idea of a general plan well fixed in my mind. I did not find my school teacher friend at home, so I did not see him again. I swallowed a few mouthfuls of food, packed my bag, and caught the afternoon train.

When I reached Macon, I stopped only long enough to get the main part of my luggage and to buy a ticket for New York. All along the journey I was occupied in debating with myself the step which I had decided to take. I argued that to forsake one's race to better one's condition was no less worthy an action than to forsake one's country for the same purpose. I finally made up my mind that I would neither disclaim the black race nor claim the white race; but that I would change my name, raise a mustache, and let the world take me for what it would; that it was not necessary for me to go about with a label of inferiority pasted across my forehead. All the while I understood that it was not discouragement or fear or search for a larger field of action and opportunity that was driving me out of the Negro race. I knew that it was shame, unbearable shame. Shame at being identified with a people that could with impunity be treated worse than animals. For certainly the law would restrain and punish the malicious burning alive of animals.

So once again I found myself gazing at the towers of New York and wondering what future that city held in store for me.

From *The Autobiography of an Ex-Colored Man* (Boston: Sherman, French, 1912).

—— Brothers ——

See! There he stands; not brave, but with an air
Of sullen stupor. Mark him well! Is he
Not more like brute than man? Look in his eye!
No light is there, none, save the light that shines
In the now glaring, and now shifting orbs
Of some wild animal in the hunter's trap.

How came this beast in human shape and form?
Speak man!—We call you man because you wear
His shape—How are you thus? Are you not from
That docile, child-like, tender-hearted race
Which we have known three centuries? Not from
That more than faithful race which through three wars
Fed our dear wives and nursed our helpless babes
Without a single breach of trust? Speak out?

I am, and am not.

Then who, why are you?

I am a thing not new, I am as old
As human nature. I am that which lurks,
Ready to spring whenever a bar is loosed;
The ancient trait which fights incessantly
Against restraint, balks at the upward climb;
The weight forever seeking to obey
The law of downward pull,—and I am more:
The bitter fruit am I of planted seed,
The resultant, the inevitable end
Of evil forces and the powers of wrong.

Lessons in degradation, taught and learned,
The memories of cruel sights and deeds,
The pent up bitterness, the unspent hate
Filtered through fifteen generations have
Sprung up and found in me sporadic life.
In me the muttered curse of dying men,
On me the stain of conquered women, and
Consuming me the fearful fires of lust,
Lit long ago by other hands than mine.
In me the down-crushed spirit, the hurled-back prayers
Of wretches now long dead,—their dire bequests,—
In me the echo of the stifled cry
Of children for their bartered mothers' breasts.

I claim no race, no race claims me; I am
No more than human dregs; degenerate;
The monstrous offspring of the monster, Sin;
I am—just what I am—The race that fed
Your wives and nursed your babes would do the same
To-day, but I—

Enough, the brute must die!
Quick! Chain him to that oak! It will resist
The fire much longer than this slender pine.
Now bring the fuel! Pile it 'round him! Wait!
Pile not so fast or high! or we shall lose
The agony and terror in his face.

And now the torch! Good fuel that! the flames
Already leap head-high. Ha! Hear that shriek!
And there's another wilder than the first.
Fetch water! Water! Pour a little on
The fire, lest it should burn too fast. Hold so!
Now let it slowly blaze again. See there!
He squirms, he groans, his eyes bulge wildly out,
Searching around in vain appeal for help.
Another shriek, the last! Watch how the flesh
Grows crisp and hangs till, turned to ash, it sifts
Down through the coils of chain that hold erect
The ghastly frame against the bark-scorched tree.

Stop! to each man no more than one man's share
You take that bone, and you this tooth; the chain
Let us divide its links; this skull, of course,
In fair division, to the leader comes.

And now his fiendish crime has been avenged;
Let us back to our wives and children.—Say,
What did he mean by those last muttered words,
"Brothers in spirit, brothers in deed are we"?

From *Crisis*, February 1916, 199–200.

French Wilson

Fl. 1914

The author of "Jimmy" has slipped into obscurity, leaving nothing but the name French Wilson. Apart from the story's listing in an index of articles, the *Crisis*, which published "Jimmy" in April 1914, has no information about French Wilson in its files. I found no record of any other publications by this author, whose race and gender remain unclear, as does the question of whether the author is writing under a pseudonym.

French Wilson's story is included in this volume because it ties enforced child labor and peonage to the system of racial oppression that produced lynching. While writers such as Bertha Johnston and Alice French worried about the effect of racial violence on white children, Wilson describes the harrowing effects of racial violence on black children who are its direct victims. Like the child attempting to burn the cat in Alice French's story, Jimmy too is "only a baby," but he has already suffered tremendous physical and psychological trauma from his time at the reform farm. The upwardly mobile bourgeois black couple who adopts Jimmy are believers in striving and racial uplift as the keys to a better future. Jimmy's fate under their care represents the fulfillment of warnings by many black leaders that white violence will inevitably produce violent retribution, even at the cost of the succeeding generation's apocalyptic self-destruction.

— Jimmy —

The little boy (it was a Negro child) stirred and tossed feverishly. The woman (and she was also "colored") knelt by the cot with all a mother's agony showing in her dark moist eyes. Her husband sat beside her, his face expressing nothing but the patient, suffering, doglike humility of his race. The tall physician (he was a white man) straightened himself and slowly, sorrowfully shook his head.

"It's too bad," he said in his kindly voice. "The lad's life is wrecked, physically, and I fear mentally."

A tear welled up and dropped from the woman's eye. The man had arisen, and now gazed apathetically down upon the little patient. The doctor paused in the act of reaching for his case. Again he shook his head as he looked at the figure outlined beneath the coverlet. Bandages, he knew, covered cruel welts on breast and back. A bruise on the lip and a gap in the row of little teeth completed the story. Something choking arose in his throat. He turned swiftly away.

"By God," he muttered fiercely, "it's unbearable. This sort of thing can't go on. It must stop."

He blindly grasped his hat and strode from the room. At the door he turned:

"Don't forget. Every hour while he's awake. And if anything develops don't fail to call me."

The man followed him downstairs. In the hall below they looked into each other's eyes and their hands met in a long, firm, comprehensive grasp. And the doctor left.

The woman looked up when she felt the man's comforting arm around her.

"He'll never have to go through it again," she said.

"No, Lela, he's ours now."

"Jimmy, she whispered. "My boy."

There was a true love between these two, the man and the woman, a love that had started in childhood and remained faithful until Monroe had graduated from the law school of H_____ university and returned to take up his practice in his home town, and to marry the girl of his heart. It had been a long uphill fight for the young lawyer, but he had borne his burden unfalteringly and now was beginning to reap his reward. Certainly he was a well-known figure in court circles, and his modern, well-furnished home gave token of his material prosperity.

A staunch supporter of his race, his suspicions were continually on watch, and there was never a measure to degrade it that did not receive his bitterest opposition, and never one to help or uplift it to which he did not give his utmost zeal.

When a warden of the State reformatory surrendered his position and came before the court with a horrible tale of the mistreatment of the children at the institution, Monroe was one of the first to demand an investigation; and when, among other things, the committee discovered one little Negro lad almost dead and raving mad, it was Monroe who, in the fullness of his heart procured the child's immediate release and carried him to his own home.

Twelve years of age was "Jimmy" Brown. Twelve orphan years had he lived, and two of them had been spent under the bane of the "reform farm." Twelve years, but the little figure was frail and the face, thin and old looking as it was, held nothing of a boyish nature.

"He's only a baby." There was something of awe in her voice.

The man gulped and nodded. "Only a baby."

The boy awoke. His gaze wandered, uncomprehending, over the walls and ceiling until it rested upon the twain kneeling together by the cot. There was a sharp exclamation. A wild terror dawned and deepened in the eyes, and the child shrank to the extreme edge of the cot, his face wincing in pain.

"God," came in a hoarse whisper from the man as he turned away.

Some minutes later his wife found him in his study. Desperation was pictured on her face and her voice was tremulous as she asked:

"Won't you see what you can do with him? He won't eat or take his medicine, and every time that I come near him he screams and looks just awful."

Without a word the man arose and followed her. He noticed how the terror-stricken eyes fell upon them as they entered the door, and followed their every move. He noticed how the thin lips drew back in a snarl as he approached the bed. Then it came to him at once. Of course, force had always been used.

"Jimmy," he said in a harsh tone, "be quiet."

It hurt him to see the child cowering into whimpering obedience, but he grit his teeth and forced the boy to take and swallow the medicine. Not until they had retreated to the other side of the room, however, would the lad touch the broth which Mrs. Monroe had prepared, and then it was pitiful to see the hurried avidity with which he devoured it, keeping watchful eye, meanwhile, upon his benefactors.

For one whole delirious week they nursed him thus. And sometimes there were cries and moans, and cruel laughs, and horrible curses, things that issued strangely from the boy's lips, those baby lips that should have known nothing but childish prattle. And always there was that terror-stricken look in the eyes, and ever anon would come that ugly snarl to his lips.

But one morning the woman found a new expression on his face. The fear was still there, but a curiosity lay back of it and the wildness was gone.

"Dis hyeh fo' me?" he asked hesitantly, as she lay his breakfast before him.

"Yes, Jimmy."

And when he had finished:

" 'Scuse me, but whut's yo' name? Ah don' know whut to call yo'-all."

A great tenderness welled up in the woman's breast. She took the little face between her hands and imprinted a gentle kiss on the thin lips.

"Call me mamma, Jimmy," she said. "You're my boy now."

Jimmy improved slowly, but the doctor stopped leaving medicine and his calls became less and less frequent, some restriction on the patient's diet being removed at every call.

He was a lovable little chap, uncomplaining, grateful. They loved him and it seemed as if his frail fingers but drew their hearts the closer together. He was a born storyteller also, and many an evening was spent listening to his quaint dialect as he told queer little tales which he had picked up from somewhere, or recounted bits of conversation, scenes or incidents that he had heard or witnessed from his window. Sometimes he would break into a boisterous laugh, and the woman's hand would reach out and touch the man's; and he, understanding, would return the pressure. But sometimes the boy's voice would be grave and there would be tears in his eyes as he told some cruel story of the "reform farm." And sometimes he would tell of his own mistreatment; but then there would be no tears, only a light that softly glowed:

" 'Ah'll break yo sperit, yo' li'l brack bastard,' he sed. 'Yas, ah'll sho yo' who's de boss.' An' he beat me wid dat hosswhup. An' w'en ah cried, he hollahed: 'Shet up.' An' he hit me in de mouf, lak dat. An' den ah stahted laffin'. Ah didn' wantah laff, but hit seem lak ah jes' couldn't he'p it. An' dat made him mad an' he beat me a 'hole lot mo'. An' somehow 'r othar, ah jes' couldn't stop laffin'. An' bimbey ah jes' fell ovah an', he kep' on beatin' me. An' den—"

"And then what , Jimmy?"

"Don' know," with a tired sigh. " 'Pears lak ah jes cain't ricollec'."

Then the man would clench his hands and hurriedly leave the room and the woman would clasp the little waif to her breast. "It's all right, Jimmy. You're my boy now."

A contented smile and a murmured:

"Yas'm, 's all right now."

The summer waned into fall, and though his face brightened continually, the patient's body remained weak and he still had to be carried up and down for his few daily hours in the morning and evening air. But the remembrance of his happy, grateful eyes lightened Mrs. Monroe's household cares considerably, and the sight of them, after a hard afternoon's work, was like a tonic to the young lawyer.

But one day the woman, hearing a cry from the sickroom, hastened to find Jimmy on his knees before the window, his form stiffened in an attitude of fright. When she called him he turned with a wild grating laugh that made her heart sink; she fell to weeping softly. He yielded to her comforting arms, but in answer to her questions he only shook his head. In a few minutes, however, it was apparently all over, and if she thought it strange she kept her ponderings to herself.

Jimmy's room had now become a settled meeting place for the family at bedtime. Attired for the night's rest, they would discuss the day's happenings or lay plans for the morrow or the next day or for the time when Jimmy should have convalesced. Or maybe Monroe would talk of some of the problems that were confronting him.

One evening he seemed somewhat more morose than usual. After their conversation he told his wife, in a low tone, of several discouraging happenings, certain bills introduced into the legislature that the governor had been only too glad to commend; segregation in the civil service; discrimination politically at Washington and lynchings—two in Texas, one in Alabama, one in Pennsylvania and two in their own State. When he had finished there was silence for a while and then little Jimmy sadly shook his head:

"Dey does treat mah peop'l bad—evahwheh."

He told of incidents that had come under his small ken. But at the last the eyes took on a far-away look and the voice became weird:

"But dey'll come a time w'en mah peop'l jes' won' stan' fo' it no longah. An' dey'll be fiah, an' shootin' an' men yellin' and wimmen faintin' an' chillun cryin', an' evah-body'll be jes' wil'. An' w'en dat time gits hyeh—" He trailed off into silence.

"What then, Jimmy?"

The boy smiled and shook his head. But after the others were asleep he crawled out of bed and over to the window. One small finger pointed across the street.

"An' w'en dat time gits hyeh," he repeated, "I'se gwine ter kill *him*."

And into his mind came the picture of a big coarse-faced man holding a horsewhip—the warden who had nearly finished Jimmy's young life and who was now living in the house just opposite.

The autumn deepened into the haze of Indian summer and Jimmy advanced so far that he was able to walk downstairs. Then it was touching to witness his eagerness to work, to help with the household duties, to do something, anything, that might be a slight return for the kindness shown him. Mrs. Monroe did assign him a few tasks and the sight of his happy, busy little self made her face her own cares with singing heart, while Mr. Monroe, seeing the life shining in the little face again, began to lay plans for entering him into school at the beginning of the next term.

Came the day when the man, returning for dinner, wore a careworn expression on his usually stolid face, and would vouchsafe no reply to the woman's questions.

After the meal, in a constrained voice:

"Could you fix me a little lunch? I might not be home this evening."

But he did return that evening, and again:

"Could you fix me another lunch? I'll have to go back."

Then she caught him by the shoulders and, looking up into his eyes, said tenderly:

"Frank, you just must tell me. If anything should happen."

He sat down and covered his face with his hands.

"It's not much. Henry Tailor is hiding in my office."

"Henry Tailor hiding—in your office? Oh, Frank, what is it?"

"White girl living next door was assaulted. The family accused Tailor. That's about all."

A low groan escaped the woman's lips. The man arose.

"Well, I'm trying to get him to give himself up."

"Frank, do you think—"

He nodded.

"I'm going to try. You know the sheriff promised me that no client of mine would ever get out. Tailor's evidence is clean cut. If—"

And upstairs, crouched before the window, one tiny finger pointing across the street, Jimmy was saying:

"An' w'en dat time gits hyeh, I'se gwine ter kill him."

Two days later the man burst into the house in mid-afternoon, with a dark grimness on his lips and a shadowy light in his eyes.

"Oh, there's hell to pay," he muttered hoarsely in answer to her unspoken question. "They're trying to get him."

He dashed up the stairs, grabbed his cartridge belt with the brace of holsters, fastened it about him under his coat as he hurried down, roughly kissed his wife and, with a slam of the door, was gone.

Jimmy awoke with noise ringing in his ears. He listened eagerly. Yes, there it was. He could hear the shooting and the shouting. At last, at last. The time had arrived. He dressed with trembling, hastening fingers and stole softly into Monroe's room. He noticed that the brace of pistols was gone, but what he wanted hung on the wall beside an old rifle—a slender, stiletto-like hunting knife.

The woman did not hear the soft opening and closing of the door. Neither did she see the little figure gliding across the street. Nor did she witness the disappointment on his face as he sensed, somehow, that his enemy was out of reach, and crouched in sudden weakness beside the fence.

A discouraging fear stole over the boy's soul, and the knife in his hand seemed to mock him. Then he started and looked around the corner of the fence, realizing that the noise that awakened him had been steadily growing and now was almost deafening. He saw men and boys running back and forth, and behind, a great crowd of them, yelling like infuriated demons, pushing, pulling, dragging, knocking, kicking along one defenseless Negro, one of "his people." He shivered and a sob arose in his throat. But the next instant the starting tears drew back and his muscles tensed. For the last ray of the setting sun had fallen squarely on the distorted features of a man who had his hand twisted in the victim's collar.

"It's *him*."

A moment's hesitation and—a small dark figure shot out into the street, threading its way through the legs of the crowd toward the cruel-faced warden. One instant and the flashing blade had buried itself in the fellow's breast. The next—and the boy was knocked down and trodden under the feet of the mob.

———

The woman moaned and it seemed to the listening man that in the sound of her voice was embodied all the pulsing grief of a mother race for her sons. The boy on the cot lay very still. The flesh hung on his bones in quivering shreds, a deep furrow showed where a bullet had ploughed along his crushed face, and it seemed to the three who watched in silent woe that each feeble breath that dragged into the shattered lungs must be the last.

"Oh God, how long?" came through the gritted teeth of the physician, and the man knew that the cry was against the prejudice and vicious license that had placed the boy there.

A long stillness followed while they watched the life ebb in and out of the little body.

At last the eyes opened, and back of their poignant suffering lay the peace of great content. The lips essayed to move, and three hearts stood still as the three heads bent to catch the husky, broken whisper.

"A'—go'—got 'im."

Silence. Then one long despairing wail from the woman:

"Jimmy!"

From *Crisis*, April 1914, 294–296.

The Waco Horror

May 15, 1916

In mid-May 1916, a crowd of fifteen thousand in Waco, Texas, watched the torture and burning to death of a mentally deficient African American teenager, Jesse Washington, who had been accused of murdering and raping his white female employer. Although Washington was reported to have confessed that he "criminally assaulted" Mrs. Fryar, the medical examiner's testimony made no mention of signs of sexual assault on the woman's body, leading many historians to conclude that this was a rumor attached to what clearly seems to have been a dispute between employee and boss. Already on a speaking tour of the state, a white suffragist named Elizabeth Freeman was sent by the NAACP to Waco, where she spent ten days investigating the sham trial and lynching. The NAACP published Freeman's findings in "The Waco Horror," an eight-page supplement to the *Crisis* magazine. The editors of the *Crisis* circulated the piece to seven hundred newspapers and sent fifty African American newspapers photographs of the lynching, purchased by Freeman in Waco, along with the text. Every member of Congress received a copy of the supplement, the cover of which bore, at Du Bois's request, a photograph of Washington's charred remains. The NAACP also widely distributed "The Waco Horror" to raise funds to aid the fight for federal antilynching legislation. Public outrage over the Waco affair was, in fact, instrumental in the congressional consideration of the Dyer antilynching measure in 1919 and 1921.

— The Waco Horror —

An account of the recent burning of a human being at Waco, Tex., as reported by a special agent of the National Association for the Advancement of Colored People, 70 Fifth Avenue, New York City.

1. The City

The city of Waco, Tex., is the county seat of McLennan county. It is situated on the Brazos river, about half way between Dallas and Austin. It is the junction point of seven railways. The city is in a fertile agricultural region with grain and cotton as the chief products, and with nearly two hundred manufacturing establishments, representing some seventy different industries.

It had a population of 14,445 in 1890 which increased to 20,686 in 1900, and to 26,425 in 1910. The white population in these twenty years has almost exactly doubled. The colored population has increased from 4,069 to 6,067, forming thus 23% of the population. The bulk of the population is native white of native parentage, there being only about 1,000 foreigners in the city.

THE TORTURE (Note the "Frenzied" Mob)

that woman?' He answered, 'No.' 'If it had been a colored boy and a colored woman? No.' 'We would not have stopped the niggers doing anything they wanted to.' 'Do you think they would?' 'No.' 'Then, they prove their superior civilization.' Then he began to tell me how he knew all about the niggers and we northerners do not. He said that as an old southerner he knew perfectly well how to handle the colored population. He told me how he was raised with them, had a colored mammy, nursed at her breast, etc.

"There is a bunch of people in Waco who are dying to see someone go forward and make a protest, but no one in Waco would do it. Ex-Mayor Mackaye and Colonel Hamilton both said, 'We do not know what to do. We are not organized to do it. It is a case of race and politics.'

"I put out a lot of wires for a lawyer to take up the case, but no human

being in Waco would take it up. I wrote to a friend in Austin and one in Houston, and the Austin friend telegraphed me that he would send me word as soon as he had found someone. I had a letter from the Houston friend who gave me the names of three lawyers, but am not sure whether they would take up a case of this kind. All have their doubts of ever getting the case into court.

"I did not dare ask much about lawyers.

"As a result of the lynching a Sunday School Convention which was to have met there, with 15,000 delegates, has been stopped.

"W. A. Brazelton, the foreman of the Jury, was very outspoken against the whole affair and blames the officials for it. He felt that as foreman of the Jury he could not lead in a protest but *thought* some protest ought to be made.

"Mr. Ainsworth, one of the newspaper men, seemed the

4. "The Torture." Reprinted from "The Waco Horror," special supplement to the *Crisis*, July 1916, 7.

The whole of McLennan county contained in 1910 a population of 73,250 of whom 17,234 were Negroes. This total population has nearly doubled in the last twenty years.

Waco is well laid out. The streets are broad, over sixty miles of them being paved. The sewer system of one hundred miles is excellent. There is a fine city-owned water system, and parks on the surrounding prairies.

There are thirty-nine white and twenty-four colored churches in Waco. By denominations the white churches are: Baptist, 14; Methodist, 9; Christian, 4; Presbyterian, 3; Jewish, 2; Episcopal, 2; Evangelistic, 1; Lutheran, 1; Catholic, 1; Christian Science, 1; Salvation Army, 1.

The colleges are: Baylor University, Baylor Academy, the Catholic College, the Independent Biblical and Industrial School, all white; the Central Texas College and Paul Quinn, colored colleges. There are also the A. & M. College, the Gurley School, the Waco Business College, the Provident Sanitarium, and the Training School.

Baylor University was founded in 1854 and has between 1,200 and 1,300 students. It is coeducational. The president is running for the United States Senate.

Two high schools serve white and colored population, and there are seven banks, including four national banks.

In other words, Waco is a typical southern town, alert, pushing and rich.

2. The Crime

Near the country town of Robinson, some six miles from Waco, lived a white family of four, named Fryar, who owned a small farm. This they cultivated themselves with the help of one hired man, a colored boy of seventeen, named Jesse Washington.

Jesse was a big, well-developed fellow, but ignorant, being unable either to read or write. He seemed to have been sullen, and perhaps mentally deficient, with a strong, and even daring temper. It is said that on the Saturday night before the crime he had had a fight with a neighboring white man, and the man had threatened to kill him.

On Monday, May 8, while Mr. Fryar, his son of fourteen, and his daughter of twenty-three, were hoeing cotton in one part of their farm, the boy, Jesse, was plowing with his mules and sowing cotton seed near the house where Mrs. Fryar was alone. He went to the house for more cotton seed. As Mrs. Fryar was scooping it up for him into the bag which he held, she scolded him for beating the mules. He knocked her down with a blacksmith's hammer, and, as he confessed, criminally assaulted her; finally he killed her with the hammer. The boy then returned to the field, finished his work, and went home to his cabin, where he lived with his father and mother and several brothers and sisters.

When the murdered woman was discovered suspicion pointed to Jesse Washington, and he was found sitting in his yard whittling a stick. He was arrested and immediately taken to jail in Waco. Tuesday a mob visited the jail. They came in about thirty automobiles, each holding as many as could be crowded in. There was no noise, no tooting of horns, the lights were dim, and some had no lights at all. These were all Robinson people. They looked for the boy, but could not find him, for he had been taken to a neighboring county where the sheriff had obtained a confession from him. Another mob went to this county seat to get the boy, but he was again removed to Dallas. Finally the Robinson people pledged themselves not to lynch the boy if the authorities acted promptly, and if the boy would waive his legal rights.

A second confession in which the boy waived all his legal rights was obtained in the Dallas jail. The Grand Jury indicted him on Thursday, and the case was set for trial Monday, May 15.

Sunday night, at midnight, Jesse Washington was brought from Dallas to Waco, and secreted in the office of the judge. There was not the slightest doubt but that he would be tried and hanged the next day, if the law took its course.

There was some, but not much doubt of his guilt. The confessions were obtained, of course, under duress, and were, perhaps, suspiciously clear, and not entirely in the boy's own words. It seems, however, that the boy was guilty of murder, and possibly of pre-meditated rape.

3. Waco Politics

Meantime, the exigencies of Waco politics are said to have demanded a lynching. Our investigator says:

"They brought the boy back to Waco because a lynching was of political value to the county officials who are running for office. Every man I talked with said that politics was at the bottom of the whole business. All that element who took part in the lynching will vote for the Sheriff. The Judge is of value to his party because he appoints the three commissioners of the jury, and these commissioners pick the Grand Jury."

The District Judge of the Criminal Court is R. I. Munroe, appointed by Governor Campbell. He is a low order of politician, and a product of a local machine. His reputation for morality is bad, and his practice at the Bar has been largely on behalf of the vicious interests.

The Sheriff of the county, S. S. Fleming, is a candidate for re-election, and has made much political capital out of the lynching. He says, in an advertisement in the Waco *Semi-Weekly Tribune*:

"Mr. Fleming is diseased with a broad philanthropy. He believes in the equality of man. He carries with him in the daily walk of his officialdom none of the 'boast of heraldry or the pomp of power.' He is just as courteous, just as obliging, just as accommodating as Sheriff as he was when selling buggies and cultivators for the hardware company. He presents to the voters for their endorsement the record made by him and his corps of splendid deputies."

Our investigator says:

"When I saw the Sheriff (Fleming) he had a beautiful story to tell. He had his story fixed up so that the entire responsibility was shifted on the Judge. The Judge admitted he could have had a change of venue, but said the mob anywhere would have done the same thing."

Meantime, the tip went out:

"The crowd began pouring into the town the day before and continued early Monday morning. The court room was packed full and a crowd of 2,000 was on the outside. The jurors could scarcely get in and out from their seats. I asked the Judge if he could not have cleared the court room, and he answered that I did not know the South. I said, 'If a person is big enough, he can get up and stop the biggest mob.' He asked, 'Do you want to spill innocent blood for a nigger?'

"Someone had arranged it so that it would be easy to get the boy out of the courtroom. A door which opened by a peculiar device had been fixed so that it would open. One of the jurors was a convicted murderer with a suspended sentence over him.

"Lee Jenkins is the best deputy sheriff, but he is under Fleming. Barney Goldberg, the other deputy sheriff, said, 'If Lee Jenkins had had it, it would never have been, but we are working for the man higher up and must take our orders from him.' Barney Goldberg knows perfectly well that if Fleming is not re-elected, and the other candidate gets in, he will be out of a job. The other nominee for sheriff, Buchanan, is reported to be unable to read and write, but is said to have three dead 'niggers' to his 'credit.'

"The boy, Jesse Washington, was asked what he thought about the mob coming after him. He said, 'They promised they would not if I would tell them about it.' He seemed not to care, but was thoroughly indifferent."

The trial was hurried through. The Waco *Semi-Weekly Tribune*, May 17, says:

"The jury returned into court at 11:22 a.m., and presented a verdict: 'We, the jury, find the defendant guilty of murder as charged in the indictment and assess his punishment at death.' This was signed by W. B. Brazleton, foreman.

" 'Is that your verdict, gentlemen?' asked Judge Monroe.

"They answered 'yes.'

"Judge Monroe began writing in his docket. He had written: 'May 15, 1916: Jury verdict of guilty,' and as he wrote there was a hush over the entire court room. It was a moment of hesitation, but just a moment. Then the tall man started [stared?] over the heads of the crowd. Fred H. Kingsbury, who was standing alongside of Judge Munroe, said, 'They are coming after him,' and as the judge looked up, the wave of people surged forward." The court room accommodates 500 persons, but the Judge had allowed 1,500 persons to crowd in.

Our investigator continues:

"The stenographer told me that there was a pause of a full minute. He said the people crowded around him and he knew what was coming, so he slipped out of the door back of the Sheriff, with his records; and Sheriff Fleming slipped out also.

"Fleming claims that all he was called upon to do in the way of protecting the boy was to get him to court.

"A fellow in the back of the court room yelled, 'Get the Nigger!' Barney Goldberg, one of the deputy sheriffs, told me that he did not know that Fleming had dropped orders to let them get the Negro, and pulled his revolver. Afterwards he got his friends to swear to an affidavit that he was not present. Fleming said he had sworn in fifty deputies. I asked him where they were. He asked, 'Would you want to protect the nigger?' The judge made no effort to stop the mob, although he had firearms in his desk."

4. The Burning

"They dragged the boy down the stairs, put a chain around his body and hitched it to an automobile. The chain broke. The big fellow took the chain off the Negro under the cover of the crowd and wound it around his own wrist, so that the crowd jerking at the chain was jerking at the man's wrist and he was holding the boy. The boy shrieked and struggled.

"The mob ripped the boy's clothes off, cut them in bits and even cut the boy. Someone cut his ear off; someone else unsexed him. A little girl working for the firm of Goldstein and Mingle told me that she saw this done.

"I went over the route the boy had been taken and saw that they dragged him between a quarter and a half a mile from the Court House to the bridge and then dragged him up two blocks and another block over to the City Hall. After they had gotten him up to the bridge, someone said that a fire was already going up at City Hall, and they turned around and went back. Several people denied that this fire was going, but the photograph shows that it was. They got a little boy to light the fire.

"While a fire was being prepared of boxes, the naked boy was stabbed and the chain put over the tree. He tried to get away, but could not. He reached up to grab the chain and they cut off his fingers. The big man struck the boy on the back of the neck with a knife just as they were pulling him up on the tree. Mr. Lester thought that was practically the death blow. He was lowered into the fire several times by means of the chain around his neck. Someone said they would estimate the boy had about twenty-five stab wounds, none of them death-dealing.

"About a quarter past one a fiend got the torso, lassoed it, hung a rope over the pummel of a saddle, and dragged it around through the streets of Waco.

"Very little drinking was done.

"The tree where the lynching occurred was right under the Mayor's window. Mayor Dollins was standing in the window, not concerned about what they were doing to the boy, but that the tree would be destroyed. The Chief of Police also witnessed the lynching. The names of five of the leaders of the mob are known to this Association, and can be had on application by responsible parties.

"Women and children saw the lynching. One man held up his little boy above the heads of the crowd so that he could see, and a little boy was in the top of the very tree to which the colored boy was hung, where he stayed until the fire became too hot."

Another account, in the Waco *Times Herald*, Monday night, says:

"Great masses of humanity flew as swiftly as possible through the streets of the city in order to be present at the bridge when the hanging took place, but when it was learned that the Negro was being taken to the City Hall lawn, crowds of men, women and children turned and hastened to the lawn.

"On the way to the scene of the burning people on every hand took a hand in showing their feelings in the matter by striking the Negro with anything obtainable, some struck him with shovels, bricks, clubs, and others stabbed him and cut him until when he was strung up his body was a solid color of red, the blood of the many wounds inflicted covered him from head to foot.

"Dry goods boxes and all kinds of inflammable material were gathered, and it required but an instant to convert this into seething flames. When the Negro was first hoisted into the air his tongue protruded from his mouth and his face was besmeared with blood.

"Life was not extinct within the Negro's body, although nearly so, when another chain was placed around his neck and thrown over the limb of a tree on the lawn, everybody trying to get to the Negro and have some part in his death. The infuriated mob then leaned the Negro, who was half alive and half dead, against the tree, he having just enough strength within his limbs to support him. As rapidly as possible the Negro was then jerked into the air at which a shout from thousands of throats went up on the morning air and dry goods boxes, excelsior, wood, and every other article that would burn was then in evidence, appearing as if by magic. A huge dry goods box was then produced and filled to the top with all of the material that had been secured. The Negro's body was swaying in the air, and all of the time a noise as of thousands was heard and the Negro's body was lowered into the box.

"No sooner had his body touched the box than people pressed forward, each eager to be the first to light the fire, matches were touched to the inflammable material and as smoke rapidly rose in the air, such a demonstration as of people gone mad was never heard before. Everybody pressed closer to get souvenirs of the affair. When they had finished with the Negro his body was mutilated.

"Fingers, ears, pieces of clothing, toes and other parts of the Negro's body were cut off by members of the mob that had crowded to the scene as if by magic when the word that the Negro had been taken in charge by the mob was heralded over the city. As the smoke rose to the heavens, the mass of people, numbering in the neighborhood of 10,000, crowding the City Hall lawn and overflowing the square, hanging from the windows of buildings, viewing the scene from the tops of buildings and trees, set up a shout that was heard blocks away.

"Onlookers were hanging from the windows of City Hall and every other building that commanded a sight of the burning, and as the Negro's body commenced to burn, shouts of delight went up from the thousands of throats and apparently everybody demonstrated in some way their satisfaction at the retribution that was being visited on the perpetrator of such a horrible crime, the worst in the annals of McLennan county's history.

"The body of the Negro was burned to a crisp and left for some time in the smoldering remains of the fire. Women and children who desired to view the scene were allowed to do so, the crowds parting to let them look on the scene. After some time the body of the Negro was jerked into the air where everybody could view the remains, and a mighty shout rose on the air. Photographer Gildersleeve made several pictures of the body as well as the large crowd which surrounded the scene as spectators."

The photographer knew where the lynching was to take place, and had his camera and paraphernalia in the City Hall. He was called by telephone at the proper moment. He writes us:

"We have quit selling the mob photos, this step was taken because our 'City dads' objected on the grounds of 'bad publicity,' as we wanted to be boosters and not knockers, we agreed to stop all sale.

"F. A. GILDERSLEEVE."

Our agent continues:

"While the torso of the boy was being dragged through the streets behind the horse, the limbs dropped off and the head was put on the stoop of a disreputable woman in the reservation district. Some little boys pulled out the teeth and sold them to some men for five dollars apiece. The chain was sold for twenty-five cents a link.

"From the pictures, the boy was apparently a wonderfully built boy. The torso was taken to Robinson, hung to a tree, and shown off for a while, then they took it down again and dragged it back to town and put it on the fire again at five o'clock."

5. The Aftermath

"I tried to talk to the Judge. I met him on the street and said, 'I want to talk with you about something very important.' He asked, 'What is the nature of it?' I said, 'I want to get your opinion of that lynching.' He said, 'No, I refuse to talk with you about that. What do you want it for?' I said, 'If you refuse to talk to me, there is no use of telling you what I want it for.'

"When I met him the second time, with different clothes on, he did not recognize me. I put on a strong English accent and said I was interested in clippings from New York papers which showed that Waco had made for itself an awful name, and I wanted to go back and make the northerners feel that Waco was not so bad as the papers had represented. Then he gave me the Court records."

Our investigator continues: "I went to the newspaper offices. They were all of the opinion that the best thing to do was to hush it up. They used it as a news item, and that finished it. The Dallas *News* did not cite anything editorially because not long ago they had done something quite as bad and the boy was not guilty.

"With the exception of the *Tribune*, all the papers had simply used it as a news item and let it drop. The *Tribune* is owned by Judge McCullum, who says anything he pleases. He is nearly blind. When I read the article to him I said, 'I would like to ask you, if that had been a colored woman and a white boy, would you have protected that woman?' He answered, 'No.' 'If it had been a colored boy and a colored woman?' 'No. We would not have stopped the niggers doing anything they wanted to.' 'Do you think they would?' 'No.' 'Then they prove their superior civilization.' Then he began to tell me how he knew all about the niggers and we northerners do not. He said that as an old southerner he knew perfectly well how to handle the colored population. He told me how he was raised with them, had a colored mammy, nursed at her breast, etc.

"There is a bunch of people in Waco who are dying to see someone go forward and make a protest, but no one in Waco would do it. Ex-Mayor Mackaye and Colonel Hamilton both said, 'We do not know what to do. We are not organized to do it. It is a case of race and politics.'

"I put out a lot of wires for lawyers to take up the case, but no human being in Waco would take it up. I wrote to a friend in Austin and one in Houston, and the Austin friend telegraphed me that he would send me word as soon as he had found someone. I had a letter from the Houston friend who gave me the names of three lawyers, but am not sure whether they would take up a case of this kind. All have their doubts of ever getting the case into court.

"I did not dare ask much about lawyers.

"As a result of the lynching a Sunday School Convention which was to have met there, with 15,000 delegates, has been stopped.

"W. A. Brazleton, the foreman of the Jury, was very outspoken against the whole affair and blames the officials for it. He felt that as foreman of the Jury he could not lead in a protest but *thought* some protest ought to be made.

"Mr. Ainsworth, one of the newspaper men, seemed the only one who wanted to start a protest.

"Colonel Hamilton, a man of high standing, a northerner, and at one time a big railroad man, was outspoken against the whole affair, but said that if he led in a protest they would do the same thing to him. He said he would never register in any hotel that he came from Waco. Two Waco men who did not register from Waco.

"Allan Stanford, ex-Mayor of Waco, saw the Sheriff and the Judge before the trial and received assurances that the lynching would not take place. They shut the mouths of the better element of Waco by telling them that the Robinson people had promised not to do it. They had gotten the promise of the Robinson people during the trial that they would not touch the boy during the trial, but they did not get the pledge of the disreputable bunch of Waco that they would not start the affair.

"Judge Spell said the affair was deplorable, but the best thing was to forget it.

"When representing myself as a news reporter, I asked, 'What shall I tell the people up North?' Ex-Mayor Mackaye said, 'Fix it up as well as you can for Waco, and make them understand that the better thinking men and women were not in it.' I said, 'But some of your better men were down there.' The whole thing savors so rotten because the better men have not tried to protest against it. Your churches have not said a word. Dr. Caldwell was the only man who made any protest at all."

6. The Lynching Industry

This is an account of one lynching. It is horrible, but it is matched in horror by scores of others in the last thirty years, and in its illegal, law-defying, race-hating aspect, it is matched by 2842 other lynchings which have taken place between January 1, 1885, and June 1, 1916. These lynchings are as follows:

COLORED MEN LYNCHED BY YEARS
1885–1916

Year	Count	Year	Count
1885	78	1902	86
1886	71	1903	86
1887	80	1904	83
1888	95	1905	61
1889	95	1906	64
1890	90	1907	60
1891	121	1908	93
1892	155	1909	73
1893	154	1910	65
1894	134	1911	63
1895	112	1912	63
1896	80	1913	79
1897	122	1914	69
1898	102	1915	80
1899	84	1916 (5 mos.)	31
1900	107		
1901	107	**TOTAL:**	**2,843**

What are we going to do about this record? The civilization of America is at stake. The sincerity of Christianity is challenged. The National Association for the Advancement of Colored People proposes immediately to raise a fund of at least $10,000 to start a crusade against this modern barbarism. Already $2,000 is promised, conditional on our raising the whole amount.

Interested persons may write to Roy Nash, secretary, 70 Fifth Avenue, New York City.

Supplement to the *Crisis*, July 1916.

Theodore Dreiser

1871–1945

Born in Terre Haute, Indiana, into a rigid and impoverished German Catholic family, Theodore Dreiser left home for Chicago while still a teenager. He worked a variety of menial jobs until a former teacher's encouragement convinced him to enroll at Indiana University, which he attended for only one year. Like many U.S. novelists, Dreiser began his writing career as a journalist, working as a reporter in Chicago, St. Louis, and Pittsburgh, and for several years as a magazine editor in New York. Widely considered the premier novelist in the tradition of U.S. literary naturalism, Dreiser combined his depiction of life as a bleak, unforgiving battle for survival with a deep compassion for the doomed, particularly the working classes and "fallen women." His best novels include *Sister Carrie* (1900), *The Financier* (1912), and *An American Tragedy* (1925). The American Academy of Arts and Letters awarded him its Gold Medal for Fiction in 1944.

Long a critic of industrialized America's obsession with materialism and of the societal inequalities produced by capitalism, Dreiser became politically active during the Great Depression, speaking out in support of striking mine workers in Kentucky and joining efforts to obtain a pardon for militant labor leader Tom Mooney, sentenced to death in a frame-up for bombing San Francisco's Market Street during a 1916 rally that supported America's entry into the First World War. (Mooney was granted an unconditional pardon by California Governor Culburt Olsen in 1939.) As chair of the National Committee for the Defense of Political Prisoners, Dreiser worked with the International Labor Defense to gain freedom for the Scottsboro Boys, nine African American youths unjustly convicted of rape. He was also a member of the NAACP's Writers' League Against Lynching.

Dreiser based his short story "Nigger Jeff" on a lynching he witnessed in the fall of 1893 as a reporter for the *St. Louis Republic*, when a Missouri mob killed a young black man accused of raping two women. *Ainslee's Magazine* published the story in 1901; a later revised version appears here. (Dreiser's abbreviation "Ko." in the telegram is a thin attempt to disguise the location of the real-life lynching, Missouri.)

—— Nigger Jeff ——

The city editor was waiting for one of his best reporters, Elmer Davies by name, a vain and rather self-sufficient youth who was inclined to be of that turn of mind which sees in life only a fixed and ordered process of rewards and punishments. If one did not do exactly right, one did not get along well. On the contrary, if one did, one did. Only the so-called evil were really punished, only the good truly rewarded—or Mr. Davies had heard this so long in his youth that he had come nearly to believe it. Presently he appeared. He was dressed in a new spring suit, a new hat and new shoes. In the lapel of his coat was a small bunch of violets. It was one o'clock of a sunny spring afternoon, and he was feeling exceedingly well and good-natured—quite fit, indeed. The world was going unusually well with him. It seemed worth singing about.

"Read that, Davies," said the city editor, handing him the clipping. "I'll tell you afterward what I want you to do."

The reporter stood by the editorial chair and read:

Pleasant Valley, Ko., April 16.

"A most dastardly crime has just been reported here. Jeff Ingalls, a negro, this morning assaulted Ada Whitaker, the nineteen-year-old daughter of Morgan Whitaker, a well-to-do farmer, whose home is four miles south of this place. A posse, headed by Sheriff Mathews, has started in pursuit. If he is caught, it is thought he will be lynched."

The reporter raised his eyes as he finished. What a terrible crime! What evil people there were in the world! No doubt such a creature ought to be lynched, and that quickly.

"You had better go out there, Davies," said the city editor. "It looks as if something might come of that. A lynching up here would be a big thing. There's never been one in this state."

Davies smiled. He was always pleased to be sent out of town. It was a mark of appreciation. The city editor rarely sent any of the other men on these big stories. What a nice ride he would have!

As he went along, however, a few minutes later he began to meditate on this. Perhaps, as the city editor had suggested, he might be compelled to witness an actual lynching. That was by no means so pleasant in itself. In his fixed code of rewards and punishments he had no particular place for lynchings, even for crimes of the nature described, especially if he had to witness the lynching. It was too horrible a kind of reward or punishment. Once, in line of duty, he had been compelled to witness a hanging, and that had made him sick—deathly so—even though carried out as a part of the due process of law of his day and place. Now, as he looked at this fine day and his excellent clothes, he was not so sure that this was a worthwhile assignment. Why should he always be selected for such things—just because he could write? There were others— lots of men on the staff. He began to hope as he went along that nothing really serious would come of it, that they would catch the man before he got there and put him in jail—or, if the worst had to be—painful thought!—that it would be all over by the time he got there. Let's see—the telegram had been filed at nine a.m. It was now one-thirty and would be three by the time he got out there, all of that. That would give him time enough, and then, if all were well, or ill, as it were, he could just gather the details of the crime and the—aftermath—and return. The mere thought of an approaching lynching troubled him greatly, and the farther he went the less he liked it.

He found the village of Pleasant Valley a very small affair indeed, just a few dozen houses nestling between green slopes of low hills, with one small business corner and a rambling array of lanes. One or two merchants of K——, the city from which he had just arrived, lived out here, but otherwise it was very rural. He took notes of the whiteness of the little houses, the shimmering beauty of the small stream one had to cross in going from the depot. At the one main corner a few men were gathered about a typical village barroom. Davies headed for this as being the most likely source of information.

In mingling with this company at first he said nothing about his being a newspaper man, being very doubtful as to its effect upon them, their freedom of speech and manner.

The whole company was apparently tense with interest in the crime which still remained unpunished, seemingly craving excitement and desirous of seeing something done about it. No such opportunity to work up wrath and vent their stored-up animal propensities had probably occurred here in years. He took this occasion to inquire into the exact details of the attack, where it had occurred, where the Whitakers lived. Then, seeing that mere talk prevailed here, he went away thinking that he had best find out for himself how the victim was. As yet she had not been described, and it was necessary to know a little something about her. Accordingly, he sought an old man who kept a stable in the village, and procured a horse. No carriage was to be had. Davies was not an excellent rider, but he made a shift of it. The Whitaker home was not so very far away—about four miles out—and before long he was knocking at its front door, set back a hundred feet from the rough country road.

"I'm from the *Times*," he said to the tall, rawboned woman who opened the door, with an attempt at being impressive. His position as reporter in this matter was a little dubious; he might be welcome, and he might not. Then he asked if this were Mrs. Whitaker, and how Miss Whitaker was by now.

"She's doing very well," answered the woman, who seemed decidedly stern, if repressed and nervous, a Spartan type. "Won't you come in? She's rather feverish, but the doctor says she'll probably be all right later on." She said no more.

Davies acknowledged the invitation by entering. He was very anxious to see the girl, but she was sleeping under the influence of an opiate, and he did not care to press the matter at once.

"When did this happen?" he asked.

"About eight o'clock this morning," said the woman. "She started to go over to our next door neighbor here, Mr. Edmonds, and this negro met her. We didn't know anything about it until she came crying through the gate and dropped down in here."

"Were you the first one to meet her?" asked Davies.

"Yes, I was the only one," said Mrs. Whitaker. "The men had all gone to the fields."

Davies listened to more of the details, the type and history of the man, and then rose to go. Before doing so he was allowed to have a look at the girl, who was still sleeping. She was young and rather pretty. In the yard he met a country man who was just coming to get home news. The latter imparted more information.

"They're lookin' all around south of here," he said, speaking of a crowd which was supposed to be searching. "I expect they'll make short work of him if they get him. He can't get away very well, for he's on foot, wherever he is. The sheriff's after him too, with a deputy or two, I believe. He'll be tryin' to save him an' take him over to Clayton, but I don't believe he'll be able to do it, not if the crowd catches him first."

So, thought Davies, he would probably have to witness a lynching after all. The prospect was most unhappy.

"Does any one know where this negro lived?" he asked heavily, a growing sense of his duty weighing upon him.

"Oh, right down here a little way," replied the farmer. "Jeff Ingalls was his name. We all know him around here. He worked for one and another of the farmers hereabouts, and don't appear to have had such a bad record, either, except for drinkin' a little now and then. Miss Ada recognized him, all right. You follow this road to the next crossing and turn to the right. It's a little log house that sets back off the road— something like that one you see down the lane there, only it's got lots o' chips scattered about."

Davies decided to go there first, but changed his mind. It was growing late, and he thought he had better return to the village. Perhaps by now developments in connection with the sheriff or the posse were to be learned.

Accordingly, he rode back and put the horse in the hands of its owner, hoping that all had been concluded and that he might learn of it here. At the principal corner much the same company was still present, arguing, fomenting, gesticulating. They seemed parts of different companies that earlier in the day had been out searching. He wondered what they had been doing since, and then decided to ingratiate himself by telling them he had just come from the Whitakers and what he had learned there of the present condition of the girl and the movements of the sheriff.

Just then a young farmer came galloping up. He was coatless, hatless, breathless.

"They've got him!" he shouted excitedly. "They've got him!"

A chorus of "whos," "wheres" and "whens" greeted this information as the crowd gathered about the rider.

"Why, Mathews caught him up here at his own house!" exclaimed the latter, pulling out a handkerchief and wiping his face. "He must 'a' gone back there for something. Mathews's takin' him over to Clayton, so they think, but they don't project he'll ever get there. They're after him now, but Mathews says he'll shoot the first man that tries to take him away."

"Which way'd he go?" exclaimed the men in chorus, stirring as if to make an attack.

"'Cross Sellers' Lane," said the rider. "The boys think he's goin' by way of Baldwin."

"Whoopee!" yelled one of the listeners. "We'll get him away from him, all right! Are you goin', Sam?"

"You bet!" said the latter. "Wait'll I get my horse!"

"Lord!" thought Davies. "To think of being (perforce) one of a lynching party—a hired spectator!"

He delayed no longer, however, but hastened to secure his horse again. He saw that the crowd would be off in a minute to catch up with the sheriff. There would be information in that quarter, drama very likely.

"What's doin'?" inquired the liveryman as he noted Davies's excited appearance.

"They're after him," replied the latter nervously. "The sheriff's caught him. They're going now to try to take him away from him, or that's what they say. The sheriff is taking him over to Clayton, by way of Baldwin. I want to get over there if I can. Give me the horse again, and I'll give you a couple of dollars more."

The liveryman led the horse out, but not without many provisionary cautions as to the care which was to be taken of him, the damages which would ensue if it were not. He was not to be ridden beyond midnight. If one were wanted for longer than that Davies must get him elsewhere or come and get another, to all of which Davies promptly agreed. He then mounted and rode away.

When he reached the corner again several of the men who had gone for their horses were already there, ready to start. The young man who had brought the news had long since dashed off to other parts.

Davies waited to see which road this new company would take. Then through as pleasant a country as one would wish to see, up hill and down dale, with charming vistas breaking upon the gaze at every turn, he did the riding of his life. So disturbed was the reporter by the grim turn things had taken that he scarcely noted the beauty that was stretched before him, save to note that it was so. Death! Death! The proximity of involuntary and enforced death was what weighed upon him now.

In about an hour the company had come in sight of the sheriff, who, with two other men, was driving a wagon he had borrowed along a lone country road. The latter was sitting at the back, a revolver in each hand, his face toward the group, which at sight of him trailed after at a respectful distance. Excited as everyone was, there was no disposition, for the time being at least, to halt the progress of the law.

"He's in that wagon," Davies heard one man say. "Don't you see they've got him in there tied and laid down?"

Davies looked.

"That's right," said another. "I see him now."

"What we ought to do," said a third, who was riding near the front, "is to take him away and hang him. That's just what he deserves, and that's what he'll get before we're through to-day."

"Yes!" called the sheriff, who seemed to have heard this. "You're not goin' to do any hangin' this day, so you just might as well go on back." He did not appear to be much troubled by the appearance of the crowd.

"Where's old man Whitaker?" asked one of the men who seemed to feel that they needed a leader. "He'd get him quick enough!"

"He's with the other crowd, down below Olney," was the reply.

"Somebody ought to go an' tell him."

"Clark's gone," assured another, who hoped for the worst.

Davies rode among the company a prey to mingled and singular feelings. He was very much excited and yet depressed by the character of the crowd which, in so far as he could see, was largely impelled to its jaunt by curiosity and yet also able under sufficient motivation on the part of some one—any one, really—to kill too. There was not so much daring as a desire to gain daring from others, an unconscious wish or impulse to organize the total strength or will of those present into one strength or one will, sufficient to overcome the sheriff and inflict death upon his charge. It was strange—almost intellectually incomprehensible—and yet so it was. The men were plainly afraid of the determined sheriff. They thought something ought to be done, but they did not feel like getting into trouble.

Mathews, a large solemn, sage, brown man in worn clothes and a faded brown hat, contemplated the recent addition to his trailers with apparent indifference. Seemingly he was determined to protect his man and avoid mob justice, come what may. A mob should not have him if he had to shoot, and if he shot it would be to kill. Finally, since the company thus added to did not dash upon him, he seemingly decided to scare them off. Apparently he thought he could do this, since they trailed like calves.

"Stop a minute!" he called to his driver.

The latter pulled up. So did the crowd behind. Then the sheriff stood over the prostrate body of the negro, who lay in the jolting wagon beneath him, and called back:

"Go 'way from here, you people! Go on, now! I won't have you follerin' after me!"

"Give us the nigger!" yelled one in a half-bantering, half-derisive tone of voice.

"I'll give ye just two minutes to go on back out o' this road," returned the sheriff grimly, pulling out his watch and looking at it. They were about a hundred feet apart. "If you don't, I'll clear you out!"

"Give us the nigger!"

"I know you, Scott," answered Mathews, recognizing the voice. "I'll arrest every last one of ye tomorrow. Mark my word!"

The company listened in silence, the horses champing and twisting.

"We've got a right to foller," answered one of the men.

"I give ye fair warning," said the sheriff, jumping from his wagon and leveling his pistols as he approached. "When I count to five I'll begin to shoot!"

He was a serious and stalwart figure as he approached, and the crowd fell back a little.

"Git out o' this now'" he yelled. "One—Two—"

The company turned completely and retreated, Davies among them.

"We'll foller him when he gits further on," said one of the men in explanation.

"He's got to do it," said another—"Let him git a little ways ahead."

The sheriff returned to his wagon and drove on. He seemed, however, to realize that he would not be obeyed and that safety lay in traveling fast. If only he could lose them or get a good start he might possibly get to Clayton and the strong county jail by morning. His followers, however, trailed him swiftly as might be, determined not to be left behind.

"He's goin' to Baldwin," said one of the company of which Davies was a member.

"Where's that?" asked Davies.

"Over west o' here, about four miles."

"Why is he going there?"

"That's where he lives. I guess he thinks if he kin git 'im over there he kin purtect 'im till he kin get more help from Clayton. I cal'late he'll try an' take 'im over yet to-night, or early in the mornin' shore."

Davies smiled at the man's English. This country-side lingo always fascinated him.

Yet the men lagged, hesitating as to what to do. They did not want to lose sight of Mathews, and yet cowardice controlled them. They did not want to get into direct altercation with the law. It wasn't their place to hang the man, although plainly they felt that he ought to be hanged, and that it would be a stirring and exciting thing if he were. Consequently they desired to watch and be on hand—to get old Whitaker and his son Jake, if they could, who were out looking elsewhere. They wanted to see what the father and brother would do.

The quandary was solved by one of the men, who suggested that they could get to Baldwin by going back to Pleasant Valley and taking the Sand River Pike, and that in the meantime they might come upon Whitaker and his son en route, or leave word at his house. It was a shorter cut than this the sheriff was taking, although he would get there first now. Possibly they could beat him at least to Clayton, if he attempted to go on. The Clayton road was back via Pleasant Valley, or near it, and easily intercepted. Therefore, while one or two remained to trail the sheriff and give the alarm in case he did attempt to go on to Clayton, the rest, followed by Davies, set off at a gallop to Pleasant Valley. It was nearly dusk now when they arrived and stopped at the corner store—supper time. The fires of evening meals were marked by upcurling smoke from chimneys. Here, somehow, the zest to follow seemed to depart. Evidently the sheriff had worsted them for the night. Morg Whitaker, the father, had not been found; neither had Jake. Perhaps they had better eat. Two or three had already secretly fallen away.

They were telling the news of what had occurred so far to one of the two storekeepers who kept the place, when suddenly Jake Whitaker, the girl's brother, and several companions came riding up. They had been scouring the territory to the north of the town, and were hot and tired. Plainly they were unaware of the developments of which the crowd had been a part.

"The sheriff's got 'im!" exclaimed one of the company, with that blatance which always accompanies the telling of great news in small rural companies. "He taken him over to Baldwin in a wagon a coupla hours ago."

"Which way did he go?" asked the son, whose hardy figure, worn, hand-me-down clothes and rakish hat showed up picturesquely as he turned here and there on his horse.

"'Cross Seller Lane. You won't git 'em that-a-way, though, Jake. He's already over there by now. Better take the short cut."

A babble of voices now made the scene more interesting. One told how the negro had been caught, another that the sheriff was defiant, a third that men were still tracking him or over there watching, until all the chief points of the drama had been spoken if not heard.

Instantly suppers were forgotten. The whole customary order of the evening was overturned once more. The company started off on another excited jaunt, up hill and down dale, through the lovely country that lay between Baldwin and Pleasant Valley.

By now Davies was very weary of this procedure and of his saddle. He wondered when, if ever, this story was to culminate, let alone he write it. Tragic as it might prove, he could not nevertheless spend an indefinite period trailing a possibility, and yet, so great was the potentiality of the present situation, he dared not leave. By contrast with the horror impending, as he now noted, the night was so beautiful that it was all but poignant. Stars were already beginning to shine. Distant lamps twinkled like yellow eyes from the cottages in the valleys and on the hillsides. The air was fresh and tender. Some pea-fowls were crying afar off, and the east promised a golden moon.

Silently the assembled company trotted on—no more than a score in all. In the dusk, and with Jake ahead, it seemed too grim a pilgrimage for joking. Young Jake, riding silently toward the front, looked as if tragedy were all he craved. His friends seemed considerately to withdraw from him, seeing that he was the aggrieved.

After an hour's riding Baldwin came into view, lying in a sheltering cup of low hills. Already its lights were twinkling softly and there was still an air of honest firesides and cheery suppers about it which appealed to Davies in his hungry state. Still, he had no thought now of anything save this pursuit.

Once in the village, the company was greeted by calls of recognition. Everybody seemed to know what they had come for. The sheriff and his charge were still there, so a dozen citizens volunteered. The local storekeepers and loungers followed the cavalcade up the street to the sheriff's house, for the riders had now fallen into a solemn walk.

"You won't get him though, boys," said one whom Davies later learned was Seavey, the village postmaster and telegraph operator, a rather youthful person of between twenty-five and thirty, as they passed his door. "He's got two deputies in there with him, or did have, and they say he's going to take him over to Clayton."

At the first street corner they were joined by the several men who had followed the sheriff.

"He tried to give us the slip," they volunteered excitedly, "but he's got the nigger in the house, there, down in the cellar. The deputies ain't with him. They've gone somewhere for help—Clayton, maybe."

"How do you know?"

"We saw 'em go out that back way. We think we did, anyhow."

A hundred feet from the sheriff's little white cottage, which backed up against a sloping field, the men parleyed. Then Jake announced that he proposed to go boldly up to the sheriff's door and demand the negro.

"If he don't turn him out I'll break in the door an' take him!" he said.

"That's right! We'll stand by you, Whitaker," commented several.

By now the throng of unmounted natives had gathered. The whole village was up and about, its one street alive and running with people. Heads appeared at doors and windows. Riders pranced up and down, hallooing. A few revolver shots were heard. Presently the mob gathered even closer to the sheriff's gate, and Jake stepped forward as leader. Instead, however, of going boldly up to the door as at first it appeared he would, he stopped at the gate, calling to the sheriff.

"Hello, Mathews!"

"Eh, eh, eh!" bellowed the crowd.

The call was repeated. Still no answer. Apparently to the sheriff delay appeared to be his one best weapon.

Their coming, however, was not as unexpected as some might have thought. The figure of the sheriff was plainly to be seen close to one of the front windows. He appeared to be holding a double-barreled shotgun. The negro, as it developed later, was cowering and chattering in the darkest corner of the cellar, hearkening no doubt to the voices and firing of the revolvers outside.

Suddenly, and just as Jake was about to go forward, the front door of the house flew open, and in the glow of a single lamp inside appeared first the double-barreled end of the gun, followed immediately by the form of Mathews, who held the weapon poised ready for a quick throw to the shoulder. All except Jake fell back.

"Mr. Mathews," he called deliberately, "we want that nigger!"

"Well, you can't git 'em!" replied the sheriff. "He's not here."

"Then what you got that gun fer?" yelled a voice.

Mathews made no answer.

"Better give him up, Mathews," called another, who was safe in the crowd, "or we'll come in an' take him!"

"No you won't," said the sheriff defiantly. "I said the man wasn't here. I say it ag'in. You couldn't have him if he was, an' you can't come in my house! Now if you people don't want trouble you'd better go on away."

"He's down in the cellar!" yelled another.

"Why don't you let us see?" asked another.

Mathews waved his gun slightly.

"You'd better go away from here now," cautioned the sheriff. "I'm tellin' ye! I'll have warrants out for the lot o' ye, if ye don't mind!"

The crowd continued to simmer and stew, while Jake stood as before. He was very pale and tense, but lacked initiative.

"He won't shoot," called some one at the back of the crowd. "Why don't you go in, Jake, an' git him?"

"Sure! Rush in. That's it!" observed a second.

"He won't, eh?" replied the sheriff softly. Then he added in a lower tone, "The first man that comes inside that gate takes the consequences."

No one ventured inside the gate; many even fell back. It seemed as if the planned assault had come to nothing.

"Why not go around the back way?" called someone else.

"Try it!" replied the sheriff. "See what you find on that side! I told you you couldn't come inside. You'd better go away from here now before ye git into trouble," he repeated. "You can't come in, an' it'll only mean bloodshed."

There was more chattering and jesting while the sheriff stood on guard. He, however, said no more. Nor did he allow the banter, turmoil and lust for tragedy to disturb him. Only, he kept his eye on Jake, on whose movements the crowd seemed to hang.

Time passed, and still nothing was done. The truth was that, young Jake, put to the test, was not sufficiently courageous himself, for all his daring, and felt the weakness of the crowd behind him. To all intents and purposes he was alone, for he did not inspire confidence. He finally fell back a little, observing, "I'll git 'im before mornin', all right," and now the crowd itself began to disperse, returning to its stores and homes or standing about the post office and the one village drugstore. Finally, Davies smiled and came away. He was sure he had the story of a defeated mob. The sheriff was to be his great hero. He proposed to interview him later. For the present he meant to seek out Seavey, the telegraph operator, and arrange to file a message, then see if something to eat was not to be had somewhere.

After a time he found the operator and told him what he wanted—to write and file a story as he wrote it. The latter indicated a table in the little post office and telegraph station which he could use. He became very much interested in the reporter when he learned he was from the *Times,* and when Davies asked where he could get something to eat said he would run across the street and tell the proprietor of the only boarding-house to fix him something which he could consume as he wrote. He appeared to be interested in how a newspaper man would go about telling a story of this kind over a wire.

"You start your story," he said, "and I'll come back and see if I can get the *Times* on the wire."

Davies sat down and began his account. He was intent on describing things to date, the uncertainty and turmoil, the apparent victory of the sheriff. Plainly the courage of the latter had won, and it was all so picturesque. "A foiled lynching," he began, and as he wrote the obliging postmaster, who had by now returned, picked up the pages and carefully deciphered them for himself.

"That's all right. I'll see if I can get the *Times* now," he commented.

"Very obliging postmaster," thought Davies as he wrote, but he had so often encountered pleasant and obliging people on his rounds that he soon dropped that thought.

The food was brought, and still Davies wrote on, munching as he did so. In a little while the *Times* answered an often-repeated call.

"Davies at Baldwin," ticked the postmaster, "get ready for quite a story!"

"Let 'er go!" answered the operator at the *Times*, who had been expecting this dispatch.

As the events of the day formulated themselves in his mind, Davies wrote and turned over page after page. Between whiles he looked out through the small window before him where afar off he could see a lonely light twinkling against a hillside. Not in frequently he stopped his work to see if anything new was happening, whether the situation was in any danger of changing, but apparently it was not. He then proposed to remain until all possibility of a tragedy, this night anyhow, was eliminated. The operator also wandered about, waiting for an accumulation of pages upon which he could work but making sure to keep up with the writer. The two became quite friendly.

Finally, his dispatch nearly finished, he asked the postmaster to caution the night editor at K—— to the effect, that if anything more happened before one in the morning he would file it, but not to expect anything more as nothing might happen. The reply came that he was to remain and await developments. Then he and the postmaster sat down to talk.

About eleven o'clock, when both had about convinced themselves that all was over for this night anyhow, and the lights in the village had all but vanished, a stillness of the purest, summery-est, country-est quality having settled down, a faint beating of hoofs, which seemed to suggest the approach of a large cavalcade, could be heard out on the Sand River Pike as Davies by now had come to learn it was, back or northwest of the post-office. At the sound the postmaster got up, as did Davies, both stepping outside and listening. On it came, and as the volume increased, the former said, "Might be help for the sheriff, but I doubt it. I telegraphed Clayton six times to-day. They wouldn't come that way, though. It's the wrong road." Now, thought Davies nervously, after all there might be something to add to his story, and he had so wished that it was all over! Lynchings, as he now felt, were horrible things. He wished people wouldn't do such things—take the law, which now more than ever he respected, into their own hands. It was too brutal, cruel. That negro cowering there in the dark probably, and the sheriff all taut and tense, worrying over his charge and his duty, were not happy things to contemplate in the face of such a thing as this. It was true that the crime which had been committed was dreadful, but still why couldn't people allow the law to take its course? It was so much better. The law was powerful enough to deal with cases of this kind.

"They're comin' back, all right," said the postmaster solemnly, as he and Davies stared in the direction of the sound which grew louder from moment to moment.

"It's not any help from Clayton, I'm afraid."

"By George, I think you're right!" answered the reporter, something telling him that more trouble was at hand. "Here they come!"

As he spoke there was a clattering of hoofs and crunching of saddle girths as a large company of men dashed up the road and turned into the narrow street of the village, the figure of Jake Whitaker and an older bearded man in a wide black hat riding side by side in front.

"There's Jake," said the postmaster, "and that's his father riding beside him there. The old man's a terror when he gets his dander up. Sompin's sure to happen now."

Davies realized that in his absence writing, a new turn had been given to things. Evidently the son had returned to Pleasant Valley and organized a new posse or gone out to meet his father.

Instantly the place was astir again. Lights appeared in doorways and windows, and both were thrown open. People were leaning or gazing out to see what new movement was afoot.

Davies noted at once that there was none of the brash enthusiasm about this company such as had characterized the previous descent. There was grimness everywhere, and he now began to feel that this was the beginning of the end. After the cavalcade had passed down the street toward the sheriff's house, which was quite dark now, he ran after it, arriving a few moments after the former which was already in part dismounted. The townspeople followed. The sheriff, as it now developed, had not relaxed any of his vigilance, however; he was not sleeping, and as the crowd reappeared the light inside reappeared.

By the light of the moon, which was almost overhead, Davies was able to make out several of his companions of the afternoon, and Jake, the son. There were many more, though, now, whom he did not know, and foremost among them this old man.

The latter was strong, iron-gray, and wore a full beard. He looked very much like a blacksmith.

"Keep your eye on the old man," advised the postmaster, who had by now come up and was standing by.

While they were still looking, the old man went boldly forward to the little front porch of the house and knocked at the door. Some one lifted a curtain at the window and peeped out.

"Hello, in there!" cried the old man, knocking again.

"What do you want?" asked a voice.

"I want that nigger!"

"Well, you can't have him! I've told you people that once."

"Bring him out or I'll break down the door!" said the old man.

"If you do it's at your own risk. I know you, Whitaker, an' you know me. I'll give ye two minutes to get off that porch!"

"I want that nigger, I tell ye!"

"If ye don't git off that porch I'll fire through the door," said the voice solemnly. "One—Two—"

The old man backed cautiously away.

"Come out, Mathews!" yelled the crowd. "You've got to give him up this time. We ain't goin' back without him."

Slowly the door opened, as if the individual within were very well satisfied as to his power to handle the mob. He had done it once before this night, why not again? It revealed his tall form, armed with his shotgun. He looked around very stolidly, and then addressed the old man as one would a friend.

"Ye can't have him, Morgan," he said. "It's ag'in' the law. You know that as well as I do."

"Law or no law," said the old man, "I want that nigger!"

"I tell you I can't let you have him, Morgan. It's ag'in' the law. You know you oughtn't to be comin' around here at this time o' night actin' so."

"Well, I'll take him then," said the old man, making a move.

"Stand back!" shouted the sheriff, leveling his gun on the instant. "I'll blow ye into kingdom come, sure as hell!"

A noticeable movement on the part of the crowd ceased. The sheriff lowered his weapon as if he thought the danger were once more over.

"You-all ought to be ashamed of yerselves," he went on, his voice sinking to a gentle neighborly reproof, "tryin' to upset the law this way."

"The nigger didn't upset no law, did he?" asked one derisively.

"Well, the law's goin' to take care of the nigger now," Mathews made answer.

"Give us that scoundrel, Mathews, you'd better do it," said the old man. "It'll save a heap o' trouble."

"I'll not argue with ye, Morgan. I said ye couldn't have him an' ye can't. If ye want bloodshed, all right. But don't blame me. I'll kill the first man that tries to make a move this way."

He shifted his gun handily and waited. The crowd stood outside his little fence murmuring.

Presently the old man retired and spoke to several others. There was more murmuring, and then he came back to the dead line.

"We don't want to cause trouble, Mathews," he began explanatively, moving his hand oratorically, "but we think you ought to see that it won't do any good to stand out. We think that—"

Davies and the postmaster were watching young Jake, whose peculiar attitude attracted their attention. The latter was standing poised at the edge of the crowd, evidently seeking to remain unobserved. His eyes were on the sheriff, who was hearkening to the old man. Suddenly, as the father talked and when the sheriff seemed for a moment mollified and unsuspecting, he made a quick run for the porch. There was an intense movement all along the line as the life and death of the deed became apparent. Quickly the sheriff drew his gun to his shoulder. Both triggers were pressed at the same time, and the gun spoke, but not before Jake was in and under him. The latter had been in sufficient time to knock the gun barrel upward and fall upon his man. Both shots blazed harmlessly over the heads of the crowd in red puffs, and then followed a general onslaught. Men leaped the fence by tens and crowded upon the little cottage. They swarmed about every side of the house and crowded upon the porch, where four men were scuffling with the sheriff. The latter soon gave up, vowing vengeance and the law. Torches were brought, and a rope. A wagon drove up and was backed into the yard. Then began the calls for the negro.

As Davies contemplated all this he could not help thinking of the negro who during all this turmoil must have been crouching in his corner in the cellar, trembling for his fate. Now indeed he must realize that his end was near. He could not have dozed or lost consciousness during the intervening hours, but must have been cowering there, wondering and praying. All the while he must have been terrified lest the sheriff might not get him away in time. Now, at the sound of horses' feet and the new murmurs of contention, how must his body quake and his teeth chatter!

"I'd hate to be that nigger," commented the postmaster grimly, "but you can't do anything with 'em. The county oughta sent help."

"It's horrible, horrible!" was all Davies could say.

He moved closer to the house, with the crowd, eager to observe every detail of the procedure. Now it was that a number of the men, as eager in their search as bloodhounds, appeared at a low cellar entryway at the side of the house carrying a rope. Others followed with torches. Headed by father and son they began to descend into the dark hole. With impressive daring, Davies, who was by no means sure that he would be allowed but who was also determined if possible to see, followed.

Suddenly, in the farthest corner, he espied Ingalls. The latter in his fear and agony had worked himself into a crouching position, as if he were about to spring. His nails were apparently forced into the earth. His eyes were rolling, his mouth foaming.

"Oh, my Lawd, boss," he moaned, gazing almost as one blind, at the lights, "oh, my Lawd, boss, don't kill me! I won't do it no mo'. I didn't go to do it. I didn't mean to dis time. I was just drunk, boss. Oh, my Lawd! My Lawd!" His teeth chattered the while his mouth seemed to gape open. He was no longer sane really, but kept repeating monotonously, "Oh, my Lawd!"

"Here he is, boys! Pull him out," cried the father.

The negro now gave one yell of terror and collapsed, falling prone. He quite bounded as he did so, coming down with a dead chug on the earthen floor. Reason had forsaken him. He was by now a groveling, foaming brute. The last gleam of intelligence was that which notified him of the set eyes of his pursuers.

Davies, who by now had retreated to the grass outside before this sight, was standing but ten feet back when they began to reappear after seizing and binding him. Although shaken to the roots of his being, he still had all the cool observing powers of the trained and relentless reporter. Even now he noted the color values of the scene, the red, smoky heads of the torches, the disheveled appearance of the men, the scuffling and pulling. Then all at once he clapped his hands over his mouth, almost unconscious of what he was doing.

"Oh, my God!" he whispered, his voice losing power.

The sickening sight was that of the negro, foaming at the mouth, bloodshot as to his eyes, his hands working convulsively, being dragged up the cellar steps feet foremost. They had tied a rope about his waist and feet, and so had hauled him out, leaving his head to hang and drag. The black face was distorted beyond all human semblance.

"Oh, my God!" said Davies again, biting his fingers unconsciously.

The crowd gathered about now more closely than ever, more horror-stricken than gleeful at their own work. None apparently had either the courage or the charity to gainsay what was being done. With a kind of mechanical deftness now the negro was rudely lifted and like a sack of wheat thrown into the wagon. Father and son now mounted in front to drive and the crowd took to their horses, content to clatter, a silent cavalcade, behind. As Davies afterwards concluded, they were not so much hardened lynchers perhaps as curious spectators, the majority of them, eager for any variation— any excuse for one—to the dreary commonplaces of their existences. The task to most— all indeed—was entirely new. Wide-eyed and nerve-racked, Davies ran for his own horse and mounting followed. He was so excited he scarcely knew what he was doing.

Slowly the silent company now took its way up the Sand River Pike whence it had come. The moon was still high, pouring down a wash of silvery light. As Davies rode he wondered how he was to complete his telegram, but decided that he could not. When this was over there would be no time. How long would it be before they would really hang him? And would they? The whole procedure seemed so unreal, so barbaric that he could scarcely believe it—that he was a part of it. Still they rode on.

"Are they really going to hang him?" he asked of one who rode beside him, a total stranger who seemed however not to resent his presence.

"That's what they got 'im fer," answered the stranger.

And think, he thought to himself, to-morrow night he would be resting in his own good bed back in K——!

Davies dropped behind again and into silence and tried to recover his nerves. He could scarcely realize that he, ordinarily accustomed to the routine of the city, its hum-drum and at least outward social regularity, was a part of this. The night was so soft, the air so refreshing. The shadowy trees were stirring with a cool night wind. Why should anyone have to die this way? Why couldn't the people of Baldwin or elsewhere have bestirred themselves on the side of the law before this, just let it take its course? Both father and son now seemed brutal, the injury to the daughter and sister not so vital as all this. Still, also, custom seemed to require death in this way for this. It was like some axiomatic, mathematic law—hard, but custom. The silent company, an articulated, mechanical and therefore terrible thing, moved on. It also was axiomatic, mathematic. After a time he drew near to the wagon and looked at the negro again.

The latter, as Davies was glad to note, seemed still out of his sense. He was breathing heavily and groaning, but probably not with any conscious pain. His eyes were fixed and staring, his face and hands bleeding as if they had been scratched or trampled upon. He was crumpled limply.

But Davies could stand it no longer now. He fell back, sick at heart, content to see no more. It seemed a ghastly, murderous thing to do. Still the company moved on and he followed, past fields lit white by the moon, under dark, silent groups of trees through which the moonlight fell in patches, up low hills and down into valleys, until at last a little stream came into view, the same little stream, as it proved, which he had seen earlier to-day and for a bridge over which they were heading. Here it ran now, sparkling like electricity in the night. After a time the road drew closer to the water and then crossed directly over the bridge, which could be seen a little way ahead.

Up to this the company now rode and then halted. The wagon was driven up on the bridge, and father and son got out. All the riders, including Davies, dismounted, and a full score of them gathered about the wagon from which the negro was lifted, quite as one might a bag. Fortunately, as Davies now told himself, he was still unconscious, an accidental mercy. Nevertheless he decided now that he could not witness the end, and went down by the waterside slightly above the bridge. He was not, after all, the utterly relentless reporter. From where he stood, however, he could see long beams of iron projecting out over the water, where the bridge was braced, and some of the men fastening a rope to a beam, and then he could see that they were fixing the other end around the negro's neck.

Finally the curious company stood back, and he turned his face away.

"Have you anything to say?" a voice demanded.

There was no answer. The negro was probably lolling and groaning, quite as unconscious as he was before.

Then came the concerted action of a dozen men, the lifting of the black mass into the air, and then Davies saw the limp form plunge down and pull up with a creaking sound of rope. In the weak moonlight it seemed as if the body were struggling but he could not tell. He watched, wide-mouthed and silent, and then the body ceased moving. Then after a time he heard the company making ready to depart, and finally it did so, leaving him quite indifferently to himself and his thoughts. Only the black mass swaying in the pale light over the glimmering water seemed human and alive, his sole companion.

He sat down upon the bank and gazed in silence. Now the horror was gone. The suffering was ended. He was no longer afraid. Everything was summery and beautiful. The whole cavalcade had disappeared, the moon finally sank. His horse, tethered to a sapling beyond the bridge, waited patiently. Still he sat. He might now have hurried back to the small post office in Baldwin and attempted to file additional details of this story, providing he could find Seavey, but it would have done no good. It was quite too late, and anyhow what did it matter? No other reporter had been present, and he could write a fuller, sadder, more colorful story on the morrow. He wondered idly what had become of Seavey? Why had he not followed? Life seemed so sad, so strange, so mysterious, so inexplicable.

As he still sat there the light of morning broke, a tender lavender and gray in the east. Then came the roseate hues of dawn, all the wondrous coloring of celestial halls, to which the waters of the stream responded. The white pebbles shone pinkily at the bottom, the grass and sedges first black now gleamed a translucent green. Still the body hung there black and limp against the sky, and now a light breeze sprang up and stirred it visibly. At last he arose, mounted his horse and made his way back to Pleasant Valley, too full of the late tragedy to be much interested in anything else. Rousing his liveryman, he adjusted his difficulties with him by telling him the whole story, assuring him of his horse's care and handing him a five-dollar bill. Then he left, to walk and think again.

Since there was no train before noon and his duty plainly called him to a portion of another day's work here, he decided to make a day of it, idling about and getting additional details as to what further might be done. Who would cut the body down? What about arresting the lynchers—the father and son, for instance? What about the sheriff now? Would he act as he threatened? If he telegraphed the main fact of the lynching his city editor would not mind, he knew, his coming late, and the day here was so beautiful. He proceeded to talk with citizens and officials, rode out to the injured girl's home, rode to Baldwin to see the sheriff. There was a singular silence and placidity in that corner. The latter assured him that he knew nearly all of those who had taken part, and proposed to swear out warrants for them, but just the same Davies noted that he took his defeat as he did his danger, philosophically. There was no real activity in that corner later. He wished to remain a popular sheriff, no doubt.

It was sundown again before he remembered that he had not discovered whether the body had been removed. Nor had he heard why the negro came back, nor exactly how he was caught. A nine o'clock evening train to the city giving him a little more time for investigation, he decided to avail himself of it. The negro's cabin was two miles out along a pine-shaded road, but so pleasant was the evening that he decided to walk. En route, the last rays of the sinking sun stretched long shadows of budding trees across his path. It was not long before he came upon the cabin, a one-story affair set well back from the road and surrounded with a few scattered trees. By now it was quite dark. The ground between the cabin and the road was open, and strewn with the chips of a woodpile. The roof was sagged, and the windows patched in places, but for all that it had the glow of a home. Through the front door, which stood open, the blaze of a wood-fire might be seen, its yellow light filling the interior with a golden glow.

Hesitating before the door, Davies finally knocked. Receiving no answer he looked in on the battered cane chairs and aged furniture with considerable interest. It was a typical negro cabin, poor beyond the need of description. After a time a door in the rear of the room opened and a little negro girl entered carrying a battered tin lamp without any chimney. She had not heard his knock and started perceptibly at the sight of his figure in the doorway. Then she raised her smoking lamp above her head in order to see better, and approached.

There was something ridiculous about her unformed figure and loose gingham dress, as he noted. Her feet and hands were so large. Her black head was strongly emphasized by little pigtails of hair done up in white twine, which stood out all over her head. Her dark skin was made apparently more so by contrast with her white teeth and the whites of her eyes.

Davies looked at her for a moment but little moved now by the oddity which ordinarily would have amused him, and asked, "Is this where Ingalls lived?"

The girl nodded her head. She was exceedingly subdued, and looked as if she might have been crying.

"Has the body been brought here?"

"Yes, suh," she answered, with a soft negro accent.

"When did they bring it?"

"Dis moanin'."

"Are you his sister?"

"Yes, suh."

"Well can you tell me how they caught him? When did he come back, and what for?" He was feeling slightly ashamed to intrude thus.

"In de afternoon, about two."

"And what for?" repeated Davies.

"To see us," answered the girl. "To see my motha'."

"Well, did he want anything? He didn't come just to see her, did he?"

"Yes, suh," said the girl, "he come to say good-by. We doan know when dey caught him." Her voice wavered.

"Well, didn't he know he might get caught?" asked Davies sympathetically, seeing that the girl was so moved.

"Yes, suh, I think he did."

She still stood very quietly holding the poor battered lamp up, and looking down.

"Well, what did he have to say?" asked Davies.

"He didn' have nothin' much to say, suh. He said he wanted to see motha'. He was a-goin' away."

The girl seemed to regard Davies as an official of some sort, and he knew it.

"Can I have a look at the body?" he asked.

The girl did not answer, but started as if to lead the way.

"When is the funeral?" he asked.

"Tomorra'."

The girl then led him through several bare sheds of rooms strung in a row to the furthermost one of the line. This last seemed a sort of storage shed for odds and ends. It had several windows, but they were quite bare of glass and open to the moonlight save for a few wooden boards nailed across from the outside. Davies had been wondering all the while where the body was and at the lonely and forsaken air of the place. No one but this little pig-tailed girl seemed about. If they had any colored neighbors they were probably afraid to be seen here.

Now as he stepped into this cool, dark, exposed outer room, the desolation seemed quite complete. It was very bare, a mere shed or wash-room. There was the body in the middle of the room, stretched upon an ironing board which rested on a box and a chair, and covered with a white sheet. All the corners of the room were quite dark. Only its middle was brightened by splotches of silvery light.

Davies came forward, the while the girl left him, still carrying her lamp. Evidently she thought the moon lighted up the room sufficiently, and she did not feel equal to remaining. He lifted the sheet quite boldly, for he could see well enough, and looked at the still black form. The face was extremely distorted, even in death, and he could see where the rope had been tightened. A bar of cool moonlight lay just across the face and breast. He was still looking, thinking soon to restore the covering when a sound, half sigh, half groan, reached his ears.

At it he started as if a ghost had made it. It was so eerie and unexpected in this dark place. His muscles tightened. Instantly his heart went hammering like mad. His first impression was that it must have come from the dead.

"Oo-o-ohh!" came the sound again, this time whimpering as if someone were crying.

Instantly he turned, for now it seemed to come from a corner of the room, the extreme corner to his right, back of him. Greatly disturbed he approached, and then as his eyes strained he seemed to catch the shadow of something, the figure of a woman, perhaps, crouching against the walls, huddled up, dark, almost indistinguishable.

"Oh, oh, oh!" the sound now repeated itself, even more plaintively than before.

Davies began to understand. He approached slowly, then more swiftly desired to withdraw, for he was in the presence of an old black mammy, doubled up and weeping. She was in the very niche of the two walls, her head sunk on her knees, her body quite still. "Oh, oh, oh!" she repeated, as he stood there near her.

Davies drew silently back. Before such grief his intrusion seemed cold and unwarranted. The guiltlessness of the mother—her love—how could one balance that against the other? The sensation of tears came to his eyes. He instantly covered the dead and withdrew.

Out in the moonlight he struck a brisk pace, but soon stopped and looked back. The whole dreary cabin, with its one golden eye, the door, seemed such a pitiful thing. The weeping mammy, alone in her corner—and he had come back to say "Good-by!" Davies swelled with feeling. The night, the tragedy, the grief, he saw it all. But also with the cruel instinct of the budding artist that he already was, he was beginning to meditate on the character of story it would make—the color, the pathos. The knowledge now that it was not always exact justice that was meted out to all and that it was not so much the business of the writer to indict as to interpret was borne in on him with distinctness by the cruel sorrow of the mother, whose blame, if any, was infinitesimal.

"I'll get it all in!" he exclaimed feelingly, if triumphantly at last. "I'll get it all in!"

From *Free and Other Stories* (New York: Boni and Liveright, 1918), 76–111.

Carl Sandburg

1878–1967

Prize-winning U.S. poet, journalist, historian, folk-song collector, and biographer, Carl Sandburg was born in Galesburg, Illinois, the son of working-class Swedish immigrants. He left school after the eighth grade to go to work. When he was nineteen, Sandburg traveled as a hobo, working odd jobs through Iowa, Missouri, Kansas, Nebraska, and Colorado and absorbing the nuances of the American vernacular that would mark the distinctive voice of his poetry. The disparity between rich and poor that he saw on his travels contributed to his disenchantment with capitalism. When the Spanish American War broke out, Sandburg volunteered for the army, serving in Puerto Rico in July and August of 1898.

As a veteran, he received free tuition to Lombard College in Galesburg. He studied there until 1902, leaving without enough credits to graduate. While at Lombard, Sandburg joined the Poor Writers' Club, a literary organization whose founder, Professor Phillip Green Wright, encouraged the development of Sandburg's poetic talents and socialist views. While working as an organizer for the Wisconsin Social Democratic Party, he met Lilian Steichen, an active socialist and sister of the photographer Edward Steichen. The two married in 1908 and in 1912 moved to Chicago, where Sandburg began his career as an investigative reporter and editor.

Sandburg's first book of poetry, *Chicago Poems*, was published in 1916. While the book was generally well received, Sandburg's socialist themes (Amy Lowell saw the poetry as propaganda) and use of free-verse form startled many critics, who wondered if he were writing poetry at all. Another volume of poems, *Cornhuskers*, appeared in 1918. After a stint in Sweden as Eastern European correspondent for the Newspaper Enterprise Association, Sandburg returned to the *Daily News*, where he covered the building racial and labor unrest in Chicago during the summer of 1919. After Sandburg published two children's books, *Rootabaga Stories* (1922) and *Rootabaga Pigeons* (1923), his publisher suggested he write a juvenile biography of Abraham Lincoln, beginning the author's seventeen-year obsession with Lincoln. His two-volume biography for adults, *Abraham Lincoln: The Prairie Years* (1926), brought Sandburg's first financial success. In 1940, Sandburg won the Pulitzer Prize for his four-volume *Abraham Lincoln: The War Years* (1939). He published several other volumes of poetry, two collections of folk songs, a novel, a screenplay, and an autobiography. In 1951, he won another Pulitzer Prize for his *Complete Poems* (1950).

Sandburg once said that "a writer's silence on living issues can in itself constitute a propaganda of conduct leading toward the deterioration of freedom." Largely remembered as a folksy poet of the American vernacular and biographer of Lincoln, Sandburg was active in radical politics between 1905 and 1920, including his involvement with the Industrial Workers of the World (the most radical and racially progressive of the unions) and the Socialist Party. These affiliations are reflected in his series on conditions in Chicago's black belt. Collected in *The Chicago Race Riots, July* 1919, and first published two to three weeks before the riot, these articles document an impending crisis in race relations. In the spring of 1919, as riots broke out across the country from Arkansas to Washington, D.C., journalists in Chicago warned that inadequate housing, unemployment, and simmering animosity between Irish and black workers would lead to violence.

On Sunday morning, July 27, 1919, groups of whites and blacks had been competing for territory between the Twenty-sixth and Twenty-ninth Street beaches. When a group of African American teenagers swam across an imaginary segregation line, a white man began to stone them, and one boy, Eugene Williams, drowned. Officer Daniel Callahan refused to arrest the man whom blacks identified as causing the drowning, instead placing a black man under arrest for harassment. As the black child's body was being taken from the beach, rocks were thrown on both sides. The officer still refused to make any arrests. Fighting then spread across the borders of the black belt. After two weeks, the death toll included fifteen whites and thirty blacks (seven killed by the police). African American homes were burned, and the police arrested blacks at twice the rate of whites.

The excerpts here from *The Chicago Race Riots, July* 1919 give a picture of life inside the black belt drawn by a white reporter sympathetic to black civil rights issues. A striking feature of the series is Sandburg's willingness to make room for the voices of African Americans in his analysis; he quotes local residents and passages from the letters of southern blacks to the *Chicago Defender*. Recording the collective hatred of a mob out for the pleasure of a kill, Sandburg's poem, "Man, the Man Hunter," which follows, appeared in *Smoke and Steel*, a volume in which the inflection of the gratuitous violence of 1919 is clearly present, particularly in poems about the working class.

— Excerpts from — *The Chicago Race Riots, July 1919*

The Background

Chicago's "black belt," so called, to-day holds at least 125,000 persons. This is double the number that same district held five years ago, when the world war began.

Chicago is probably the third city in the United States in number of colored persons and, at the lowest, ranks as fifth in this regard, according to estimates of Frederick Rex, municipal reference librarian. The four cities that may possibly exceed Chicago in this population group are New York, which had 91,709 at the last census; Baltimore, with

84,749; Philadelphia, with 84,459; and Washington, with 94,466. The colored population in all these cities has increased since the last census.

New Orleans, which had 89,262, has decreased instead of gaining, and the same will apply to three other large southern cities where the colored population at the beginning of the war was slightly above 50,000 and just about equal to that of Chicago. These are Birmingham, Ala., Atlanta, Ga., and Memphis, Tenn., all reported to have decreased, while Chicago has gained.

During interviews with some forty persons more or less expert on the question the lowest estimate of the present colored population of Chicago was 100,000 and the highest 200,000. The figure most commonly agreed on was 125,000. There is no doubt that upward of 150,000 have arrived here. The number that have departed for other points is unknown.

Under the pressure of the biggest over-crowding problem any race or nation has faced in a Chicago neighborhood, the population of the district is spilling over, or rather is being irresistibly squeezed out into other residence districts.

Such is the immediately large and notable fact touching what is generally called "the race problem."

Other facts pertaining to the situation, each one indicating a trend of importance, are the following:

Local draft board No. 4 in a district surrounding State and 35th streets, containing 30,000 persons, of whom 90 per cent are colored, registered upward of 9,000 and sent 1,850 colored men to cantonments. Of these 1,850 there were only 125 rejections. On Nov. 11, when the armistice was declared, this district had 7,832 men passed by examiners and ready for the call to the colors. So it is clear that in one neighborhood are thousands of strong young men who have been talking to each other on topics more or less intimately related to the questions, "What are we ready to die for? Why do we live? What is democracy? What is the meaning of freedom; of self-determination?"

In barber shop windows and in cigar stores and haberdasheries are helmets, rifles, cartridges, canteens and haversacks and photographs of negro regiments that were sent to France.

Walk around this district and talk with the black folk and leaders of the black folk. Ask them, "What about the future of the colored people?" The reply that comes most often and the thought that seems uppermost is: "We made the supreme sacrifice; they didn't need any work or fight law for us; our record, like Old Glory, the flag we love because it stands for our freedom, hasn't got a spot on it; we 'come clean'; now we want to see our country live up to the constitution and the declaration of independence."

Soldiers, minister, lawyers, doctors, politicians, machinists, teamsters, day laborers—this is the inevitable outstanding thought they offer when consulted about tomorrow, next week, next year or the next century for the colored race in America. There is no approaching the matters of housing, jobs or political relations of the colored people to-day without taking consideration of their own vivid conception of what they consider their unquestioned Americanism.

They had one bank three years ago. Now they have five. Three co-operative societies to run stores are forming. Five new weekly papers, two new monthly magazines, seven drug stores, one hospital—all of these have come since Junius B. Wood's encyclopedic recital of negro activities in Chicago appeared in *The Daily News* in December, 1916. Also since then a life insurance company and a building and loan association have been organized. In one district where there were counted sixty-nine neighborhood agencies of demoralization there have been established within two years under negro auspices, a cafe, a drug store, a laundry, a bakery, a shoe repair shop, a tailor shop, a fish market, a dry goods store—all told, twenty-four constructive agencies entered the contest against sixty-nine of the destructive kind.

The colored people of Chicago seem to have more big organizations with fewer press agents and less publicity than any other group in the city. They have, for instance, the largest single protestant church membership in North America in the Olivet Baptist church at South Park avenue and East 31st street. It has more than 8,500 members. The "miscellaneous" local of the Meat Cutters and Butcher Workmen's union, at 43rd and State streets, reports that upward of 10,000 colored workmen are affiliated. The People's Movement club has moved into a $50,000 clubhouse, has 2,000 active and 6,000 associate members.

There is apparent an active home buying, home owning movement, with many circumstances indicating that the colored people coming in with the new influx are making preparations to stay, their viewpoint being that of the boll weevil in that famous negro song, "This'll Be My Home." In nearly all circles the opinion is voiced that Chicago is the most liberal all around town in the country, and the constitution of Illinois the most liberal of all state constitutions. And so if they can't make Chicago a good place for their people to live in the colored people wonder where they can go.

Their houses, jobs, politics, their hope and outlook in the "black belt," are topics to be considered in this series of articles.

After Each Lynching

Chicago is a receiving station that connects directly with every town or city where the people conduct a lynching.

"Every time a lynching takes place in a community down south you can depend on it that colored people from that community will arrive in Chicago inside of two weeks," says Secretary Arnold Hill of the Chicago Urban league, 3032 South Wabash avenue. "We have seen it happen so often that now whenever we read newspaper dispatches of a public hanging or burning in Texas or a Mississippi town, we get ready to extend greetings to people from the immediate vicinity of the scene of the lynching. If it is Arkansas or Georgia, where a series of lynchings is going on this week, then you may reckon with certainty that there will be large representations from those states among the colored folks getting off the trains at the Illinois Central station two or three weeks from to-day."

Better jobs, the right to vote and have the vote counted at elections, no Jim Crow cars, less race discrimination and a more tolerant attitude on the part of the whites, equal rights with white people in education—these are among the attractions that keep up the steady movement of colored people from southern districts to the north.

"Opportunity, not alms," is the slogan of the educated, while the same thought comes over and over again from the illiterate in their letters, saying, "All we want is a chanst," or, as one spells it, "Let me have a chanch, please."

Hundreds of letters written to The Chicago Defender, the newspaper, and to the Urban league reflect the causes of the migration. Charles Johnson, an investigator for the Carnegie foundation, a lieutenant from overseas with the 803d infantry, believes the economic motive is foremost. He says:

"There are several ways of arriving at a conclusion regarding the economic forces behind the movement of the colored race northward. The factors might be determined by the amount of unemployment or the extent of poverty. These facts are important, but may or may not account for individual action.

"Except in a few localities of the south there was no actual misery or starvation. Nor is it evident that those who left would have perished from want had they remained. Large numbers of negroes have frequently moved around from state to state and even within the states of the south in search of more remunerative employment. The migrations to Arkansas and Oklahoma were expressions of the economic force.

"A striking feature of the northern migration was its individualism. Motives prompting the thousands of negroes were not always the same, not even in the case of close neighbors. The economic motive was foremost, a desire simply to improve their living standards when opportunity beckoned. A movement to the west or even about the south could have proceeded from the same cause.

"Some of the letters reveal a praiseworthy solicitude for their families on the part of the writers. Other letters are an index to poverty and helplessness of home communities.

"In this type of migration the old order is strangely reversed. Instead of leaving an overdeveloped and overcrowded country for undeveloped new territory, they have left the south, backward as it is in development of its resources, for the highly industrialized north. Out of letters from the south we listed seventy-nine different occupations among 1,000 persons asking for information and aid. Property holders, impecunious adventurers, tradesmen, entire labor unions, business and professional men, families, boys and girls, all registered their protests, mildly but determinately, against their homes and sought to move."

From Pensacola, Fla., in May, 1917, came a letter saying, "Would you please let me know what is the price of boarding and rooming in Chicago and where is the best place to get a job before the draft will work? I would rather join the army 1,000 times up there than to join it once down here."

"What I want to say is I am coming north," wrote another, "and thought I would write you and list a few of the things I can do and see if you can find a place for me anywhere north of the Mason and Dixon line, and I will present myself in person at your office as soon as I hear from you. I am now employed in the R.R. shops at Memphis. I am an engine watchman, hostler, rod cup man, pipe fitter, oil house man, shipping clerk, telephone lineman, freight caller, an expert soaking vat man who can make dope for packing hot boxes on engines. I am capable of giving satisfaction in either of the above-named positions."

"I wish very much to come north," wrote a New Orleans man. "Anywhere in Illinois will do if I am away from the lynchmen's noose and the torchmen's fire. We are firemen, machinist helpers, practical painters and general laborers. And most of all, ministers of the gospel who are not afraid of labor, for it put us where we are."

"I want to ask you for information as to what steps I should take to secure a good position as a first class automobeal blacksmith or any kind pertaining to such," is an inquiry from a large Georgia city. "I have been operating a first class white shop here for quite a number of years, and if I must say, the only colored man in the city that does. Any charges, why notify me, but do not publish my name."

"Please don't publish this in any paper," and "I would not like for my name to be published in the paper," are requests that accompanied two letters from communities where lynchings had occurred.

From *The Chicago Race Riots, July 1919* (1919; reprint, New York: Harcourt, Brace and World, 1969), 7–11, 31–35.

—— Man, the Man-Hunter ——

I saw Man, the man-hunter,
Hunting with a torch in one hand
And a kerosene can in the other,
Hunting with guns, ropes, shackles.

   I listened
   And the high cry rang.
The high cry of Man, the man-hunter:
We'll get you yet, you sbxyzch!

   I listened later.
   The high cry rang.
Kill him! Kill him! the sbxyzch!

In the morning the sun saw
Two butts of something, a smoking rump,
And a warning in charred wood.
   Well, we got him,
   The sbxyzch.

From *Smoke and Steel* (New York: Harcourt, Brace and Howe, 1920), 48.

Mary Powell Burrill

1879–1946

Mary Powell Burrill was an outspoken antilynching activist and advocate for the rights of African American women. Born in Washington, D.C., Burrill graduated from the famous M Street School (later named Dunbar High School) in Washington, then continued her studies at Emerson College in Boston. After receiving her diploma in 1904, Burrill returned to Washington to teach drama at M Street School and to serve as director of the Washington Conservatory of Music's School of Expression. A close friend (and according to Gloria Hull, at one time a lover) of Angelina Weld Grimké, Burrill was for twenty-five years the companion of Lucy Diggs Slowe, dean of women at Howard University.

Over the years, Burrill staged numerous dramatic productions throughout the Washington area. Her published plays were radical in their racial and gender politics. In her 1919 play *They That Sit in Darkness*, an impoverished mother dies from bearing too many children, forcing her eldest daughter to give up her college scholarship and her future to raise her siblings. The play appeared in a special issue of Margaret Sanger's *Birth Control Review* on "The Negroes' Need for Birth Control, As Seen by Themselves," along with Angelina Weld Grimké's short story "The Closing Door," in which a mother kills her baby boy to save him from the possibility of being lynched when he is older.

First published in 1919, *Aftermath* shows the reaction of a black soldier when he returns from France to rural South Carolina to find that, while he was away, his father has been lynched over a wage dispute. Most antilynching plays were written by women, and many, like *Aftermath*, were written in support of the NAACP's campaign for antilynching legislation. *Aftermath* was produced as part of the competition in the David Belasco Sixth Annual Little Theatre Tournament on May 8, 1928, in New York City as part of a collaborative effort between the Krigwa Players Little Negro Theatre and the Workers' Drama League. The white producers decided to change the play's ending without consulting the author. Burrill was angered by the new ending, in which John is shot offstage and then staggers back to die, because it twisted the message of militancy her play was meant to project.

— Aftermath —

Characters

MILLIE, *a young woman*

MAM SUE, *an old woman*

REV. LUKE MOSEBY, *a clergyman*

LONNIE, *a young man*

MRS. HAWKINS, *a friend*

JOHN, *a soldier*

TIME: *The present*

PLACE: *The Thornton cabin in South Carolina*

It is late afternoon of a cool day in early spring. A soft afterglow pours in at the little window of the Thornton cabin. The light falls on MILLIE, *a slender brown girl of sixteen, who stands near the window, ironing. She wears a black dress and a big gingham apron. A clothes-horse weighted down with freshly ironed garments is nearby. In the rear there is a door leading out to the road. To the left, another door leads into the other room of the cabin. To the right there is a great stone hearth blackened by age. A Bible rests on the mantel over the hearth. An old armchair and a small table on which is a kerosene lamp are near the hearth. In the center of the room sits a well-scrubbed kitchen table and a substantial wooden chair. In front of the hearth, in a low rocking chair drawn close to the smouldering woodfire, sits* MAM SUE *busily sewing. The many colors in the old patchwork quilt that she is mending, together with the faded red of the bandanna on her head, contrast strangely with her black dress. Mam Sue is very old. Her ebony face is seamed with wrinkles; and in her bleared, watery eyes there is a world-old sorrow. A service flag containing one star hangs in the little window of the cabin.*

MAM SUE: (*Crooning the old melody*)

    O, yes, yonder comes mah Lawd,

    He is comin' dis way

    Wid his sword in his han'

    O, yes, yonder comes—

(*A burning log falls apart, and Mam Sue suddenly stops singing and gazes intently at the fire. She speaks in deep mysterious tones to Millie, who has finished her task and has come to the hearth to put up her irons.*) See dat log dah, Millie? De one fallin' tuh de side dah wid de big flame lappin' 'round hit? Dat means big doin's 'round heah tonight!

MILLIE: (*With a start*) Oh Mam Sue, don' you go proph'sying no mo'! You seen big doing's in dat fire de night befo' them w'ite devuls come in heah an' tuk'n po' dad out and bu'nt him!"

MAM SUE: (*Calmly*) No Millie, Ah didn' see no big doin's dat night—Ah see'd evul doin's an' Ah tole yo' po' daddy to keep erway f'om town de nex' day wid his cotton. Ah jes knowed dat he wuz gwine to git in a row wid dem w'ite debbils—but he wou'd'n lis'n tuh his ole mammy—De good Lawd sen' me deses warnin's in dis fiah, jes lak He sen' His messiges in de fiah to Moses. Yo' chillun bettah lis'n to—

MILLIE: (*Nervously*) Oh, Mam Sue, you skeers me when you talks erbout seein' all them things in de fire—

MAM SUE: Yuh gits skeered cause yuh don' put yo' trus' in de good Lawd! He kin tek keer o' yuh no mattuh whut com'!

MILLIE: (*Bitterly*) Sometimes I thinks that Gawd's done fu'got us po' cullud people. Gawd didn' tek no keer o' po' dad and *he* put *his* trus' in Him! He useter set evah night by dis fire at dis here table and read his Bible an' pray—but jes' look whut happen' to dad! That don' look like Gawd wuz tekin' keer—

MAM SUE: (*Sharply*) Heish yo' mouf, Millie! Ah ain't a-gwine to 'ave dat sinner-talk 'roun' hyeah! (*Derisively*) Gawd don't tek no keer o' yuh? Ain't yuh bin prayin' night an' mawnin' fo' Gawd to sen' yo' brudder back f'om de war 'live an' whole? An' ain't yuh git dat lettah no longer'n yistiddy sayin' dat de fightin's all done stopp't an' dat de blessid Lawd's done brung yo' brudder thoo all dem battuls live an' whole? Don' dat look lak de Lawd's done 'membered yuh?

MILLIE: (*Thoughtfully*) I reckon youse right, Mam Sue. But ef anything had a-happen' to John I wuz' nevah going to pray no mo'!

(*Millie goes to the clothes-horse and folds the garments and lays them carefully into a large basket. Mam Sue falls again to her crooning.*)

MAM SUE:

O, yes, yonder comes mah Lawd,
He's comin' dis way-a.

MILLIE: Lonnie's so late gittin' home tonight; I guess I'd bettah tek Mis' Hart's wash home tonight myse'f.

MAM SUE: Yas, Lonnie's mighty late. Ah reckons you'd bettah slip erlon' wid hit. (*Millie gets her hat from the adjoining room and is about to leave with the basket when Mam Sue calls significantly.*) Millie?

MILLIE: Yas, Mam Sue.

MAM SUE: (*Firmly*) Don' yo' fu'git to drap dat lettah fu' John in de Pos' Awfus ez yuh goes by. Whah's de lettah?

MILLIE: (*Reluctantly*) But, Mam Sue, please don' let's—

(*A knock is heard. Millie opens the door and REV. LUKE MOSEBY enters. Moseby is a wiry little old man with a black, kindly face, and bright, searching eyes; his woolly hair and beard are snow-white. He is dressed in a rusty black suit with a coat of clerical cut that comes to his knees. In one hand he carries a large Bible, and in the other, a stout walking stick.*)

MILLIE: Good evenin', Brother Moseby, come right in.

MOSEBY: Good eben', Millie. Good eben', Mam Sue. Ah jes drap't in to see ef you-all is still trus'in de good Lawd an'—

MAM SUE: Lor', Brudder Moseby, ain't Ah bin trus'n de good Lawd nigh onter dese eighty yeah! Whut fu' yuh think Ah's agwine to quit w'en Ah'm in sight o' de Promis' Lan'? Millie, fetch Brudder Moseby dat cheer.

MOSEBY: (*Drawing his chair to the fire*) Dat's right, Mam Sue, you jes a-keep on trus'n an prayin' an evahthing's gwine to come aw-right. (*Observing Millie is about to leave*) Don lemme 'tain yuh, Millie, but whut's all dis good news wese bin heahin' bout yo' brudder John? Dey say he's done won some kind o' medal ober dah in France?

MILLIE: (*Brightening up*) Oh, yes, we got a lettah day befo' yestiddy f'om John tellin us all erbout it. He's won de War Cross! He fought off twenty Germuns all erlone an' saved his whole comp'ny an the gret French Gen'rul come an' pinned de medal on him, hisse'f.

MOSEBY: De Lawd bles' his soul! Ah know'd dat boy wud mek good!

MILLIE: (*Excited by the glory of it all*) An' he's been to Paris, an' the fines' people stopp't him when they seen his medal, an' shook his han' an' smiled at him—an' he kin go evahwhere, an' dey ain't nobody all the time a-lookin' down on him, an' a-sneerin' at him 'cause he's black; but evahwhere they's jes gran' to him! An' he sez it's the firs' time evah in his life he's felt lak a real, sho-nuf man!

MOSEBY: Well, honey don't de Holy Book say, "De fust shill be las' and the las' shill be fust"?

MAM SUE: (*Fervently*) Dat hit do! An' de Holy Book ain't nebber tole no lie!

MOSEBY: Folks ober in Char'ston is sayin' dat some sojers is gwine to lan' dah today or tomorrer. Ah reckons day'll all be comin' 'long soon now dat de war's done stopp't.

MILLIE: I jes hates the thought of John comin' home an' hearin' 'bout Dad!

MOSEBY: (*In astonishment*) Whut! Yuh mean to say yuh ain't 'rite him 'bout yo' daddy, yit?

MAM SUE: Dat she ain't! Millie mus' 'ave huh way! She 'lowed huh brudder ough'n be tole, an' dat huh could keep on writin' to him jes lak huh dad wuz livin'—Millie allus done de writin'—An' Ah lets huh 'ave huh way—

MOSEBY: (*Shaking his head in disapproval*) Yuh mean tuh say—

MILLIE: (*Pleading*) But, Brother Moseby, I couldn't write John no bad news w'ilst he wuz way over there by hisse'f. He had 'nuf to worry him with death a'-starin' him in the face evah day!

MAM SUE: Yas, Brudder Moseby, Millie's bin carryin' on dem lies in huh lettahs fu' de las' six months; but today Ah jes sez to huh—Dis war done stopp't now, an' John, he gwine to be comin' home soon, an' he ain't agwine to come hyeah an' fin' me wid no lie on mah soul! An' Ah med huh set down an' tell him de whole truf. She's gwine out to pos' dat lettah dis minute.

MOSEBY: (*Still disapproving*) No good nebber come—

(*The door is pushed violently open, and* LONNIE, *a sturdy black boy of eighteen, rushes in breathlessly.*)

LONNIE: Mam Sue! Millie! Whut'da yuh think? John's come home!

MILLIE: (*Speechless with astonishment*) John? Home? Where's he at?

MAM SUE: (*Incredulously*) Whut yuh sayin'? John done come home? Bles' de Lawd! Bles' de Lawd! Millie, didn' Ah tell yuh sumpin wuz gwine tuh happen?

LONNIE: (*Excitedly*) I wuz sweepin' up de sto' jes befo' leavin' an' de phone rung—it wuz John—he wuz at Char'ston—jes landid! His comp'ny's waitin' to git de ten o'clock train fu' Camp Reed, whah dey's goin' to be mustered out.

MOSEBY: But how's he gwine to get erway?

LONNIE: Oh, good evenin', Brother Moseby, Ise jes so 'cited I didn' see yuh—Why his Cap'n done give him leave to run over heah 'tell de train's ready. He ought tuh be heah now 'cause it's mos' two hours sence he wuz talkin'—

MAM SUE: Whuffo yuh so long comin' home an' tellin' us?

LONNIE: *(Hesitatingly)* I did start right out but when I git to Sherley's corner I seen a whole lot of them w'ite hoodlums hangin' 'round de feed sto'—I jes felt like dey wuz jes waitin' dah to start sumpin, so I dodged 'em by tekin' de long way home.

MILLIE: Po' Lonnie! He's allus dodgin' po' w'ite trash!

LONNIE: *(Sullenly)* Well, yuh see whut Dad got by not dodgin' 'em.

MOSEBY: *(Rising to go)* Ah mus' be steppin' long now. Ah got to stop in to see ole man Hawkins; he's mighty sick. Ah'll drap in on mah way back fu' a word o' prayer wid John.

MAM SUE: Lonnie, yu'd bettah run erlon' as Brudder Moseby go an tote dat wash tuh Mis' Ha't. An drap in Mis' Hawkins' sto' an git some soap an' starch; an' Ah reckons yu'd bettah bring me a bottle o' linnimint—dis ole pain done come back in mah knee. *(To Moseby)* Good eben, Brudder Moseby.

MOSEBY: Good eben, Mam Sue; Good eben, Millie, an' Gawd bles' yuh.

LONNIE: *(As he is leaving)* Tell John I'll git back fo' he leaves.

(Lonnie and Moseby leave. Millie closes the door behind them and then goes to the window and looks out anxiously.)

MILLIE: *(Musingly)* Po' John! Po' John! *(Turning to Mam Sue)* Mam Sue?

MAM SUE: Yas, Millie.

MILLIE: *(Hesitatingly)* Who's goin' to tell John 'bout Dad?

MAM SUE: *(Realizing for the first time that the task must fall to someone)* Dunno. Ah reckons yu'd bettah.

MILLIE: *(Going to Mam Sue and kneeling softly at her side)* Mam Sue, don' let's tell him now! He's got only a li'l hour to spen' with us—an' it's the firs' time fu' so long! John loved Daddy so! Let 'im be happy jes a li'l longer—we kin tell 'im the truth when he comes back fu' good. Please, Mam Sue!

MAM SUE: *(Softened by Millie's pleading)* Honey chile, John gwine to be askin' for his daddy fust thing—dey ain't no way—

MILLIE: *(Gaining courage)* Oh, yes, 'tis! We kin tell 'im Dad's gone to town—anything, jes so's he kin spen' these few li'l minutes in peace! I'll fix the Bible jes like Dad's been in an' been a-readin' in it! He won't know no bettah!

(Millie takes the Bible from the mantel and opening it at random lays it on the table; she draws the old armchair close to the table as her father had been wont to do every evening when he read his Bible.)

MAM SUE: *(Shaking her head doubtfully)* Ah ain't much on actin' dis lie, Millie.

(The soft afterglow fades and the little cabin is filled with shadows. Millie goes again to the window and peers out. Mam Sue falls again to her crooning.)

MAM SUE: *(Crooning)*:

    O, yes, yonder comes mah Lawd,

He's comin' dis way
Wid his sword in his han'—

(To Millie) Millie, bettah light de lamp, it's gittin' dark.

He's gwine ter hew dem sinners down
Right lebbal to de groun'
O, yes, yonder comes mah Lawd—

(As Millie is lighting the lamp, whistling is heard in the distance. Millie listens intently, then rushes to the window. The whistling comes nearer; it rings out clear and familiar—"Though the boys are far away, they dream of home.")

MILLIE: *(Excitedly)* That's him! That's John, Mam Sue!

(Millie rushes out of doors. The voices of JOHN and Millie are heard from without in greetings. Presently, John and Millie enter the cabin. John is tall and straight—a good soldier and a strong man. He wears the uniform of a private in the American Army. One hand is clasped in both of Millie's. In the other, he carries an old-fashioned valise. The War Cross is pinned on his breast. On his sleeve three chevrons tell mutely of wounds suffered in the cause of freedom. His brown face is aglow with life and the joy of homecoming.)

JOHN: *(Eagerly)* Where's Dad? Where's Mam Sue?

MAM SUE: *(Hobbling painfully to meet him)* Heah's ole Mam Sue! *(John takes her tenderly in his arms)* Bles' yo' heart, chile, bles' yo' heart! Tuh think dat de good Lawd's done lemme live to see dis day!

JOHN: Dear old Mam Sue! Gee, but I'm glad to see you an' Millie again!

MAM SUE: Didn' Ah say dat yuh wuz comin' back hyeah?

JOHN: *(Smiling)* Same old Mam Sue with huh faith an' huh prayers. But where's Dad? *(He glances toward the open Bible)* He's been in from de field, ain't he?

MILLIE: *(Without lifting her eyes)* Yes, he's come in but he had to go out ag'in—to Sherley's feed sto'.

JOHN: *(Reaching for his cap that he has tossed upon the table)* That ain't far. I've jes a few minutes so I'd bettah run down there an' hunt him up. Won't he be surprised!

MILLIE: *(Confused)* No—no, John—I fu'got; he ain't gone to Sherley's, he's gone to town.

JOHN: *(Disappointed)* To town? I hope he'll git in befo I'm leavin'. There's no tellin' how long they'll keep me at Camp Reed. Where's Lonnie?

MAM SUE: Lonnie's done gone to Mis' Ha't's wid de wash. He'll be back toreckly.

MILLIE: *(Admiring the medal on his breast)* An' this is the medal? Tell us all erbout it, John.

JOHN: Oh, Sis, it's an awful story—wait 'til I git back fu' good. Let's see whut I've got in dis bag fu' you. *(He places the worn valise on the table and opens it. He takes out a bright-colored dress pattern)* That's fu' you, Millie, and quit wearin' them black clothes.

(Millie takes the silk and hugs it eagerly to her breast; suddenly there sweeps into her mind the realization that she cannot wear it, and the silk falls to the floor)

MILLIE: *(Trying to be brave)* Oh, John, it's jes lovely! *(As she shows it to Mam Sue)* Look, Mam Sue!

JOHN: *(Flourishing a bright shawl)* An this is fu' Mam Sue. Mam Sue'll be so gay!

MAM SUE: (*Admiring the gift*) Who'd evah b'lieved dat yo' ole Mam Sue would live to be wearin' clo'es whut huh gran'chile done brung huh f'om Eu'ope!

JOHN. Never you mind, Mam Sue, one of these days I'm goin to tek you an' Millie over there, so's you kin breathe free jes once befo' yuh die.

MAM SUE: It's got tuh be soon, 'cause dis ole body's mos' wo'e out; an de good Lawd s gwine to be callin' me to pay mah debt 'fo' long.

JOHN: (*Showing some handkerchiefs, with gay borders*) These are fu' Lonnie. (*He next takes out a tiny box that might contain a bit of jewelry.*) An this is fu' dad. Sum'pin he's been wantin' fu' years. I ain't goin' to open it 'till he comes.

(*Millie walks into the shadows and furtively wipes a tear from her eyes.*)

JOHN: (*Taking two army pistols from his bag and placing them on the table*)An' these las' are fu' youahs truly.

MILLIE: (*Looking at them, fearfully*) Oh, John, are them youahs?

JOHN: One of' 'em's mine; the other's my Lieutenant's. I've been cleanin' it fu' him. Don' tech 'em—'cause mine's loaded.

MILLIE: (*Still looking at them in fearful wonder*) Did they learn yuh how to shoot 'em?

JOHN: Yep, an' I kin evah mo' pick 'em off!

MILLIE: (*Reproachfully*) Oh, John!

JOHN: Nevah you worry, li'l Sis, John's nevah goin' to use 'em less it's right fu' him to. (*He places the pistols on the mantel—on the very spot where the Bible has lain.*) My! but it's good to be home! I've been erway only two years but it seems like two cent'ries. All that life ovah there seems like some awful dream!

MAM SUE: (*Fervently*) Ah know it do! Many's de day yo' ole Mam Sue set in dis cheer an' prayed fu' yuh.

JOHN: Lots of times, too, in the trenches when I wuz dog-tired, an' sick, an' achin' wid the cold I uster say: well, if we're sufferin' all this for the oppressed, like they tell us, then Mam Sue, an' Dad, an Millie come in on that—they'll git some good ou'n it if I don't! An' I'd shet my eyes an' fu'git the cold, an' the pain, an' them old guns spit-tin' death all 'round us; an' see you folks settin' here by this fire—Mam Sue, noddin', an' singin'; Dad a spellin' out his Bible—(*He glances toward the open book.*) Let's see whut he's been readin'— (*John takes up the Bible and reads the first passage upon which his eye falls.*) "But I say unto you, love your enemies, bless them that curse you, an' do good to them that hate you"—(*He lets the Bible fall to the table.*) That ain't the dope they been feedin' us soljers on! "Love your enemies?" It's been—git a good aim at 'em, an' let huh go!

MAM SUE: (*Surprised*) Honey, Ah hates to hyeah yuh talkin' lak dat! It sound lak yuh done fu'git yuh Gawd!

JOHN: No, Mam Sue, I ain't fu'got God, but I've quit thinkin' that prayers kin do ever'thing. I've seen a whole lot sence I've been erway from here. I've seen some men go into battle with a curse on their lips, and I've seen them same men come back with never a scratch; an' I've seen men whut read their Bibles befo' battle, an' prayed to live, left dead on the field. Yes, Mam Sue, I've seen a heap an' I've done a tall lot o' thinkin' sence I've been erway from here. An' I b'lieve it's jes like this—beyon' a certain point prayers ain't no good! The Lawd does jes so much for you, then it's up to you to do the res' fu' yourse'f. The Lawd's done His part when He's done give me strength an' courage; I got tuh do the res' fu' myse'f!

MAM SUE: (*Shaking her head*) Ah don' lak dat kin' o' talk—it don' bode no good.

(*The door opens and Lonnie enters with packages. He slips the bolt across the door.*)

JOHN: (*Rushing to Lonnie and seizing his hand*) Hello, Lonnie, ole man!

LONNIE: Hello, John, gee, but Ah'm glad tuh see yuh!

JOHN: Boy, you should 'ave been with me! It would 'ave taken some of the skeeriness out o' yuh, an' done yuh a worl' o' good.

LONNIE: (*Ignoring John's remark*) Here's the soap an' starch, Millie.

MAM SUE: Has yuh brung mah linimint?

LONNIE: Yassum, it's in de packige.

MILLIE: (*Unwrapping the package*) No, it ain't, Lonnie.

LONNIE: Mis' Hawkins give it tuh me. Ah mus' a lef' it on de counter. Ah'll git it w'en Ah goes to de train wid John.

MILLIE: (*Showing him the handkerchief*) See whut John done brought you! An' look on de mantel! (*Pointing to the pistols*)

LONNIE: (*Drawing back in fear as he glances at the pistols*) You'd bettah hide them things! No cullud man bettah be seen wid dem things down heah!

JOHN: That's all right, Lonnie, nevah you fear. I'm goin' to keep 'em an' I ain't a-goin' to hide 'em either. See them. (*Pointing to the wound chevrons on his arm*) Well, when I got them wounds, I let out all the rabbit-blood 'at wuz in me! (*Defiantly*) Ef I kin be trusted with a gun in France, I kin be trusted with one in South Car'lina.

MAM SUE: (*Sensing trouble*) Millie, yu'd bettah fix some suppah fu' John.

JOHN: (*Looking at his watch*) I don' want a thing. I've got to be leavin' in a little while. I'm 'fraid I'm goin' to miss Dad after all.

(*The knob of the door is turned as though someone is trying to enter. Then there is a loud knock on the door.*)

JOHN: (*Excitedly*) That's Dad! Don't tell him I'm here!

(*John tips hurriedly into the adjoining room. Lonnie unbolts the door and* MRS. SELENA HAWKINS *enters.*)

MRS. HAWKINS: Lonnie fu'got de liniment so I thought I' bettah run ovah wid hit, 'cause when Mam Sue sen' fu' dis stuff she sho' needs hit. Brudder Moseby's been tellin' me dat John's done come home.

JOHN: (*Coming from his hiding place and trying to conceal his disappointment*) Yes, I'm here. Good evenin' Mis' Hawkins. Glad to see you.

MRS. HAWKINS: (*Shaking hands with John*) Well, lan' sakes alive! Ef it ain't John sho' nuf! An' ain't he lookin' gran'! Jes look at dat medal a-shinin' on his coat! Put on yuh cap, boy, an' lemme see how yuh look!

JOHN: Sure! (*John puts on his overseas cap and, smiling, stands at attention a few paces off, while Mam Sue, Lonnie, and Millie form an admiring circle around him.*)

MRS. HAWKINS: Now don' he sholy look gran'! I knows yo' sistah an' gran' mammy's proud o' yuh! (*A note of sadness creeps into her voice.*) Ef only yuh po' Daddy had a-lived to see dis day!

(*John looks at her in amazement. Millie and Mam Sue stand transfixed with terror over the sudden betrayal.*)

JOHN: (*Looking from one to the other and repeating her words as though he can scarcely realize their meaning*) "Ef your po' Daddy had lived—" (*To Millie*) Whut does this mean?

(*Millie sinks sobbing into the chair at the table and buries her face in her hands.*)

MRS. HAWKINS: Lor' Millie, I thought you'd tole him!

(*Bewildered by the catastrophe that she has precipitated, Mrs. Hawkins slips out of the cabin.*)

JOHN: (*Shaking Millie almost roughly*) Come, Millie, have you been lyin' to me? Is Dad gone?

MILLIE: (*Through her sobs*) I jes hated to tell you—you wuz so far erway—

JOHN: (*Nervously*) Come, Millie, for God's sake don' keep me in this su'pense! I'm a brave soldier—I kin stan' it—did he suffer much? Wuz he sick long?

MILLIE: He wuzn't sick no time—them w'ite devuls come in heah an' dragged him—

JOHN: (*Desperately*) My God! You mean they lynched Dad?

MILLIE: (*Sobbing piteously*) They burnt him down by the big gum tree!

JOHN: (*Desperately*) Whut fu', Millie? Whut fu'?

MILLIE: He got in a row wid ole Mister Withrow 'bout the price of cotton—an' he called Dad a liar an' struck him—an' Dad he up an' struck him back—

JOHN: (*Brokenly*) Didn' they try him? Didn' they give him a chance? Whut'd the Sheriff do? An' the Gov'nur?

MILLIE: (*Through her sobs*) They didn't do nothin'!

JOHN: Oh, God! Oh, God! (*Then recovering [from his] first bitter anguish and speaking*) So they've come into ouah home, have they! (*He strides over to Lonnie and seizes him by the collar.*) An' whut wuz you doin' when them hounds come in here after Dad?

LONNIE: (*Hopelessly*) They wuz so many of 'em come an' git 'im—whut could Ah do?

JOHN: Do? You could 'ave fought 'em like a man!

MAM SUE: (*Pleadingly*) Don't be too hard on 'im, John, we'se ain't got no gun 'round heah!

JOHN: Then he should 'ave burnt their damn kennels ovah their heads! Who was it leadin' 'em?

MILLIE: Old man Withrow and the Sherley boys, they started it all.

(*Gradually assuming the look of a man who has determined to do some terrible work that must be done, John walks deliberately toward the mantel where the revolvers are lying.*)

JOHN: (*Bitterly*) I've been helpin' the w'ite man git his freedom, I reckon I'd bettah try now to get my own!

MAM SUE: (*Terrified*) Whut yuh gwine ter do?

JOHN: (*With bitterness growing in his voice*) I'm sick o' these w'ite folks doin's—we're "fine, trus'worthy feller citizuns" when they're handin' us out guns, an' Liberty

Bonds, an' chuckin' us off to die; but we ain't a damn thing when it comes to handin' us the rights we done fought an' bled fu'! I'm sick o' this sort o' life—an' I'm goin' to put an end to it!

MILLIE: (*Rushing to the mantel, and covering the revolvers with her hands*) Oh, no, no, John! Mam Sue, John's gwine to kill hisse'f!

MAM SUE: (*Piteously*) Oh, mah honey, don' yuh go do nothin' to bring sin on yo' soul! Pray to de good Lawd to tek all dis fiery feelin' out'n yo' heart! Wait 'tel Brudder Moseby come back—he's gwine ter pray—

JOHN: (*His speech growing more impassioned and bitter*) This ain't no time fu' preachers or prayers! You mean to tell me I mus' let them w'ite devuls send me miles erway to suffer an' be shot up fu' the freedom of people I ain't nevah seen, while they're burnin' an' killin' my folks here at home! To Hell with 'em!

(*He pushes Millie aside, and, seizing the revolvers, thrusts the loaded one into his pocket and begins deliberately to load the other.*)

MILLIE: (*Throwing her arms about his neck*) Oh, John, they'll kill yuh!

JOHN: (*Defiantly*) Whut ef they do! I ain't skeered o' none of 'em! I've faced worse guns than any sneakin' hounds kin show me! To Hell with 'em! (*He thrusts the revolver that he has just loaded into Lonnie's hands.*) Take this, an' come on here, boy, an' we'll see what Withrow an' his gang have got to say!

(*Followed by Lonnie, who is bewildered and speechless, John rushes out of the cabin and disappears in the gathering darkness.*)

Curtain

From *Liberator*, April 1919, 10–14.

Claude McKay

1889–1948

Claude McKay's "If We Must Die" has often been identified as the penultimate articulation of the militant spirit of the Harlem Renaissance. With its publication in the *Liberator* in 1919 and with the subsequent publication of *Harlem Shadows* in 1922, McKay established himself as a new—and radical—voice in American poetry.

Festus Claudius McKay was born in Clarendon Parish, Jamaica, the youngest of eleven children. His father raised him with an awareness of his grandfather's enslavement and with an appreciation for the Ashanti traditions of their ancestors. McKay received a scholarship to become an apprentice carpenter in Brownstown. After his mother's death in 1910, he became a police constable in Kingston but left a year later, unwilling to serve the colonial order. Upon his return to Clarendon Parish, he took up with Walter Jekyll, an English collector of island folklore who encouraged McKay to write Jamaican dialect poetry. In 1912, McKay published *Constab Ballads* and *Song of Jamaica*, for which he became the first black person awarded the medal of the Jamaican Institute of Arts and Sciences. McKay used his award money to enroll in Tuskeegee Institute in Alabama. Appalled at the racism of the Jim Crow South, McKay transferred to Kansas State College, where he studied agriculture before leaving to resume his writing career in New York. There he became friendly with the poet Edward Arlington Robinson and the novelist Waldo Frank. He published his first American poetry under the pseudonym Eli Edwards in *Pearson's Review* and the *Liberator*.

During the First World War, working on the Pennsylvania Railroad as stevedore, porter, houseman, and waiter provided material for McKay's poetry and reinforced his working-class politics. In 1919, McKay moved to London, where he read the works of Marx and Lenin and worked for Sylvia Pankhurst at the Communist newspaper the *Worker's Dreadnought*. C. K. Ogden published almost two dozen of his poems in the summer issue of *Cambridge Magazine*, and the critic I. A. Richards wrote a preface for McKay's third volume of verse, *Summer in New Hampshire*.

In 1922, McKay published *Harlem Shadows*, widely considered his most important poetry collection. Harlem's most famous poet, however, grew increasingly disenchanted with U.S. race relations and with many of the political and artistic leaders of the Harlem Renaissance. For the next twelve years, he traveled the world, living in the Soviet Union, France, Spain, and North Africa. His publications while abroad include the novels *Home to Harlem* (1928), *Banjo, a Story Without a Plot* (1929), and *Banana Bottom* (1933), as well as the collection *Gingertown and Other Stories* (1932). McKay returned to the United States in 1934 and published his autobiography, *A Long Way from Home*, in 1937. His last book, the essay collection *Harlem: Negro Metropolis*, was published in 1940. In addition to working for the Federal Writers' Project, in later years McKay became involved with Friendship House, the Catholic-sponsored community center in Harlem, where he befriended the African American writer and devout Catholic Ellen Terry. McKay eventually converted to Catholicism, teaching from 1944 to his death in 1948 at the Catholic Youth Organization in Chicago.

Recited by Winston Churchill in a speech against the Nazis, "If We Must Die" became an unofficial anthem for Allied Forces in the Second World War. The poem's universal call to courageous resistance explains why it remains one of the most anthologized of all modern poems. Yet even if there is no internal evidence to suggest that "If We Must Die" is about race, the poem's reception and McKay's recollection of the conditions of production during the Red Summer of 1919 establish its importance in the canon of antilynching representations. In *A Long Way from Home*, McKay describes the unbearable tension he and his fellow railroad workers endured during the racial clashes of the Red Summer of 1919:

> Our Negro newspapers were morbid, full of details of clashes between colored and white, murderous shootings and hangings. Traveling from city to city and unable to gauge the attitude and temper of each one, we Negro railroad men were nervous. . . . We stuck together, some of us armed, going from railroad station to our quarters. We stayed in our quarters all through the dreary ominous nights, for we never knew what was going to happen
>
> It was during those days that the sonnet, "If We Must Die," exploded out of me. And for it the Negro people unanimously hailed me as a poet. . . . It was the only poem I ever read to members of my crew.

Reprinted in the September 1919 issue of the militant African American newspaper the *Crusader* and in dozens of African American journals throughout the 1920s, the poem, with its celebration of manly courage against oppression, perfectly captured the determined spirit of the age. "The Lynching," which follows here, was published in 1922 and belongs with protest poetry like Anne Spencer's "White Things" and McKay's own "White Fiends"; all fight oppression by exposing the barbarism of white supremacy.

—— If We Must Die ——

If we must die, let it not be like hogs
Hunted and penned in an inglorious spot,
While round us bark the mad and hungry dogs,
Making their mock at our accursed lot.
If we must die, O let us nobly die,
So that our precious blood may not be shed
In vain; then even the monsters we defy
Shall be constrained to honor us though dead!
O kinsmen! We must meet the common foe!
Though far outnumbered let us show us brave,
And for their thousand blows deal one deathblow!
What though before us lies the open grave?
Like men we'll face the murderous, cowardly pack,
Pressed to the wall, dying, but fighting back!

From *Liberator*, July 1919, 21.

—— The Lynching ——

His Spirit in smoke ascended to high heaven.
His father, by the cruelest way of pain,
Had bidden him to his bosom once again;
The awful sin remained still unforgiven.
All night a bright and solitary star
(Perchance the one that ever guided him,
Yet gave him up at last to Fate's wild whim)
Hung pitifully o'er the swinging char.
Day dawned, and soon the mixed crowds came to view
The ghastly body swaying in the sun:
The women thronged to look, but never a one
Showed sorrow in her eyes of steely blue;
And little lads, lynchers that were to be,
Danced round the dreadful thing in fiendish glee.

From *Harlem Shadows: The Poems of Claude McKay*
(New York: Harcourt, Brace, 1922), 51.

Angelina Weld Grimké

1880–1958

Poet, playwright, essayist, feminist, and antilynching activist, Angelina Weld Grimké was born in Boston, the only child of a Harvard Law School graduate Archibald Henry Grimké. Her paternal grandparents were Henry Grimké and Nancy Weston, a slave on the Grimkés' Caneacre Plantation. Henry's half-sisters, the famous abolitionists Sarah Moore and Angelina Grimké, publicly acknowledged Archibald as their nephew and helped with his education. Angelina Weld Grimké's family, a microcosm of the post–Civil War United States, included ex-slaveholders and white abolitionists, free-born and formerly enslaved black people, and Grimké experienced the trauma of racial division in her primary relationship. Her mother, Sarah Stanley, a white woman whose family opposed her interracial marriage, deserted the family (presumably because of mental and physical illness) when Angelina was a child. Angelina never saw her mother again. This abandonment may inform her constant return to issues of motherhood in her fiction. Grimké graduated from the Boston Normal School of Gymnastics in 1902. She taught at the renowned Dunbar High School in Washington, D.C., from 1916 until 1933. Although much of her poetry was not published during her lifetime, some of Grimké's poems appeared in journals such as the *Colored American*, the *Boston Transcript*, and *Opportunity* and in most major anthologies of the Harlem Renaissance. The first successful drama written by an African American and interpreted by African American actors, Grimké's three-act antilynching play *Rachel* was performed in Washington in 1916. The NAACP production program described *Rachel*, which aimed to counter the impact of the motion picture *Birth of a Nation*, as "the first attempt to use the stage for race propaganda in order to enlighten the American people relating to the lamentable condition of ten millions of Colored citizens in this free republic." *Rachel* was also produced at the Neighborhood Theatre in New York City on April 26, 1917, and was published by Cornhill Publishers in 1920. A second antilynching play, *Mara*, was never published or produced.

Most of Grimké's fiction expresses her passionate opposition to lynching. Her 1919 short story "The Closing Door," which appeared in the *Birth Control Review*, ends with a hysterical black woman killing her infant son to prevent him from possible torture and death at the hands of a lynch mob when he is older. Grimké's short story "Goldie," which was serialized in the *Birth Control Review*, reflects the violent death of Mary Turner, her unborn child, and her husband in Georgia in 1918. (See also Anne Spencer's "White Things" and Walter White's "I Investigate Lynchings" in this volume.) In Grimké's fiction and poetry, the lynching tree operates as a complex, sometimes occult symbol of the African American experience (see her poem "Tenebris" in this volume). The name of the protagonist in "Goldie," Victor Forrest, marks him as a kind of African American Everyman, struggling on an arduous journey toward redemption. An earlier version of the story, "Blackness," ends with the lynched woman's brother escaping punishment for avenging her death. The publishers of the Birth Control Review evidently preferred the later version, in which Victor's retribution brings about his own lynching. As with the unauthorized revision of Mary Burrill's Aftermath, the changed ending of "Goldie" keeps outside the limits of discursive possibility the idea that successful African American revenge for lynching could go unpunished.

—— Goldie ——

He had never thought of the night, before, as so sharply black and white; but then he had never walked before, three long miles, after midnight, over a country road. A short distance only, after leaving the railroad station, the road plunged into the woods and stayed there most of the way. Even in the day, he remembered, although he had not traveled over it for five years, it had not been the easiest to journey over. Now, in the almost palpable darkness, the going was hard, indeed; and he was compelled to proceed, it almost seemed to him, one careful step after another careful step.

Singular fancies may come to one, at such times: and, as he plodded forward, one came, quite unceremoniously, quite unsolicited, to him and fastened its tentacles upon him. Perhaps it was born of the darkness and the utter windlessness with the resulting great stillness; perhaps—but who knows from what fancies spring? At any rate, it seemed to him, the woods, on either side of him, were really not woods at all but an ocean that had flowed down in a great rolling black wave of flood to the very lips of the road itself and paused there as though suddenly arrested and held poised in some strange and sinister spell. Of course, all of this came, he told himself over and over, from having such a cursed imagination; but whether he would or not, the fancy persisted and the growing feeling with it, that he, Victor Forrest, went in actual danger, for at any second the spell might snap and with that snapping, this boundless deep upon deep of horrible, waiting sea, would move, rush, hurl itself heavily and swiftly together from the two sides, thus engulfing, grinding, crushing, blotting out all in its path, not excluding what he now knew to be that most insignificant of insignificant pigmies, Victor Forrest.

But there were bright spots, here and there in the going—he found himself calling them white islands of safety. These occurred where the woods receded at some little distance from the road.

"It's as though," he thought aloud, "they drew back here in order to get a good deep breath before plunging forward again. Well, all I hope is, the spell holds O.K. beyond."

He always paused, a moment or so, on one of these islands to drive out expulsively the dank, black oppressiveness of the air he had been breathing and to fill his lungs anew with God's night air, that here, at least, was sweet and untroubled. Here, too, his eyes were free again and he could see the dimmed white blur of road for a space each way; and above, the stars, millions upon millions of them, each one hardly brilliant, stabbing its way whitely through the black heavens. And if the island were large enough there was a glimpse, scarcely more, of a very pallid, slightly crumpled moon sliding furtively down the west. —Yes, sharply black and sharply white, that was it, but mostly it was black.

And as he went, his mind busy enough with many thoughts, many memories, sub-consciously always the aforementioned fancy persisted, clung to him; and he was never entirely able to throw off the feeling of his very probable and imminent danger in the midst of this arrested wood-ocean.

—Of course, he thought, it was downright foolishness, his expecting Goldie, or rather Cy, to meet him. He hadn't written or telegraphed. —Instinct he guessed, must have warned him that wouldn't be safe; but, confound it all! This was the devil of a road. —Gosh! What a lot of noise a man's feet could make—couldn't they? —All alone like this. —Well, Goldie and Cy would feel a lot worse over the whole business than he did. —After all it was only once in a lifetime, wasn't it? —Hoofing it was good for him, any-way. —No doubt about his having grown soft. —He'd be as lame as the dickens tomorrow. —Well, Goldie would enjoy that—liked nothing better than fussing over a fellow. —If (But he very resolutely turned away from that if.)

—In one way, it didn't seem like five years and yet, in another, it seemed longer— since he'd been over this road last. It had been the sunshiniest and the saddest May morning he ever remembered. —He'd been going in the opposite direction, then; and that little sister of his, Goldie, had been sitting very straight beside him, the two lines held rigidly in her two little gold paws and her little gold face stiff with repressed emo-tion. He felt a twinge, yet, as he remembered her face and the way the great tears would well up and run over down her cheeks at intervals. —Proud little thing! —She had dis-dained even to notice them and treated them as a matter with which she had no con-cern. —No, she hadn't wanted him to go. —Good, little Goldie! —Well, she never knew, how close, how very close he had been to putting his hand out and telling her to turn back—he'd changed his mind and wasn't going after all.—

He drew a sharp breath. —He hadn't put out his hand.

—And at the station, her face there below him, as he looked down at her through the open window of the train. —The unwavering way her eyes had held his—and the look in them, he hadn't understood then, or didn't now, for that matter.

"Don't," he had said. "Don't, Goldie!"

"I must. Vic, I must. —I don't know. —Don't you understand I may never see you again?"

"Rot!" he had said. "Am I not going to send for you?"

—And then she had tried to smile and that had been worse than her eyes.

"You think so, now, Vic—but will you?"

"Of course."

"Vic!"

"Yes."

"Remember, whatever it is—it's all right. *It's all right.* —I mean it. —See! I couldn't smile could I?—if I didn't?"

And then, when it had seemed as if he couldn't stand any more—he had leaned over, even to pick up his bag to get off, give it all up—the train had started and it was too late. The last he had seen of her, she had been standing there, very straight, her arms at sides and her little gold paws little tight fists. —And her eyes! —And her twisted smile! —God! That was about enough of that. —He was going to her, now, wasn't he?

—Had he been wrong to go? —Had he? —Somehow, now, it seemed that way. —And yet, at the time, he had felt he was right. —He still did for that matter. —His chance, that's what it had meant. —Oughtn't he to have had it? —Certainly a colored man couldn't do the things that counted in the South. —To live here, just to *live* here, he had to swallow his self-respect. —Well, he had tried, honestly, too, for Goldie's sake, to swallow his. — The trouble was he couldn't keep it swallowed—it nauseated him. —The thing for him to have done, he saw that now, was to have risked everything and taken Goldie with him. —He shouldn't have waited, as he had from year to year, to send for her. —It would have meant hard sledding, but they could have managed somehow. —Of course, it wouldn't have been the home she had had with her Uncle Ray and her Aunt Millie, still. —Well, there wasn't any use in crying over spilt milk. One thing was certain, never mind how much you might wish to, you couldn't recall the past.—

—Two years ago—(gosh!) but time flew!—when her letter had come telling him she had married Cy Harper. —Queer thing, this life! —Darned queer thing!— Why, he had been in the very midst of debating whether or not he could afford to send for her— had almost decided he could. —Well, sisters, even the very best of them, it turned out, were not above marrying and going off and leaving you high and dry—just like this. —Oh! of course Cy was a good enough fellow, clean, steady going, true, and all the rest of it—no one could deny that—still, confound it all! how could Goldie prefer a fathead like Cy to him. —Hm!—peeved yet, it seemed! —Well, he'd acknowledge it—he was peeved all right.

Involuntarily he began to slow up.

—Good! Since he was acknowledging things—why not get along and acknowledge the rest. —Might just as well have this out with himself here and now.— Peeved first, then what?

He came to an abrupt stop in the midst of the black silence of the arrested wood-ocean.

—There was one thing, it appeared, a dark road could do for you—it could make it possible for you to see yourself quite plainly—almost too plainly. —Peeved first, then what? —No blinking now, the truth. —He'd evaded himself very cleverly—hadn't he?—up until tonight? —No use any more. —Well, what was he waiting for—Out with it—Peeved first; go ahead, now. —Louder! —*Relief!* —Honest, at last. —Relief! Think of it, he had felt relief when he had learned he wasn't to be bothered, after all, with little, loyal, big-hearted Goldie. —*Bothered!* —And he had prided himself upon being rather a decent, upright, respectable fellow. —Why, if he had heard this about anybody else, he wouldn't have been able to find language strong enough to describe him—a rotter, that's what he was, and a cad.

"And Goldie would have sacrificed herself for you any time, and gladly, and you know it."

To his surprise he found himself speaking aloud.

—Why once, when the kid had been only eight years old and he had been taken with a cramp while in swimming, she had jumped in too! —Goldie, who couldn't swim a single stroke! —Her screams had done it and they were saved. He could see his mother's face yet, quizzical, a little puzzled, a little worried.

"But what on earth, Goldie, possessed you to jump in too?" she had asked. "Didn't you *know* you couldn't save him?"

"Yes, I knew it."

"Then, why?"

"I don't know. It just seemed that if Vic had to drown, why, I had to drown with him. —Just couldn't live *afterwards*, Momsey. If I lived *then* and he drowned."

"Goldie! Goldie! —If Vic fell out of a tree, would you have to fall out too?"

"Proberbly." Goldie had never been able to master "probably," but it fascinated her.

"Well, for Heaven's sake. Vic, do be careful of yourself hereafter. You see how it is," his mother had said.

And Goldie had answered—how serious, how quaint, how true her little face had been.—

"Yes, that's how it is, isn't it?" Another trick of hers, ending so often what she had to say with a question. —And he hadn't wished to be bothered with her!

He groaned and started again.

—Well, he'd try to even things up a little, now. —He'd show her (there was a lump in his throat) if he could—

For the first time Victor Forrest began to understand the possibilities of tragedy that may lie in those three little words, "If I can."

—Perhaps Goldie had understood and married Cy so that he needn't bother anymore about having to have her with him. He hoped, as he had never hoped for anything before, that this hadn't been her reason. She was quite equal to marrying, he knew, for such a motive—and so game, too, you'd never dream it was a sacrifice she was making. He'd rather believe, even, that it had been just to get the little home all her own. — When Goldie was only a little thing and you asked her what she wanted most in all the world when she grew up, she had always answered:

"Why, a little home—all my own—a cunning one—and young things in it and about it."

And if you asked her to explain, she had said:

"Don't you *know?*—not *really?*"

And, then, if you had suggested children, she had answered:

"Of course, all my own; and kittens and puppies and little fluffy chickens and ducks and little birds in my trees, who will make little nests and little songs there because they will know that the trees near the little home all my own are the very nicest ever and ever."—

—Once, she must have been around fifteen, then—how well he remembered that once—he had said:

"Look here, Goldie, isn't this an awful lot you're asking God to put over for you?"

Only teasing, he had been—but Goldie's face!

"Oh! Vic, am I? —Do you *really* think that?"

And then, before he could reply, in little, eager, humble rushes:

"I hadn't thought of it— *that* way—before. —Maybe you're right. —If—if—I gave up something, perhaps—the ducks—or the chickens—or the—birds—or the kittens—or the puppies?"

Then very slowly:

"Or—the—children? —Oh! —But I couldn't! —Not any of them. —Don't you think, perhaps—just perhaps, Vic—if—if—I'm—good—always—from now on—that—that— maybe—maybe—sometime, Vic, sometime—I—I—might? —Oh! Don't you?"—

He shut his mouth hard.

—Well, she had had the little home all her own. Cy had made a little clearing, she had written, just beyond the great live oak. Did he remember it? And did he remember, too, how much Cy loved the trees?—

—No, he hadn't forgotten that live oak—not the way he had played in it—and carved his initials all over it; and he hadn't forgotten Cy and the trees, either. —Silly way, Cy had had, even after he grew up, of mooning among them.

"Talk to me—they do—sometimes. —Tell me big, quiet things, nice things."

—Gosh! After *his* experience, *this* night among them. *Love* 'em! —Hm! —Damned, waiting, greedy things! —Cy could have them and welcome.—

—It had been last year Goldie had written about the clearing with the little home all her own in the very "prezact" middle of it.—They had had to wait a whole year after they were married before they could move in—not finished or something—he'd forgotten the reason.—How had the rest of that letter gone? —Goldie's letters were easy to remember—had, somehow, a sort of burrlike quality about them. He had it, now, something like this:

She wished she could tell him how cunning the little home all her own was, but there was really no cunning word cunning enough to describe it. —Why even the very trees came right down to the very edges of the clearing on all four sides just to look at it. —

If he could only *see* how proudly they stood there and nodded their entire approval one to the other!—

Four rooms the little home, all her own, had—Four! —And a little porch in the front and a "littler" one in the back, and a hall that had really the most absurd way of trying to get out both the front and rear doors at the same time. Would he believe it they had to keep both the doors shut tight in order to hold that ridiculous hall in. Had he ever in all his life, heard of such a thing? And just off of this little hall, at the right of the front door, was their bedroom, and back of this, at the end of this same very silly hall, was their dining room, and opposite, across the hall again—she hoped he saw how this hall simply refused to be ignored—again—opposite was the kitchen. —He was then to step back into the hall once more, but *this* time he was to pretend very hard not to see it. There was no telling, its vanity was so great, if you paid too much attention to it what it might do. Why, the unbearable little thing might rise up, break down the front and back doors and escape; and then where'd they be, she'd like to know, without any little hall at all? —He was to step, then, quite nonchalantly—if he knew what that was—back into the hall and come forward, but this time he was to look at the room at the left of the front door; and *there,* if he pleased, he would see something really to repay him for his trouble, for here he would behold her sitting room and parlor both in one And if he couldn't believe how perfectly adorable this little room could be and was, why she was right there to tell him all about it. —Every single bit of the little home all her own was built just as she had wished and furnished just as she had hoped. And, well, to sum it all up, it wasn't safe, if you had any kind of heart trouble at all, to stand in the road in front of the little home all her own, because it had such a way of calling you that before you knew it, you were running to it and running fast. She could vouch for the absolute truth of this statement.

And she had a puppy, yellow all over, all but his little heart—she dared him even to suggest such a thing!—with a funny wrinkled forehead and a most impudent grin And he insisted upon eating up all the uneatable things they possessed, including Cy's best straw hat and her own Sunday-go-to-meeting slippers. And she had a kitten, a grey one—and the busiest things he did were to eat and sleep. Sometimes he condescended to play with his tail and to keep the puppy in his place. He had a way of looking at you out of blue, very young, very innocent eyes that you knew perfectly well were not a bit young nor yet a bit innocent. And she had the darlingest, downiest little chickens and ducks and a canary bird, which Emma Elizabeth lent her sometimes when she went away to work and the canary had been made of two golden songs. And outside of the little home all her own—in the closest trees—the birds were, lots of them, and they had nested there—If, of a morning, he could only hear them singing! —As if they knew— and did it on purpose—just as she had wished. —How happy it had all sounded—and yet—and yet—once or twice—he had had the feeling that something wasn't quite right.

—He hoped it didn't mean she wasn't caring for Cy. —He would rather believe it was because there hadn't been children. —The latter could be remedied—from little hints he had been gathering lately, he rather thought it was already being remedied; but if she didn't *care* for Cy, there wasn't much to be done about that. —Well, he was going to her at last. —She couldn't fool him—couldn't Goldie; and if that fathead, Cy, couldn't take care of her, now. Just let somebody start something.—

—That break ahead there, in the darkness, ought to be just about where the settlement was. —No one need ever tell *him* again it was only three miles from the station— he guessed he knew better. —More like ten or twenty. —The settlement, all right. —Thought he hadn't been mistaken. —So far, then, so good.

The road, here, became the main street of the little colored settlement. Three or four smaller ones cut it at right angles and then ran off into the darkness. The houses, for the most part, sat back, not very far apart; and, as the shamed moon had entirely disappeared, all he could make out of them was their silent, black little masses. His quick eyes and his ears were busy. No sound broke the stillness. He drew a deep breath of relief. As nearly as he could make out, everything was as it should be.

He did not pause until he was about midway of the settlement. Here he set his bag down, sat on it and looked at the illuminated hands of his watch. It was half past two. In the woods he had found it almost cold, but in this spot the air was warm and close. He pulled out his handkerchief, took off his hat, mopped his face, head and neck, finally the sweatband of his hat.

—Queer! —But he wouldn't have believed that the mere sight of all this, after five years, could make him feel this way. There was something to this home idea, after all. —Didn't feel, hardly, as though he had ever been away.—

Suddenly he wondered if old man Tom Jackson had fixed that gate of his yet. Curiosity got the better of him. He arose, went over and looked. Sure enough the gate swung outward on a broken hinge. Forrest grinned.

"Don't believe over much here in change, do they? —That gate was that way ever since I can remember. —Bet every window is shut tight too. Turrible, the night air always used to be. —Wonder if my people will ever get over these things."

He came back and sat down again. He was facing a house that his eyes had returned to more than any other.

"Looks just the same. —Wonder who lives there now. —Suppose someone does. — Looks like it. —Mother sure had courage—more than I would have had—to give up a good job in the North, teaching school, to come down here and marry a poor doctor in a colored settlement. I give it to her. —Game! —Goldie's just like her—she'd have done it too."

—How long had it been since his father had died? —Nine—ten—why, it was ten years and eight since his mother—. They'd both been born there—he and Goldie. — What was that story his mother had used to tell about him when he had first been brought in to see her? —He had been six at the time.

"Mother," he had asked, "is her gold?"

"What, son?"

"I say, is her gold?"

"Oh! I see," his mother had said and smiled, he was sure, that very nice understanding smile of hers. "Why, she is gold, isn't she?"

"Yes, all of her. What's her name?"

"She hasn't any yet, son."

"She ain't got no name? —Too bad! —I give her one. Her name's Goldie, 'cause."

"All right, son, Goldie it shall be." And Goldie it had always been.

—No, you couldn't call Goldie pretty exactly. —Something about her, though, mighty attractive. —Different looking! —That was it. —Like herself. —She had never lost that beautiful even gold color of hers. —Even her hair was "goldeny" and her long eyelashes. Nice eyes Goldie had, big and brown with flecks of gold in them—set in a little wistful, pointed face.—

He came to his feet suddenly and picked up his bag. He moved swiftly now, but not so swiftly as not to notice things still as he went.

"Why, hello!" he exclaimed and paused a second or so before going on again. "What's happened to Uncle Ray's house? —Something's not the same. —Seems larger, somehow. —Wonder what it is? —Maybe a porch. —So they do change here a little. —That there ought to be Aunt Phoebe's house. —But she must be dead—though I don't remember Goldie's saying so. —Why, she'd be way over ninety. — Used to be afraid of the dark or something and never slept without a dim light. —Gosh! If there isn't the light—just the same as ever. —And way over ninety. —Whew! —Wonder how it feels to be that old. —Bet I wouldn't like it. —Gee! What's that?"

Victor Forrest stopped short and listened. The sound was muffled but continuous; it seemed to come from the closed, faintly lighted pane of Aunt Phoebe's room. It was a sound, it struck him, remarkably like the keening he had heard in an Irish play. It died slowly and, though he waited, it did not begin again.

"Probably dreaming or something and woke herself up," and he started on once more.

He soon left the settlement behind and, continuing along the same road, found himself (he hoped for the last time) in the midst of the arrested wood-ocean.

But the sound of that keening, although he had explained it quite satisfactorily to himself, had left him disturbed. Thoughts, conjectures, fears that he had refused, until now, quite resolutely to entertain no longer would be denied. They were rooted in Goldie's last two letters, the cause of his hurried trip South.

"Of course, there's no *real* danger. —I'm foolish, even, to entertain such a thought. —Women get like that sometimes—nervous and overwrought. —And if it is with her as I suspect and hope—why the whole matter's explained. —Why it had really sounded *frightened!* —And parts of it were—hm!—almost incoherent. —The whole thing's too ridiculous, however, to believe. —Well, when she sees me we'll have a good big laugh over it all. —Just the same, I'm glad I came. —Rather funny—somehow—thinking of Goldie—with a kid—in her arms. —Nice, though."

—Lafe Coleman! —Lafe Coleman! —He seemed to remember dimly a stringy, long white man with stringy colorless hair quite disagreeably unclean; eyes a pale grey and fishlike. —He associated a sort of toothless grin with that face. —No, that wasn't it, either. —Ah! That was it! —He had it clearly, now. —The grin was all right but it displayed the dark and rotting remains of tooth stumps.—

He made a grimace of strong disgust and loathing.

—And—this—this—*thing* had been annoying Goldie, had been in fact, for years. — She hadn't told anybody, it seems, because she had been able to take care of herself. — But since she had married and been living away from the settlement—it had been easier for him, and much more difficult for her. He wasn't to worry, though, for the man was stupid and so far she'd always been able to outwit [him]— What she feared was Cy. It was true Cy was amiability itself—but—well—she had seen him angry once. —Ought she to tell him? —She didn't believe Cy would kill the creature—not outright—but it would be pretty close to it. —The feeling between the races was running higher than it used to. —There had been a very terrible lynching in the next county only last year. — She hadn't spoken of it before—for there didn't seem any use going into it. —As he had never mentioned it, she supposed it had never gotten into the papers. Nothing, of course, had been done about it, nothing ever was. Everybody knew who was in the mob. —Even he would be surprised at some of the names. —The brother of the lynched man, quite naturally, had tried to bring some of the leaders to justice; and he, too, had paid with his life. Then the mob, not satisfied, had threatened, terrorized, cowed all the colored people in the locality. —He was to remember that when you were under the heel it wasn't the most difficult of matters to be terrorized and cowed. There was absolutely no law, as he knew, to protect a colored man. —That was one of the reasons she had hesitated to tell Cy, for not only Cy and she might be made to pay for what Cy might do, but the little settlement as well. Now, keeping all this in mind, ought she to tell Cy?

And the letter had ended:

"I'm a little nervous, Vic, and frightened and not quite sure of my judgment. Whatever you advise me to do, I am sure will be right."

—On the very heels of this had come the "special" mailed by Goldie in another town. —She hadn't dared, it seems, to post it in Hopewood. —It had contained just twelve words, but they had brought him South on the next train.

"Cy knows," it had said, "and O! Vic, if you love me, come, come, come!"

Way down inside of him, in the very depths, a dull, cold rage began to glow, but he banked it down again, carefully, very carefully, as he had been able to do, so far, each time before that the thoughts of Lafe Coleman and little Goldie's helplessness had threatened anew to stir it.

—That there ought to be the great live oak—and beyond should be the clearing, in the very "prezact" middle of which should be the little home all Goldie's own.—

For some inexplicable reason his feet suddenly began to show a strange reluctance to go forward. "Damned silly ass!" he said to himself. "There wasn't a thing wrong with the settlement. That ought to be a good enough sign for anybody with a grain of sense."

And then, quite suddenly, he remembered the keening.

He did not turn back to pause; still his feet showed no tendency to hasten. Of necessity, however, it was only a matter of time before he reached the live oak. He came to a halt beside it, ears and every sense keenly on the alert. Save for the stabbing, white stars above the clearing, there was nothing else in all the world, it seemed, but himself and the heavy black silence.

Once more he advanced but, this time, by an act of sheer will. He paused, set his jaw and faced the clearing. In the very center was a small dark mass; it must be the little home. The breath he had drawn in sharply, while turning, he emitted in a deep sigh. His knees felt strangely weak. —What he had expected to see exactly, he hardly knew. He was almost afraid of the reaction going on inside of him. The relief, the blessed relief at merely finding it there, the little house all her own!

It made him feel suddenly very young and joyous and the world, bad as it was, a pretty decent old place after all. Danger! —Of course, there was no danger. —How could he have been so absurd? —Just wait until he had teased Goldie aplenty about this. He started to laugh aloud but caught himself in time. —No use awaking them. —He'd steal up and sit on the porch—there'd probably be a chair there or something—and wait until dawn. —They shouldn't be allowed to sleep one single second after that. —And then he'd bang on their window, and call out quite casually:

"O, Goldie Harper, this is a nice way—isn't it?—to treat a fellow; not even to leave a latch string out for him?"

He could hear Goldie's little squeal now.

And then he'd say to Cy:

"Hello, you big fathead, you! —What do you mean, anyhow, by making a perfectly good brother-in-law hoof it the whole way here, like this?"

He had reached the steps by this time and he began softly to mount them. It was very dark on the little porch and he wished he dared to light a match, but he mustn't risk anything that might spoil the little surprise he was planning. He transferred his bag from his right to his left hand, the better to feel his way. With his fingers outstretched in front of him he took a cautious step forward and stumbled over something.

"Clumsy chump!" he exclaimed below his breath. "That will about finish your little surprise I am thinking." He stood stockstill for several seconds, but there was no sound.

"Some sleepers," he commented.

He leaned over to find out what it was he had stumbled against and discovered that it was a broken chair lying on its side. Slowly he came to a standing posture. He was not as happy for some reason. He stood there, very quiet, for several moments. Then his hand stretched out before he started forward again. This time, after only a couple of steps, his hand came in contact with the housefront. He was feeling his way along, cautiously still, when all of a sudden his fingers encountered nothing but air. Surprised, he paused. He thought, at first, he had come to the end of the porch. He put out a carefully exploring foot only to find firm boards beneath. A second time he experimented, with the same result. And then, as suddenly, he felt the housefront once more beneath his fingers. Gradually it came to him where he must be. He was standing before the door and it was open, wide open!

He could not have moved if he had wished. He made no sound and none broke the blackness all about.

It was sometime afterwards when he put his bag down upon the porch, took a box of matches out of his pocket, lit one and held it up. His hand was trembling, but he managed, before it burned his fingers and he blew it out automatically, to see four things—two open doors to right and left, a lamp in a bracket just beyond the door at the left and a dirty mud-trodden floor.

The minutes went by and then it seemed to him, somebody else called out:

"Goldie! Cy!" This was followed by silence only.

Again the voice tried, a little louder this time:

"Goldie! Cy!" —There was no response.

————

This other person, who seemed, somehow, to have entered into his body, moved forward, struck another match, lit the lamp and took it down out of the bracket. Nothing seemed to make very much difference to this stranger. He moved his body stiffly; his eyes felt large and dry. He passed through the open door at the left and what he saw there did not surprise him in the least. In some dim way, only he knew that it affected him.

There was not, in this room, one single whole piece of furniture. Chairs, tables, sofa, a whatnot, all had been smashed, broken, torn apart; the stuffing of the upholstery completely ripped out; and the entirety thrown, scattered, here, there and everywhere. The piano lay on one side, its other staved in. —Something, it reminded him of—something to do with a grin—the black notes like the rotting stumps of teeth. Oh, yes! Lafe Coleman! —That was it. The thought aroused no particular emotion in him. Only, again he knew it affected him in some far off way.

Every picture on the walls had been wrenched down and the molding with it, the pictures themselves defaced and torn, and the glass splintered and crushed under foot. Knickknacks, vases, a china clock, all lay smashed and broken. Even the rug upon the floor had not escaped, but had been ripped up, torn into shreds and fouled by many dirty feet. The frail white curtains and window shades had gone down too in this human whirlwind; not a pane of glass was whole. The white woodwork and the white walls were soiled and smeared. Over and over the splay-fingered imprint of one dirty hand repeated itself on the walls. A wanton boot had kicked through the plastering in places.

This someone else went out of the door, down the hall, into the little kitchen and dining room. In each room he found precisely the same conditions prevailing.

There was one left, he remembered, so he turned back into the hall, went along to the open door and entered in. —What was the matter, here, with the air? —He raised the lamp higher above his head. He saw the same confusion as elsewhere. A brass bed was overturned and all things else shattered and topsy-turvy. There was something dark at the foot of the bed. He moved nearer, and understood why the air was not pleasant. The dark object was a little dead dog, a yellow one, with a wrinkled forehead. His teeth were bared in a snarl. A kick in the belly had done for him. He leaned over; the little leg was quite stiff. Less dimly this time, he knew that this affected him.

He straightened up. When he had entered the room there had been something else he had noticed for him to do. But what was it? This stranger's memory was not all that it should be. —Oh, yes! He knew, now. The bed. He was to right the bed. With some difficulty he cleared a space for the lamp and set it down carefully. He raised the bed. Nothing but the mattress and the rumpled and twisted bed clothing. He didn't know exactly just what this person was expecting to find.

He was sitting on the steps, the extinguished lamp at his side. It was dawn. Everything was veiled over with grey. As the day came on, a breeze followed softly after, and with the breeze there came to him there on the steps a creaking, two creakings! — Somewhere there to the right they were, among the trees. The grey world became a shining green one. Why were the birds singing like that, he wondered. —It didn't take the day long to get here—did it?—once it started. A second time his eyes went to the woods at the right. He was able to see now. Nothing there, as far as he could make out. His eyes dropped from the trees to the ground and he beheld what looked to him like a trampled path. It began there at the trees; it approached the house; it passed over a circular bed of little pansies. It ended at the steps. Again his eyes traversed the path, but this time from the steps to the trees.

Quite automatically he arose and followed the path. Quite automatically he drew the branches aside and saw what he saw. Underneath those two terribly mutilated swinging bodies, lay a tiny unborn child, its head crushed in by a deliberate heel.

Something went very wrong in his head. He dropped the branches, turned and sat down. A spider, in the sunshine, was reweaving the web someone had just destroyed while passing through the grass. He sat slouched far forward, watching the spider for hours. He wished the birds wouldn't sing so. —Somebody had said something once about them. He wished, too, he could remember who it was.

About midday, the children of the colored settlement, playing in the road, looked up and saw a man approaching. There was something about him that frightened them, the little ones in particular, for they ran screaming to their mothers. The larger ones drew back as unobtrusively as possible into their own yards. The man came on with a high head and an unhurried gait. His should have been a young face, but it was not. Out of its set sternness looked his eyes, and they were very terrible eyes indeed. Mothers with children, hanging to them from behind and peering around, came to their doors. The man was passing through the settlement now. A woman, startled, recognized him and called the news out shrilly to her man eating his dinner within. He came out, went down to the road rather reluctantly. The news spread. Other men from other houses followed the first man's example. They stood about him, quite a crowd of them. The stranger, of necessity, came to a pause. There were no greetings on either side. He eyed them over, this crowd, coolly, appraisingly, contemptuously. They eyed him, in turn, but surreptitiously. They were plainly very uncomfortable. Wiping their hands on aprons, women joined the crowd. A larger child or two dared the outskirts. No one would meet his eye.

Suddenly a man was speaking. His voice came sharply, jerkily. He was telling a story. Another took it up and another.

One added a detail here; one a detail there. Heated arguments arose over insignificant particulars; angry words were passed. Then came too noisy explanations, excuses, speeches in extenuation of their own actions, pleas, attempted exoneration of themselves. The strange man said never a word. He listened to each and to all. His contemptuous eyes made each writhe in turn. They had finished. There was nothing more that they could see to be said. They waited, eyes on the ground, for him to speak.

But what he said was:

"Where is Uncle Ray?"

Uncle Ray, it seemed, was away—had been for two weeks. His Aunt Millie with him. No one had written to him, for his address was not known.

The strange man made no comment.

"Where is Lafe Coleman?" he asked.

No one there knew where he was to be found—no one. They regretted the fact, they were sorry, but they couldn't say. They spoke with lowered eyes, shifting their bodies uneasily from foot to foot.

Watching their faces he saw their eyes suddenly lift, as if with one accord, and focus upon something behind him and to his right. He turned his head. In the brilliant sunshine, a very old, very bent form leaning heavily on a cane was coming down the path from the house in whose window he had seen the dimmed light. It was Aunt Phoebe.

He left the crowd abruptly and went to meet her. When she was quite sure he was coming she paused where she was, bent over double, her two hands, one over the other, on the knob of her cane, and waited for him. No words, either, between these two. He looked down at her and she bent back her head, tremulous from age, and looked up at him.

The wrinkles were many and deep-bitten in Aunt Phoebe's dark skin. A border of white wool fringed the bright bandana tied tightly around her head. There were grey hairs in her chin; two blue rings encircled the irises of her dim eyes. But all her ugliness could not hide the big heart of her, kind yet, and brave, after ninety years on earth.

And as he stood gazing down at her, quite suddenly he remembered what Goldie had once said about those circled eyes.

"Kings and Queens may have *their* crowns and welcome. What's there to *them*? — But the kind Aunt Phoebe wears—that's different. She earned hers, Vic, earned them through many years and long of sorrow, and heartbreak and bitter, bitter tears. She bears with her the unforgetting heart. —And though they could take husband and children and sell them South, though she lost them in the body—never a word of them, since—she keeps them always in her heart. —I know, Vic, I know—and God who is good and God who is just touched her eyes, both of them and gave her blue crowns, beautiful ones, a crown for each. Don't you see *she is of God's Elect*?"

For a long time Victor Forrest stood looking down into those crowned eyes. No one disturbed these two in the sun-drenched little yard. They, in the road, drew closer and watched silently.

And then he spoke:

"You are to tell me, Aunt Phoebe—aren't you?—where I am to find Lafe Coleman?"

Aunt Phoebe did not hesitate a second. —"Yes," she said, and told him.

The crowd in the road moved uneasily, but no one spoke.

And then Victor Forrest did a thing he had never done before: he leaned over swiftly and kissed the wrinkled parchment cheek of Aunt Phoebe.

"Goldie loved you," he said and straightened up, turned on his heel without another word and went down the path to the road. Those there made no attempt to speak. They drew closer together and made way for him. He looked neither to the right nor to the left. He passed them without a glance. He went with a steady, purposeful gait and a high head. All watched him for they knew they were never to see him alive again. The wood swallowed Victor Forrest. A low keening was to be heard. Aunt Phoebe had turned and was going more feebly, more slowly than ever toward her house.

———

Those that know whereof they speak say that when Lafe Coleman was found he was not a pleasant object to see. There was no bullet in him—nothing like that. It was the marks upon his neck and the horror of his blackened face.

And Victor Forrest died, as the other two had died, upon another tree.

———

There is a country road upon either side of which grow trees even to its very edges. Each tree has been chosen and transplanted here for a reason and the reason is that at some time each has borne upon its boughs a creaking victim. Hundreds of these trees there are, thousands of them. They form a forest—"Creaking Forest" it is called. And over this road many pass, very, very many. And they go jauntily, joyously here—even at night. They do not go as Victor Forrest went, they do not sense the things that Victor Forrest sensed. If their souls were not deaf, there would be many things for them to hear in Creaking Forest. At night the trees become an ocean dark and sinister, for it is made up of all the evil in all the hearts of all the mobs that have done to death their creaking victims. It is an ocean arrested at the very edges of the road by a strange spell. But this spell may snap at any second and with that snapping this sea of evil will move, rush, hurl itself heavily and swiftly together from the two sides of the road, engulfing, grinding, crushing, blotting out all in its way.

From *Birth Control Review* 4 (1920), November: 7–11; December: 10–14.

1921–1930

William Pickens

1881–1954

Educator, college dean, NAACP activist, and government employee William Pickens was born in Anderson County, South Carolina. While enslaved, Pickens's maternal grandmother had received a beating that broke her spine, causing her to walk with a crooked back for forty of her eighty years. After Pickens's mother died in 1888, the family moved to rural Arkansas, where his father worked as a sharecropper for a year but fell so deeply into debt that the family ran away to North Little Rock. Pickens attended segregated schools in Little Rock and graduated first in his class from high school. He earned a bachelor's degree from Talladega College in Alabama in 1902, a second bachelor's degree from Yale in 1904, where he was elected to Phi Beta Kappa, and a master's degree from Fisk in 1908. Pickens taught literature, classics, and sociology at Talladega College from 1904 to 1914; at Wiley University in Marshall, Texas, from 1914 to 1915; and at Morgan College in Baltimore, where he became the college's first black dean, from 1915 to 1920.

Part of Du Bois's Niagara movement, Pickens wrote for its magazine, the *Voice of the Negro*. A founding member of the NAACP, Pickens delivered major addresses at the association's 1915 convention and its National Conference on Lynching in May 1919. Pickens's speaking skills earned praise from Langston Hughes, who dubbed him "one of the most popular platform orators in America." Pickens left education to become field secretary for the NAACP in 1920. Unlike many NAACP leaders, Pickens was no stranger to working with his hands and was particularly sensitive to the plight of labor. To put himself through college, he had joined his father on the railroad, working with rough laborers laying track. While attending Yale, Pickens had spent his summers working at a Chicago ironworks. During his twenty-two years working for the NAACP, he was a tireless activist, taking to the road for six or seven months a year and maintaining a daunting public-speaking schedule. According to the historian Sheldon Avery, "Pickens came into more direct contact with the Negro masses than any other black leader of his time" (1988, 9).

As a contributing editor for the Associated Negro Press beginning in 1920, Pickens would for the next twenty years write columns that appeared in over one hundred newspapers. He often took controversial positions, joining Robert Bagnall in the crusade to deport United Negro Improvement Association leader Marcus Garvey, whom they denounced for his alliance with the Klan and his back-to-Africa scheme. Although he worked with communist organizations on other issues, Pickens was sharply critical of the American Communist Party's handling of the Scottsboro case, in which nine young men were falsely accused of rape. Pickens left the NAACP in 1942 to serve as director of the Interracial Section of the Treasury Department's Savings (later War) Bonds Division.

In 1911, Pickens published his autobiography, *The Heir of Slaves*, which he updated in 1923 as *Bursting Bonds* to include the increasingly more militant positions outlined in his 1916 collection of essays, *The New Negro: His Political, Civil, and Mental Status*. In 1922, Pickens published a collection of short fiction, *The Vengeance of the Gods and Three Other Stories of the Real American Color Line*. During his time working for the NAACP, Pickens publicized in widely circulated pamphlets and articles his investigations of several notorious lynchings. His pamphlet "The American Congo: The Burning of Henry Lowry" was reprinted in Nancy Cunard's *Negro Anthology*, as was his article "Aftermath of a Lynching" about the effects of a lynching on an Indiana town. (See James Madison's recent *A Lynching in the Heartland* and James Cameron's *Time of Terror* for further writing on the Marion, Indiana, lynchings.)

In this selection from *Lynching and Debt Slavery*, a pamphlet issued by the American Civil Liberties Union in 1921, Pickens describes the effect of debt slavery on hundreds of thousands of African Americans and analyzes how lynching represents an eruption of a systemic violence operating to maintain sharecroppers in a condition of virtual slavery. The primary example he uses is the Elaine, Arkansas, race massacre of 1919, in which federal troops supposedly brought in to keep order were responsible for the killing and torture of countless black citizens.

The cover of the pamphlet reads:

¶ The exploitation of black labor by white land-owners is here shown to be the underlying cause of this most barbarous of social crimes. Lynching is but one method of the "White Terror" of the rural South, where civil rights for Negroes do not and cannot exist. With it goes the Ku Klux Klan, whose avowed object is the "maintenance of white supremacy."

¶ In the South today no man, white or black, is really free publicly to speak the truth about the race problem. We believe this pamphlet to be the essential truth. We have consulted Southern white men and women who tell us privately that it is the truth.

¶ Mr. Pickens writes as a Negro from a rich experience as Field Secretary of the National Association for the Advancement of Colored People, and as a teacher in the South. We publish the pamphlet in the belief that only by frankly recognizing the economic basis of lynching can we even begin to solve the problem.

¶ Its solution is obviously bound up with the cause of exploited labor— white and black alike. And that solution will become possible only as the black and white workers of the South both achieve the right to meet, speak freely, organize, and strike.

— Excerpt from —
Lynching and Debt Slavery

The race problem in the United States is only an intensification of the wrongs of our economic system. It is fundamentally one with the difference between labor and capital, employee and employer, wages and unearned income.

Lynching and mob violence are only methods of economic repression. Lynching is most prevalent where Negro labor is most exploited; and the spread of mob violence against colored people has followed the spread of this exploitation. It is either due directly to efforts of the exploiting class to repress the Negro, or it is the indirect resentment of the laborers of other racial groups against the exploitation of Negro labor to their disadvantage. This is the difference between Georgia and East St. Louis. The chain of causes which leads from the economic wrong to the lynching may take different directions. It may be that the Negro is the chief labor element, as on the farms of Arkansas, and that the landed employer class will resort to lynching to keep Negroes down, even by a great massacre, as at Elaine, Ark., in 1919. Or it may be that the Negro is a newcomer in need of a job, used by the employers as a tool with which to beat down all labor, and we may therefore see the spectacle of white laborers making an indirect attack upon the system by killing black laborers, as in East St. Louis, in 1917.

Where Lynchings Occur

It is instructive to note where most lynchings take place. In thirty years, the seven states which led in lynching are in the order of their evil eminence: Georgia, Mississippi, Texas, Louisiana, Alabama, Arkansas and Tennessee. Along with Alabama, Georgia, and Texas, therefore, we have the great southern Mississippi Valley, a region which might be termed "the American Congo."

Debt Slavery

The quest of this Congo is not for rubber and ivory, but for cotton and sugar. Here labor is forced, and the laborer is a slave. The slavery is a cunningly contrived debt slavery to give the appearance of civilization and the sanction of law. A debt of a few hundred dollars may tie a black man and his family of ten as securely in bondage to a great white planter as if he had purchased their bodies. If the Thirteenth Amendment, which has never been enforced in this region, means anything, it is that a man's body cannot be held for an honestly contracted debt; that only his property can be held; and that if a contracting debtor has no property, the creditor takes the risk in advancing credit. Otherwise a law abolishing slavery could be easily evaded, for the wealthy enslaver could get the poor victim into debt and then hold his body in default of payment. Wages could then be so adjusted to expenses and the cost of "keep" that the slavery would be unending.

And that is precisely the system of debt-slavery. The only way for this debt-slave to get free from such a master is to get someone else to pay this debt; that is, to sell himself to another, with added charges, expenses of moving and bonuses. By this method the enslaver gets his bondmen cheaper than in a regular slave system, for in the debt system he does not have to pay the full market price of a man.

The effect is to allow the ignorant and the poor unwittingly and unwillingly to sell themselves for much less than an old slaveholder would have sold them. The debt-master has other advantages. He is free from liabilities on account of the debtor's ill-health or the failure of his crops. The debtor takes all risk. In case of misfortune or crop failure, he gets deeper into debt, more securely tied in bondage.

This is the system that obtains in the great Mississippi Valley, and it has not been modified for thirty years or more. The evil of this system is responsible for all of the massacres of colored people and for nearly all of the horrible lynchings and burnings of individual Negroes that have lately taken place in this region.

As long as this system lasts there will be lynching and burning and occasional great outbreaks against the colored populations of these states. And of course, under the influence of suggestion, there will be sporadic attacks upon colored people in other parts of the nation. To attack lynching without attacking this system is like trying to be rid of the phenomena of smoke and heat without disturbing the basic fire. If we examine any, even the most complicated, of these "race" troubles, we will find some economic wrong at the bottom, some trouble about wages or work or property. The existence side by side of two races, one powerful and the other weak, simply lends greater opportunity and freer play to human greed and social injustice.

The Massacre at Elaine, Arkansas

For example, there was the alleged "Negro insurrection" at Elaine, near Helena, Ark., on the last day of September and the first days of October, 1919. In this case the planters and landlords overreached credulity by charging too much. They charged that the black peons and tenants had plotted to murder all the whites, to take possession of all the land and seize the government of Arkansas! Such a wild charge discredited itself with all fair-minded people who know Arkansas or any other part of the South. If all the Negroes from all the insane asylums of all the South were gathered together in one state, they would not attempt such a thing.

It is instructive to review the cause of all this trouble which resulted in the immediate slaughter of at least twenty-five helpless colored people (nobody knows exactly how many), the condemning of twelve to the electric chair by mere travesties of trials, the imprisonment of more than three score in the state penitentiary for life or long terms, and the terrorizing of the colored population of the whole state. The cause of all this was the attempt of the Negro tenants and sharecroppers to sell their cotton in the open market for a price between 30 and 40 cents a pound, instead of selling it to their respective landlords for prices ranging around 15 cents. The landlord wanted to be a middle-man with 100 percent profit.

The colored tenants organized a farmer's union, a labor union if you will, for the pur-pose of mutual support in getting the best price for their cotton and to raise funds to sue the landlords for their right to such prices, when necessary. It is pathetic to think that these colored tenants would have had to sue these planters in the planters' own courts, where planters would sit as judge and jurors, where even their own lawyers would be white men. And yet this feeble attack upon their debt-slave system made the landlords so nervous that they seized the first opportunity to accuse the Negroes of a general plot of treason and murder and they shouted for troops ostensibly to put down "rebellion," but in reality to smash this union of Negro farm laborers.

If it had not led to so great a tragedy, it would now be amusing to review the evidence on which the landlords based their charge of a general conspiracy to "murder all whites." While the planters were in a state of nervous tension over this union move-ment, the colored organization was holding a public meeting in a church; and two white men passing by proceeded to "shoot up" the church and the congregation. It may be that the white men intended merely to frighten the colored folk and discourage union meetings, but those in the church could not guess that secret and so fired back, killing one of the whites. This one homicide in self-defense convinced the landlords and Governor Brough that the colored farmers' union was organized to kill off the entire white population, and he immediately seized all the state troops he could lay hands on, borrowed all the Federal troops they would lend him at Camp Pike and hurried down to Phillips County to join the landlords and the great white mobs that poured in from the nearby counties of Tennessee and Mississippi to clean out the Negroes.

No War Profits for Debt Slaves

Why were these landlords so desperately opposed to war profits in cotton going to their tenants? Not simply because they themselves wanted to profit as middlemen, but also because they knew that if those Negroes ever got hold of so much money, it would spell the doom of debt slavery. This slavery is based on debt, to avoid the technicalities involved in the 13th Amendment, and if the tenants ever got free from debt the sys-tem would fall. It is a religious dogma in the South that you cannot keep the free (?) Negro working unless you keep him hopelessly in debt. It is indeed the only way to keep him working for such starvation wages. In 1914, cotton could hardly be sold for seven cents a pound, and it took only a small debt of a few hundred dollars or less to hold a colored man and his family bound to the landlord. But these sharecroppers and renters and those who were attempting to buy a small farm from the landlord by paying installments on an endless mortgage, could have become independent in 1918–19 if they had been allowed to get the huge war price for their cotton.

Most of these debts and mortgages had been contracted and made when money was dear and scarce, and they might have been paid in full while money was cheap and plentiful. Millions and millions of other Americans reaped in the benefit of this economic change, of this war stimulation of the market, but if Negro tenants in Arkansas had been permitted to get their share, it would have injured debt slavery. One Arkansan said to Walter F. White, of the National Association for the Advancement of Colored People, whom he mistook for a white person also: "Why, if we settled with these niggers accordin' to the law, they would soon own half of Arkansas!"

Just as unusual prosperity of the working class anywhere threatens the security of wage slavery, so would any real prosperity among the farm-tenants undermine the system of debt-bondage which obtains in the Mississippi Valley states of the South. Therefore, the landlord, who generally "furnishes rations" and supplies to his tenants at his own figure, endeavored to prevent "war prices" of farm products from increasing the prosperity of his tenants, by raising rations and supplies to a price-level which made war prices look tame. Mr. White found that the tenant had been charged $58.00 for cotton seed worth $4.20; $25.00 for a second-hand plow worth $16.00 when new; and $3.50 for a piece of rope that cost 30 cents.

Why Henry Lowry Was Burned

Is it any wonder that such a monstrous economic system should be the hotbed of the most terrible social crimes? The burning of Henry Lowry at Nodena, Ark., on January 26, 1921 was *occasioned* by the fact that Lowry had killed two white people in a fight, but the cause of the fight was Lowry's persistence in demanding a settlement for two years' work on the farms of a big planter. The debt-slave system could not survive regular and actual accounting on the part of the debt-master to the debt-bondsmen, even if such accounts were rendered only once in two years. And so Lowry was beaten when he first insisted upon a settlement for his work, and when he dared to come three weeks later and renew his insistence, he was murderously assaulted with a gun. Shooting back, he killed two from the group of his assailants. For this he was made the victim of what is perhaps the most barbarous burning of a human being in the history of man.

All the other big planters in Mississippi County, Ark., naturally sympathized with the burning of Lowry, and many of them helped to burn him. According to the sheriff, "every (white) man, woman and child in the county" wanted the Negro burned. This indicates some deeper and more primal feeling than mere aversion to color or even anger at homicide in self-defense. Lowry's act awakened in the landed class a feeling akin to horror at insurrection. It was like a threat of rebellion on the part of the submerged class to overthrow the system on which the power of the landlords rests.

Convict Slavery

The temptation of the large plantation owner to exploit the brawn of the defenseless Negro avails itself of another unfair advantage in which the state becomes a party to the wrong. It is the custom of farming out prisoners—state prisoners and even county and city prisoners. A Negro who has been jailed for some misdemeanor or fined for vagrancy, may be "sold" to some landlord who needs farm hands, for the price of the Negro's fine. The farmer pays the fine and is supposed to work it out of the Negro in a specified time. This colored man is still a prisoner of the state and is kept in chains and stockades, maybe on the landlord's private estate, under guards who may shoot him down if he attempts to escape, or whip his naked back if he does not work to suit them. Thus the state, under the technical right of law, does a slave business.

It can be readily understood why this system is so much more vicious than was the old slave system. In a regular slave system, the owner might have such selfish interest in the slave as any man may have in the preservation of his valuable property. But in the convict lease system of Georgia, it is to the landlord's advantage to put the least into the Negro and get the most out of him whom he owns for a limited time only.

This farming out of convicts also leads to great lynching debauches. In May of 1918, in Georgia, at least eleven colored people were killed in consequence of trouble between a Negro convict-slave named Johnson, and his temporary slave-holder, Smith, who, it appears, had worked the colored man for a longer time than the period for which he had bought him from the state. And when Johnson demanded pay for the considerable overtime, a quarrel ensued and the white man was killed. This white man could not afford to pay Johnson, for then the other overworked convicts might make similar demands.

Even in April, 1921, we read in the daily news that a white man in Georgia who was using such farmed-out Negro convict labor, deliberately murdered a dozen or so of the victims because he feared that if they were ever released at all, they might "squeal" on his system and his crimes. It is one of the greatest horrors of our history that colored women have been thus farmed out to work and live in stockades under the absolute control of brutal men. The multiple lynchings in Brooks and Lowndes Counties, Georgia, which were caused by this system in May, 1918, are among the most savage of such occurrences. The unspeakable vivisection of Mary Turner, a colored woman whose baby was to be born about four weeks later, was one in this carnival.

There is seldom an effort to avenge anything; there is seldom anything to avenge which the constituted authorities and the law could not avenge. It is a passion, allied with the deepest instincts of greed, to keep a submerged group submerged and to keep a downed group down. It is an appeal to the extra legal, because no law—even the most defective law of the most backward state—could keep a race wholly and forever down. The deepest and ugliest human passions are based on greed.

From *Lynching and Debt Slavery*, American Civil Liberties Union pamphlet, May 1921.

Leslie Pinckney Hill

1880–1960

Leslie Pinckney Hill was a notable educator, poet, and civic leader who devoted his life to securing full citizenship for African Americans. Born in Lynchburg, Virginia, Hill moved as a teenager to East Orange, New Jersey. He earned a bachelor's degree in 1903 and a master's degree in 1904 from Harvard University, where he was elected to Phi Beta Kappa. Hill taught at Tuskeegee under Booker T. Washington from 1904 to 1907, when he was appointed principal at the Manassas Industrial Training School in Manassas, Virginia. In 1913, Hill became head of the Institute for Colored Youth in Cheyney, Pennsylvania (later Cheyney State College).

Believing above all in education as the key to fighting racism, Hill embraced a vision of a one-world consciousness for all people. He belonged to many civic organizations that pursued peace and universal brotherhood, including the Interracial Committee of Philadelphia, the Peace Section for the American Friends Service Committee, the Committee of National Councils of Student Christian Associations, and the National Education Association's Committee on the Defense of Democracy Through Education. His poetry appeared in many anthologies, including James Weldon Johnson's *Book of American Negro Poetry* (1922), Robert T. Kerlin's *Negro Poets and Their Poems* (1923), and Sterling Brown's *Negro Caravan* (1941). Hill also published an extended blank-verse portrait of the famous Haitian leader, *Touissant L'Ouverture: A Dramatic History* (1928).

Hill's 1921 poetry collection, *The Wings of Oppression*, consists of sixty-nine poems on themes that included one-world consciousness, the dignity and bravery of black soldiers in the First World War, and Jim Crow segregation. Advocating endurance and patience in the face of persecution, Hill saw the oppressed as particularly blessed and predicted that they would soar "on the wings of oppression." This vision of harmony and transcendence did not prevent Hill, however, from articulating anger over the scourge of racial violence. After reading a *New York Times* article on the lynching of a black man in Smithville, Georgia, on December 21, 1919, he penned a scathing reply in "So Quietly." One of Hill's finest poems, this indictment of the hypocrisy of the press has appeared in many anthologies.

─── So Quietly ───

News item from the *New York Times* on the lynching of a Negro at Smithville, Georgia, December 21, 1919.

> "The train was boarded so quietly . . . that members of the train crew did not know that the mob had seized the Negro until informed by the prisoner's guard after the train had left the town. . . . A coroner's inquest held immediately returned the verdict that West came to his death at the hands of unidentified men."

So quietly they stole upon their prey
And dragged him out to death, so without flaw
Their black design that they to whom the law
Gave him in keeping, in the broad, bright day,
Were not aware when he was snatched away;
And when the people, with a shrinking awe,
The horror of that mangled body saw,
"By unknown hands!" was all that they could say.

So, too, my country, stealeth on apace
The soul-blight of a nation. Not with drums
Or trumpet blare is that corruption sown,
But quietly—now in the open face
Of day—now in the dark—and when it comes,
Stern truth will never write, "By hands unknown."

From *The Wings of Oppression* (Boston: Stratford, 1921), 17–18.

Carrie Williams Clifford

1862–1934

Suffragist, civil rights activist, club woman, and writer, Carrie Williams Clifford was born and raised in Chillicothe, Ohio, and attended high school in Columbus, Ohio. She married William H. Clifford, a lawyer and member of the Ohio state legislature, with whom she had two sons. Clifford served as editor-in-chief of the women's edition of the *Cleveland Journal* and contributed to numerous other publications, including *Alexander's Magazine*. She was involved with the National Association of Colored Women and participated in demonstrations by black and white women's-rights activists. The founder of the Ohio Federation of Colored Women's Clubs, she was a major force in that organization's promotion of women's rights.

Around 1910, the Cliffords moved to Washington, D.C. There Clifford hosted salons in her home, where famous black intellectuals such as Mary Church Terrell, W.E.B. Du Bois, Alain Locke, and Georgia Douglas Johnson would gather for literary and political discussions. A member of the Niagara movement, Clifford also held leadership roles in the NAACP.

Particularly concerned with the oppression of women of color, Clifford in her writing highlights discrimination of every form. She published two volumes of poetry and contributed numerous short stories, articles, and poems to such periodicals as *Opportunity* and the *Crisis*. "The Black Draftee from Dixie," which appeared in Clifford's *Widening Light* and was reprinted in *The Negro Anthology* in 1934, protests the southern lynching of African American soldiers returning from the First World War.

—— The Black Draftee from Dixie ——

(Twelve Negro soldiers who had served overseas were lynched upon their return to their homes in the South.)

Upon his dull ear fell the stern command;
And though scarce knowing why or whither, he
Went forth prepared to battle loyally,
And questioned not your faith, O Dixie-land!

And though the task assigned were small or grand,
If toiling at mean tasks ingloriously,
Or in fierce combat fighting valiantly,
With poise magnificent he took his stand!

What though the hero-warrior was black?
His heart was white and loyal to the core;
And when to his loved Dixie he came back,
Maimed, in the duty done on foreign shore,
Where from the hell of war he never flinched,
Because he cried, "Democracy," was lynched.

From *The Widening Light* (Boston: Walter Reid, 1922), 22.

Countee Cullen

1903–1946

Poet, essayist, anthologist, children's writer, and playwright, Countee Cullen was one of the major literary contributors to the Harlem Renaissance. Born in Louisville, Kentucky, Cullen was adopted after his mother's death by Rev. Frederick Cullen, a prominent and conservative Harlem minister. He attended the prestigious, almost entirely white DeWitt Clinton High School in New York City and burst onto the literary scene in his senior year when his "I Have a Rendezvous with Life" won a citywide poetry contest. When he published "Shroud of Color" in H. L. Mencken's *American Mercury* at the age of nineteen, many saw him as one of the most exciting poets on the U.S. scene. Cullen received a B.A. in 1925 from New York University, which he attended on a New York State Regents scholarship. During his senior year, his first collection of poetry, *Color*, appeared to critical acclaim. He received his master's degree from Harvard in 1926. Cullen's other verse collections include *Copper Sun* (1927), *The Ballad of the Brown Girl* (1927), and *The Black Christ* (1929). His novel, *One Way to Heaven*, appeared in 1932.

Cullen gathered more prizes and enjoyed wider acclaim than any other black writer during the 1920s: first prize in the Witter Bynner Poetry contest at New York University in 1925, *Poetry* magazine's John Reed Memorial Prize, the Amy Spingarn Award from *Crisis* magazine, and prizes in poetry contests sponsored by *Palms* and *Opportunity* magazines. Cullen's academic training and ability to write lyric poetry in the tradition of Shelley and Keats while retaining color consciousness gave him cross-racial appeal. Although Cullen said he wanted to be remembered as a poet rather than as a "Negro poet," his major poems and most of those still being anthologized have racial themes.

In 1928, the year he received a Guggenheim fellowship to study in Paris, Cullen married Nina Yolande Du Bois, only child of W.E.B. Du Bois, in one of the major social events of the Harlem Renaissance. By 1930, the marriage had failed because of Cullen's attraction to men. From 1932 until his death, Cullen taught French at Frederick Douglas Junior High School, where one of his pupils was James Baldwin. At the time of his death he was working on a musical with his friend the writer Arna Bontemps.

"Christ Recrucified" appeared in 1922, when Cullen was only nineteen years old, and was not included in any of his subsequent verse collections. The poem presents, in sonnet form, an earlier version of Cullen's longest and most complicated

"O say, can you see by the Dawn's early light,
What so proudly we hailed at the Twilight's last gleaming!"

5. "O Say Can You See . . . ?" Reprinted from the *Crisis*, February 1915, 97.

poem, "The Black Christ," which appeared in the volume of that name in 1929 to unfavorable reviews. While uneven in parts, "The Black Christ" embraces some major themes in antilynching poetry, including the depiction of the southern landscape as a hell on earth and the awestruck recognition that lynching has transfigured the ordinary person into Christ.

—— Christ Recrucified ——

The South is crucifying Christ again
By all the laws of ancient rote and rule:
The ribald cries of "Save Yourself" and "Fool"
Din in his ears, the thorns grope for his brain,
And where they bite, swift springing rivers stain
His gaudy, purple robe of ridicule
With sullen red; and acid wine to cool
His thirst is thrust at him, with lurking pain.
Christ's awful wrong is that he's dark of hue,
The sin for which no blamelessness atones;

But lest the sameness of the cross should tire
They kill him now with famished tongues of fire,
And while he burns, good men, and women, too,
Shout, battling for his black and brittle bones.

From *Kelley's Magazine*, October 1922, 13.

Langston Hughes

1902–1967

Poet, playwright, novelist, anthologist, and historian, James Langston Hughes enjoyed a career in African American letters that stretched from the Harlem Renaissance in the early 1920s to the black arts movement of the late 1960s. Born in Joplin, Mississippi, Hughes came from an illustrious family. His maternal grandfather was abolitionist Charles Langston, who fought with John Brown at Harper's Ferry, and his half brother was John Mercer Langston, a U.S. congressman from Virginia. His parents separated when he was a child after his father, angered by U.S. racism, moved to Mexico, where he worked successfully as a lawyer and engineer. His mother remarried, and in 1916 the family moved to Cleveland. Attending Cleveland's Central High School exposed Hughes to the vernacular poetry of the Chicago School, Carl Sandburg's in particular, and to socialism—two influences of life-long importance.

Hughes enrolled in Columbia University but dropped out after one year. He published several poems in the *Crisis* in 1922, including "The South." In 1923, Hughes took a job on a freighter, voyaging to West Africa and seeing firsthand the operation of white colonialism and black subjugation. For the next several years, he traveled extensively in Mexico, Europe, Africa, and the United States, often working as a waiter or a manservant. He was "discovered" while working as a busboy after leaving three of his best poems on the dinner plate of Vachel Lindsay. With financial aid from Amy Spingarn, Hughes returned to school at Lincoln University, from which he graduated in 1930. Hughes published his first book of poetry, *The Weary Blues*, in 1926, followed by *Fine Clothes to the Jew* in 1927. His poetry, which won praise from both jazz and literary patrons, is best known for its innovations in literary blues and jazz and for its adaptations of black street vernacular. In 1926, he published his famous manifesto for artistic freedom, "The Negro Artist and the Racial Mountain."

During his years at Lincoln, Hughes met Charlotte Mason, an elderly white woman who became the patron of both Hughes and Zora Neale Hurston. Mason, who insisted on being called "Godmother," wanted her artists to embrace primitivism rather than politics. Her relationship with Hughes ended in 1930 after he wrote a poem, "Advertisement for the Waldorf Astoria," that attacked the hotel's racism in choosing employees and guests. After his split with Mason, Hughes traveled to the U.S. South and West and to Haiti. His politics moved to the left and he published frequently in the leftist journal *New Masses*. Hughes visited the Soviet Union to make a movie about race relations, but the project fell apart. In 1937, he reported on the Spanish Civil War for the *Afro-American*. From 1938 to 1940, Hughes established black theaters in Harlem, Los Angeles, and Chicago. He later collaborated with Arna Bontemps on anthologies and children's works and funded theater groups in Harlem, Chicago, and Los Angeles. Hughes wrote a number of plays, including *Mulatto* (1935), which enjoyed a highly successful Broadway run from 1935 to 1937, and *Scottsboro Limited* (1932). His first published collection of short stories was *Ways of White Folks* (1934). He published humorous accounts of his memorable character Jesse B. Semple in *Simple Speaks His Mind* (1950) and *Simple Stakes a Claim* (1957) and also produced a Broadway musical, *Simply Heavenly* (1957), with Simple/Semple as its focus. Hughes worked as a visiting professor at Atlanta University, served as poet in residence at the University of Chicago's laboratory school, and lectured in Europe for the U.S. Information Agency. He received the Spingarn Medal, the NAACP's highest honor, in 1960.

One of Hughes's earliest poems, "The South" plays on the conventions of the Plantation School's nostalgia industry, which celebrated a pastoral, chivalrous Dixieland. Useful comparisons can be made between his deployment of gender in this poem and in "Christ in Alabama," which appears later in this volume.

— The South —

The lazy, laughing South
With blood on its mouth;
The sunny-faced South,
Beast-strong,
Idiot-brained;
The child-minded South
Scratching in the dead fire's ashes
For a Negro's bones.
Cotton and the moon,
Warmth, earth, warmth,
The sky, the sun, the stars,
The magnolia-scented South;
Beautiful, like a woman,
Seductive as a dark-eyed whore,
Passionate, cruel,
Honey-lipped, syphilitic—
That is the South.
And I, who am black, would love her
But she spits in my face;
And I, who am black,
Would give her many rare gifts
But she turns her back upon me;
So now I seek the North—
The cold-faced North,
For she, they say,
Is a kinder mistress,
And in her house my children
May escape the spell of the South.

From *Crisis*, June 1922, 72.

Jean Toomer

1894–1967

Novelist, philosopher, poet, essayist, and dramatist Jean Toomer was born Nathan Pinchback Toomer in Washington, D.C., the son of Nathan Toomer, a Georgia planter, and Nina Pinchback Toomer, the daughter of Pinckney Benton Stewart Pinchback, who had been governor of Louisiana during Reconstruction. Toomer's father left the family when Jean was one year old, and Nina took her son to live with her father, who agreed to help raise the boy only if he changed his name. His grandparents called him Eugene Pinchback, although in school he was known as Eugene Pinchback Toomer. When he began to write, he shortened his name to Jean Toomer. The name shift is indicative of Toomer's lifelong preoccupation with identity. His family was racially mixed and could have passed for white. (He would later claim that P.B.S. Pinchback identified as African American solely to win black votes.) During his own childhood, Toomer lived alternately as white and African American. In Washington, the boy lived in a white neighborhood but attended the all-black Garnet Elementary School. When his mother remarried in 1906, Toomer moved to New Rochelle, New York, where he lived with and attended school with whites. When he returned to Washington in 1909 after his mother's death, Toomer attended the all-black Dunbar High School. Upon his graduation in 1914, Toomer rejected racial classifications, proclaiming himself a member of the "human race" and an American.

During the next three years, Toomer went to several universities in Wisconsin, Massachusetts, Chicago, and New York but never took a degree. After leaving City College in New York in 1917, he spent the next four years writing and publishing poetry in *Broom*, the *Liberator*, the *Little Review*, and other literary magazines. During this time he became part of Greenwich Village's artistic society, befriending prominent intellectuals such as the poets Edward Arlington Robinson and Hart Crane, the photographer Alfred Steiglitz, and the critic Kenneth Burke. He became close friends with the writer Waldo Frank, who acted as his mentor. Toomer made extensive revisions to Frank's own antilynching novel, *Holiday* (1923).

In 1921, Toomer returned to Washington to take care of his aging grandparents. He was struggling with their care and trying to write when he received an offer for a temporary teaching position at the Sparta Agricultural and Industrial Institute in Sparta, Georgia. His experiences during his two months there became the basis for *Cane* (1923), a three-part collection of interlocking poems, tales, sketches, and impressions that record Toomer's discovery of his southern heritage. *Cane* pays homage to the beauty of African American vernacular culture but also laments its passing with the exodus to the North and the industrialization of the South. *Cane's* modernist experimentalism and innovation set the standard for writers of the New Negro movement, but it was the last time Toomer chose to take African American life as his subject. He went on to write several autobiographies, four novels, plays, poetry, short stories, and articles.

In the first section of *Cane*, Toomer interweaves six stories with twelve poems to create lyrical portraits of six southern women. The second section consists of seven prose sketches and five poems set in urban Chicago and Washington, D.C., that show black southerners and their children struggling to build a life in the North. The third and longest section (written first), "Kabnis," embraces the themes of the first two as it explores the identity conflicts of an educated black northerner teaching school in Georgia. As Barbara Foley points out, the lynching of Mame Lakins in the "Kabnis" section closely parallels the real-life lynching of Mary Turner for trying to save her husband during a massacre that followed a violent dispute over wages. Foley also points out unmistakable references in "Kabnis" to the multiple murders on a Jasper County debt farm about thirty miles from Sparta just months before Toomer's visit. In February 1921, a series of bodies of drowned black men who had worked for John S. Williams on his Monticello farms were found in the Yellow, Alcovy, and South Rivers. Most of them had been chained together in pairs and weighted down with bags of rocks. Between Reconstruction and 1966, Williams was the only southern white convicted of killing a black person. (For more detail on these murders, see Gregory A. Freeman's *Lay This Body Down*.)

Appearing together in *Cane's* first section, "Portrait in Georgia" and "Blood Burning Moon" explore the racial violence that spurs the northward migration of the book's second part. Although some critics have faulted Toomer's portrayal of violence as too lyrical and aesthetic, both these selections make important points about the economic and sexual underpinnings of the southern racial caste system.

—— Portrait in Georgia ——

Hair—braided chestnut,
coiled like a lyncher's rope,
Eyes—fagots,
Lips—old scars, or the first red blisters,
Breath—the last sweet scent of cane,
And her slim body, white as the ash
of black flesh after flame.

From "Georgia Portraits" (second of three), *Modern Review* 1 (January 1923): 81;
reprinted in *Cane* (Boni and Liveright, 1923), 50.

—— Blood-Burning Moon ——

1

Up from the skeleton stone walls, up from the rotting floor boards and the solid hand-hewn beams of oak of the pre-war cotton factory, dusk came. Up from the dusk the full moon came. Glowing like a fired pine-knot, it illumined the great door and soft showered the Negro shanties aligned along the single street of factory town. The full moon in the great door was an omen. Negro women improvised songs against its spell.

Louisa sang as she came over the crest of the hill from the white folks' kitchen. Her skin was the color of oak leaves on young trees in fall. Her breasts, firm and up-pointed like ripe acorns. And her singing had the low murmur of winds in fig trees. Bob Stone, younger son of the people she worked for, loved her. By the way the world reckons things, he had won her. By measure of that warm glow which came into her mind at thought of him, he had won her. Tom Burwell, whom the whole town called Big Boy, also loved her. But working in the fields all day, and far away from her, gave him no chance to show it. Though often enough of evenings he had tried to. Somehow, he never got along. Strong as he was with hands upon the ax or plow, he found it difficult to hold her. Or so he thought. But the fact was that he held her to factory town more firmly than he thought for. His black balanced, and pulled against, the white of Stone, when she thought of them. And her mind was vaguely upon them as she came over the crest of the hill, coming from the white folks' kitchen. As she sang softly at the evil face of the full moon.

A strange stir was in her. Indolently, she tried to fix upon Bob or Tom as the cause of it. To meet Bob in the canebrake, as she was going to do an hour or so later, was nothing new. And Tom's proposal which she felt on its way to her could be indefinitely put off. Separately, there was no unusual significance to either one. But for some reason, they jumbled when her eyes gazed vacantly at the rising moon. And from the jumble came the stir that was strangely within her. Her lips trembled. The slow rhythm of her song grew agitant and restless. Rusty black and tan spotted hounds, lying in the dark corners of porches or prowling around back yards, put their noses in the air and caught its tremor. They began plaintively to yelp and howl. Chickens woke up and cackled. Intermittently, all over the countryside dogs barked and roosters crowed as if heralding a weird dawn or some ungodly awakening. The women sang lustily. Their songs were cotton-wads to stop their ears. Louisa came down into factory town and sank wearily upon the step before her home. The moon was rising towards a thick cloud-bank which soon would hide it.

> Red nigger moon. Sinner!
> Blood-burning moon. Sinner!
> Come out that fact'ry door.

2

Up from the deep dusk of a cleared spot on the edge of the forest a mellow glow arose and spread fan-wise into the low-hanging heavens. And all around the air was heavy with the scent of boiling cane. A large pile of cane-stalks lay like ribboned shadows upon the ground. A mule, harnessed to a pole, trudged lazily round and round the pivot of the grinder. Beneath a swaying oil lamp, a Negro alternately whipped out at the mule, and fed cane-stalks to the grinder. A fat boy waddled pails of fresh ground juice between the grinder and the boiling stove. Steam came from the copper boiling pan. The scent of cane came from the copper pan and drenched the forest and the hill that sloped to factory town, beneath its fragrance. It drenched the men in a circle seated around the stove. Some of them chewed at the white pulp of stalks, but there was no need for them to, if all they wanted was to taste the cane. One tasted it in factory town. And from factory town one could see the soft haze thrown by the glowing stove upon the low-hanging heavens.

Old David Georgia stirred the thickening syrup with a long ladle, and ever so often drew it off. Old David Georgia tended his stove and told tales about the white folks, about moonshining and cotton picking, and about sweet nigger gals, to the men who sat there about his stove to listen to him. Tom Burwell chewed cane-stalk and laughed with the others till some one mentioned Louisa. Till some one said something about Louisa and Bob Stone, about the silk stockings she must have gotten from him. Blood ran up Tom's neck hotter than the glow that flooded from the stove. He sprang up. Glared at the men and said, "She's my gal." Will Manning laughed. Tom strode over to him. Yanked him up and knocked him to the ground. Several of Manning's friends got up to fight for him. Tom whipped out a long knife and would have cut them to shreds if they hadnt ducked into the woods. Tom had had enough. He nodded to Old David Georgia and swung down the path to factory town. Just then, the dogs started barking and the roosters began to crow. Tom felt funny. Away from the fight, away from the stove, chill got to him. He shivered. He shuddered when he saw the full moon rising towards the cloud-bank. He who didnt give a godam for the fears of old women. He forced his mind to fasten on Louisa. Bob Stone. Better not be. He turned into the street and saw Louisa sitting before her home. He went towards her, ambling, touched the brim of a marvelously shaped, spotted, felt hat, said he wanted to say something to her, and then found that he didnt know what he had to say, or if he did, that he couldnt say it. He shoved his big fists in his overalls, grinned, and started to move off.

"Youall want me, Tom?"

"Thats sho what us wants, sho, Louisa."

"Well, here I am—"

"An here I is, but that aint ahelpin none, all th same."

"You wanted to say something?"

"I did that, sho. But words is like th spots on dice: no matter how y fumbles em, there's times when they jes wont come. I dunno why. Seems like th love I feels fo yo done stole m tongue. I got it now. Whee! Louisa, honey, I oughtnt tell y, I feel I oughtnt cause yo is young an goes t church an I has had other gals, but Louisa I sho do love y. Lil gal, Ise watched y from them first days when youall sat right here befo yo door befo th well an sang sometimes in a way that like t broke m heart. Ise carried y with me into th fields, day after day, an after that, an I sho can plow when yo is there, an I can pick cotton. Yassur! Come near beatin Barlo yesterday. I sho did. Yassur! An next year if ole Stone'll trust me, I'll have a farm. My own. My bales will buy yo what y gets from white folks now. Silk stockings an purple dresses—course I dont believe what some folks been whisperin as t how y gets them things now. White folks always did do for niggers what they likes. An they jes cant help alikin yo, Louisa. Bob Stone likes y. Course he does. But not th way folks is awhisperin. Does he, hon?"

"I dont know what you mean, Tom."

"Course y dont. Ise already cut two niggers. Had t hon, t tell em so. Niggers always tryin t make somethin out a nothin. An then besides, white folks aint up t them tricks so much nowadays. Godam better not be. Leastawise not with yo. Cause I wouldnt stand f it. Nassur."

"What would you do, Tom?"

"Cut him jes like I cut a nigger."

"No, Tom—"

"I said I would an there aint no mo to it. But that aint th talk f now. Sing, honey Louisa, an while I'm listenin t y I'll be makin love."

Tom took her hand in his. Against the tough thickness of his own, hers felt soft and small. His huge body slipped down to the step beside her. The full moon sank upward into the deep purple of the cloud-bank. An old woman brought a lighted lamp and hung it on the common well whose bulky shadow squatted in the middle of the road, opposite Tom and Louisa. The old woman lifted the well-lid, took hold the chain, and began drawing up the heavy bucket. As she did so, she sang. Figures shifted, restlesslike, between lamp and window in the front rooms of the shanties. Shadows of the figures fought each other on the gray dust of the road. Figures raised the windows and joined the old woman in song. Louisa and Tom, the whole street, singing:

> Red nigger moon. Sinner!
> Blood-burning moon. Sinner!
> Come out that fact'ry door.

3

Bob Stone sauntered from his veranda out into the gloom of fir trees and magnolias. The clear white of his skin paled, and the flush of his cheeks turned purple. As if to balance this outer change, his mind became consciously a white man's. He passed the house with its huge open hearth which, in the days of slavery, was the plantation cook-ery. He saw Louisa bent over that hearth. He went in as a master should and took her. Direct, honest, bold. None of this sneaking that he had to go through now. The contrast was repulsive to him. His family had lost ground. Hell no, his family still owned the nig-gers, practically. Damned if they did, or he wouldnt have to duck around so. What would they think if they knew? His mother? His sister? He shouldnt mention them, shouldnt think of them in this connection. There in the dusk he blushed at doing so. Fellows about town were all right, but how about his friends up North? He could see them incredible, repulsed. They didnt know. The thought first made him laugh. Then, with their eyes still upon him, he began to feel embarrassed. He felt the need of explain-ing things to them. Explain hell. They wouldnt understand, and moreover, who ever heard of a Southerner getting on his knees to any Yankee, or anyone. No sir. He was going to see Louisa to-night, and love her. She was lovely—in her way. Nigger way. What way was that?

Damned if he knew. Must know. He'd known her long enough to know. Was there something about niggers that you couldnt know? Listening to them at church didnt tell you anything. Looking at them didnt tell you anything. Talking to them didnt tell you anything—unless it was gossip, unless they wanted to talk. Of course, about farming, and licker, and craps—but those werent nigger. Nigger was some-thing more. How much more? Something to be afraid of, more? Hell no. Who ever heard of being afraid of a nigger? Tom Burwell. Cartwell had told him that Tom went with Louisa after she reached home. No sir. No nigger had ever been with his girl. He'd like to see one try. Some position for him to be in. Him, Bob Stone, of the old Stone family, in a scrap with a nigger over a nigger girl. In the good old days. . . . Ha! Those were the days. His family had lost ground. Not so much, though. Enough for him to have to cut through old Lemon's canefield by way of the woods, that he might meet her. She was worth it. Beautiful nigger gal. Why nigger? Why not, just gal? No, it was because she was nigger that he went to her. Sweet . . . The scent of boiling cane came to him. Then he saw the rich glow of the stove. He heard the voices of the men circled around it. He was about to skirt the clearing when he heard his own name mentioned. He stopped. Quivering. Leaning against a tree, he listened.

"Bad nigger. Yassur, he sho is one bad nigger when he gets started."

"Tom Burwell's been on th gang three times fo cuttin men."

"What y think he's agwine t do t Bob Stone?"

"Dunno yet. He aint found out. When he does— Baby!"

"Aint no tellin."

"Young Stone aint no quitter an I ken tell y that. Blood of th old uns in his veins."

"That's right. He'll scrap, sho."

"Be getting too hot f niggers round this away."

"Shut up, nigger. Y dont know what y talkin bout."

Bob Stone's ears burned as though he had been holding them over the stove. Sizzling heat welled up within him. His feet felt as if they rested on red-hot coals. They stung him to quick movement. He circled the fringe of the glowing. Not a twig cracked beneath his feet. He reached the path that led to factory town. Plunged furiously down it. Halfway along, a blindness within him veered him aside. He crashed into the bordering cane brake. Cane leaves cut his face and lips. He tasted blood. He threw himself down and dug his fingers in the ground. The earth was cool. Cane-roots took the fever from his hands. After a long while, or so it seemed to him, the thought came to him that it must be time to see Louisa. He got to his feet and walked calmly to their meeting place. No Louisa. Tom Burwell had her. Veins in his forehead bulged and distended. Saliva moistened the dried blood on his lips. He bit down on his lips. He tasted blood. Not his own blood. Tom Burwell's blood. Bob drove through the cane and out again upon the road. A hound swung down the path before him towards factory town. Bob couldnt see it. The dog loped aside to let him pass. Bob's blind rushing made him stumble over it. He fell with a thud that dazed him. The hound yelped. Answering yelps came from all over the countryside.

Chickens cackled. Roosters crowed, heralding the bloodshot eyes of southern awakening. Singers in the town were silenced. They shut their windows down. Palpitant between the rooster crows, a chill hush settled upon the huddled forms of Tom and Louisa. A figure rushed from the shadow and stood before them. Tom popped to his feet.

"Whats y want?"

"I'm Bob Stone."

"Yassur—an I'm Tom Burwell. Whats y want?"

Bob lunged at him. Tom side-stepped, caught him by the shoulder, and flung him to the ground. Straddled him.

"Let me up."

"Yassur—but watch yo doins, Bob Stone."

A few dark figures, drawn by the sound of scuffle, stood about them. Bob sprang to his feet.

"Fight like a man, Tom Burwell, an I'll lick y."

Again he lunged. Tom side-stepped and flung him to the ground. Straddled him.

"Get off me, you godam nigger you."

"Yo sho has started somethin now. Get up."

Tom yanked him up and began hammering at him. Each blow sounded as if it smashed into a precious, irreplaceable soft something. Beneath them, Bob staggered back. He reached in his pocket and whipped out a knife.

"Thats my game, sho."

Blue flash, a steel blade slashed across Bob Stone's throat. He had a sweetish sick feeling. Blood began to flow. Then he felt a sharp twitch of pain. He let his knife drop. He slapped one hand against his neck. He pressed the other on top of his head as if to hold it down. He groaned. He turned, and staggered towards the crest of the hill in the direction of white town. Negroes who had seen the fight slunk into their homes and blew the lamps out. Louisa, dazed, hysterical, refused to go indoors. She slipped, crumbled, her body loosely propped against the woodwork of the well. Tom Burwell leaned against it. He seemed rooted there.

Bob reached Broad Street. White men rushed up to him. He collapsed in their arms. "Tom Burwell . . ."

White men like ants upon a forage rushed about. Except for the taut hum of their moving, all was silent. Shotguns, revolvers, rope, kerosene, torches. Two high-powered cars with glaring search-lights. They came together. The taut hum rose to a low roar. Then nothing could be heard but the flop of their feet in the thick dust of the road. The moving body of their silence preceded them over the crest of the hill into factory town. It flattened the Negroes beneath it. It rolled to the wall of the factory, where it stopped. Tom knew that they were coming. He couldnt move. And then he saw the search-lights of the two cars glaring down on him. A quick shock went through him. He stiffened. He started to run. A yell went up from the mob. Tom wheeled about and faced them. They poured down on him. They swarmed. A large man with dead-white face and flabby cheeks came to him and almost jabbed a gun-barrel through his guts.

"Hands behind y, nigger."

Tom's wrists were bound. The big man shoved him to the well. Burn him over it, and when the woodwork caved in, his body would drop to the bottom. Two deaths for a godam nigger. Louisa was driven back. The mob pushed in. Its pressure, its momentum was too great. Drag him to the factory. Wood and stakes already there. Tom moved in the direction indicated. But they had to drag him. They reached the great door. Too many to get in there. The mob divided and flowed around the walls to either side. The big man shoved him through the door. The mob pressed in from the sides. Taut humming. No words. A stake was sunk into the ground. Rotting floor boards piled around it. Kerosene poured on the rotting floor boards. Tom bound to the stake. His breast was bare. Nails' scratches let little lines of blood trickle down and mat into the hair. His face, his eyes were set and stony. Except for irregular breathing, one would have thought him already dead. Torches were flung onto the pile. A great flare muffled in black smoke shot upward. The mob yelled. The mob was silent. Now Tom could be seen within the flames. Only his head, erect, lean, like a blackened stone. Stench of burning flesh soaked the air. Tom's eyes popped. His head settled downward. The mob yelled. Its yell echoed against the skeleton stone walls and sounded like a hundred yells. Like a hundred mobs yelling. Its yell thudded against the thick front wall and fell back. Ghost of a yell slipped through the flames and out the great door of the factory. It fluttered like a dying thing down the single street of factory town. Louisa, upon the step before her home, did not hear it, but her eyes opened slowly. They saw the full moon glowing in the great door. The full moon, an evil thing, an omen, soft showering the homes of folks she knew. Where were they, these people? She'd sing, and perhaps they'd come out and join her. Perhaps Tom Burwell would come. At any rate, the full moon in the great door was an omen which she must sing to:

> Red nigger moon. Sinner!
> Blood-burning moon. Sinner!
> Come out that fact'ry door.

From *Prairie*, March–April 1923, 18. Reprinted in *Cane*
(Boni and Liveright, 1923), 51–67.

Anne Spencer

1882–1975

Poet, feminist, community activist, librarian, and intellectual Anne Spencer was born on a Virginia plantation to parents who separated when she was five. Her mother took Anne to Bramwell, West Virginia, where Anne lived with a foster family while her mother worked as an itinerant cook in the mining camps. Spencer's mother refused to allow her to attend school with the miners' children, so Anne received no formal education until she was eleven years old, when she was sent to the Virginia Seminary and College in Lynchburg, from which she graduated as valedictorian in 1899. Two years later, she married fellow student Edward Spencer, who became the first black parcel postman in Lynchburg. The couple had an unusually egalitarian marriage; Edward Spencer hired housekeepers so that Anne could write and built her a room in her beloved garden at the back of the house so that she could find the solitude she craved. The couple had three children.

Spencer's home and elaborate garden in Lynchburg, like Georgia Douglas Johnson's home in Washington, D.C., served as a literary haven during segregation. In 1920, when Spencer was almost forty, her first published poem appeared in the *Crisis* through the help of James Weldon Johnson, who stayed at the Spencers' home on his travels between North and South as field secretary for the NAACP. Other notable figures of the black intelligentsia who visited the Spencers included Langston Hughes, Georgia Douglas Johnson, Paul Robeson, W.E.B. Du Bois, and Claude McKay. Anne Spencer was one of the most respected poets in the Harlem Renaissance. Her work appeared in most of the major anthologies of the twenties, and she is one of the few women poets included in later anthologies of the Harlem Renaissance. Although long considered a nature poet, Spencer also wrote verse that engages racial and gender issues that is beginning to receive more attention.

An activist against racism in her own community, Anne Spencer refused to use—or to let her children use—public transportation. Spencer opened a library at Lynchburg's black Dunbar High School, where she worked until her retirement in 1943, and remained adamantly opposed to the integration of public schools. She offered sanctuary in her home to Ota Benga, an African pygmy tribesman first exhibited at the 1904 Saint Louis World's Fair, then transferred to New York's Natural History Museum, and, finally, to the monkey house in the Bronx Zoo before he was rescued and brought to Lynchburg.

Anne Spencer wrote "White Things" to protest the lynching of Mary Turner and her unborn baby, an atrocity so traumatic to the African American community that it drew an immediate and anguished response from black artists, as well as journalists. Jean Toomer describes this lynching in the "Kabnis" section of *Cane*, and Angelina Weld Grimké wrote about it repeatedly in her fiction. In "White Things," considered by many to rank among the finest protest poems of the twentieth century, Spencer depicts Euro-American "civilization" as a pestilence sweeping the land.

—— White Things ——

Most things are colorful things—the sky, earth, and sea.
Black men are most men; but the white are free!
White things are rare things; so rare, so rare
They stole from out a silvered world—somewhere.
Finding earth-plains fair plains, save greenly grassed,
They strewed white feathers of cowardice, as they passed;
   The golden stars with lances fine,
   The hills all red and darkened pine,
They blanched with their wand of power;
And turned the blood in a ruby rose
To a poor white poppy flower.

They pyred a race of black, black men,
And burned them to ashes white; then,
Laughing, a young one claimed a skull,
For the skull of a black is white, not dull,
   But a glistening awful thing;
   Made, it seems, for this ghoul to swing
In the face of God with all his might,
And swear by the hell that sired him:
   "Man-maker, make white!"

From *Crisis*, March 1923, 204.

Floyd J. Calvin

1904–1939

Floyd J. Calvin was a well-known reporter whose column, "Calvin's Digest," was serialized in many African American newspapers. He also headed Calvin's News Service, which at the time of his death at thirty-five supplied news to 151 African American newspapers throughout the nation. Head of the New York office of the *Pittsburgh Courier*, Calvin was also an associate editor of the *Messenger*, in which his investigative series about conditions in the Jim Crow South, "Eight Weeks in Dixie," appeared in 1923. In the final installment of the series, "The Present South," Calvin reports on the reverberations of a single lynching in his native Arkansas—from the immediate consequence, the flight of young people to the industrial cities of the North, to the more pernicious impact, the community's general unease over threats to their property and their lives.

—— The Present South ——

(Mister Calvin this month takes up his narrative at Hope, Arkansas, where the second installment, last month, was concluded.)

But in the midst of it all came a shock—what may never happen at a given place, and still may occur today or tomorrow, anywhere. It's like a riddle: *It is at all times possible and yet may never be probable.*

On July 27th, John West, Negro, was taken from the streets of Hope and lynched.

I didn't see it. I saw its effect.

John West was an elderly man, concrete finisher, from Emporia, Kansas; imported by a paving company then engaged in paving the streets. He was one of the highest paid men on the job and had white men as subordinates. He drank from the same cup the white men used. One white man objected and an argument and fight ensued. West whipped the white man up terribly, then said in public what he thought of the White South in general. Both men paid fines for disturbing the peace—West about three times what the white man paid. Then he (West) bought a ticket for Texarkana and boarded train No. 35, at 12:10 P.M., starting home. The mob knew his moves and had everything planned. Six miles below Hope the train stopped for water. A crowd of white men rushed into the colored coach, overpowered the Negro, took him off and there was the mob which took him into the woods and shot him to death.

The afternoon papers reported the fate that met a "presumptuous nigger" and that was all.

The town moved on quite normally and I went ahead enjoying myself. It was the second Negro lynched in Hope within eighteen months. The first I knew personally, and his wife's voice tremored when she spoke to me. One of his friends explained the tragedy as she pointed out his grave in the colored cemetery where the white people dumped him and called it a burial. Those were *"the good 100 per cent American white people"* the Superintendent referred to when he was imploring Negroes not to join the Catholics. That is why I laughed! *"How can I hear what you say, when what you are is continually ringing in my ears?"*

The tragedy was on Friday. The following Monday a crowd of the younger set left for Detroit, Chicago and Gary, some declaring they never wanted to see the town again.

———

Politics timidly showed itself too. I say timidly—referring, of course, to its bearing on Negroes. The one party—the Democratic—held its primary during my sojourn, for the entire state as well as for local offices which I could observe at close range. The newspapers were always filled with the regular political activities of the Klan, from paid advertisements espousing the cause of their candidates to front-page news features describing their sensational campaign meetings. In the end the Klan triumphed.

No Negroes voted. They are plainly told they are not wanted in the Democratic party. Many attend the "stump speech" gatherings, and others even do much minor work in behalf of long-standing friends, but that is all. (I heard of rare instances where sentimental servants were taken along and allowed to vote with their employers, but this was both "personal and private.") The City (white) Superintendent of the Hope public schools (including the Negro) however, did say before the colored teachers assembled that he wished the Democrats would change the law and allow Negroes to vote the Democratic ticket, for he felt sure the time would come when the ("100 per centers") would need good, loyal, colored people to help defeat the Catholics. . . .

———

Out of this mass of observation and experience I have attempted to reach some conclusions, to wit:

On the surface the black people of Dixie seem happy enough: but underneath a peaceful revolution is slowly but surely making headway. *Times are surely growing worse.* There is a reason. Progress means change. When the change among the Negroes is for the better the Southern whites can't stand it. Theoretically they want the Negro to go to school, become educated, acquire property. But with that comes something else. *A man of education and property is a man of standing.* He should be consulted on important questions. He should be respected. He shouldn't have to suffer petty indignities.

But where is the Southerner who won't tell you:

"Education is all right, *but a nigger is a nigger just the same.*" The theory and practice are different. They produce a paradox. One side must give way—must concede. *The Negro knows nothing else but concede—"but he's getting damn tired of conceding ALL the time."*

There will always be some poor Southern whites. They are the proudest people in the world. *You can't insist that they treat you as a human being.* They do so if they want to—but it is optional with them. The better element may sympathize with you, but you are still helpless. "A chain is no stronger than its weakest link." *Basically the most prosperous Southern Negro is at the mercy of the most ignoble Southern white. There is no law* when it comes to a *showdown* between black and white.

All Negroes know this. Some may live 40 years and never have a single instance of trouble. But the brutal fact stares them in the face—*if it ever comes to a showdown.* And the *least thing* can bring this showdown. *"Would you put a nigger before a white man?"* (That "nigger" may be Major Moton or he may be any obscure Southern peon.)* Where is the Southerner who wouldn't quail? They may *all* regret it afterwards—but for the moment: *"White Supremacy"* with capital letters. And those whites who would bravely stand out against it—*"they are 'nigger' lovers—shoot 'em like dogs!"*

This is the actual situation. It is not true in *every* case, but it may be true in *any* case. And every Negro knows that *any* case might be *his own.*

Underneath the revel and merrymaking is a nervous tremor. *Always be careful.* The *mob* is a *possibility* for *any* Negro. Each fine house and each automobile may be in ashes next week this time, or they may be here indefinitely.

From "Eight Weeks in Dixie," *Messenger*, January 1923, 576–577.

---

*Robert Russa Moton (1867–1940) succeeeded Booker T. Washington as head of Tuskeegee Institute.

Robert Bagnall

1883–1943

Born in Norfolk, Virginia, Robert Bagnall, like his father before him, joined the Episcopal priesthood, serving congregations in Pennsylvania, Maryland, and Ohio. In 1911 Bagnall became rector of St. Matthew's Episcopal Church in Detroit, where he helped struggling migrants from the South find housing and jobs. A gifted orator, Bagnall delivered the keynote address at the 1914 inaugural session of the NAACP's Detroit branch, which he had been instrumental in organizing. He was appointed NAACP district organizer for the Michigan area in 1918, recruiting migrant factory workers to the new branches he founded. A tireless community activist, Bagnall battled successfully against school segregation in Ypsilanti, fought against police brutality, and persuaded the Ford Motor Company in Dearborn to hire more African American workers.

In 1921, Bagnall left Michigan for New York City, where he took over from James Weldon Johnson as national director of the NAACP branches. For the next twelve years, he visited hundreds of cities, helping to raise funds for the local branches and offering encouragement to local activists. Throughout the 1920s, Bagnall contributed articles to the *Crisis* and the *Messenger*. "The Unquenchable Fire" appeared in the *Messenger* when Bagnall was most active in his campaign to deport Marcus Garvey, the charismatic pan-Africanist leader whom Bagnall denounced as a race traitor for associating with the Ku Klux Klan at a time of continued lynching and racial violence. Among those who joined Bagnall in the "Garvey Must Go!" campaign were William Pickens, field secretary of the NAACP, and *Messenger* editors A. Philip Randolph and Chandler Owen. Bagnall resigned from the NAACP in 1931 during a time of fiscal retrenchment under newly appointed national secretary Walter White. In 1932, he became pastor of St. Thomas's Episcopal Church in Philadelphia, where he remained until his death in 1943.

"The Unquenchable Fire" shows the unmistakable influence of a lifetime of delivering sermons. On one level a haunt tale (a genre Bruce E. Baker in "North Carolina Lynching Ballads" includes in the "folk culture" of lynching) told to emphasize lynching's corrosive effect on white America's soul, the work also explores the construction of the color line and the incest anxiety underlying white patriarchal edicts against miscegenation.

—— The Unquenchable Fire ——

Three hundred miles of Kentucky roads that day the speedometer had registered. It was cold and my motor coat seemed to be powerless to keep me warm. Chilled to the bone, dog tired, and as hungry as a famished timber wolf, I saw at last a farmhouse in the distance. Houses were few and far between in this region of heavy timber, and night, bleak and black, was rapidly outstriding me. I decided to seek shelter.

As I turned into the long lane leading to the solitary farmhouse, I thought with pleasurable anticipation of the warm fire, the hot food, and the bed, I expected to find. All day the chill wind had been blowing an intermittent gale. Like a banshee or a weir wolf it howled. Ragged clouds raced across a dim moon like witches playing hide and seek. The shadows of the dark woods on either side of the country lane seemed to conceal unwholesome figures that were lurking there, watching for a chance to spring at my throat. Dark, desolate, chill, and cheerless, the night held but two comforting things— the patch of light from the farmhouse window, and the pencil beams of light cast by my motor lamps.

At the end of the lane, a big gate barred the way, and as I climbed from my seat to open this, I was greeted by the hollow and furious baying of two great black hounds which stood with straddled legs on the other side, and bared their fangs, reminding me of the "hound of the Baskervilles."

"Hello! Hello! The house!" I shouted. It seemed an interminable time before there came a response. A chain clanked, there was the sound of bars removed, and *slowly the door opened, the light within rushing out, like an imprisoned fairy.*

In the doorway, outlined by the light within, stood the gigantic figure of a man, whose head nearly touched the lintel. He stood with his hands shading his eyes, peering out of the half-opened door.

"Who's that?" he called. "What do ye want?" The voice was that of an old man and it contained a note of fear. It was a monotone—a dead voice, which seemed to belong to one in whom hope had died, and in it was dread. "Shut up, ye varmints," he called to the dogs, and at his voice, with tails between their legs, they slunk to cover.

"I am lost, tired, and hungry," I called, "and I want a place to stop tonight."

There was a long pause which startled me, for this was a hospitable country.

At length, the man spoke: "Wal, open the gate and drive in. The dogs won't bother you. I guess I've got to put ye up."

"A boot-legger," I said to myself, "who doesn't relish a possible prohibition officer entertained unawares." I parked my car in front of the house and entered. It was a typical farmhouse into which I came. The lamp failed to light all the big space and the dark shadows caused my eyes, unused to the glare, to be blinded to much of it. But the fireplace held a big, warm blaze which bade me a glowing welcome.

I turned to look at the man of the house and saw a once powerful figure over six feet four, now emaciated and worn. His great gnarled hands showed the strength that had been his. His face was the color of old parchment and seamed with wrinkles. The skin was drawn tightly on the cheek bones like a death mask, and his mouth constantly twitched. This spasm and the man's whole appearance revealed that he had suffered some great shock. His hair, snow-white and shaggy, stood up on his head in a most peculiar manner. It seemed to be literally standing up with fright. My gaze would stray to it. But one was most haunted by that man's eyes. They were the eyes of a trapped animal. They were filled with such horror and terror that they chilled my blood. At the slightest sound they would glance here and there like a hunted beast and glare as if in a frenzy of fear.

"Make yourself at home, stranger," said my host. "My name's Tower." As I told my name and removed my coat, there was the feeling that the name sounded vaguely familiar, but I could not remember where I had heard it.

"I'll see what Mandy can git fer you to eat. Warm yerself." With that he strode out of the room and in the distance I could hear his voice calling: "Mandy! You Mandy!" A dim voice answered—a woman's voice.

What is the matter with this man, I wondered. Some awful tragedy has overshadowed him. Just this way might Oedipus have looked when he learned that he had slain his father and taken his mother to wife.

I walked over to the fireplace and stooped to warm my hands. Suddenly behind me came a woman's voice, tired, hopeless, fearful.

"Did you see him in the lane?"

Startled, I wheeled, for I had thought myself alone in the room. Then I saw her. She sat in a rocker amid the shadows on the other side of the room. Her blue eyes burned with madness as she looked at me. Her face was pitiably thin and pinched. She wore a red calico wrapper which seemed without shape or form. *Her mouth hung open now and I could see she was insane.* Just then the fire flared up and revealed her hair. Masses of disheveled gold, falling in glistening showers around her, the light from the flames dancing upon its rippling sheen. As she sat, she rocked and rocked without cessation, and her fingers never ended pulling at her locks.

"I saw nobody," I answered, but already her attention was gone, and her wild eyes stared into space.

"What have I come upon, a mad house?" I whispered to myself. "What awful thing has happened here?"

Then the man stood in the door. "Come and git some grub," he said.

The meal was indifferent, but my hunger was a sufficient appetizer. It was served by a middle-aged mulatto woman, who gave evidence of having been very comely. My host stood by the mantel in silence and smoked as I ate. Every little while, the mulatto would glance at him with a concentrated look of hatred. At these times his mouth would twitch more rapidly and with greater violence.

I didn't sleep well, tired as I was. I didn't like the house nor its occupants, and outside the wind howled as if a thousand demons had been let loose out of hell.

It must have been about three o'clock when a wild scream awoke me. It came again and again, the long drawn-out cry of a tortured and anguished soul, and then came that moaning cry: "O pappy, O pappy, why, Oh why did we do it?"

I crept to my door and heard the murmur of voices, and that heartrending sobbing of a woman, the sobbing of a woman whose heart is broken beyond cure.

At the sound of that sobbing, like a flash came to me the memory which had eluded me all the evening. I knew now who these people were and what was their tragedy. It was a year ago that I had heard their tale, and now for the first time I recognized them as the subjects of the story told me.

Seated in the smoking compartment of a Pullman car a year ago, with the hazy outline of the same Kentucky mountains looking like purple shadows against a pale sky, my fellow travelers and I had talked about lynching. It was then that one of them, a gentleman stock breeder said: "Don't imagine that those lynched are the only ones who suffer as the result of it all. Let me tell you that often the white lyncher pays a bigger price than the Negro victim. The black man's torture is soon ended; his life snuffed out in a little while, but often, there's hell to pay for a long time afterwards for the whites who lynch."

Someone started to speak when the stock breeder continued: "May I tell you a story of what happened in this section less than a year ago?" He began: "Just twenty miles from my home is the farm of John Tower. Tower was one of the most popular men in this country. The strong man of this region, the champion amateur boxer and wrestler, the jolly spirit at gatherings, his blue eyes crinkling with his sunny smiles, his infectious laugh resounding on every occasion—he was the local hero. His golden hair and huge bulk made him look like one of the old Vikings. Women adored him, but while he had a pleasant word for all, he paid no serious attention to any of them. Tower had lost his wife, and many of the women thought that he needed a mother for his five-year-old girl, a winsome thing with her father's hair and eyes, but he did not seem to agree with them. He was immensely proud of her and while she sat on his knee and rumpled his hair by the hour, his face would light in a wonderful way. Every night, as he drove down the lane, a rare smile of joy would irradiate his countenance as the little girl would run out to the gate, and waving her arms and jumping up and down in glee, would shout, 'Here comes Daddy!'

"From some place up the state, Tower had brought a mulatto woman to keep house for him. She was a fine looking woman who had a little son about six years old. The boy had blue eyes and jet black curls and showed little trace of Negro blood. It wasn't long before the gossips were whispering that Mandy was more than a housekeeper and remarking about the boy's eyes resembling Tower's. It may have been a chance resemblance, but the boy did somehow remind one of Tower. At any rate, you know, gentlemen, that the sort of relationship implied is not uncommon here in the South. But whatever Tower and his mulatto housekeeper were to each other, everyone agreed that the boy never dreamed that Tower was his father, although he adored the man.

Wherever Tower went, you would see seated on the wagon beside him the little colored lad and, until she began to get around eleven or twelve, his little girl. The boy showed so little trace of color that strangers thought they were brother and sister. They were great chums—the two children, and Tower's friends at times warned him that it wasn't well for even the children of the two races to be so intimate.

"The boy had the habit of waiting at the end of that farmhouse lane for Tower when he did not accompany him. He would climb on the seat beside Tower and ride down the lane to open the big gate at the end. The lad's affection for Tower seemed to be returned in full measure. He wanted the boy near him, it appeared, and apparently forgot his race.

"I remember an incident when the boy sat on a box in a corner of the store where Tower was chatting with acquaintances. One of these called to the lad, "Say, little nigger, bring me that bag near you.' The boy's form grew tense but he didn't move. In one stride, Tower stood in front of the man, his fists clenched, his face white with fury. 'Call Jimmie a nigger again,' he said, 'an' I'll knock yer teeth down yer throat.'

"As a result of all this people said Tower was spoiling the boy, and that no good would come from a nigger being taught to forget his place.

"In a little while, the boy and girl had passed childhood. She was as pretty as a sunset, with something of its dazzling effect. The boy now called her Miss Annie and appeared to know his place. He was a huge lad for his twenty years, six feet two, and had the habit of holding high his head and looking you straight in the eyes—a habit that made it hard for you to remember that he was not white.

"It was shortly after this that the thunderbolt fell. Tower's girl had not been well for some time. She grew thin; her color left; she couldn't eat, and she appeared melancholy. Tower wanted to send for a physician, but she persuaded him that soon she would be well again. Mandy it was who told Tower something that caused him to send post-haste for the doctor. When he learned that Annie was to be a mother, he was like one stricken. And then he became furious. He swore that he would wring the neck of the man who had ruined his little girl, and then he began to try to force her secret from her. She had his will, and it wasn't until he reluctantly swore on her mother's bible to do no harm to her lover that Annie told his name. It was Jimmie, the colored boy, who had grown up with her. They loved each other; they knew it would not be permitted and so they had met secretly for over a year. He had wanted her to go North to marry him but she wouldn't. It was not his fault; she had loved him so much, and she had made him do her will. As she sobbed out her tale, Tower looked at her as if she were a monster. Then, white as salt, without a word, he strode over to the mantel, caught down his rifle, and started for the door. With a wild cry, the girl caught his arm, but with a shrug he flung her to the end of the room where she lay in an unconscious heap.

"The night had just fallen when he left, but the clock had struck midnight when he returned. Warned in some way, Jimmie was gone. Tower's quest had been in vain.

"No one knows what he did to that girl during the night, but in the morning when all the country round belched forth grim-faced white men with guns and dogs, the girl told a different tale. The Negro, Jim, had raped her and threatened her life, if she told; forcing her again and again to do his bidding on pain of death.

"Death was in the air when she finished her story. You could smell its acrid odor, you could taste it, you could see it reflected in the stark gleaming eye-balls of these erstwhile kindly Kentucky farmers. You could hear it in the hoarse growl of their voices—in the sharp baying of their hounds. These men, in a moment, had shed like an irksome garment centuries of civilization. They had become the man beast whose sole lust was to kill—to kill! The blood lust was theirs, and the thrall of that most ancient and exciting of sports—the man hunt.

"It wasn't much of a chase. Two hours had not gone before they found the hapless wretch in the woods near the farm.

"Like a pack of wolves, pulling down their quarry, they were upon him. Down he went under the struggling mass of frenzied men, each seeming to strike, to tear, to destroy him. Tower tore through them, throwing them aside as a hunter scatters a pack of hounds lest they ruin the skin of the kill. The men fell back, and Tower stood face to face with Jimmie. Gripping the boy's shoulders with a grasp that almost crunched the bones, his nostrils dilated, his face contorted into a horrible mask, he glared into the boy's face. The boy's eyes did not sink before his glare. His face white, but his head erect, looking for a moment like Tower's other self, he met look with look, cold blue steel meeting cold blue steel. Tower's huge hands reached for the boy's throat and then dropped to his sides. 'Take him!' he growled.

"With a beast-like snarl, the mob was upon him. Ox chains fastened him to a sturdy oak. Leaves and faggots in feverish haste were heaped around him. The blood lust hurried them. The mob had made its preparation. They poured gasoline over the faggots, over his clothing.

"All the while the boy and Tower stared each at the other. Tower's fingers opened and shut like talons—his face a grimace of hate. Whatever the boy had been to him was past. He was now only a nigger who had ruined his daughter, just as he was to the mob—a nigger who had raped a white girl.

"Someone placed a lighted torch in Tower's hand. With a snarling oath, he lighted the faggot. The flames leaped up, but before the smoke blotted out his face, Jimmie looked the last time at Tower—a look not to be forgotten. Higher leaped the flames, thicker swirled the smoke. More fuel! More gasoline! It was over and the boy had not uttered a word or cry. Unsatisfied, the mob pumped bullets into the charred body until it was literally torn to pieces.

"Things will leak out. The girl went raving mad and babbled the truth. But the mob had no remorse. 'He got what was coming to him,' they said, 'daring to have a white girl for a sweetheart!' They envisioned themselves as heroes, protectors of white womanhood and Anglo-Saxon purity of blood.

"The child came before its time—dead. The girl has never recovered her mind. She believes her Negro lover comes back to reproach her for betraying him. And Tower has become the broken, fear-haunted wretch. The neighbors leave them alone. They dwell there. The man, the girl, and Mandy—the boy's mother. Why this woman stays or why Tower permits her to stay, no one knows. She hates him. Her every gesture shows it, and some think she will yet kill him in revenge.

"Tower, it is said, believes that whenever he drives into that lane, the lad comes as he did in life, climbs to the seat beside him, and at the end, opens the gate. He says that the boy stares at him with his somber blue eyes as he did on the day of the lynching, and it causes his flesh to run cold. Tower will not leave the house after dark—for he says Jimmie is waiting outside for him. Remorse and terror stalk over at his side. The Negro lad's fate was far easier."

The stock breeder ended. There was a silence and then a mining engineer started to make some comment. Just then the porter called another station stop, and I hurried out to get together my luggage.

All this now came back to me as the echo of that cry of despair rang in my ears, "O pappy, why, O why, did we do it?"

I didn't sleep any more that night, haunted by the thought of the tragedy in that house. When gray dawn was breaking, I dressed and came down stairs, and there in front of the fireplace, with his head in his hands, as if he had not been to bed, sat Tower. In the wan light of the morning he looked more forlorn and distressed than ever.

I greeted him in as bright a manner as possible, but received no reply. Thinking that the old man, weary with his remorse had at length fallen asleep, I came nearer, when I noticed that his eyes were wide open, a look of stark horror and animal terror in them. The man was dead.

As I turned to call some occupant of the house, I noticed on a table nearby an open Bible, with the words underlined in red ink: "Where the worm dieth not, and the fire is not quenched."

From *Messenger*, November 1924, 274–276.

Lola Ridge

1873–1941

Modernist poet and political activist Lola Ridge was born in Dublin, Ireland, in 1873 and emigrated with her mother to New Zealand in 1887. In 1885 she married Peter Webster, the manager of a gold mine, then after the marriage failed, moved to Sydney to study painting. When her mother died, Ridge emigrated to the United States, where she refashioned herself as an Australian poet and painter. In 1909, she moved to Greenwich Village, where she at first earned her living writing fiction and ad copy for popular magazines; she eventually stopped because the work was so at odds with her increasingly radical beliefs. Supporting herself through a variety of jobs, including factory worker and artist's model, Ridge continued writing, publishing two poems in Emma Goldman's radical monthly *Mother Earth* in 1909 and 1911.

Ridge counted among her friends the poets William Carlos Williams and Marianne Moore, writer Jean Toomer, composer Aaron Copeland, and photographer and filmmaker Paul Strand. She held salons at her small Manhattan apartment, first for those who wrote for the *Others* magazine, of which Ridge was associate editor, and, after her appointment in 1922 as U.S. editor of *Broom*, for contributors to that magazine. In 1918, when she was forty-five, Ridge published her first book of poetry, *The Ghetto and Other Poems*, which was critically acclaimed, as was her 1920 volume *Sun-Up*. In 1927 she published *Red Flag*; in 1929, *Firehead*, a long verse poem on the Crucifixion presented as an allegory of the government execution of Sacco and Vanzetti (immigrant Italian anarchists framed for a Massachusetts robbery); and in 1935, *Dance of Fire*. None of these books is in print today.

Ridge's protest poetry includes "Frank Little at Calvary" (1918), which describes the lynching of Frank Little, a union organizer for the Industrial Workers of the World, by hired guns for the Anaconda Copper Company. Her 1919 "Lullaby," as Ridge explains in a parenthetical note to the poem, is based on "an incident of the East St. Louis Race Riots when some white women flung a living colored baby into the heart of a blazing fire." On July 2, 1917, a mob of white men, women, and children burned and destroyed nearly half a million dollars' worth of black-owned property, drove six thousand African Americans out of their homes, and shot, burned, and hanged to death by low estimates thirty-nine African American men, women, and children. By choosing one incident in which the mothers of other children viciously rock and sing to their victim before tossing it into the fire, Ridge captures a barbarity that transcends gender and age. In response and in contrast to

6. Silent protest parade on Fifth Avenue, New York City, July 28, 1917,
in response to East St. Louis Massacre. *Front row (behind drummers), from right*:
James Weldon Johnson; W.E.B. Du Bois; Rev. Hutchens Chew Bishop, rector of
St. Philip's Episcopal Church; and realtor John Nail; the other men are unidentified.
(Photographs and Prints Division, Schomburg Center for Research in Black Culture,
The New York Public Library, Astor, Lenox and Tilden Foundations.)

the riot, African Americans organized a protest parade up New York's Fifth Avenue
in which both marchers and spectators observed a solemn silence to commemorate
the victims.

"Morning Ride," from *Red Flag*, takes as its subject the 1915 lynching of Leo
Frank, a Jewish New Yorker who managed his uncle's pencil factory in Georgia
and was convicted of murdering Mary Phagan, his thirteen-year-old employee.
Frank was an upstanding, religious family man, and incriminating evidence
clearly pointed toward Jim Conley, a black sweeper at the factory with a criminal
record, as the killer. Anger over economic conditions that forced young girls to
leave the country and work in factories owned by Yankee capitalists combined
with anti-Semitism to convince the jury to accept Conley's word over Frank's,
after Frank's reputation had been vilified in a vicious smear campaign by Tom
Watson, a populist turned rabid racist, anti-Semite, and anti-Catholic. Drawing
from a stock of images similar to those used against black males, Watson por-

trayed Frank as a bestial Jewish pervert who had tried to rape and then murder an innocent Christian girl. Frank was tried, convicted, and sentenced to death in the midst of a lynch mob, as the spectators brought their weapons to court and prominently displayed banners outside that read "Hang the Jew or We'll Hang You."

There was such an outcry across the country, however, that Georgia governor John Marshall Slaton commuted the sentence to life in prison, a move that signed the death warrant of his own political career and that led to such serious threats against him he declared martial law to prevent his own lynching. On August 16, 1915, Frank was taken from a prison farm at Milledgeville by an armed mob that called itself the Knights of Mary Phagan (and that would re-form into the Knights of the Ku Klux Klan after Franks' murder). They drove Frank more than one hundred miles toward her hometown of Marietta to lynch him at her grave, but daybreak intervened and instead they hanged him from a tree on the city's outskirts.

Philip Dray calls the Frank case "one of the great national criminal dramas, on a par with the Lizzie Borden trial, the Lindbergh kidnapping, and the O. J. Simpson case" (2002, 207). In "Morning Ride," Ridge comments on lynching's pervasive influence in national popular culture, as headlines about Frank's lynching and advertisements merge with a whirling cityscape seen from the window of a New York elevated train.

—— Morning Ride ——

HEADLINES chanting—
y o u t h
l y n c h e d   t e n   y e a r s   a g o
                        c l e a r e d —
Skyscrapers
seeming still
whirling on their concrete
bases,
windows fanged—
l e o   f r a n k
l y n c h e d   t e n
     s a y   i t   w i t h   f l o w e r s
w r i g l e y ' s   s p e a r m i n t   g u m
   c a r t e r ' s   l i t t l e   l i v e r —
lean
to the soft blarney of the wind
fooling with your hair,
look
milk-clouds oozing over the blue
        Step Lively Please
        Let 'Em Out First Let 'Em Out

did he too feel it on his forehead,
the gentle raillery of the wind,
as the rope pulled taut over the tree
in the cool dawn?

From *Red Flag* (New York: Viking, 1927), 67.

Angelina Weld Grimké

1880–1958

Angelina Weld Grimké's "Tenebris" appeared in *Caroling Dusk*, a 1927 anthology edited by Countee Cullen. Trees have a special significance in Grimké's work as living symbols of traumatic violation and retribution; "Tenebris" can be usefully read alongside her undated poem "Trees," which begins with a conventional salute to trees as special symbols of God's providence that is cancelled out by an uncanny eruption of evil in the tranquil landscape, as amid the "wistful sounds of leaves" the speaker becomes aware of a "black hued something" that "swings and swings." The traumatic rupture of the everyday in "Trees" is answered in "Tenebris" by the indeterminacy of dread, an excruciating aftermath for the perpetrators of evil. (Grimké's biography appears with her story "Goldie" in this volume.)

—— Tenebris ——

There is a tree, by day,
That, at night,
Has a shadow,
A hand huge and black,
With fingers long and black.
   All through the dark,
Against the white man's house,
   In the little wind,
The black hand plucks and plucks
   At the bricks.
The bricks are the color of blood and very small.
   Is it a black hand,
   Or is it a shadow?

From *Caroling Dusk* (New York: Harper, 1927).

Walter Francis White

1893–1955

The great antilynching and civil rights advocate, novelist, and essayist Walter White was born in Atlanta in 1893. With blond hair and blue eyes, White chose to live as a black man, strategically passing for white to personally investigate dozens of lynchings and race riots. His narrow escape from harm during the Atlanta race terrorization of 1906 when he was thirteen left White forever committed to the struggle for civil rights. After graduating from Atlanta University in 1916, he began a career with the Standard Life Insurance Company, an African American–owned business. White helped organize the Atlanta branch of the NAACP, and in 1918 he accepted James Weldon Johnson's offer of the position of assistant executive secretary of the association.

In his early days with the NAACP, White "passed" to infiltrate vigilante and Klan groups of the Deep South for evidence of mob violence against African Americans. He published the results of his investigations in articles that stunned America and the world. In his classic study *Rope and Faggot* (1929), White became the first author to present a comprehensive analysis of lynching based on sociological, historical, cultural, and economic considerations. His conclusions continue to influence scholarly research and writing about lynching. The factors White cited as contributing to the lynching epidemic include the South's general backwardness, alarm over African American economic advances since the Civil War, and a complex of white southern sexual obsessions, particularly those inflamed by evangelical Christianity. Lynching's decline in the face of African American outmigration confirmed White's conclusions that the practice was primarily used as a tool to control the southern labor force.

Although his tireless lobbying for antilynching legislation did not bear fruit, White's visible and vocal agitation undoubtedly helped persuade public opinion against lynching. In 1930 White successfully lobbied the Senate against Hoover's Supreme Court nomination of North Carolina judge John Parker, a public opponent of black voting rights. White was also instrumental in ending discrimination in wartime industry and the armed services during the Second World War, and he helped convince Truman to order the desegregation of troops in 1948. In recognition of his long career as civil rights activist and executive secretary of the NAACP, White received several awards, including the Star of Ethiopia, the Haitian Order of Merit, an honorary doctorate in law from Howard University, and the prestigious Spingarn Medal in 1937.

White wrote two novels, *The Fire in the Flint* (1924), an exposé of southern lynching, and *Flight* (1926), a less successful novel of passing. In addition to his weekly column in the *Chicago Defender*, White's work also appeared in the *New York Herald Tribune*, and he served as wartime correspondent reporting on African American servicemen for the *New York Post*.

—— I Investigate Lynchings ——

Nothing contributes so much to the continued life of an investigator of lynchings and his tranquil possession of all his limbs as the obtuseness of the lynchers themselves. Like most boastful people who practice direct action when it involves no personal risk, they just can't help talk about their deeds to any person who manifests even the slightest interest in them.

Most lynchings take place in small towns and rural regions where the natives know practically nothing of what is going on outside their own immediate neighborhoods. Newspapers, books, magazines, theatres, visitors and other vehicles for the transmission of information and ideas are usually as strange among them as dry-point etchings. But

7. Flag in front of NAACP headquarters, Fifth Avenue, New York City, around 1936.
(Bettman/CORBIS.)

those who live in so sterile an atmosphere usually esteem their own perspicacity in about the same degree as they are isolated from the world of ideas. They gabble *ad infinitum* apparently unable to keep from talking.

———————

Of the forty-one lynchings and eight race riots I have investigated for the National Association for the Advancement of Colored People during the past ten years all of the lynchings and seven of the riots occurred in rural or semi-rural communities. The towns ranged in population from around one hundred to ten thousand or so. The lynchings were not difficult to inquire into because of the fact already noted that those who perpetrated them were in nearly every instance simple-minded and easily fooled individuals. On but three occasions were suspicions aroused by my too definite questions or by informers who had seen me in other places. These three times I found it rather desirable to disappear slightly in advance of reception committees imbued with the desire to make an addition to the lynching record. One other time the possession of a light skin and blue eyes (though I consider myself a colored man) almost cost me my life when (it was during the Chicago race riots in 1919) a Negro shot at me thinking me to be a white man.

II

In 1918 a Negro woman, about to give birth to a child, was lynched with almost unmentionable brutality along with ten men in Georgia.* I reached the scene shortly after the butchery and while excitement yet ran high. It was a prosperous community. Forests of pine trees gave rich returns in turpentine, tar and pitch. The small towns where the farmers and turpentine hands traded were fat and rich. The main streets of the largest of these towns were well paved and lighted. The stores were well stocked. The white inhabitants belonged to the class of Georgia crackers—lanky, slow of movement and of speech, long-necked, with small eyes set close together and skin tanned by the hot sun to a reddish-yellow hue.

As I was born in Georgia and spent twenty years of my life there, my accent is sufficiently Southern to enable me to talk with Southerners and not arouse their suspicion that I am an outsider. (In the rural South hatred of Yankees is not much less than hatred of Negroes.) On the morning of my arrival in the town I casually dropped into the store of one of the general merchants who, I had been informed, had been one of the lead-

———————

*A May 1918 lynching in Valdosta, Georgia, during mayhem that ensued when a mob, unable to find the suspected killer of white planter Hampton Smith, lynched a number of innocent men. Mary Turner, the wife of one of the slain men, denounced the lynchers and vowed to seek justice. She and the child in her womb were both killed. Turner's lynching inspired Anne Spencer's "White Things" and Angelina Grimké's "Goldie." Jean Toomer refers to the lynching in the "Kabnis" section of *Cane*.

ers of the mob. After making a small purchase I engaged the merchant in conversation. There was, at the time, no other customer in the store. We spoke of the weather, the possibility of good crops in the Fall, the political situation, the latest news from the war in Europe. As his manner became more and more friendly I ventured to mention guardedly the recent lynchings.

Instantly he became cautious—until I hinted that I had great admiration for the manly spirit the men of the town had exhibited. I mentioned the newspaper accounts I had read and confessed that I had never been so fortunate as to see a lynching. My words or tone seemed to disarm his suspicions. He offered me a box on which to sit, drew up another one for himself, and gave me a bottle of Coca-Cola.

"You'll pardon me, Mister," he began, "for seeming suspicious but we have to be careful. In ordinary times we wouldn't have anything to worry about, but with the war there's been some talk of the Federal government looking into lynchings. It seems there's some sort of law during wartime making it treason to lower the manpower of the country."

"In that case I don't blame you for being careful," I assured him. "But couldn't the Federal government do something if it wanted to when a lynching takes place, even if no war is going on at the moment?"

"Naw," he said, confidently, obviously proud of displaying his store of information to one whom he assumed knew nothing whatever about the subject. "There's no such law, in spite of all the agitation by a lot of fools who don't know the niggers as we do. States' rights won't permit Congress to meddle in lynchings in peace time."

"But what about your State government—your Governor, your sheriff, your police officers?"

"Humph! Them? We elected them to office, didn't we? And the niggers, we've got them disfranchised, ain't we? Sheriffs and police and Governors and prosecuting attorneys have got too much sense to mix in lynching-bees. If they do they know they might as well give up all idea of running for office any more—if something worse don't happen to them—" This last with a tightening of the lips and a hard look in the eyes.

I sought to lead the conversation into less dangerous channels. "Who was the white man who was killed—whose killing caused the lynchings?" I asked.

"Oh, he was a hard one, all right. Never paid his debts to white men or niggers and wasn't liked much around here. He was a mean 'un, all right, all right."

"Why, then, did you lynch the niggers for killing such a man?"

"It's a matter of safety—we gotta show niggers that they mustn't touch a white man, no matter how low-down and ornery he is."

Little by little he revealed the whole story. When he told of the manner in which the pregnant woman had been killed he chuckled and slapped his thigh and declared it to be "the best show, Mister, I ever did see. You ought to have heard the wench howl when we strung her up."

Covering the nausea the story caused me as best I could, I slowly gained the whole story, with the names of the other participants. Among them were prosperous farmers, businessmen, bankers, newspaper reporters and editors, and several law enforcement officers.

My several days of discreet inquiry began to arouse suspicions in the town. On the third day of my stay I went once more into the store of the man with whom I had first talked. He asked me to wait until he had finished serving the sole customer. When she had gone he came from behind the counter and with secretive manner and lowered voice he asked, "You're a government man, ain't you?" (An agent of the Federal Department of Justice was what he meant.)

"Who said so?" I countered.

"Never mind who told me; I know one when I see him," he replied, with a shrewd hardness in his face and voice.

Ignorant of what might have taken place since last I had talked with him, I thought it wise to learn all I could and say nothing which might commit me. "Don't you tell anyone I am a government man; if I *am* one, you're the only one in town who knows it," I told him cryptically. I knew that within an hour everybody in town would share his "information."

An hour or so later I went in at nightfall to the little but not uncomfortable hotel where I was staying. As I was about to enter a Negro approached me and, with an air of great mystery, told me that he had just heard a group of white men discussing me and declaring that if I remained in the town overnight "something would happen" to me.

The thought raced through my mind before I replied that it was hardly likely that, following so terrible a series of lynchings, a Negro would voluntarily approach a supposedly white man whom he did not know and deliver such a message. He had been sent, and no doubt the persons who sent him were white and for some reason did not dare tackle me themselves. Had they dared there would have been no warning in advance—simply an attack. Though I had no weapon with me, it occurred to me that there was no reason why two should not play at the game of bluffing. I looked straight into my informant's eyes and said, in as convincing a tone as I could muster: "You go back to the ones who sent you and tell them this: that I have a damned good automatic and I know how to use it. If anybody attempts to molest me tonight or any other time, somebody is going to get hurt."

That night I did not take off my clothes nor did I sleep. Ordinarily in such small Southern towns everyone is snoring by nine o'clock. That night, however, there was much passing and re-passing of the hotel. I learned afterward that the merchant had, as I expected, told generally that I was an agent of the Department of Justice, and my empty threat had served to reinforce his assertion. The Negro had been sent to me in the hope that I might be frightened enough to leave before I had secured evidence against the members of the mob. I remained in town two more days. My every movement was watched, but I was not molested. But when, later, it became known that not only was I not an agent of the Department of Justice but a Negro, the fury of the inhabitants of the region was unlimited—particularly when it was found that evidence I gathered had been placed in the hands of the Governor of Georgia. It happened that he was a man genuinely eager to stop lynching—but restrictive laws against which he had appealed in vain effectively prevented him from acting upon the evidence. And the Federal government declared itself unable to proceed against the lynchers.

————

On another occasion, a serious race riot occurred in Tulsa, Okla., a bustling town of 100,000 inhabitants. In the early days Tulsa had been a lifeless and unimportant village of not more than five thousand people, and its Negro residents had been forced to live in what was considered the least desirable section of the village, down near the railroad. Then oil was discovered nearby and almost overnight the village grew into a prosperous town. The Negroes prospered along with the whites, and began to erect comfortable homes, business establishments, a hotel, two cinemas and other enterprises, all of these springing up in the section to which they had been relegated. This was, as I have said, down near the railroad tracks. The swift growth of the town made this hitherto disregarded land of great value for business purposes. Efforts to purchase the land from the Negro owners at prices far below its value were unavailing. Having built up the neighborhood and knowing its value, the owners refused to be victimized.

One afternoon in 1921 a Negro messenger boy went to deliver a package in an office building on the main street of Tulsa. His errand done, he rang the bell for the elevator in order that he might descend. The operator, a young white girl, on finding that she had been summoned by a Negro, opened the door of the car ungraciously. Two versions there are of what happened then. The boy declared that she started the car on its downward plunge when he was only halfway in, and that to save himself from being killed he had to throw himself into the car, stepping on the girl's foot in doing so. The girl, on the other hand, asserted that the boy attempted to rape her in the elevator. The latter story, at best, seemed highly dubious—that an attempted criminal assault would be made by any person in an open elevator of a crowded office building on the main street of a town of 100,000 inhabitants—and in open daylight!

Whatever the truth, the local press, with scant investigation, published lurid accounts of the alleged assault. That night a mob started to the jail to lynch the Negro boy. A group of Negroes offered their services to the jailer and sheriff in protecting the prisoner. The offer was declined, and when the Negroes started to leave the sheriff's office a clash occurred between them and the mob. Instantly the mob swung into action.

The Negroes, outnumbered, were forced back to their own neighborhood. Rapidly the news spread of the clash and the numbers of mobbers grew hourly. By daybreak of the following day the mob numbered around five thousand, and was armed with machine-guns, dynamite, rifles, revolvers and shotguns, cans of gasoline and kerosene, and—such are the blessings of invention!—airplanes. Surrounding the Negro section, it attacked, led by men who had been officers in the American army in France. Outnumbered and out-equipped, the plight of the Negroes was a hopeless one from the beginning. Driven further and further back, many of them were killed or wounded, among them an aged man and his wife, who were slain as they knelt at prayer for deliverance. Forty-four blocks of property were burned after homes and stores had been pillaged.

I arrived in Tulsa while the excitement was at its peak. Within a few hours I met a commercial photographer who had worked for five years on a New York newspaper and he welcomed me with open arms when he found out that I represented a New York paper. From him I learned that special deputy sheriffs were being sworn in to guard the town from a rumored counter attack by the Negroes. It occurred to me that I could get myself sworn in as one of these deputies.

It was even easier to do than I had expected. That evening in the City Hall I had to answer only three questions—name, age, and address. I might have been a thug, a murderer, an escaped convict, a member of the mob itself which had laid waste to a large area of the city—none of these mattered; my skin was apparently white, and that was enough. After we—some fifty or sixty of us—had been sworn in, solemnly declaring we would do our utmost to uphold the laws and constitutions of the United States and the State of Oklahoma, a villainous-looking man next to me turned and remarked casually, even with a note of happiness in his voice: "Now you can go out and shoot any nigger you see and the law'll be behind you."

As we stood in the wide marble corridor of the not unimposing City Hall waiting to be assigned to automobiles which were to patrol the city during the night, I noticed a man, clad in the uniform of a captain of the United States Army, watching me closely. I imagined I saw in his very swarthy face (he was much darker than I, but was classed as a white man while I am deemed a Negro) mingled inquiry and hostility. I kept my eye on him without appearing to do so. Tulsa would not have been a very healthy place for me had my race or my previous investigations of other race riots been known there. At last the man seemed certain he knew me and started toward me.

He drew me aside into a deserted corner on the excuse that he had something he wished to ask me, and I noticed that four other men with whom he had been talking detached themselves from the crowd and followed us.

Without further introduction or apology my dark-skinned newly-made acquaintance, putting his face close to mine and looking into my eyes with a steely, unfriendly glance, demanded challengingly:

"You say that your name is White?"

I answered affirmatively.

"You say you're a newspaper man?"

"Yes, I represent the New York——. Would you care to see my credentials?"

"No, but I want to tell you something. There's an organization in the South that doesn't love niggers. It has branches everywhere. You needn't ask me the name—I can't tell you. But it has come back into existence to fight this damned nigger Advancement Association. We watch every movement of the officers of this nigger society and we're out to get them for putting notions of equality into the heads of our niggers down South here."

There could be no question that he referred to the Ku Klux Klan on the one hand and the National Association for the Advancement of Colored People on the other. As coolly as I could, the circumstances being what they were, I took a cigarette from my case and lighted it, trying to keep my hand from betraying my nervousness. When he finished speaking I asked him:

"All this is very interesting, but what, if anything, has it to do with the story of the race riot here which I've come to get?"

For a full minute we looked straight into each other's eyes, his four companions meanwhile crowding close about us. At length his eyes fell. With a shrug of his shoulders and a half-apologetic smile, he replied as he turned away, "Oh, nothing except I wanted you to know what's back of the trouble here."

It is hardly necessary to add that all that night, assigned to the same car with this man and his four companions, I maintained a considerable vigilance. When the news stories I wrote about the riot (the boy accused of attempted assault was acquitted in magistrate's court after nearly one million dollars of property and a number of lives had been destroyed) revealed my identity—that I was a Negro and an officer of the Advancement Society—more than a hundred anonymous letters threatening my life came to me. I was also threatened with a suit for criminal libel by a local paper, but nothing came of it after my willingness to defend it was indicated.

———

A narrower escape came during an investigation of an alleged plot by Negroes in Arkansas to "massacre" all the white people of the State. It later developed that the Negroes had simply organized a cooperative society to combat their economic exploitation by landlords, merchants, and bankers, many of whom openly practiced peonage. I went as a representative of a Chicago newspaper to get the facts. Going first to the capital of the State, Little Rock, I interviewed the Governor and other officials and then proceeded to the scene of the trouble, Phillips county, in the heart of the cotton-raising area close to the Mississippi.

As I stepped from the train at Elaine, the county seat, I was closely watched by a crowd of men. Within half an hour of my arrival I had been asked by two shopkeepers, a restaurant waiter, and a ticket agent why I had come to Elaine, what my business was, and what I thought of the recent riot. The tension relaxed somewhat when I implied I was in sympathy with the mob. Little by little suspicion was lessened and then, the people being eager to have a metropolitan newspaper give their side of the story, I was shown "evidence" that the story of the massacre plot was well-founded, and not very clever attempts were made to guide me away from the truth.

Suspicion was given new birth when I pressed my inquiries too insistently concerning the share-cropping and tenant farming system, which works somewhat as follows: Negro farmers enter into agreements to till specified plots of land, they to receive usually half of the crop for their labor. Should they be too poor to buy food, seed, clothing and other supplies, they are supplied these commodities by their landlords at designated stores. When the crop is gathered the landowner takes it and sells it. By declaring that he has sold it at a figure far below the market price and by refusing to give itemized accounts of the supplies purchased during the year by the tenant, a landlord can (and in that region almost always does) so arrange it that the bill for the supplies always exceeds the tenant's share of the crop. Individual Negroes who had protested against such thievery had been lynched. The new organization was simply a union to secure relief through the courts, which relief those who profited from the system meant to prevent. Thus the story of a "massacre" plot.

Suspicion of me took definite form when word was sent to Phillips county from Little Rock that it had been discovered that I was a Negro, though I knew nothing about the message at the time. I walked down West Cherry street, the main thoroughfare of Elaine, one day on my way to the jail, where I had an appointment with the sheriff, who was going to permit me to interview some of the Negro prisoners who were being implicated in the alleged plot. A tall, heavy-set Negro passed me and, *sotto voce*, told me as he passed that he had something important to tell me, and that I should turn to the right at the next corner and follow him. Some inner sense bade me obey. When we had got out of sight of other persons the Negro told me not to go to the jail, that there was great hostility in the town against me and that they planned harming me. In the man's manner there was something which made me certain he was telling the truth. Making my way to the railroad station, since my interview with the prisoners (the sheriff and jailer being present) was unlikely to add anything to my story, I was able to board one of the two trains a day out of Elaine. When I explained to the conductor—he looked at me so inquiringly—that I had no ticket because delays in Elaine had given me no time to purchase one, he exclaimed, "Why, Mister, you're leaving just when the fun is going to start! There's a damned yaller nigger down here passing for white and the boys are going to have some fun with him."

I asked him the nature of the fun.

"Wal, when they get through with him," he explained grimly, "he won't pass for white no more."

From *American Mercury*, January 1929, 77–84.

1931–1935

Sterling Brown

1901–1989

Poet, critic, educator, and folklorist Sterling Brown was born in Washington, D.C. The son of a distinguished theologian and professor, Brown grew up at Howard University and attended the famed Dunbar High School, where his teachers included the poet Angelina Weld Grimké and the writer and editor Jessie Fauset. Brown received his B.A. from Williams College, where he was Phi Beta Kappa. He received his M.A. in English from Harvard in 1923.

After graduation, Brown taught at African American colleges such as Virginia Seminary in Lynchburg, Virginia, and Lincoln University in Missouri. In 1929, he joined the faculty of Howard University, where he would teach until his retirement in 1969. While at Virginia Seminary, Brown conceived a lifelong fascination for the folk life, stories, and language of the rural black poor. In his poetry and his criticism, Brown's folk-based aesthetic united a passion for jazz and the blues with a joy in the rhythm of speech. His own poetry was strongly influenced by such poets as Edwin Arlington Robinson, Robert Frost, Vachel Lindsay, and Carl Sandburg, whose poems celebrated vernacular language and daily life. It was Brown's practice to visit rural communities, spending time collecting folklore at local barbershops and jook joints. The colorful characters such as Slim Greer, Calvin "Big Boy" Davis, and Mrs. Bibby who appear in his poetry were inspired by the people he met on these excursions.

Throughout the twenties, Brown published poems in the *Crisis*, *Opportunity*, *Contempo*, *Ebony*, and *Topaz*. His first collection of poetry, *Southern Road*, was published in 1932, and he would not publish another until 1975, *The Last Ride of Wild Bill and Eleven Narratives*. Throughout the 1930s, Brown worked as literary editor of *Opportunity* and served as Negro-affairs editor for the Federal Writers Project. He also served on the editorial board of the *Crisis* and was involved with the American Council of Learned Societies, the American Folklore Society, the Carnegie Myrdal Study of Race Relations in the United States, and the Institute of Jazz Studies.

Many consider Brown's critical and scholarly study of African American literature his most important legacy. His foundational writings on the African American literary tradition include his essay "Negro Characters as Seen by White Authors," published in the *Journal of Negro Education* in 1933; his critical studies *The Negro in American Fiction* and *Negro Poetry and Drama* (both 1937); and the 1941 anthology *Negro Caravan*, which he edited with Arthur P. Davis and Ulysses Lee.

Brown based his poems "He Was a Man" and "Let Us Suppose," published in *Opportunity* in 1932 and 1935, on actual lynchings. On December 4, 1931, a mob of two thousand in Salisbury, Maryland, took Mack Williams, an African American man charged with murdering his employer, from his hospital cot, hanged him in front of the courthouse, and cremated his body. Brown's ballad "He Was a Man" enshrines Williams as a folk hero for his unassuming dignity and courage. "Let Us Suppose" was based on the September 26, 1933, lynching of John White, a young African American accused of rape in Opelousas, a part of Louisiana with a long history of racial violence. Sixty-five years earlier, on September 28, 1868, a mob of violent whites (many of them prominent citizens) beat up Emerson Bentley, an eighteen-year-old white teacher with the Freedmen's Bureau and editor of the Republican newspaper in Opelousas. When blacks came to his rescue, twelve were arrested by the sheriff, only to be taken from jail and lynched that night. For the next few days terror reigned, as whites hunted the fields and swamps surrounding Opelousas and massacred every African American they could find. It is estimated that two hundred people lost their lives in the mayhem. In the 1933 lynching, the Opelousas mob seized White from law officers and shot him to death, riddling his body with bullets. Brown's elegiac lament manages to celebrate White's life while painting a bleak portrait of the peril remarkable individuals faced under the Jim Crow regime.

—— He Was a Man ——

It wasn't about no woman,
It wasn't about no rape,
He wasn't crazy, and he wasn't drunk,
An' it wasn't no shooting scrape,
He was a man, and they laid him down.

He wasn't no quarrelsome feller,
And he let other folks alone,
But he took a life, as a man will do,
In a fight to save his own,
He was a man, and they laid him down.

He worked on his little homeplace
Down on the Eastern Shore;
He had his family, and he had his friends,
And he didn't expect much more,
He was a man, and they laid him down.

He wasn't nobody's great man,
He wasn't nobody's good,
Was a po' boy tried to get from life
What happiness he could,
He was a man and they laid him down.

He didn't abuse Tom Wickley,
Said nothing when the white man curst,
But when Tom grabbed his gun, he pulled his own,
And his bullet got there first,
He was a man, and they laid him down.

Didn't catch him in no manhunt
But they took him from a hospital bed,
Stretched on his back in the nigger ward,
With a bullet wound in his head,
He was a man, and they laid him down.

It didn't come off at midnight
Nor yet at the break of day,
It was in the broad noon daylight,
When they put po' Will away,
He was a man, and they laid him down.

Didn't take him to no swampland,
Didn't take him to no woods,
Didn't hide themselves, didn't have no masks,
Didn't wear no Ku Klux hoods,
He was a man, and they laid him down.

They strung him up on Main Street,
On a tree in the Court House Square,
And people came from miles around
To enjoy a holiday there,
He was a man, and they laid him down.

They hung him and they shot him,
They piled packing cases around,
They burnt up Will's black body,
Cause he shot a white man down;
"He was a man, and we'll lay him down."

It wasn't no solemn business,
Was more like a barbecue,
The crackers yelled when the fire blazed,
And the women and the children too—
"He was a man, and we laid him down."

The Coroner and the Sheriff
Said "Death by Hands Unknown."
The mob broke up by midnight,
"Another uppity Nigger gone—
He was a man, an' we laid him down."

From *Opportunity*, June 1932, 17–19.

—— Let Us Suppose ——

Let us suppose him differently placed
In wider fields than these bounded by bayous
And the fringes of moss-hung trees
Over which, in lazy spirals, the caranc[h]os soar and dip.

Let us suppose these horizons pushed farther,
So that his eager mind,
His restless senses, his swift eyes,
Could glean more than the sheaves he stored
Time and time again:
Let us suppose him far away from here.

Or let us, keeping him here; suppose him
More submissive, less ready for the torrent of hot Cajan speech,
The clenched fist, the flushed face,
The proud scorn and the spurting anger;
Let us suppose him with his hat crumpled in his hand,
The proper slant to his neck, the eyes abashed,
Let us suppose his tender respect for his honor
Calloused, his debt to himself outlawed.

Let us suppose him what he could never be.

Let us suppose him less thrifty
Less the hustler from early morning until first dark,
Let us suppose his corn weedy,
His cotton rusty, scantily fruited, and his fat mules poor.
His cane a sickly yellow
Like his white neighbor's.

Let us suppose his burnt brick color,
His shining hair thrown back from his forehead,
His stalwart shoulders, his lean hips,
His gently fused patois of Cajan, Indian, African,
Let us suppose these less the dragnet
To her, who might have been less lonesome
Less driven by Louisiana heat, by lone flat days,
And less hungry.

Let us suppose his full-throated laugh
Less repulsive to the crabbed husband,
Let us suppose his swinging strides
Less of an insult to the half-alive scarecrow
Of the neighboring fields:
Let us suppose him less fermenting to hate.

Let us suppose that there had been
In this tiny forgotten parish, among these lost bayous,
No imperative need
Of preserving unsullied, Anglo-Saxon mastery.

Let us suppose. . . .
Oh, let us suppose him alive.

(Opelousas, La.)

From *Opportunity*, September 1935, 281.

Langston Hughes

1902–1967

One of the most influential black U.S. writers of the twentieth century, Langston Hughes, set off with his friend Zell Ingram on March 22, 1931, for a brief tour of the South. While driving to Florida they read about the arrest of nine black youths on March 25, 1931, for raping two white women aboard a freight train as it passed near the town of Scottsboro, Alabama. The youths narrowly escaped lynching only to be convicted in a legal lynching, a show trial attended by an angry mob. The International Labor Defense, the American Communist Party's legal arm, took over the boy's defense, widely publicizing the case and further exacerbating regional and racial antagonisms.

In July 1931, in an incident reminiscent of the 1919 Elaine, Arkansas, massacre, an armed white mob attacked a black church in Camp Hill, Alabama, where a sharecropper's union was meeting. (For an account of the Elaine massacre, see William Pickens's "Lynching and Debt Slavery" in this volume.) A number of African Americans were wounded in the ensuing exchange of gunfire. In the next few days, armed posses of five hundred whites roamed the countryside hunting blacks. The official death toll stood at one black murdered and five wounded, but the actual number was probably higher.

It was into this charged atmosphere that Langston Hughes returned on a $1,000 grant from the Rosenwald Fund to undertake a reading tour of the South. When the editors of *Contempo*, an unofficial student magazine at the all-white University of North Carolina at Chapel Hill, asked Hughes for a contribution to their December 1931 issue, he responded with a blistering essay on the Scottsboro case, which was featured on the front cover of the magazine. "Christ in Alabama" appeared inside. Hughes was incensed that black colleges remained silent about the case, asking when he visited Tuskeegee in February 1932, "If the Communists don't awaken the Negroes of the South, who will?" "Christ in Alabama" was reprinted in a pamphlet entitled *Scottsboro Limited*, published with the assistance of Carl Van Vechten and Prentiss Taylor through their Golden Stair Press in 1932. (Hughes's biography appears with his poem "The South" in this volume.)

—— **Christ in Alabama** ——

Christ is a Nigger,
Beaten and black—
O, bare your back.

Mary is His Mother
Mammy of the South,
Silence your Mouth.

God's his father—
White Master above
Grant us your love.

Most holy bastard
Of the bleeding mouth:
Nigger Christ
On the cross of the South.

From *Contempo*, December 1931, 1; reprinted in *Scottsboro, Limited*
(New York: Golden Stair Press, 1932), n.p.

Nancy Clara Cunard

1896–1965

Poet, radical activist, journalist, publisher, and collector of African art Nancy Cunard was a central figure in the avant-garde movement of the 1920s. Striking in looks and manner, Cunard inspired many artists to make her the subject of their work. Man Ray photographed her, and Constanin Brancusi made a famous sculpture of Cunard that paid homage to her fascination with African art. No mere bohemian, Cunard was also a fervent supporter of antifascist causes and black civil rights: her crusades included Ethiopia, the Scottsboro Boys, and Republican Spain. The only child of the American socialite Maude Burke and Sir Bache Cunard of the famous shipping family, Cunard enjoyed an extremely privileged upbringing. She received her education at several exclusive schools in London, Germany, and Paris, where she became friends with a literary circle that included writer Osbert Sitwell and poet Ezra Pound. After a brief and disastrous marriage, Cunard turned seriously to the business of writing. Her poetry first appeared in magazines in 1916. She moved to Paris in 1920, where she became associated with the Dada and Modernist movements. She published three volumes of poetry—*Outlaws* (1921); *Sublunary* (1923); and *Parallax* (1925)—the last brought out by Virginia Woolf and her husband, Leonard's, Hogarth Press.

In 1928, Cunard founded the Hours Press, which published the works of such authors as Samuel Beckett, Richard Aldington, Ezra Pound, Norman Douglas, Laura Riding, and George Moore. That same year, she met and fell in love with the African American jazz musician Henry Crowder. Through Crowder, Cunard discovered the *Crisis*, the *Liberator*, and the writings of W.E.B. Du Bois, Walter White, and William Pickens—and began a lifelong commitment to alleviating racial oppression. The couple's cohabitation in London caused a major scandal in the British press, leading to Cunard's total estrangement from her mother and to her libel suit against the British papers. After fleeing to the continent, Cunard published a highly personalized attack, *Black Man and White Ladyship* (1931), that criticized her mother's life and values. In 1932, she became involved in the campaign to free the Scottsboro Boys, fund-raising and serving as head of their defense committee in England.

With Crowder she published *Negro, an Anthology* (1934), a comprehensive history that celebrates the social, political, cultural, and artistic achievements of the African diaspora and makes an eloquent plea for civil rights. Cunard used her connections brilliantly to secure 150 contributors preeminent in contemporary art, lit-

8. May 14, 1934, Mother's Day. Appealing for presidential intervention on behalf of their sons
on death row, the mothers of some of the Scottsboro Boys, with Richard B. Moore
of the International Labor Defense, and Ruby Bates, one of the alleged victims.
From left: Ida Norris, Janine Patterson, Bates, Mamie Williams, Viola Montgomery, and Moore.
(AP/Wide World Photos.)

erature, and intellectual thought, including Louis Armstrong, Samuel Beckett, Norman Douglas, Theodore Dreiser, W.E.B. Du Bois, Langston Hughes, Zora Neale Hurston, William Plomer, Arthur Schomburg, and William Carlos Williams. International in approach, the anthology included sections on the United States, Europe, Africa, the West Indies, and South America. Passionately devoted to the project, Cunard paid for the printing of the anthology herself using proceeds from the settlement of her lawsuit against the British press.

At the outbreak of the Spanish Civil War, Cunard went to Spain as a freelance writer for the *Manchester Guardian* and other publications. She polled British writers on their attitudes toward the conflict and published their comments in the pamphlet *Authors Take Sides on the Spanish Civil War* (1937). Cunard also agitated for better treatment for the Spanish refugees and Republican prisoners. Along with writers Sylvia Townsend Warner and Valentine Ackland, she joined the British delegation to the Second Congress of the International Association of Writers for the Defense of Culture held in Madrid in 1937. Traveling extensively in South America, the Caribbean, and Tunisia, she wrote critically of colonialism abroad and of racism in

England and the United States. Other publications included *Poems for France* (1944), *Grand Man: Memories of Norman Douglas* (1954), *GM: Memories of George Moore* (1956), and a posthumously published memoir, *These Were the Hours* (1965).

Although Cunard never joined the Communist Party, she declares in *Negro* that "the Communist world order is the solution of the race problem of the Negro," a position that led to her vociferous support of the party's legal arm, the International Labor Defense, in its dispute with the NAACP over the defense of the Scottsboro Boys. Her coverage of the case transcends such partisanship, however, because of her important positioning of the "Scottsboro frame-up" as part of the economic exploitation of the African American worker. Cunard begins "Scottsboro—and Other Scottsboros" with a summary of the incident for which nine black youths, the youngest thirteen, were accused of raping two white women on an Alabama train and convicted in a trial so prejudiced it drew international condemnation. The ILD took the boys' appeal all the way to the Supreme Court, which in its 1932 ruling in *Powell v. Alabama* ordered a retrial. The selection that follows is Cunard's account of the second trial. She makes clear her opinion of southern "justice" by refusing to capitalize the honorific "sheriff" or "judge." Cunard's impassioned polemic reveals how what initially began as a quarrel over the right of black men to inhabit space became charged with the sexual mythology used to justify segregation and racial violence, a mythology discredited forever by the courage of a poor white woman who finally told the truth.

—— Excerpt from ——
"Scottsboro—and Other Scottsboros"

To bring out the absolute fiendishness of the treatment of Negro workers by the governing white class in America, more specifically, but by no means restrictedly, in the Southern States, I am going to start with what may seem a fantastic statement—I am going to say that the Scottsboro case is not such an astounding and unbelievable thing as it must, as it certainly does, appear to the public at large. What? 9 provenly innocent Negro boys, falsely accused of raping two white prostitutes, tried and re-tried, still held in death cells after 2 1/2 years. . . . It is unparalleled. It is not *primarily* a case that can be called political as is that of Tom Mooney, still held for 18 years in St. Quentin, a California jail, on an equally vicious frame-up because he was an active strike-leader; nor at first sight do the same elements predominate as in Meerut and the murder-by-law of Sacco and Vanzetti.* But the same capitalist oppression and brutality are at the root—

---

*Tom Mooney, a San Francisco labor leader sentenced to death for the 1916 Preparedness Day bombing, was pardoned by Governor Culburt Olson in 1939. The Meerut trial (1929–1933) followed a wave of strikes in 1928 and 1929 in the railroad, ironworks, and textile industries; thirty-three trade unionists were found guilty of conspiracy. Although their sentences were later reduced, the arrests effectively dismantled the fledgling Communist Party of India. Sacco and Vanzetti were Italian immigrant anarchists convicted of a 1920 Massachusetts payroll robbery. In spite of the public outcry protesting their innocence, the two were executed in 1927. In 1977, Governor Michael Dukakis cleared their names.

because every Negro worker is the potential victim of lynching, murder and legal lynching by the white ruling class, simply because he is a worker and black. No, this frame-up is not unparalleled, though the scale of it and its colossal development into what is now really a world-issue, are so. No previous Negro case has aroused such a universal outcry against the abomination of American "law."

> [Cunard goes on to list a number of "other Scottsboros" in which obviously innocent men and women have been lynched, "legally" and otherwise, in the past two years. She then summarizes the first trial and subsequent efforts by the ILD to achieve justice in the case.]

Ruby Bates Repudiates the Rape Lie

About two or three months after [the end of the first trial], while the I.L.D. was preparing the whole of the case anew for rehearing, it became public that a letter written by Ruby Bates to a boy friend, in which she stated that she had lied about the "rape," had been seized and kept by the police. The defence forced this to be handed over to the court as evidence. Ruby Bates had written:

> Jan. 5, 1932, Huntsville, Alabama.

> dearest Earl, I want too make a statement too you. Mary Sanders is a god-damn lie about those Negroes, those policemen made me tell a lie. that is my stement because i want too clear myself that is all too if you want to belive me ok. if not that is ok. you will be sorry some day. if you had too stay in jail with 8 Negroes you would tell a lie two. those Negroes did not touch me or those white boys. i hope you will belive me the law dont. i love you better than Mary does ore any body else in the world that is why i am telling you of this thing. i was drunk at the time and did not know what i was doing. i know it was wrong to let those Negroes die on account of me. i hope you will believe my statement because it is the god's truth. i wish those Negroes are not Burnt on account of me. it is these white boys fault. that is my statement and that is all i know. I hope you tell the law; hope you will answer. Ruby Bates. P.S. this is one time that i might tell a lie but it is the truth so god help me.

The Decatur Re-Trial

March 27 had been set for the re-trial in Decatur, Alabama, although the defence had asked for a change of venue to the large town of Birmingham as less likely to contain the lynch spirit so dominant in Scottsboro. Decatur is under 40 miles from Scottsboro and as frantically, bitterly prejudiced. But change of venue had been denied. At this time prosecuting attorney Knight made statements to the press that the boys had had a fair trial and would have a fair re-trial. It has been seen how fair the first trial was. At this time also Knight opposed the defence lawyers when they asked that action be taken against the militiaman who had stuck a bayonet into Roy Wright's face in addition to the beating and torturing that he had undergone in the attempt to make him testify against the other boys. Knight said a Negro's accusation was of no value, and covertly opposed demands from the defence for private interviews with the boys prior to the trial; the presence of guards of course preventing prisoners from speaking openly.

On March 27 the trial opened. The chief figures in it are:

Samuel Leibowitz, defence counsel, a celebrated criminal lawyer from the North, who had never yet lost one of his very numerous cases.

Joseph Brodsky, chief lawyer of the International Labor Defense.

General George Chamlee, of Chattanooga.

State Attoney Prosecutor Knight, who had prosecuted the cases at Scottsboro, a Southerner, of the rankest cracker type.

Judge Horton, the same who was later to hear the 2nd Alabama Supreme Court appeal.

Ruby Bates, one of the two white girls, who had repudiated her false testimony and whose letter to a white boy friend confessing she had lied had been stolen and kept for months by the police.

Lester Carter, one of the white boys on the train, who now came forward to testify to the Negroes' innocence and to denounce the frame-up.

Although all the boys were brought to Decatur, only *Heywood Patterson* was tried.

As at Scottsboro, the crowd began to collect early; the courtroom was jammed. There were soldiers everywhere, by the judge's desk, and outside, hedging in the courthouse with drawn bayonets. About 400 people inside the court, of whom a third were Negroes. These last were of course in the separate jim-crow pen, including the two Negro reporters from the *Afro-American* and the *Norfolk Journal and Guide*. To leave at the end of each session the Negroes had to wait seated until the whites had gone out first. Meanwhile the Southerners were proclaiming *there is no discrimination*. In the same breath they would say that men of dark skins are not "of sound mind." This idiocy was thrown into sharp relief by the courageous and intelligent testimony of a Negro plasterer from Scottsboro put on the stand for the defence the first day. At two o'clock a van rolled up with the boys from Birmingham jail, preceded and followed by squads with riot guns and tear gas. Olin Montgomery is nearly blind. He stumbled as he got out. A wave went through the crowd. They thought he'd been shot; they thought the shootings were beginning. That was the state of tension the townsfolk were in. As Roy Wright entered the court Leibowitz came and shook him by the hand, to the angry stupor of court officials. By now the audience had increased to about 600, and half of these were Negro.

A Southerner, Mary Heaton Vorse, a white author, who was present throughout the entire trial, told me that the Negroes and whites were "perfectly friendly, fraternising even" everywhere except in court, where the tension was bitter, violent, at times positively frantic, so that you didn't know what mightn't happen. I find this "friendliness" too difficult to believe; one cannot see how this could happen, with the daily insults flung by Knight at the Negroes, with his appeals based on race difference and prejudice made continuously to the only-too-appreciative jury. I think her desire that it should be so made it seem so to her—as also her statement that judge Horton was just and well-disposed . . . a fact that I will come to presently proved it otherwise. We know there are degrees in the visibility of prejudice.

All through the day small organized bands of whites from surrounding communities such as Scottsboro, Huntsville and Athens kept filtering into the town, adding to the danger of "extra-legal" action, a danger to the boys, to witnesses called for the defence, to the defence itself. "There is no danger whatever to the prisoners," proclaimed the authorities. The jail the boys were kept in during the two weeks of the trial was so rotten and old it had been abandoned for white prisoners. "Why you could break out of it with a spoon," said a sheriff—indicating unwittingly it could be broken into as easily.

The first proceedings were statements by defending counsel Leibowitz that *no Negroes had been employed on juries for 40 years. This is illegal*; this is in exact opposition to the 13th, 14th and 15th amendments to the U.S. Constitution, which guarantee that Negroes shall serve. These amendments had to be made in 1865, for until Abolition no Negroes had any rights, civic, legal or political. These amendments are systematically, unfailingly disregarded in all the Southern States, as Leibowitz proceeded to show when he called for the jury roll. There was not a name on it of any Negro citizen qualified to serve; not one had served within living memory. Knight refused to answer on this point. "Prove it," was his retort. And Leibowitz proved it.

An arc light was thrown on the cracker mentality when Benson, of the Scottsboro Progressive Age, was called in. Leibowitz asked him if he had ever known a Negro to be placed on the jury roll. "Never heard of one, never noticed one," answered Benson with apologetic glances at prosecutor Knight. "There are 666 Negroes of serving age in Jackson county [where Scottsboro is situated], were none of these qualified to serve as jurors?" continued Leibowitz. "Some of them are good Negroes as far as Negroes go," said Benson, "but they couldn't be said to possess sound judgment, they couldn't get round that clause, and they all steal; they haven't been trained for jury duty" (!) "I might say the same thing about women—the Negroes haven't been trained, not made a study of justice and law, and such." The defence collected evidence showing that there were 26 Negroes at least who could have served in the Scottsboro trial.

No, it was not the trial of the nine boys, particularly during the whole first week in Decatur; it was the trying and proving guilty of the entire Southern manner of denying to the Negro his constitutional rights.

Meanwhile, and throughout the trial, and ever since, and without doubt in the future too, the Southern authorities, press, etc., proclaim that there is neither discrimination nor prejudice; and that these fiendish and scandalous trials were "fair." William Patterson, national secretary of the American I.L.D., himself a Negro, and a lawyer, analysing, commenting on the whole matter wrote: "If the authorities of Alabama had been or were in any way sincere in their claim to a desire to give the boys a fair trial and to prevent them being lynched, they themselves, through their organ the capitalist press, would issue a call for full social, political and economic equalities for the Negro, and expose the real reason why the Negro people are now in such a state of oppression, and why the Scottsboro boys are framed on faked charges. But this they cannot do, for capitalism would then no longer be capitalism."

The sheriff of Morgan county, in which Decatur is situated, needed 30 national guardsmen to "prevent the boys escaping"; the same troops which had beaten and mistreated them previously and were soon to do so again. It is a recognised provocation to lynch mobs to call in the aid of the National Guard; double provocation to call in, as was suggested, the Federal troops.

On this first trial day, the judge, Horton, overrules the defence's demand that all the indictments be quashed on the ground of the absence of Negro jurors. Knight's cracker spirit begins to rise. He addresses the witness Tom Sanford, Negro plasterer, as "John," bullies and browbeats him. Leibowitz remarks sharply, "Call witness Mr. Sanford." "Not doing that," answers Knight. Then a lynching pamphlet is discovered. It is being hawked about in the crowd. A battle opens between defence and prosecution; Leibowitz demands its suppression, Knight defends its right to be circulated. Finally the judge has it confiscated.

A day or two later Knight jumps to his feet clapping his hands during the declaration of a prosecution witness that the boys took a penknife from Victoria Price. Constantly there are little incidents of this sort, rabid pin-pricks of hatred studding the whole of the trial. The testimonies of state (prosecution) witnesses form an indescribable jumble of lies and contradictions, each more stupefying than the last. They are contrasted against each other by Leibowitz. For example: Price said she fainted after the "rape" in the train; but a state witness affirmed he saw her walking and talking. Another had seen a Negro prevent a white girl from jumping off the train—but the photograph taken subsequently from the spot where he stood showed that he could have seen nothing at all. Price's overalls, she said, were torn and stained; yet they were neither when produced in court. "And why were they not introduced into the first trial?" asked Leibowitz. Knight and the judge made objection to this query. Throughout, Price spoke mechanically, maintaining the whole of the rape story with its knives and guns, but only answered questions at the direct prompting of Knight. And the two doctors, Bridges and Lynch, called by the State, branded as false the story she told of being battered and bleeding. She was without any marks or wounds, save a few scratches which would be likely to come from clambering about on the train and from the gravel in the freight-car she'd travelled in. While she was being cross-examined a man got up in court. "Let's get Leibowitz now," he muttered. The soldiers seized and searched him for arms and put him out. Also were put out two others who had begun a struggle.

The lives of Leibowitz, Brodsky, Ruby Bates, Lester Carter and the boys were in constant danger from mobs or gangs forming daily, broadcasting their intention of lynching them. Well it would have been too much even for the State of Alabama if four white people, the four chief protagonists in this case angrily watched by a universe, had been murdered. So all the time a handful of soldiers was set around lawyers and witnesses. They didn't know it perhaps, but at the time that Ruby Bates and Lester Carter were giving evidence two lynch-mobs had already started out from Huntsville and Scottsboro to get them. The militia posted along and across the roads outside Decatur turned them back. In keeping with the reiterated lie that nothing at all was going on, given out by the authorities, the press were asked not to mention this. But the press said they had come to send news and to take photos. "Send it only if something happens." Terrorisation or interference with the press was a strong feature throughout. Photographers were threatened at Paint Rock while taking pictures of the scene of arrest. A group of black and white people were arrested because found together in a Negro neighbourhood; charged with contempt of court (!) they were then brought before judge Horton. A white journalist, Fuller, had already been run out of the town because he was reporting for a Negro daily, the *Atlanta World*. As to Leibowitz, they called him "a Russian Jew Nigger who ought to be hung." But the attitude and spirit of the Negro population were stirringly militant. "If a mob comes we're not running," they said. They were told, of course, that the Communists were only making propaganda and that they did not care about the issue of the trials. "If the reds are responsible for all this," said the Negro workers, "then we are with them."

And the boys in the rotten jail you could break out of with a spoon. . . . A special correspondent went to see them: Thirteen iron steps and the shadow of the hangman's noose. So, for two years, they'd been face to face with the electric chair across the passage in front of their cells and now they had the gallows to stare at in the electric light. On the last step was the trap-door to eternity—a painting of Christ at Gethsemane, done by some dead convict, above it. The correspondent looked at the gallows and the Christ. Then he saw the eyes—the Scottsboro boys were looking at him. It was full of shadows in the place—jailors and guards moving about, the shadow of the actual noose, shadows of themselves shuffling round, straining ears for the rumble of mobs. They couldn't sleep; they were wondering all time if they would die in Decatur, lynched, or be convicted again. Did they dare even to think of possibility of acquittal? Vermin was on them, the cockroaches crept over the filthy cell floor; the bed bugs lived in their clothes, they couldn't get them out; jail gives no change of clothes. "What'll you do when you are freed?" asked the journalist. "Olin Montgomery seized one of the greasy bars and leaned against it, peering intently with his one near-sighted eye, 'Go home,' he said simply. 'Oh boss, I wants to go home. I been here 2 years and 9 days, 2 years and 9 days.'"

Between the scenes in court, the gallows and the mob threats, the blood-lust outside and the agony, terror and despair within, the brutalities of the jailors and the thought of death that must never leave them, how is it that these boys did not go insane?

In court the "lantern-jowled morons," as Leibowitz ended by calling them, are sitting and smoking, very informal. Plenty of them out of work in this impoverished, rotting

South always 50 years behind the times in everything. Hard eyes staring at judge and counsel. Only a whetting of the appetite so far to be sure, the death hunger will be sated all right, for haven't they been assured again and again that the boys won't get out of Decatur if the jury does acquit them? The Negroes sit apart, straining to hear and see, grim and silent. Other Negroes outside, trying to see into the court. Leibowitz and Chamlee keep Heywood Patterson between them. There's a photo in a French paper, Heywood Patterson is holding a horseshoe. . . . "Were you tried at Scottsboro?" "I was *framed* in Scottsboro."

They try to force him to admit he pronounced a phrase they have invented themselves: "I told you if we had killed those girls we wouldn't be here." Knight has announced that he will simply *ignore* Ruby Bates' repudiation of her Scottsboro testimony, her admittance of perjury. A little later Knight says he'll have her arrested for perjury. Leibowitz tells the world that the Negroes are being framed up—he says he will fight like hell to save them.

"The Negroes Never Touched Me,
As They Never Touched Victoria Price"

This is what Ruby Bates told the court. Though they had heard she was coming now to be a witness for the boys, and that she had publicly repudiated the rape lie, to hear this Southern white girl, one of themselves utter this statement, made them aghast and convulsed them with fury. It is the first great crack in the old Southern structure of white supremacy. It will never be forgotten, it is a very high and splendid point in the history of black and white. Realise too that it needed very great courage, physical and moral in these two young white Southerners, Ruby Bates and Lester Carter. With their testimony they were piercing the whole of the rotten Southern fabric of lies and race hatred, holding it up to the entire world, tearing it inside out.

Knight and other court authorities said Lester Carter and Ruby Bates had been "bought" by the Communists, pointed at the different clothes the latter was now wearing (most ordinary city girl's clothes). "We didn't dress Victoria Price up like a lily of the valley," vociferated the state prosecutor. Until her appearance in court Knight had been angrily shouting: " Produce Ruby Bates!" and saying it could not be done. She came in with Brodsky and Mrs. Jones, a social worker. "You have been asking for Ruby," said Leibowitz quietly, "here she is. I ask that she be sworn." An electric shock went through the court. An I.L.D. Scottsboro release says: "Knight, who had been in the witness room preparing rebuttal witnesses, rushed back into the courtroom. Judge Horton called for order; an extra cordon of soldiers was thrown round the courthouse. Victoria Price was called in and stood staring at Ruby as she was asked to identify her as her companion on the trip."

Cross-examined by Knight with all the rancour and viciousness that one can visualise, she made a flat denial of the rape, could not identify Heywood Patterson, explained that she had lied out of excitement, ignorance, terrorisation by the police and at Victoria's prompting to escape jail. "The whole thing was a frame-up," she said. And it had troubled her so long that finally she had left her home in Huntsville in February 1933 and gone to New York, and seen Rev. Dr. Fosdyck, and he had told her to go back South and tell the truth at Decatur. She had not even known the meaning of the word "rape"; she had had to ask her mother what it meant; that was after the Scottsboro trial. No, the boys had certainly not touched her or Victoria.

Lester Carter, a tall blond Southern boy, gave evidence too. His conscience had been at him for two years, since the frame-up. Now, here, it was "like getting well from being dead." His story tallied with Ruby's; he had been on the train with the girls—he was very detailed. He'd met them both in Huntsville jail in 1931; he was then doing 50 days on a chain gang. Victoria was under sentence too. And Ruby had come to see her. After they'd got out they had met again and planned the trip. They'd spent that night in the Chattanooga jungle. The other boy who was along was married, so he hadn't accompanied them on the journey; he was going to follow later. On the train, he (Lester) had seen some white boys throwing stones at some Negroes; they'd shouted to him to come and join them, so he'd gone along. Then he jumped off the train when one of the Negroes took a swing at him. They did not have either knives or guns. He had been one of those who had notified the authorities about the fight. At Paint Rock, later, he'd overheard Victoria ask Orvil Gilley to pass as her brother, so that she wouldn't be arrested for hoboing. And in Scottsboro jail, where they had all been locked up without knowing on what charge, he heard those two having a quarrel, Victoria telling Gilley he must keep to her story, and what did niggers matter anyway? let 'em all go to jail. But Gilley had said she was mad, and that "some time a nigger may have to testify to save *your* life." Of course the State interjected here that Carter had been coached to say all this. So Carter told how he had been in the Scottsboro prison for 16 days and barred from testifying because they saw he wouldn't lie. After that he'd been so uneasy in his mind he had bummed his way to Albany in New York State to see Governor Roosevelt, who refused to see him. And finally he had heard that the I.L.D. in New York was defending the boys and had gone to them.

What did Knight do in the face of this testimony?

He asked Lester Carter if he had syphilis!

This attempt to damage his character drew an immediate protest from Leibowitz indicating that this astounding question was sufficient for a mistrial to be declared. The judge overruled this, and Knight said, "I am not ashamed of the way I am treating this witness."

A gynecologist from Chattanooga, Dr. Reisman, had proved with charts and diagrams of feminine anatomy that it was not possible the alleged rape could have occurred at the time stated, backing up the declaration of the other two doctors. (It goes without saying that these doctors were also threatened by lynchers.)

Knight is now again browbeating Heywood Patterson. "Did you pick up Victoria Price and hold her over the side of the train? Who did you see raping the girls?" Patterson repeats he'd seen no girls at any time, admits freely to the fight when the white boys had attacked him and the others. And he tells his mother—she is sitting beside him, she hasn't seen him for over a year (they allow her to see him sentenced to death again), "I'm afraid of what'll happen if they free me."

Another mob formed; led by Ku Klux Klan men, 200 of them were coming to the courthouse for Leibowitz. Sheriff Davis argued with and "cajoled" them (yes that is the word used), but they wouldn't go away till they saw the soldiers were at the point of firing. This is when most of the press agreed to withhold news. The Klansmen however boasted of it, and the I.L.D. forced the truth of this and other incidents into the open.

As the trial went on 5 of the Negro boys were put on the stand by the defence. And then the very initial start of the whole thing came out. It was Eugene Williams who told how the white boys were climbing from one car to another and one of them had walked on Heywood Patterson's hand. Heywood had asked him couldn't he be more careful . . . and so the fight had begun. And then Heywood had pulled back Orvil Gilley as he was about to jump off. Why would he save a white life to let him see a white girl raped afterwards? asked Heywood Patterson.

Victoria Price had said she'd never seen Carter or Gilley, but Dallas Ramsay, a Negro witness had seen them all together on the morning of the freight-ride, when she had asked him when there was a train to Memphis. Both General Chamlee and a sister of the Wright boys, who live in Chatanooga said how they had searched it for the [woman named] Callie Broochie and her house where Price said they had spent the night, but in two years' investigation had never found either. Further "character testimony" was ruled out by the judge, who had allowed Knight to insult and attack defence witnesses as much as he pleased.

"That Black Thing"

Knight is shaking his fist at Heywood Patterson and calling him "that black thing over there." Leibowitz has made a four-hour summing up. Insults to Ruby Bates, Lester Carter, Leibowitz and Brodsky have been spat out by Knight and other prosecuting counsel. Leibowitz and Brodsky are "New York jews but jew money can't buy Alabama justice"; all four have received many death threats. And another of the prosecuting attorneys has made a lynch-inciting speech which has increased the number of fiery crosses (Ku Klux manifestations) that have burned nightly for over a week in all the surrounding villages. The ammunition stores report they are sold out, "but no cartridges sold to niggers." The jury deliberates all night. Then they actually ask if they can give their decision based on the Scottsboro trial!! They don't want to take into account any of the Decatur hearing. Next morning the jury file in, many of them with broad grins. Horton reads out their verdict: "Guilty. We ask for the death penalty." The court empties in a flash; the news is shouted all over the town. The first case is settled, and now they can get on with that of Charlie Weems. . . .

One would like to engrave the entire report, the whole detail of these trial testimonies of both sides, the false along with the real, on some matter that would last as long as humanity; to record forever also the moment of this cutting open of the plague of hatred, the exposure of Southern courts' "justice."

From *Negro: An Anthology* (Made by Nancy Cunard,
1931–1933; London: Wishart, 1934), 245–269.

Esther Popel

1896–1958

Educator and poet Esther Popel grew up in Harrisburg, Pennsylvania, and graduated Phi Beta Kappa from Dickinson College in Carlisle, Pennsylvania, in 1919. She
held a government position with the War Risk Insurance Department and taught in
Baltimore for two years. Popel then moved to Washington, D.C., where she taught
French and Spanish at Shaw Junior High School. A member of the Lincoln Memorial Congregational Temple, Popel was a popular public speaker. Her speech "Personal Adventures in Race Relations" was published by the Women's Press of the
YMCA in New York. In addition to writing six plays for junior high school students,
Popel also published poetry in the *Crisis* and *Opportunity* from 1925 to 1934. Her
work tends to fall into lyrical, religious, and political categories.

"Flag Salute," which appeared in 1934, was written in response to a lynching
and riot on Maryland's Eastern Shore in 1933 that received widespread coverage
because of the area's proximity to Washington and New York. An area hard hit by
the Depression, the Eastern Shore had been simmering with racial tension since
the ILD prevented the lynching of a sixty-three-year-old black man for murdering
a white family and successfully appealed his conviction twice. In the 1933 case,
twenty-eight-year-old George Armwood was accused of raping Mary Denston, a
white woman in her late seventies. As reported in the *Nation* in December 1933,
the more likely story is that a robbery planned by Armwood's white employer and
conducted by Armwood had gone wrong when Denston resisted. Armwood had
been removed to Baltimore for his own safety, but then was sent back to jail in
the Eastern Shore town of Princess Anne, where a lynch mob was waiting for him.
Two thousand people used a battering ram to break down the front door of the
jail. State troopers fought the intruders and even hurled tear gas bombs, but
many in the crowd had brought along their army-issue gas masks from the First
World War. The crowd then broke through three interior doors to get to Armwood.
The gruesome details of what transpired next are much as Popel reports in her
poem, in which she presents the lynching in ironic counterpoint to the Pledge of
Allegiance.

—— Flag Salute ——

(Note: In a classroom in a Negro school a pupil gave as his news topic during the opening exercises of the morning, a report of the Princess Anne Lynching of October 18, 1933. A brief discussion of the facts of the case followed, after which the student in charge gave this direction: pupils, rise, and give the flag salute! They did so without hesitation!)

"I pledge allegiance to the flag"—
They dragged him naked
Through the muddy streets,
A feeble-minded black boy!
And the charge? Supposed assault
Upon an aged woman!
"Of the United States of America"—
One mile they dragged him
Like a sack of meal,
A rope around his neck,
A bloody ear
Left dangling by the patriotic hand
Of Nordic youth! (A boy of seventeen!)
"And to the Republic for which it stands"—
And then they hanged his body to a tree,
Below the window of the county judge
Whose pleadings for that battered human flesh
Were stifled by the brutish, raucous howls
Of men, and boys, and women with their babes,
Brought out to see the bloody spectacle
Of murder in the style of '33!
(Three thousand strong, they were!)
"One Nation, Indivisible"—
To make the tale complete
They built a fire—
What matters that the stuff they burned
Was flesh—and bone—and hair—
And reeking gasoline!
"With Liberty—and Justice"—
They cut the rope in bits
And passed them out,
For souvenirs, among the men and boys!
The teeth no doubt, on golden chains
Will hang
About the favored necks of sweethearts, wives,
And daughters, mothers, sisters, babies, too!
"For ALL!"

From *Crisis*, August 1934, 231.

Erskine Caldwell

1903–1987

Novelist, essayist, and short-story writer Erskine Caldwell was born in White Oak, Georgia, the son of a Presbyterian minister who provided his son with an upbringing as free of racial prejudice as was possible in the Deep South. Caldwell attended Erskine College, the University of Pennsylvania, and the University of Virginia, the last of which he left without obtaining a degree in 1925. Caldwell then worked as a reporter for the *Atlanta Journal* before moving to Maine in 1926 to become a full-time writer. After years of surviving on a meager living eked out writing book reviews, Caldwell had his first piece of fiction accepted for publication in Lewis Mumford's *New American Caravan* in 1929. Success followed quickly and by the end of the 1930s he was well known as both a short-story writer and a novelist. He would produce more than fifty volumes of fiction and nonfiction and become one of the world's most widely read authors.

In 1932, Caldwell published a critically acclaimed novel, *Tobacco Road*, which became a bestseller following its dramatization by James Kirkland. His next novel, *God's Little Acre*, enjoyed an even-more-positive critical reception. In 1935, he began collaborations with photographer Margaret Bourke-White, whom he later married, that would result in their photo documentary of the Deep South, *Now You Have Seen Their Faces* (1940). Caldwell's best fiction shines a searchlight on the southern pockets of rural poverty and near starvation that he documented with Bourke-White. In 1935, the same year in which "Kneel to the Rising Sun" appeared, Caldwell published *Some American People*, which included exposés of the Ford Motor Company's exploitation of its assembly-line workers and of the exploitation of rural Southerners by the tenant-farming system. Combined with his concern for the worker, Caldwell had an abhorrence for racial violence and a keen understanding of the economic origins of white supremacy as a system that used racism to oppress and divide all workers.

Caldwell also published a novel about a lynching, *Trouble in July* (1940), in which a sheriff "attempts" to save an obviously innocent black boy from a mob intent on executing him for raping a white woman. Once put in motion, the machine of racism—the minister, the politicians, the lawmakers, the farmer cowed by the social pressures of a white supremacist society—rolls along until the boy is killed. In a surprising denouement, however, the crowd stones the woman to death after she reveals that she had in fact attempted to initiate a sexual encounter. In "Saturday

Afternoon," a short story published in *Nativity* in 1930, Caldwell describes—from the perspective of the town butcher who speculates on the commercial value of the event—the lynching of a black man who is hated for his intelligence, industry, and prosperity. In addition to his fiction, Caldwell also wrote dispatches for the *New Masses* that publicized and condemned lynchings in his native Georgia. "Kneel to the Rising Sun" dramatizes how racial violence ensures the survival of a peonage system that keeps both white and black enduring each day on the knife-edge of starvation.

— Kneel to the Rising Sun —

A shiver went through Lonnie. He drew his hand away from his sharp chin, remembering what Clem had said. It made him feel now as if he were committing a crime by standing in Arch Gunnard's presence and allowing his face to be seen.

He and Clem had been walking up the road together that afternoon on their way to the filling station when he told Clem how much he needed rations. Clem stopped a moment to kick a rock out of the road, and said that if you worked for Arch Gunnard

9. "When they get together they'll dump us off."
Reprinted from the *Messenger*, August 1919, 4.

long enough, your face would be sharp enough to split the boards for your own coffin.

As Lonnie turned away to sit down on an empty box beside the gasoline pump, he could not help wishing that he could be as unafraid of Arch Gunnard as Clem was. Even if Clem was a Negro, he never hesitated to ask for rations when he needed something to eat; and when he and his family did not get enough, Clem came right out and told Arch so. Arch stood for that, but he swore that he was going to run Clem out of the country the first chance he got.

Lonnie knew without turning around that Clem was standing at the corner of the filling station with two or three other Negroes and looking at him, but for some reason he was unable to meet Clem's eyes.

Arch Gunnard was sitting in the sun, honing his jackknife blade on his boot top. He glanced once or twice at Lonnie's hound, Nancy, who was lying in the middle of the road waiting for Lonnie to go home.

"That your dog, Lonnie?"

Jumping with fear, Lonnie's hand went to his chin to hide the lean face that would accuse Arch of short-rationing.

Arch snapped his fingers and the hound stood up, wagging her tail. She waited to be called.

"Mr. Arch, I—"

Arch called the dog. She began crawling towards them on her belly, wagging her tail a little faster each time Arch's fingers snapped. When she was several feet away, she turned over on her back and lay on the ground with her four paws in the air.

Dudley Smith and Jim Weaver, who were lounging around the filling station, laughed. They had been leaning against the side of the building, but they straightened up to see what Arch was up to.

Arch spat some more tobacco juice on his boot top and whetted the jackknife blade some more.

"What kind of a hound dog is that, anyway, Lonnie?" Arch said. "Looks like to me it might be a ketch hound."

Lonnie could feel Clem Henry's eyes boring into the back of his head. He wondered what Clem would do if it had been his dog Arch Gunnard was snapping his fingers at and calling like that.

"His tail's way too long for a coon hound or a bird dog, ain't it, Arch?" somebody behind Lonnie said, laughing out loud.

Everybody laughed then, including Arch. They looked at Lonnie, waiting to hear what he was going to say to Arch.

"Is he a ketch hound, Lonnie?" Arch said, snapping his finger again.

"Mr. Arch, I—"

"Don't be ashamed of him, Lonnie, if he don't show signs of turning out to be a bird dog or a foxhound. Everybody needs a hound around the house that can go out and catch pigs and rabbits when you are in a hurry for them. A ketch hound is a mighty respectable animal. I've known the time when I was mighty proud to own one."

Everybody laughed.

Arch Gunnard was getting ready to grab Nancy by the tail. Lonnie sat up, twisting his neck until he caught a glimpse of Clem Henry at the other corner of the filling station. Clem was staring at him with unmistakable meaning, with the same look in his eyes he had had that afternoon when he said that nobody who worked for Arch Gunnard ought to stand for short-rationing. Lonnie lowered his eyes. He could not figure out how a Negro could be braver than he was. There were a lot of times like that when he would have given anything he had to be able to jump into Clem's shoes and change places with him.

"The trouble with this hound of yours, Lonnie, is that he's too heavy on his feet. Don't you reckon it would be a pretty slick little trick to lighten the load some, being as how he's a ketch hound to begin with?"

Lonnie remembered then what Clem Henry had said he would do if Arch Gunnard ever tried to cut off his dog's tail. Lonnie knew, and Clem knew, and everybody else knew, that that would give Arch the chance he was waiting for. All Arch asked, he had said, was for Clem Henry to overstep his place just one little half inch, or to talk back to him with just one little short word, and he would do the rest. Everybody knew what Arch meant by that, especially if Clem did not turn and run. And Clem had not been known to run from anybody, after fifteen years in the country.

Arch reached down and grabbed Nancy's tail while Lonnie was wondering about Clem. Nancy acted as if she thought Arch were playing some kind of a game with her. She turned her head around until she could reach Arch's hand to lick it. He cracked her on the bridge of the nose with the end of the jackknife.

"He's a mighty playful dog, Lonnie," Arch said, catching up a shorter grip on the tail, "but his wagpole is way too long for a dog his size especially when he wants to be a ketch hound."

Lonnie swallowed hard.

"Mr. Arch, she's a mighty fine rabbit tracker. I—"

"Shucks, Lonnie," Arch said, whetting the knife blade on the dog's tail. "I ain't ever seen a hound in all my life that needed a tail that long to hunt rabbits with. It's way too long for just a common, ordinary, everyday ketch hound."

Lonnie looked up hopefully at Dudley Smith and the others. None of them offered any help. It was useless for him to try to stop Arch, because Arch Gunnard would let nothing stand in his way when once he had set his head on what he wished to do. Lonnie knew that if he should let himself show any anger or resentment, Arch would drive him off the farm before sundown that night. Clem Henry was the only person there who would help him, but Clem . . .

The white men and the Negroes at both corners of the filling station waited to see what Lonnie was going to do about it. All of them hoped he would put up a fight for his hound. If anyone ever had the nerve to stop Arch Gunnard from cutting off a dog's tail, it might put an end to it. It was plain, though, that Lonnie, who was one of Arch's sharecroppers, was afraid to speak up. Clem Henry might; Clem was the only one who might try to stop Arch, even if it meant trouble. And all of them knew that Arch would insist on running Clem out of the country or filling him full of lead.

"I reckon it's all right with you, ain't it, Lonnie?" Arch said. "I don't seem to hear no objections."

Clem Henry stepped forward several paces, and stopped.

Arch laughed, watching Lonnie's face, and jerked Nancy to her feet. The hound cried out in pain and surprise, but Arch made her be quiet by kicking her in the belly.

Lonnie winced. He could hardly bear to see anybody kick his dog like that.

"Mr. Arch, I . . ."

A contraction in his throat almost choked him for several moments, and he had to open his mouth wide and fight for breath. The other white men around him were silent. Nobody liked to see a dog kicked in the belly like that.

Lonnie could see the other end of the filling station from the corner of his eye. He saw a couple of Negroes go up behind Clem and grasp his overalls. Clem spat on the ground, between outspread feet, but he did not try to break away from them.

"Being as how I don't hear no objections, I reckon it's all right to go ahead and cut it off," Arch said, spitting.

Lonnie's head went forward and all he could see of Nancy was her hind feet. He had come to ask for a slab of sowbelly and some molasses or something. Now he did not know if he could ever bring himself to ask for rations, no matter how much hungrier they became at home

"I always make it a habit of asking a man first," Arch said. "I wouldn't want to go ahead and cut off a tail if a man had any objections. That wouldn't be right. No, sir, it just wouldn't be fair and square."

Arch caught a shorter grip on the hound's tail and placed the knife blade on it two or three inches from the rump. It looked to those who were watching as if his mouth were watering, because tobacco juice began to trickle down the corners of his lips. He brought up the back of his hand and wiped his mouth.

A noisy automobile came plowing down the road through the deep red dust. Everyone looked up as it passed in order to see who was in it.

Lonnie glanced at it, but he could not keep his eyes raised. His head fell downward once more until he could feel his sharp chin cutting into his chest. He wondered then if Arch had noticed how lean his face was.

"I keep two or three ketch hounds around my place," Arch said, honing the blade on the tail of the dog as if it were a razor strop until his actions brought smiles to the faces of the men grouped around him, "but I never could see the sense of a ketch hound having a long tail. It only gets in their way when I send them out to catch a pig or a rabbit for my supper."

Pulling with his left hand and pushing with his right, Arch Gunnard docked the hound's tail as quickly and as easily as if he were cutting a willow switch in the pasture to drive the cows home with. The dog sprang forward with the release of her tail until she was far beyond Arch's reach, and began howling so loud she could be heard half a mile away. Nancy stopped once and looked back at Arch, and then she sprang to the middle of the road and began leaping and twisting in circles. All that time she was yelping and biting at the bleeding stub of her tail.

Arch leaned backward and twirled the severed tail in one hand while he wiped the jackknife blade on his boot sole. He watched Lonnie's dog chasing herself around in circles in the red dust.

Nobody had anything to say then. Lonnie tried not to watch his dog's agony, and he forced himself to keep from looking at Clem Henry. Then, with his eyes shut, he wondered why he had remained on Arch Gunnard's plantation all those past years, sharecropping for a mere living on short rations, and becoming leaner and leaner all the time. He knew then how true it was what Clem had said about Arch's sharecroppers' faces becoming sharp enough to hew their own coffins. His hands went to his chin before he knew what he was doing. His hand dropped when he had felt the bones of jaw and the exposed tendons of his cheeks.

As hungry as he was, he knew that even if Arch did give him some rations then, there would not be nearly enough for them to eat for the following week. Hatty, his wife, was already broken down from hunger and work in the fields, and his father, Mark Newsome, stone-deaf for the past twenty years, was always asking him why there was never enough food in the house for them to have a solid meal. Lonnie's head fell forward a little more, and he could feel his eyes becoming damp.

The pressure of his sharp chin against his chest made him so uncomfortable that he had to raise his head at last in order to ease the pain of it.

The first thing he saw when he looked up was Arch Gunnard twirling Nancy's tail in his left hand. Arch Gunnard had a trunk full of dogs' tails at home. He had been cutting off tails ever since anyone could remember, and during all those years he had accumulated a collection of which he was so proud that he kept the trunk locked and the key tied around his neck on a string. On Sunday afternoons when the preacher came to visit, or when a crowd was there to loll on the front porch and swap stories, Arch showed them off, naming each tail from memory just as well as if he had had a tag on it.

Clem Henry had left the filling station and was walking alone down the road towards the plantation. Clem Henry's house was in a cluster of Negro cabins below Arch's big house, and he had to pass Lonnie's house to get there. Lonnie was on the verge of getting up and leaving when he saw Arch looking at him. He did not know whether Arch was looking at his lean face, or whether he was watching to see if he were going to get up and go down the road with Clem.

The thought of leaving reminded him of his reason for being there. He had to have some rations before suppertime that night, no matter how short they were.

"Mr. Arch, I . . ."

Arch stared at him for a moment, appearing as if he had turned to listen to some strange sound unheard of before that moment.

Lonnie bit his lips, wondering if Arch was going to say anything about how lean and hungry he looked. But Arch was thinking about something else. He slapped his hand on his leg and laughed out loud.

"I sometimes wish niggers had tails," Arch said, coiling Nancy's tail into a ball and putting it into his pocket. "I'd a heap rather cut off nigger tails than dog tails. There'd be more to cut, for one thing."

Dudley Smith and somebody else behind them laughed for a brief moment. The laughter died out almost as suddenly as it had risen.

The Negroes who had heard Arch shuffled their feet in the dust and moved backwards. It was only a few minutes until not one was left at the filling station. They went up the road behind the red wooden building until they were out of sight.

Arch got up and stretched. The sun was getting low, and it was no longer comfortable in the October air. "Well, I reckon I'll be getting on home to get me some supper," he said.

He walked slowly to the middle of the road and stopped to look at Nancy retreating along the ditch.

"Nobody going my way?" he asked. "What's wrong with you, Lonnie? Going home to supper, ain't you?"

"Mr. Arch, I . . ."

Lonnie found himself jumping to his feet. His first thought was to ask for the sow-belly and molasses, and maybe some corn meal; but when he opened his mouth, the words refused to come out. He took several steps forward and shook his head. He did not know what Arch might say or do if he said "No."

"Hatty'll be looking for you," Arch said, turning his back and walking off.

He reached into his hip pocket and took out Nancy's tail. He began twirling it as he walked down the road towards the big house in the distance.

Dudley Smith went inside the filling station, and the others walked away.

After Arch had gone several hundred yards, Lonnie sat down heavily on the box beside the gas pump from which he had got up when Arch spoke to him. He sat down heavily, his shoulders drooping, his arms falling between his outspread legs.

Lonnie did not know how long his eyes had been closed, but when he opened them, he saw Nancy lying between his feet, licking the docked tail. While he watched her, he felt the sharp point of his chin cutting into his chest again. Presently the door behind him was slammed shut, and a minute later he could hear Dudley Smith walking away from the filling station on his way home.

II

Lonnie had been sleeping fitfully for several hours when he suddenly found himself wide awake. Hatty shook him again. He raised himself on his elbow and tried to see into the darkness of the room. Without knowing what time it was, he was able to determine that it was still nearly two hours until sunrise.

"Lonnie," Hatty said again, trembling in the cold night air, "Lonnie, your pa ain't in the house."

Lonnie sat upright in bed.

"How do you know he ain't?" he said.

"I've been lying here wide awake ever since I got in bed, and I heard him when he went out. He's been gone all that time."

"Maybe he just stepped out for a while," Lonnie said, turning and trying to see through the bedroom window.

"I know what I'm saying, Lonnie," Hatty insisted. "Your pa's been gone a heap too long."

Both of them sat without a sound for several minutes while they listened for Mark Newsome.

Lonnie got up and lit a lamp. He shivered while he was putting on his shirt, overalls, and shoes. He tied his shoelaces in hard knots because he couldn't see in the faint light. Outside the window it was almost pitch-dark, and Lonnie could feel the damp October air blowing against his face.

"I'll go help look," Hatty said, throwing the covers off and starting to get up.

Lonnie went to the bed and drew the covers back over her and pushed her back into place.

"You try to get some sleep, Hatty," he said; "you can't stay awake the whole night. I'll go bring Pa back."

He left Hatty, blowing out the lamp, and stumbled through the dark hall, feeling his way to the front porch by touching the wall with his hands. When he got to the porch, he could still barely see any distance ahead, but his eyes were becoming more accustomed to the darkness. He waited a minute, listening.

Feeling his way down the steps into the yard, he walked around the corner of the house and stopped to listen again before calling his father.

"Oh, Pa!" he said loudly. "Oh, Pa!"

He stopped under the bedroom window when he realized what he had been doing.

"Now that's a fool thing for me to be out here doing," he said, scolding himself. "Pa couldn't hear it thunder."

He heard a rustling of the bed.

"He's been gone long enough to get clear to the crossroads, or more," Hatty said, calling through the window.

"Now you lay down and try to get a little sleep, Hatty," Lonnie told her. "I'll bring him back in no time."

He could hear Nancy scratching fleas under the house, but he knew she was in no condition to help look for Mark. It would be several days before she recovered from the shock of losing her tail.

"He's been gone a long time," Hatty said, unable to keep still.

"That don't make no difference," Lonnie said. "I'll find him sooner or later. Now you go on to sleep like I told you, Hatty."

Lonnie walked towards the barn, listening for some sound. Over at the big house he could hear the hogs grunting and squealing, and he wished they would be quiet so he could hear other sounds. Arch Gunnard's dogs were howling occasionally, but they were not making any more noise than they usually did at night, and he was accustomed to their howling.

Lonnie went to the barn, looking inside and out. After walking around the barn, he went into the field as far as the cotton shed. He knew it was useless, but he could not keep from calling his father time after time.

"Oh, Pa!" he said, trying to penetrate the darkness.

He went farther into the field.

"Now, what in the world could have become of Pa?" he said, stopping and wondering where to look next.

After he had gone back to the front yard, he began to feel uneasy for the first time. Mark had not acted any more strangely during the past week than he ordinarily did, but Lonnie knew he was upset over the way Arch Gunnard was giving out short rations. Mark had even said that, at the rate they were being fed, all of them would starve to death inside another three months.

Lonnie left the yard and went down the road towards the Negro cabins. When he got to Clem's house, he turned and walked the path to the door. He knocked several times and waited. There was no answer, and he rapped louder.

"Who's that?" he heard Clem say from bed.

"It's me," Lonnie said. "I've got to see you a minute, Clem. I'm out in the front yard."

He sat down and waited for Clem to dress and come outside. While he waited, he strained his ears to catch any sound that might be in the air. Over the fields towards the big house he could hear the fattening hogs grunt and squeal.

Clem came out and shut the door. He stood on the doorsill a moment speaking to his wife in bed, telling her he would be back and not to worry.

"Who's that?" Clem said, coming down into the yard.

Lonnie got up and met Clem halfway.

"What's the trouble?" Clem asked then, buttoning up his overall jumper.

"Pa's not in his bed," Lonnie said, "and Hatty says he's been gone from the house most all night. I went out in the field, and all around the barn, but I couldn't find a trace of him anywhere."

Clem then finished buttoning his jumper and began rolling a cigarette. He walked slowly down the path to the road. It was still dark, and it would be at least an hour before dawn made it any lighter.

"Maybe he was too hungry to stay in bed any longer," Clem said. "When I saw him yesterday, he said he was so shrunk up and weak he didn't know if he could last much longer. He looked like his skin and bones couldn't shrivel much more."

"I asked Arch last night after suppertime for some rations—just a little piece of sow-belly and some molasses. He said he'd get around to letting me have some the first thing this morning."

"Why don't you tell him to give you full rations or none?" Clem said. "If you knew you wasn't going to get none at all, you could move and find a better man to sharecrop for, couldn't you?"

"I've been loyal to Arch Gunnard for a long time now," Lonnie said. "I'd hate to haul off and leave him like that."

Clem looked at Lonnie, but he did not say anything more just then. They turned up the road towards the driveway that led up to the big house. The fattening hogs were still grunting and squealing in the pen, and one of Arch's hounds came down a cotton row beside the driveway to smell their shoes.

"Them fattening hogs always get enough to eat," Clem said. "There's not a one of them that don't weigh seven hundred pounds right now, and they're getting bigger every day. Besides taking all that's thrown to them, they make a lot of meals off the chickens that get in there to peck around."

Lonnie listened to the grunting of the hogs as they walked up the driveway towards the big house.

"Reckon we'd better get Arch up to help look for Pa?" Lonnie said. "I'd hate to wake him up, but I'm scared Pa might stray off into the swamp and get lost for good. He couldn't hear it thunder, even. I never could find him back there in all that tangle if he got into it."

Clem said something under his breath and went on towards the barn and hog pen. He reached the pen before Lonnie got there.

"You'd better come here quick," Clem said, turning around to see where Lonnie was.

Lonnie ran to the hog pen. He stopped and climbed halfway up the wooden-and-wire sides of the fence. At first he could see nothing, but gradually he was able to see the moving mass of black fattening hogs on the other side of the pen. They were biting and snarling at each other like a pack of hungry hounds turned loose on a dead rabbit.

Lonnie scrambled to the top of the fence, but Clem caught him and pulled him back.

"Don't go in that hog pen that way," he said. "Them hogs will tear you to pieces, they're that wild. They're fighting over something."

Both of them ran around the corner of the pen and got to the side where the hogs were. Down under their feet on the ground Lonnie caught a glimpse of a dark mass splotched with white. He was able to see it for a moment only, because one of the hogs trampled over it.

Clem opened and closed his mouth several times before he was able to say anything at all. He clutched at Lonnie's arm, shaking him. "That looks like it might be your pa," he said. "I swear before goodness, Lonnie, it does look like it."

Lonnie still could not believe it. He climbed to the top of the fence and began kicking his feet at the hogs, trying to drive them away. They paid no attention to him.

While Lonnie was perched there, Clem had gone to the wagon shed, and he ran back with two singletrees he had somehow managed to find there in the dark. He handed one to Lonnie, poking it at him until Lonnie's attention was drawn from the hogs long enough to take it.

Clem leaped over the fence and began swinging the singletree at the hogs. Lonnie slid down beside him, yelling at them. One hog turned on Lonnie and snapped at him, and Clem struck it over the back of the neck with enough force to drive it off momentarily.

By then Lonnie was able to realize what had happened. He ran to the mass of hogs, kicking them with his heavy stiff shoes and striking them on their heads with the iron-tipped singletree. Once he felt a stinging sensation, and looked down to see one of the hogs biting the calf of his leg. He had just enough time to hit the hog and drive it away before his leg was torn. He knew most of his overall leg had been ripped away, because he could feel the night air on his bare wet calf.

Clem had gone ahead and had driven the hogs back. There was no other way to do anything. They were in a snarling circle around them, and both of them had to keep the singletrees swinging back and forth all the time to keep the hogs off. Finally Lonnie reached down and got a grip on Mark's leg. With Clem helping, Lonnie carried his father to the fence and lifted him over to the other side.

They were too much out of breath for a while to say anything, or to do anything else. The snarling, fattening hogs were at the fence, biting the wood and wire, and making more noise than ever.

While Lonnie was searching in his pockets for a match, Clem struck one. He held the flame close to Mark Newsome's head.

They both stared unbelievingly, and then Clem blew out the match. There was nothing said as they stared at each other in the darkness.

Clem walked several steps away, and turned and came back beside Lonnie.

"It's him, though," Clem said, sitting down on the ground. "It's him, all right."

"I reckon so," Lonnie said. He could think of nothing else to say then.

They sat on the ground, one on each side of Mark, looking at the body. There had been no sign of life in the body beside them since they had first touched it. The face, throat, and stomach had been completely devoured.

"You'd better go wake up Arch Gunnard," Clem said after a while.

"What for?" Lonnie said. "He can't help none now. It's too late for help."

"Makes no difference," Clem insisted. "You'd better go wake him up and let him see what there is to see. If you wait till morning, he might take it into his head to say the hogs didn't do it. Right now is the time to get him up so he can see what his hogs did."

Clem turned around and looked at the big house. The dark outline against the dark sky made him hesitate.

"A man who short-rations tenants ought to have to sit and look at that till it's buried."

Lonnie looked at Clem fearfully. He knew Clem was right, but he was scared to hear a Negro say anything like that about a white man.

"You oughtn't talk like that about Arch," Lonnie said. "He's in bed asleep. He didn't have a thing to do with it. He didn't have no more to do with it than I did."

Clem laughed a little, and threw the singletree on the ground between his feet. After letting it lie there a little while, he picked it up and began beating the ground with it.

Lonnie got to his feet slowly. He had never seen Clem act like that before, and he did not know what to think about it. He left without saying anything and walked stiffly to the house in the darkness to wake up Arch Gunnard.

III

Arch was hard to wake up. And even after he was awake, he was in no hurry to get up. Lonnie was standing outside the bedroom window, and Arch was lying in bed six or eight feet away. Lonnie could hear him toss and grumble.

"Who told you to come and wake me up in the middle of the night?" Arch said.

"Well, Clem Henry's out here, and he said maybe you'd like to know about it."

Arch tossed around on the bed, flailing the pillow with his fists.

"You tell Clem Henry I said that one of these days he's going to find himself turned inside out, like a coat sleeve."

Lonnie waited doggedly. He knew Clem was right in insisting that Arch ought to wake up and come out there to see what had happened. Lonnie was afraid to go back to the barnyard and tell Clem that Arch was not coming. He did not know, but he had a feeling that Clem might go into the bedroom and drag Arch out of bed. He did not like to think of anything like that taking place.

"Are you still out there, Lonnie?" Arch shouted.

"I'm right here, Mr. Arch. I—"

"If I wasn't so sleepy, I'd come out there and take a stick and—I don't know what I wouldn't do!"

Lonnie met Arch at the back step. On the way out to the hog pen Arch did not speak to him. Arch walked heavily ahead, not even waiting to see if Lonnie was coming. The lantern that Arch was carrying cast long flat beams of yellow light over the ground; and when they got to where Clem was waiting beside Mark's body, the Negro's face shone in the night like a highly polished plowshare.

"What was Mark doing in my hog pen at night, anyway?" Arch said, shouting at them both.

Neither Clem nor Lonnie replied. Arch glared at them for not answering. But no matter how many times he looked at them, his eyes returned each time to stare at the torn body of Mark Newsome on the ground at his feet.

"There's nothing to be done now," Arch said finally. "We'll just have to wait till daylight and send for the undertaker." He walked a few steps away. "Looks like you could have waited till morning in the first place. There wasn't no sense in getting me up."

He turned his back and looked sideways at Clem. Clem stood up and looked him straight in the eyes.

"What do you want, Clem Henry?" he said. "Who told you to be coming around my house in the middle of the night? I don't want niggers coming here except when I send for them."

"I couldn't stand to see anybody eaten up by the hogs, and not do anything about it," Clem said.

"You mind your own business," Arch told him. "And when you talk to me, take off your hat, or you'll be sorry for it. It wouldn't take much to make me do you up the way you belong." ·

Lonnie backed away. There was a feeling of uneasiness around them. That was how trouble between Clem and Arch always began. He had seen it start that way dozens of times before. As long as Clem turned and went away, nothing happened, but sometimes he stayed right where he was and talked up to Arch just as if he had been a white man, too.

Lonnie hoped it would not happen this time. Arch was already mad enough about being waked up in the middle of the night, and Lonnie knew there was no limit to what Arch would do when he got good and mad at a Negro. Nobody had ever seen him kill a Negro, but he had said he had, and he told people that he was not scared to do it again.

"I reckon you know how he came to get eaten up by the hogs like that," Clem said, looking straight at Arch.

Arch whirled around.

"Are you talking to me . . . ?"

"I asked you that," Clem stated.

"God damn you, yellow-blooded . . ." Arch yelled.

He swung the lantern at Clem's head. Clem dodged, but the bottom of it hit his shoulder, and it was smashed to pieces. The oil splattered on the ground, igniting in the air from the flaming wick. Clem was lucky not to have it splash on his face and overalls.

"Now, look here . . ." Clem said.

"You yellow-blooded nigger," Arch said, rushing at him. "I'll teach you to talk back to me. You've got too big for your place for the last time. I've been taking too much from you, but I ain't doing it no more."

"Mr. Arch, I . . ." Lonnie said, stepping forward partly between them. No one heard him.

Arch stood back and watched the kerosene flicker out on the ground.

"You know good and well why he got eaten up by the fattening hogs," Clem said, standing his ground. "He was so hungry he had to get up out of bed in the middle of the night and come up here in the dark trying to find something to eat. Maybe he was trying to find the smokehouse. It makes no difference, either way. He's been on short rations like everybody else working on your place, and he was so old he didn't know where else to look for food except in your smokehouse. You know good and well that's how he got lost up here in the dark and fell in the hog pen."

The kerosene had died out completely. In the last faint flare, Arch had reached down and grabbed up the singletree that had been lying on the ground where Lonnie had dropped it.

Arch raised the singletree over his head and struck with all his might at Clem. Clem dodged, but Arch drew back again quickly and landed a blow on his arm just above the elbow before Clem could dodge it. Clem's arm dropped to his side, dangling lifelessly.

"You God-damn yellow-blooded nigger!" Arch shouted. "Now's your time, you black bastard! I've been waiting for the chance to teach you your lesson. And this's going to be one you won't never forget."

Clem felt the ground with his feet until he had located the other singletree. He stooped down and got it. Raising it, he did not try to hit Arch, but held it in front of him so he could ward off Arch's blows at his head. He continued to stand his ground, not giving Arch an inch.

"Drop that singletree," Arch said.

"I won't stand here and let you beat me like that," Clem protested.

"By God, that's all I want to hear," Arch said, his mouth curling. "Nigger, your time has come, by God!"

He swung once more at Clem, but Clem turned and ran towards the barn. Arch went after him a few steps and stopped. He threw aside the singletree and turned and ran back to the house.

Lonnie went to the fence and tried to think what was best for him to do. He knew he could not take sides with a Negro, in the open, even if Clem had helped him, and especially after Clem had talked to Arch in the way he wished he could himself. He was a white man, and to save his life he could not stand to think of turning against Arch, no matter what happened.

Presently a light burst through one of the windows of the house, and he heard Arch shouting at his wife to wake her up.

When he saw Arch's wife go to the telephone, Lonnie realized what was going to happen. She was calling up the neighbors and Arch's friends. They would not mind getting up in the night when they found out what was going to take place.

Out behind the barn he could hear Clem calling him. Leaving the yard, Lonnie felt his way out there in the dark.

"What's the trouble, Clem?" he said.

"I reckon my time has come," Clem said. "Arch Gunnard talks that way when he's good and mad. He talked just like he did that time he carried Jim Moffin off to the swamp—and Jim never came back."

"Arch wouldn't do anything like that to you, Clem," Lonnie said excitedly, but he knew better.

Clem said nothing.

"Maybe you'd better strike out for the swamps till he changes his mind and cools off some," Lonnie said. "You might be right, Clem."

Lonnie could feel Clem's eyes burning into him.

"Wouldn't be no sense in that, if you'd help me," Clem said. "Wouldn't you stand by me?"

Lonnie trembled as the meaning of Clem's suggestion became clear to him. His back was to the side of the barn, and he leaned against it while sheets of black and white passed before his eyes.

"Wouldn't you stand by me?" Clem asked again.

"I don't know what Arch would say to that," Lonnie told him haltingly.

Clem walked away several paces. He stood with his back to Lonnie while he looked across the field towards the quarter where his home was.

"I could go in that little patch of woods out there and stay till they get tired of looking for me," Clem said, turning around to see Lonnie.

"You'd better go somewhere," Lonnie said uneasily. "I know Arch Gunnard. He's hard to handle when he makes up his mind to do something he wants to do. I couldn't stop him an inch. Maybe you'd better get clear out of the country, Clem."

"I couldn't do that, and leave my family down there across the field," Clem said.

"He's going to get you if you don't."

"If you'd only sort of help me out a little, he wouldn't. I would only have to go and hide out in that little patch of woods over there a while. Looks like you could do that for me, being as how I helped you find your pa when he was in the hog pen."

Lonnie nodded, listening for sounds from the big house. He continued to nod at Clem while Clem was waiting to be assured.

"If you're going to stand up for me," Clem said, "I can just go over there in the woods and wait till they get it off their minds. You won't be telling them where I'm at, and you could say I struck out for the swamp. They wouldn't ever find me without bloodhounds."

"That's right," Lonnie said, listening for sounds of Arch's coming out of the house. He did not wish to be found back there behind the barn where Arch could accuse him of talking to Clem.

The moment Lonnie replied, Clem turned and ran off into the night. Lonnie went after him a few steps, as if he had suddenly changed his mind about helping him, but Clem was lost in the darkness by then.

Lonnie waited for a few minutes, listening to Clem crashing through the underbrush in the patch of woods a quarter of a mile away. When he could hear Clem no longer, he went around the barn to meet Arch.

Arch came out of the house carrying his double-barreled shotgun and the lantern he had picked up in the house. His pockets were bulging with shells.

"Where is that damn nigger, Lonnie?" Arch asked him. "Where'd he go to?"

Lonnie opened his mouth, but no words came out.

"You know which way he went, don't you?"

Lonnie again tried to say something, but there were no sounds. He jumped when he found himself nodding his head to Arch.

"Mr. Arch, I—"

"That's all right, then," Arch said. "That's all I need to know now, Dudley Smith and Tom Hawkins and Frank and Dave Howard and the rest will be here in a minute, and you can stay right here so you can show us where he's hiding out."

Frantically Lonnie tried to say something. Then he reached for Arch's sleeve to stop him, but Arch had gone.

Arch ran around the house to the front yard. Soon a car came racing down the road, its headlights lighting up the whole place, hog pen and all. Lonnie knew it was probably Dudley Smith, because his was the first house in that direction, only half a mile away. While he was turning into the driveway, several other automobiles came into sight, both up the road and down it.

Lonnie trembled. He was afraid Arch was going to tell him to point out where Clem had gone to hide. Then he knew Arch would tell him. He had promised Clem he would not do that. But try as he might, he could not make himself believe that Arch Gunnard would do anything more than whip Clem.

Clem had not done anything that called for lynching. He had not raped a white woman, he had not shot at a white man; he had only talked back to Arch, with his hat on. But Arch was mad enough to do anything; he was mad enough at Clem not to stop at anything short of lynching.

The whole crowd of men was swarming around him before he realized it. And there was Arch clutching his arm and shouting into his face.

"Mr. Arch, I—"

Lonnie recognized every man in the feeble dawn. They were excited, and they looked like men on the last lap of an all-night fox-hunting party. Their shotguns and pistols were held at their waist, ready for the kill.

"What's the matter with you, Lonnie?" Arch said, shouting into his ear. "Wake up and say where Clem Henry went to hide out. We're ready to go get him."

Lonnie remembered looking up and seeing Frank Howard dropping yellow twelve-gauge shells into the breech of his gun. Frank bent forward so he could hear Lonnie tell Arch where Clem was hiding.

"You ain't going to kill Clem this time, are you, Mr. Arch?" Lonnie asked.

"Kill him?" Dudley Smith repeated. "What do you reckon I've been waiting all this time for if it wasn't for a chance to get Clem. That nigger has had it coming to him ever since he came to this county. He's a bad nigger, and it's coming to him."

"It wasn't exactly Clem's fault," Lonnie said. "If Pa hadn't come up here and fell in the hog pen, Clem wouldn't have had a thing to do with it. He was helping me, that's all."

"Shut up, Lonnie," somebody shouted at him. "You're so excited you don't know what you're saying. You're taking up for a nigger when you talk like that."

People were crowding around him so tightly he felt as if he were being squeezed to death. He had to get some air, get his breath, get out of the crowd.

"That's right," Lonnie said.

He heard himself speak, but he did not know what he was saying.

"But Clem helped me find Pa when he got lost looking around for something to eat."

"Shut up, Lonnie," somebody said again. "You damn fool, shut up!"

Arch grabbed his shoulder and shook him until his teeth rattled. Then Lonnie realized what he had been saying.

"Now, look here, Lonnie," Arch shouted. "You must be out of your head, because you know good and well you wouldn't talk like a nigger-lover in your right mind."

"That's right," Lonnie said, trembling all over. "I sure wouldn't want to talk like that."

He could still feel the grip on his shoulder where Arch's strong fingers had hurt him.

"Did Clem go to the swamp, Lonnie?" Dudley Smith said. "Is that right, Lonnie?"

Lonnie tried to shake his head; he tried to nod his head. Then Arch's fingers squeezed his thin neck. Lonnie looked at the men wild-eyed.

"Where's Clem hiding, Lonnie?" Arch demanded, squeezing.

Lonnie went three or four steps towards the barn. When he stopped, the men behind him pushed forward again. He found himself being rushed behind the barn and beyond it.

"All right, Lonnie," Arch said. "Now which way?"

Lonnie pointed towards the patch of woods where the creek was. The swamp was in the other direction.

"He said he was going to hide out in that little patch of woods along the creek over there, Mr. Arch," Lonnie said. "I reckon he's over there now."

Lonnie felt himself being swept forward, and he stumbled over the rough ground trying to keep from being knocked down and trampled upon. Nobody was talking, and everyone seemed to be walking on tiptoes. The gray light of early dawn was increasing enough both to hide them and to show the way ahead.

Just before they reached the fringe of the woods, the men separated, and Lonnie found himself a part of the circle that was closing in on Clem.

Lonnie was alone, and there was nobody to stop him, but he was unable to move forward or backward. It began to be clear to him what he had done.

Clem was probably up a tree somewhere in the woods ahead, but by that time he had been surrounded on all sides. If he should attempt to break and run, he would be shot down like a rabbit.

Lonnie sat down on a log and tried to think what to do. The sun would be up in a few more minutes, and as soon as it came up, the men would close in on the creek and Clem. He would have no chance at all among all those shotguns and pistols.

Once or twice he saw the flare of a match through the underbrush where some of the men were lying in wait. A whiff of cigarette smoke struck his nostrils, and he found himself wondering if Clem could smell it wherever he was in the woods.

There was still no sound anywhere around him, and he knew that Arch Gunnard and the rest of the men were waiting for the sun, which would in a few minutes come up behind him in the east.

It was light enough by that time to see plainly the rough ground and the tangled underbrush and the curling bark on the pine trees.

The men had already begun to creep forward, guns raised as if stalking a deer. The woods were not large, and the circle of men would be able to cover it in a few minutes at the rate they were going forward. There was still a chance that Clem had slipped through the circle before dawn broke, but Lonnie felt that he was still there. He began to feel then that Clem was there because he himself had placed him there for the men to find more easily.

Lonnie found himself moving forward, drawn into the narrowing circle. Presently he could see the men all around him in dim outline. Their eyes were searching the heavy green pine tops as they went forward from tree to tree.

"Oh, Pa!" he said in a hoarse whisper. "Oh, Pa!"

He went forward a few steps, looking into the bushes and up into the treetops. When he saw the other men again, he realized that it was not Mark Newsome being sought. He did not know what had made him forget like that.

The creeping forward began to work into the movement of Lonnie's body. He found himself springing forward on his toes, and his body was leaning in that direction. It was like creeping up on a rabbit when you did not have a gun to hunt with.

He forgot again what he was doing there. The springing motion in his legs seemed to be growing stronger with each step. He bent forward so far he could almost touch the ground with his fingertips. He could not stop now. He was keeping up with the circle of men.

The fifteen men were drawing closer and closer together. The dawn had broken enough to show the time on the face of a watch. The sun was beginning to color the sky above.

Lonnie was far in advance of anyone else by then. He could not hold himself back. The strength in his legs was more than he could hold in check.

He had for so long been unable to buy shells for his gun that he had forgotten how much he liked to hunt.

The sound of the men's steady creeping had become a rhythm in his ears.

"Here's the bastard!" somebody shouted, and there was a concerted crashing through the dry underbrush. Lonnie dashed forward, reaching the tree almost as quickly as anyone else.

He could see everybody with guns raised, and far into the sky above the sharply outlined face of Clem Henry gleamed in the rising sun. His body was hugging the slender top of the pine.

Lonnie did not know who was the first to fire, but the rest of the men did not hesitate. There was a deafening roar as the shotguns and revolvers flared and smoked around the trunk of the tree.

He closed his eyes; he was afraid to look again at the face above. The firing continued without break. Clem hugged the tree with all his might, and then, with the faraway sound of splintering wood, the top of the tree and Clem came crashing through the lower limbs to the ground. The body, sprawling and torn, landed on the ground with a thud that stopped Lonnie's heart for a moment.

He turned, clutching for the support of a tree, as the firing began once more. The crumpled body was tossed time after time, like a sackful of kittens being killed with an automatic shotgun, as charges of lead were fired into it from all sides. A cloud of dust rose from the ground and drifted overhead with the choking odor of burned powder.

Lonnie did not remember how long the shooting lasted. He found himself running from tree to tree, clutching at the rough pine bark, stumbling wildly towards the cleared ground. The sky had turned from gray to red when he emerged in the open, and as he ran, falling over the hard clods in the plowed field, he tried to keep his eyes on the house ahead.

Once he fell and found it almost impossible to rise again to his feet. He struggled to his knees, facing the round red sun. The warmth gave him the strength to rise to his feet, and he muttered unintelligibly to himself. He tried to say things he had never thought to say before.

When he got home, Hatty was waiting for him in the yard. She had heard the shots in the woods, and she had seen him stumbling over the hard clods in the field, and she had seen him kneeling there looking straight into the face of the sun. Hatty was trembling as she ran to Lonnie to find out what the matter was.

Once in his own yard, Lonnie turned and looked for a second over his shoulder. He saw the men climbing over the fence at Arch Gunnard's. Arch's wife was standing on the back porch, and she was speaking to them.

"Where's your pa, Lonnie?" Hatty said. "And what in the world was all that shooting in the woods for?" Lonnie stumbled forward until he had reached the front porch. He fell upon the steps.

"Lonnie, Lonnie!" Hatty was saying. "Wake up and tell me what in the world is the matter. I've never seen the like of all that is going on."

"Nothing," Lonnie said. "Nothing."

"Well, if there's nothing the matter, can't you go up to the big house and ask for a little piece of streak-of-lean? We ain't got a thing to cook for breakfast. Your pa's going to be hungrier than ever after being walking around all night."

"What?" Lonnie said, his voice rising to a shout as he jumped to his feet.

"Why, I only said go up to the big house and get a little piece of streak-of-lean, Lonnie. That's all I said."

He grabbed his wife about the shoulders.

"Meat?" he yelled, shaking her roughly.

"Yes," she said, pulling away from him in surprise. "Couldn't you go ask Arch Gunnard for a little bit of streak-of-lean?"

Lonnie slumped down on the steps, his hands falling between his outspread legs and his chin falling on his chest.

"No," he said almost inaudibly. "No, I ain't hungry."

From *Scribner's*, January–June 1935, 71–80.

Richard Wright

1908–1960

Born on Rucker's Plantation between Roxie and Natchez, Mississippi, Richard Wright was the son of Nathaniel Wright, an illiterate sharecropper, and Ella Wilson, a schoolteacher. Wright's father abandoned the family when Wright was five, forcing Ella to go into domestic service and to send Wright and his brother to an orphanage. When Ella became paralyzed around 1920, the family went to live in Jackson, Mississippi, with her parents, who were strict Seventh Day Adventists. Repudiating fiction as the devil's work, Wright's grandmother refused to allow books in her home. In 1925, Wright graduated as the class valedictorian from Smith Robertson Junior High School in Jackson. He attended Lanier High School for only a few weeks before leaving to find work. Wright took off for Memphis, where he worked as a dishwasher and delivery boy for an optical company. Using a library card borrowed from an Irish co-worker, Wright began to read American fiction, discovering the power of language as a form of resistance.

Wright fled the strictures of the Jim Crow South for Chicago in 1927. He worked a number of jobs there, including a stint at the post office, taking care of lab animals at Michael Reese Hospital, and selling insurance. In 1933, Wright joined the John Reed Club, a group of leftist writers closely affiliated with the American Communist Party. Wright joined the party in 1934, the same year he published two poems in the John Reed Club journal *Left Front*: "A Red Love Note" and "Rest for the Weary." Between 1934 and 1941, Wright published more than a dozen poems in the Left press. His protest poetry from this period. particularly his gripping images of the African American proletarian body, is seen as an important precursor of the militancy of the black arts movement of the 1960s.

Wright worked in 1935 with the Federal Negro Theater in Chicago under the Federal Writer's Project. In 1937, he moved to New York, where he worked as an editor of *Left Front*, the *Daily Worker*, and *New Challenge*. Wright's short-story collection, *Uncle Tom's Children*, won *Story Magazine*'s competition for the best book-length manuscript and was published by Harper's in 1938. This collection includes "Big Boy Leaves Home," a shocking story of a young boy's traumatic passage into adulthood through witnessing the lynching of his friend. Growing up in the Deep South, Wright felt tormented by the specter of lynching, and his fiction is haunted by the lynching scenario. His great novel *Native Son* (1940) tells the story of Bigger Thomas, a man who accidentally kills Mary Dalton, a white girl he worked for, and then commits a brutal, premeditated murder of his black girlfriend, Bessie. By the end of the novel, Bigger is convicted for his assumed rape of Mary, but not for killing Bessie. This strategic deployment of the white supremacist stereotype of the "brute Negro" made many African Americans uncomfortable, but the book became a best-seller and the first Book of the Month Club selection by an African American writer. Wright collaborated with Paul Green on a stage adaptation of *Native Son*, which ran on Broadway in 1941.

In 1941, Wright also published *Twelve Million Black Voices: A Folk History of the United States*. The book combined his prose with compelling photographs of the rural black poor, which Edwin Rosskam selected from the Depression-era Farm Security Administration collection. In 1942, Wright left the Communist Party, disillusioned with its failure to successfully integrate African American issues into its vision. Wright's 1944 essay "I Tried to Be a Communist" was reprinted in the famous collection of exposés by disillusioned leftists, *The God That Failed* (1949). In 1945, the publication of Wright's autobiography, *Black Boy*, caused an uproar; the book climbed the best-seller lists while being denounced in the U.S. Senate as "obscene." Because *Black Boy*'s publisher wanted only the story of Wright's life in the South, the section of his autobiography that deals with his life in Chicago and his experience with the American Communist Party was not published until 1977, when it appeared as *American Hunger*.

Wright moved permanently to Paris in 1947, unable to endure U.S. racism. He published three more novels: *Outsider* (1953); *Savage Holiday* (1954), in which no blacks appear; and *The Long Dream* (1958). During the mid-1950s, Wright traveled to Africa, Asia, and Spain, his outlook growing increasingly internationalist. Between 1946 and 1948, he helped found *Presence Africaine*, along with famous African intellectuals and writers Leopold Senghor, Aime Cesaire, and Alioune Diop. Wright published several nonfiction works on political and sociological topics, including *Black Power* (1954), *The Color Curtain* (1956), and *Pagan Spain* (1956). A collection of his essays, *White Man Listen!* was published in 1957.

Throughout his career, Wright strongly advanced the position that the racial violence done to a single African American reverberated throughout the community. In *Black Boy*, he compared the violent conditions of life under Jim Crow to enduring "a thousand lynchings." "Between the World and Me," which first appeared in 1935 and has since been widely anthologized, relives this deep wounding to the African American psyche through the speaker's traumatic and imaginative reenactment of a lynching.

— Between the World and Me —

And one morning while in the woods I stumbled suddenly upon the thing,
Stumbled upon it in a grassy clearing guarded by scaly oaks and elms.
And the sooty details of the scene rose, thrusting themselves between the
    world and me . . .

There was a design of white bones slumbering forgottenly upon a cushion of
   ashes.
There was a charred stump of a sapling pointing a blunt finger accusingly at
   the sky.
There were torn tree limbs, tiny veins of burnt leaves, and a scorched coil of
   greasy hemp;
A vacant shoe, an empty tie, a ripped shirt, a lonely hat, and a pair of trousers
   stiff with black blood.
And upon the trampled grass were buttons, dead matches, butt-ends of cigars
   and cigarettes, peanut shells, a drained gin-flask, and a whore's lipstick;
Scattered traces of tar, restless arrays of feathers, and the lingering smell of
   gasoline.
And through the morning air the sun poured yellow surprise into the eye
   sockets of a stony skull . . .

And while I stood my mind was frozen with a cold pity for the life that was
   gone.
The ground gripped my feet and my heart was circled by icy walls of fear—
The sun died in the sky; a night wind muttered in the grass and fumbled the
   leaves in the trees; the woods poured forth the hungry yelping of hounds;
   the darkness screamed with thirsty voices; and the witnesses rose and lived:
The dry bones stirred, rattled, lifted, melting themselves into my bones.
The grey ashes formed flesh firm and black, entering into my flesh.

The gin-flask passed from mouth to mouth; cigars and cigarettes glowed, the
   whore smeared the lipstick red upon her lips,
And a thousand faces swirled around me, clamoring that my life be burned . . .

And then they had me, stripped me, battering my teeth Into my throat till I
   swallowed my own blood.
My voice was drowned in the roar of their voices, and my black wet body
   slipped and rolled in their hands as they bound me to the sapling.
And my skin clung to the bubbling hot tar, falling from me in limp patches.
And the down and quills of the white feathers sank into my raw flesh, and I
   moaned in my agony.
Then my blood was cooled mercifully, cooled by a baptism of gasoline.
And in a blaze of red I leaped to the sky as pain rose like water, boiling my
   limbs.
Panting, begging I clutched child-like, clutched to the hot sides of death.
Now I am dry bones and my face a stony skull staring in yellow surprise at
   the sun . . .

From *Partisan Review*, July–August 1935, 18–19.

Bibliography

Primary Sources

Andrews, James E. 1939. "Burnt Offering." *Opportunity* 17.3 (March): 84.

Bruce, John Edward. 1901. *The Blood Red Record: A Review of the Horrible Lynchings and Burning of Negroes by Civilized White Men in the United States, as Taken from the Records, with Comments by John Edward Bruce* [Bruce Grit]. Albany: Argus Company, Printers, [sold by] J. E. Bruce, Albany, N.Y.

Cameron, James. 1982] 1994. *A Time of Terror.* Baltimore, Md.: Black Classic Press.

Cooper, Anna Julia. 1892. *A Voice from the South.* Xenia, Ohio: Aldine Printing House.

Cullen, Countee. 1929. *The Black Christ and Other Poems.* New York: Harper and Brothers.

Cutler, James Elbert. 1905. *Lynch Law: An Investigation into the History of Lynching in the United States.* London: Longmans, Green.

Du Bois, W.E.B. 1919. "We Return Fighting." *Crisis*, May, 13–14.

———. 1999. "The Criteria of Negro Art." In *The Crisis Reader: Stories, Poetry, and Essays from the N.A.A.C.P's "Crisis" Magazine*, ed. Sondra Kathryn Wilson, 317–325. New York: Modern Library.

Duster, Alfreda M., ed. 1970. *Crusade for Justice: The Autobiography of Ida B. Wells.* Chicago: U of Chicago P.

Griggs, Sutton. 1905. *The Hindered Hand; or, The Reign of the Repressionist.* Nashville: Orion Publishers.

Hardwick, Edward S. 1935. "The Mob." *Opportunity* 13.10 (October): 310

Harper, Frances E. W. 1894. "Women's Political Future." In *World's Congress of Representative Women*, ed. May Wright Sewell. Chicago: Rand McNally.

Hopkins, Pauline. [1900] 1988. *Contending Forces.* New York: Oxford UP.

Johnson, James Weldon. [1933] 2000. *Along This Way: The Autobiography of James Weldon Johnson.* New York: DaCapo Press.

Moorer, Lizelia Augusta Jenkins. [1907] 1988. *Prejudice Unveiled and Other Poems.* Boston: Roxburgh; facsimile reprint in *Collected Black Women's Poetry*, vol. 3, ed. Joan R. Sherman. New York: Oxford UP.

Pickens, William. [1923] 1991. *Bursting Bonds: The Heir of Slaves: The Autobiography of a "New Negro."* Reprint, Bloomington: Indiana UP.

———. 1934. "The American Congo: Burning of Henry Lowry." In *Negro: An Anthology*, ed. Nancy Cunard. London: Wishart.

Raper, Arthur. [1933] 1969. *The Tragedy of Lynching.* Reprint, Montclair, N.J.: Patterson Smith.

Sandburg, Carl. [1919] 1969. *The Chicago Race Riots, July 1919.* New York: Harcourt, Brace and World.

Twain, Mark. |1929| 1977. "The United States of Lyncherdom." In *The Portable Mark Twain*, 584–593. New York: Penguin.

White, Walter. |1924| 1995. *The Fire in the Flint*. Athens: U of Georgia P.

———. |1929| 2001. *Rope and Faggot: A Biography of Judge Lynch*. Notre Dame, Ind.: U of Notre Dame P.

———. |1948| 1995. *A Man Called White: The Autobiography of Walter White*. Athens: U of Georgia P.

Anthologies

Adoff, Arnold, ed. 1968. *I Am the Darker Brother: An Anthology of Modern Poems by Negro Americans*. New York: Macmillan.

Brown, Sterling, ed. 1941. *The Negro Caravan*. New York: Dryden Press.

Cunard, Nancy, ed. 1934. *Negro: An Anthology*. New York: Unger.

Metress, Christopher, ed. 2002. *The Lynching of Emmett Till: A Documentary Narrative*. Charlottesville: U of Virginia P.

Perkins, Kathy A., and Judith L. Stephens, eds. 1998. *Strange Fruit: Plays on Lynching by American Women*. Bloomington: Indiana UP.

Roediger, David R., ed. 1998. *Black on White: Black Writers on What It Means to Be White*. New York: Schocken Books.

Wilson, Sondra Kathryn, ed. 1999. *The Crisis Reader*. New York: Modern Library.

———. 1999. *The Opportunity Reader*. New York: Modern Library.

———. 2000. *The Messenger Reader*. New York: Modern Library.

Secondary Sources

Allen, James. 2000. *Without Sanctuary: Lynching Photography in America*. Santa Fe: Twin Palms.

Aptheker, Herbert. 1993. *A Documentary History of the Negro People in the United States*. New York: Carol Publishing.

Avery, Sheldon. 1988. *Up from Washington: William Pickens and the Negro Struggle for Equality, 1900–1954*. Newark: U of Delaware P.

Ayers, Edward L. 1984. *Vengeance and Justice: Crime and Punishment in the Nineteenth-Century American South*. New York: Oxford UP.

Baker, Bruce. 1997. "North Carolina Lynching Ballads." In *Under Sentence of Death: Lynching in the New South*, ed. W. Fitzhugh Brundage, 191–246. Chapel Hill: U of North Carolina P.

Baker, Lee. 1998. *From Savage to Negro: Anthropology and the Construction of Race, 1896–1954*. Berkeley: U of California P.

Bannister, Robert C. 1979. *Social Darwinism: Science and Myth in Anglo-American Social Thought*. Philadelphia: Temple UP.

Beck, E. M., and Stewart Tolnay. 1995. *A Festival of Violence: An Analysis of Southern Lynchings: 1882–1930*. Urbana: U of Illinois P.

Bernardi, Daniel, ed. 1996. *The Birth of Whiteness: Race and the Emergence of U.S. Cinema*. New Brunswick, N.J.: Rutgers UP.

Bowser, Pearl, and Louise Spence. 2000. *Writing Himself into History: Oscar Micheaux, His Silent Films, and His Audiences*. New Brunswick, N.J.: Rutgers UP. See "Within Our Gates," 53–147.

Brundage, W. Fitzhugh, ed. 1993. *Lynching in the New South: Georgia and Virginia, 1880–1930*. Urbana: U of Illinois P.

————. 1997. *Under Sentence of Death: Lynching in the South*. Chapel Hill: U of North Carolina P.

Carby, Hazel. 1987. *Reconstructing Womanhood: The Emergence of the Afro-American Woman Novelist*. New York: Oxford UP.

Cha-Jua, Sundiata Keita. 2000. "A Warlike Demonstration." *Journal of Urban History* 26.5 (July): 591–630.

Daniel, Pete. 1972. *The Shadow of Slavery: Peonage in the South, 1901–1969*. Urbana: U of Illinois P.

Derrida, Jacques. 1996. *Archive Fever: A Freudian Impression*. Trans. Eric Prenowitz. Chicago: U of Chicago P.

Dillard, Tom W. 2001. "Madness with a Past: An Overview of Race Violence in Arkansas History." *Arkansas Review: A Journal of Delta Studies* 32.2 (August): 93–102.

Doreski, C. K. 1992. "From News to History: Robert Abbott and Carl Sandburg Read the 1919 Chicago Riot." *African American Review* 26.4 (winter): 637–651.

Dray, Philip. 2002. *At the Hands of Persons Unknown: The Lynching of Black America*. New York: Random House.

Fedo, Michael. 2000. *The Lynchings in Duluth*. St. Paul: Minnesota Historical Society.

Foley, Barbara. 1998. "'In the Land of Cotton': Economics and Violence in Jean Toomer's *Cane*." *African American Review* 32.2 (summer): 181–198.

Freeman, Gregory A. 1999. *Lay This Body Down: The 1921 Murders of Eleven Plantation Slaves*. Chicago: Chicago Review Press.

Gaines, Jane. 1993. "Fire and Desire: Race, Melodrama, and Oscar Micheaux." In *Black American Cinema*, ed. Manthia Diawara. New York: Routledge.

Geiger, Jeffrey. 1999. "Unmaking the Body: The Politics of Masculinity in *The Long Dream*." *African American Review* 33.2 (summer): 197–208.

Gilmore, Glenda. 1996. *Gender and Jim Crow: Women and the Politics of White Supremacy in North Carolina, 1896–1920*. Chapel Hill: U of North Carolina P.

Ginzberg, Ralph. 1988. *One Hundred Years of Lynchings*. Baltimore: Black Classic Press.

Goodman, James. 1994. *Stories of Scottsboro*. New York: Pantheon.

Grant, Donald L. 1975. *The Anti-Lynching Movement, 1883–1932*. San Francisco: RE/Search Publications.

Gunning, Sandra. 1996. *Race, Rape, and Lynching: The Red Record of American Literature, 1890–1912*. New York: Oxford UP.

Hale, Grace Elizabeth. 1999. *Making Whiteness: The Culture of Segregation in the South, 1890–1940*. New York: Vintage.

Hall, Jacqueline Dowd. 1993. *Revolt Against Chivalry: Jessie Daniel Ames and the Women's Campaign Against Lynching*. New York: Columbia UP.

————. 1997. "A Later Comment." *Journal of American History* 83 (March): 1268–1273.

Harris, Trudier. 1984. *Exorcising Blackness: Historical and Literary Lynching and Burning Rituals*. Bloomington: Indiana UP.

Haynes, Robert. 1976. *A Night of Violence: The Houston Riot of 1917*. Baton Rouge: Louisiana State UP.

Hull, Gloria T. 1987. *Color, Sex, and Poetry: Three Women Writers of the Harlem Renaissance*. Bloomington: Indiana UP.

Hunter, Tera W. 1997. *To 'Joy My Freedom: Southern Black Women's Lives and Labors after the Civil War*. Cambridge: Harvard UP.

Kinney, Arthur F. 1996. *Go Down Moses: The Miscegenation of Time*. New York: Twayne.

Klotman, Phyllis R. 1985. "'Tearing a Hole in History': Lynching as Theme and Motif." *Black American Literature Forum* 19.2 (summer): 55–63.

Kornweibel, Theodore, Jr. 1975. *No Crystal Stair: Black Life and the Messenger, 1917–1928*. Westport, Conn.: Greenwood Press.

LaCapra, Dominick. 2001. *Writing History, Writing Trauma*. Baltimore: Johns Hopkins UP.

Langa, Hele. 1999. "Two Antilynching Art Exhibitions." *American Art* 13.1 (spring): 10–40.

Lewis, David Levering. 1993. *W.E.B. DuBois: Biography of a Race, 1868–1919*. New York: Henry Holt.

———. 1997. Response to Joel Williamson. "Wounds Not Scars: Lynching, the National Conscience and the American Historian." *Journal of American History* 83 (March): 1221–1253.

———. 2000. *W.E.B. DuBois: The Fight for Equality and the American Century, 1919–1963*. New York: Henry Holt.

Lichtenstein, Alex. 1996. *Twice the Work of Free Labor: The Political Economy of Convict Labor in the New South*. London: Verso.

Logan, Shirley W. 1991. "Rhetorical Strategies in Ida B. Wells's 'Southern Horrors: Lynch Law in All Its Phases.'" *SAGE: A Scholarly Journal on Black Women* 8.1 (summer): 3–9.

McMillen, Neil R. 1990. *Dark Journey: Black Mississippians in the Age of Jim Crow*. Urbana: U of Illinois P.

Madison, James. 2001. *A Lynching in the Heartland: Race and Memory in America*. New York: Palgrave/St. Martin's Press.

Mancini, Matthew. 1996. *One Dies, Get Another: Convict Leasing in the American South, 1866–1928*. Columbia: U of South Carolina P.

Marshall, Elaine. 1996. "Crane's 'The Monster' Seen in Light of Robert Lewis's Lynching." *Nineteenth Century Literature* 51.2 (September): 205–224.

Maxwell, William J. 1999. *New Negro, Old Left: African-American Writing and Communism Between the Wars*. New York: Columbia UP.

Morrison, Toni. 1992. *Playing in the Dark: Whiteness and the American Literary Imagination*. Cambridge: Harvard UP.

Myrdal, Gunnar. 1944. *An American Dilemma: The Negro Problem and American Democracy*. New York: Harper.

Nelson, Cary. 2001. *Revolutionary Memory: Recovering the Poetry of the American Left*. New York: Routledge.

Oshinsky, David. 1996. *"Worse than Slavery": Parchman Farm and the Ordeal of Jim Crow Justice*. New York: Free Press.

Ovington, Mary White. 1995. *Black and White Sat Down Together: The Reminiscences of an NAACP Founder*. Edited by Ralph E. Luker. New York: Feminist Press.

Painter, Nell Irvin. 1976. *Exodusters: Black Migration to Kansas after Reconstruction*. New York: Norton.

———. 2002. *Southern History across the Color Line*. Chapel Hill: U of North Carolina P.

Park, Marlene. 1994. "Lynching and Antilynching: Art and Politics in the 1930s." *Prospects* 18: 311–366.

Patterson, Orlando. 1998. *Rituals of Blood: Consequences of Slavery in Two American Centuries*. New York: Basic Civitas.

Salem, Dorothy. 1990. *To Better Our World: Black Women in Organized Reform, 1890–1920*. Brooklyn: Carlson Press.

Schneider, Mark Robert. 2002. *"We Return Fighting": The Civil Rights Movement in the Jazz Age.* Boston: Northeastern UP.

Shapiro, Herbert. 1988. *White Violence and Black Response: From Reconstruction to Montgomery.* Amherst: U of Massachusetts P.

Smead, Howard. 1986. *Blood Justice: The Lynching of Mack Charles Parker.* New York: Oxford UP.

Smith, Lillian. 1994. *Killers of the Dream.* New York: Norton.

Stockley, Grif. 2001. *Blood in Their Eyes: The Elaine Race Massacres of 1919.* Fayetteville: U of Arkansas P.

Sundquist, Eric. 1993. *To Wake the Nations: Race in the Making of American Literature.* Cambridge: Harvard UP.

Thurston, Michael. 1995. "Black Christ, Red Flag: Langston Hughes on Scottsboro." *College Literature* 22.3: 30–49.

Tolnay, Stuart E., and E. M. Beck. 1995. *A Festival of Violence: An Analysis of Southern Lynchings, 1882–1930.* Urbana: U of Illinois P.

Tuttle, William L., Jr. 1996. *Race Riot: Chicago in the Red Summer of 1919.* Urbana: U of Illinois P.

Wade, Wyn C. 1987. *The Fiery Cross: The Ku Klux Klan in America.* New York: Simon and Schuster.

Wallace, Michele Faith. 1999. "Passing, Lynching, and Jim Crow: A Genealogy of Race and Gender in U.S. Visual Culture, 1895–1929." Ph.D. dissertation, New York University.

Warren, Robert Penn. 1956. *Segregation: The Inner Conflict of the South.* New York: Random House.

Wexler, Laura. 2003. *Fire in a Canebrake: The Last Mass Lynching in America.* New York: Scribner.

Whitfield, Stephen J. 1988. *A Death in the Delta: The Story of Emmett Till.* Baltimore: Johns Hopkins UP.

Williams, Patricia. 2000. "Diary of a Mad Law Professor: Without Sanctuary." *Nation*, February 14, 9.

Williamson, Joel. 1997. "Wounds Not Scars: Lynching, the National Conscience, and the American Historian." *Journal of American History* 83 (March):1221–1253.

Wright, George C. 1990. *Racial Violence in Kentucky, 1865–1940: Lynchings, Mob Rule, and "Legal Lynchings."* Baton Rouge: Louisiana State UP.

Wyatt-Brown, Bertram. 1982. *Southern Honor: Ethics and Behavior in the Old South.* New York: Oxford UP.

Yaeger, Patricia. 1997. "Consuming Trauma, or, the Pleasures of Merely Circulating." *Journal X,* spring, 225–251.

Zangrando, Robert. 1980. *The NAACP Crusade Against Lynching, 1909–1950.* Philadelphia: Temple UP.

Bibliographies

Moses, Norton H. 1997. *Lynching and Vigilantism in the United States: An Annotated Bibliography.* Westport, Conn.: Greenwood Press.

Williams, Daniel T., comp. 1970. "The Lynching Records at Tuskeegee Institute; with Lynching in America: A Bibliography." In *Eight Negro Bibliographies.* New York: Kraus Reprint.

Permissions

Index

Index ■ 321

About the Authors

ANNE RICE is an adjunct lecturer in the black studies department at Lehman College. MICHELE WALLACE is a professor of English, women's studies, and film at City College of New York and the CUNY Graduate Center. She is the author of *Black Macho and the Myth of the Superwoman, Invisibility Blues,* and *Dark Designs and Visual Culture.*